Pro iPhone Development with Swift 4

Design and Manage Top Quality Apps

Molly Maskrey
Wallace Wang

Apress®

Pro iPhone Development with Swift 4: Design and Manage Top Quality Apps

Molly Maskrey
Parker, Colorado, USA

Wallace Wang
San Diego, California, USA

ISBN-13 (pbk): 978-1-4842-3380-1
https://doi.org/10.1007/978-1-4842-3381-8

ISBN-13 (electronic): 978-1-4842-3381-8

Library of Congress Control Number: 2018932359

Copyright © 2018 by Molly Maskrey and Wallace Wang

This work is subject to copyright. All rights are reserved by the Publisher, whether the whole or part of the material is concerned, specifically the rights of translation, reprinting, reuse of illustrations, recitation, broadcasting, reproduction on microfilms or in any other physical way, and transmission or information storage and retrieval, electronic adaptation, computer software, or by similar or dissimilar methodology now known or hereafter developed.

Trademarked names, logos, and images may appear in this book. Rather than use a trademark symbol with every occurrence of a trademarked name, logo, or image we use the names, logos, and images only in an editorial fashion and to the benefit of the trademark owner, with no intention of infringement of the trademark.

The use in this publication of trade names, trademarks, service marks, and similar terms, even if they are not identified as such, is not to be taken as an expression of opinion as to whether or not they are subject to proprietary rights.

While the advice and information in this book are believed to be true and accurate at the date of publication, neither the authors nor the editors nor the publisher can accept any legal responsibility for any errors or omissions that may be made. The publisher makes no warranty, express or implied, with respect to the material contained herein.

Cover image designed by Freepik

> Managing Director: Welmoed Spahr
> Editorial Director: Todd Green
> Acquisitions Editor: Aaron Black
> Development Editor: James Markham
> Technical Reviewer: Bruce Wade
> Coordinating Editor: Jessica Vakili
> Copy Editor: Karen Jameson
> Compositor: SPi Global
> Indexer: SPi Global
> Artist: SPi Global

Distributed to the book trade worldwide by Springer Science+Business Media New York, 233 Spring Street, 6th Floor, New York, NY 10013. Phone 1-800-SPRINGER, fax (201) 348-4505, e-mail orders-ny@springer-sbm.com, or visit www.springeronline.com. Apress Media, LLC is a California LLC and the sole member (owner) is Springer Science + Business Media Finance Inc (SSBM Finance Inc). SSBM Finance Inc is a **Delaware** corporation.

For information on translations, please e-mail rights@apress.com, or visit http://www.apress.com/rights-permissions.

Apress titles may be purchased in bulk for academic, corporate, or promotional use. eBook versions and licenses are also available for most titles. For more information, reference our Print and eBook Bulk Sales web page at http://www.apress.com/bulk-sales.

Any source code or other supplementary material referenced by the author in this book is available to readers on GitHub via the book's product page, located at www.apress.com/978-1-4842-3380-1. For more detailed information, please visit http://www.apress.com/source-code.

Printed on acid-free paper

This book is dedicated to everyone who has an idea for an app but didn't know what to do first or how to get started. First, believe in your idea. Second, trust that you have intelligence to achieve your dream even if you don't know how you'll get there. Third, keep learning and improving your skills all the time. Fourth, stay focused. Success will come one day as long as you persist and never give up on yourself.

Table of Contents

About the Authors .... **xi**

About the Technical Reviewer .... **xiii**

Chapter 1: Multithreaded Programming Using Grand Central Dispatch **1**

    Creating the SlowWorker Application 3

        Threading Basics 7

        Units of Work 8

        GCD: Low-Level Queuing 9

        Improving SlowWorker 10

    Background Processing 17

    Application Life Cycle 19

    State-Change Notifications 20

        Creating State Lab 22

        Exploring Execution States 23

        Using Execution State Changes 26

        Handling the Inactive State 27

        Handling the Background State 33

        Saving State When Entering the Background 37

    Summary 43

Chapter 2: Simple Games Using SpriteKit **45**

    Creating the TextShooter App 46

        Initial Scene Customization 51

        Player Movement 57

        Creating Your Enemies 63

        Putting Enemies in the Scene 65

        Start Shooting 67

TABLE OF CONTENTS

    Attacking Enemies with Physics.. 73
    Finishing Levels... 74
    Customizing Collisions... 77
    Spicing Things Up with Particles.. 83
    Putting Particles into the Scene... 87
    Ending the Game... 89
    Create a StartScene... 92
    Adding Sound Effects 95
    Making the Game a Little Harder: Force Fields 96
Summary.. 100

Chapter 3: Taps, Touches, and Gestures 103

Multitouch Terminology... 104
The Responder Chain 105
    Responding to Events.. 105
    Forwarding an Event: Keeping the Responder Chain Alive 107
The Multitouch Architecture.. 108
The Four Touch Notification Methods... 108
Creating the TouchExplorer Application 110
    Creating the Swipes Application.. 116
    Using Touch Events to Detect Swipes... 116
    Automatic Gesture Recognition 120
    Implementing Multiple Swipes 122
    Detecting Multiple Taps 125
    Detecting Pinch and Rotation Gestures 131
Summary.. 137

Chapter 4: Determining Location 139

The Location Manager 140
    Setting the Desired Accuracy 140
    Setting the Distance Filter 141
    Getting Permission to Use Location Services 142

Starting the Location Manager	142
Using the Location Manager Wisely	142
The Location Manager Delegate	143
Getting Location Updates	143
Getting Latitude and Longitude Using CLLocation	143
Error Notifications	147
Creating the WhereAmI Application	147
Using Location Manager Updates	155
Visualizing Your Movement on a Map	159
Changing Location Service Permissions	164
Summary	165

Chapter 5: Device Orientation and Motion 167

Accelerometer Physics	167
Rotation Detection Using the Gyroscope	169
Core Motion and the Motion Manager	169
Creating the MotionMonitor Application	170
Proactive Motion Access	176
Gyroscope and Attitude Results	179
Accelerometer Results	180
Detecting Shakes	182
Baked-In Shaking	182
The Shake and Break Application	183
Accelerometer as a Directional Controller	188
The Ball Application	188
Calculating Ball Movement	195
Summary	198

Chapter 6: Using the Camera and Accessing Photos 199

Using the Image Picker and UIImagePickerController	200
Using the Image Picker Controller	200
Implementing the Image Picker Controller Delegate	203

vii

TABLE OF CONTENTS

Creating the Camera Interface 205

    Privacy Options 208

    Implementing the Camera View Controller 210

Summary 215

Chapter 7: Translating Apps Using Localization 217

Localization Architecture 218

Strings Files 219

    The Strings File 220

    The Localized String Function 221

Creating the LocalizeMe App 222

    Localizing the Project 230

    Localizing the Storyboard 234

    Generating and Localizing a Strings File 242

    Localizing the App Display Name 249

    Adding Another Localization 252

Summary 253

Chapter 8: Using Machine Learning 255

Understanding Machine Learning 256

Finding a Core ML Model 257

Image Recognition 258

    Creating the Image Recognition Application 259

    Identifying Objects from the Camera 269

    Analyzing an Image 275

Summary 283

Chapter 9: Using Facial and Text Recognition 285

Recognizing Faces in Pictures 286

Highlighting Faces in an Image 293

Highlighting Parts of a Face in an Image 301

TABLE OF CONTENTS

Recognizing Text in an Image 309

Summary.. 315

Chapter 10: Using 3D Touch 317

Understanding 3D Touch 318

Detecting 3D Touch Availability 321

Detecting Pressure... 323

    Creating Home Screen Quick Actions 325

Responding to Quick Action Items 329

    Adding Dynamic Home Screen Quick Actions 333

Adding Peeking, Popping, and Previewing... 339

Summary.. 346

Chapter 11: Using Speech.. 347

Converting Speech to Text 347

Recognizing Spoken Commands.. 356

Turning Text to Speech 358

Summary.. 362

Chapter 12: Understanding SiriKit... 363

How SiriKit Works 364

Defining How Siri Interacts with the User 368

Understanding the IntentHandler.swift File 371

Understanding the ExtensionUI Folder 375

Creating a Payment App with Siri 381

Summary.. 386

Chapter 13: Understanding ARKit.. 389

How ARKit Works... 389

Drawing Augmented Reality Objects 397

Resetting the World Origin 399

TABLE OF CONTENTS

Drawing Custom Shapes	404
Modifying the Appearance of Shapes	407
Summary	418

Chapter 14: Interacting with Augmented Reality 419

Storing and Accessing Graphic Assets	420
Working with Touch Gestures	423
Detecting a Horizontal Plane	428
Modifying an Image	433
Creating Virtual Objects	435
Summary	446

Index 447

About the Authors

Molly Maskrey started as an electrical engineer in her 20s working for various large Aerospace companies including IBM Federal Systems, TRW (now Northrup-Grumman), Loral Systems, Lockheed-Martin, and Boeing. After successfully navigating the first dot.com boom, she realized that a break was in order, took took several years off, moved to Maui and taught windsurfing at the beautiful Kanaha Beach Park.

She moved back to Colorado in 2005 and, with Jennifer, formed Global Tek Labs, an iOS development and accessory design services company that is now one of the leading consulting services for new designers looking to create smart attachments to Apple devices.

In 2014 Molly and Jennifer formed Quantitative Bioanalytics Laboratories, a wholly owned subsidiary of Global Tek to bring high-resolution mobile sensor technology to physical therapy, elder balance and fall prevention, sports performance quantification and instrumented gait analysis (IGA). In a pivot, Molly changed the direction of QB Labs to a platform-based predictive analytics company seeking to democratize data science for smaller companies.

Molly's background includes advanced degrees in Electrical Engineering, Applied Mathematics, Data Science, and business development. Molly generally speaks at a large number of conferences throughout the year including the Open Data Science Conference (ODSC) 2017 West advancing the topic of moving analytics from the cloud to the fog for smart city initiatives. What fuels her to succeed is the opportunity to bring justice and equality to everyone whether it's addressing food insecurity, with her business partner, to looking at options for better management of mental health using empirical data and tools such as natural language processing, speech pattern recognition using neural networks, or analyzing perfusion in brain physiology.

ABOUT THE AUTHORS

Wallace Wang has written dozens of computer books over the years beginning with ancient MS-DOS programs like WordPerfect and Turbo Pascal, migrating to writing books on Windows programs like Visual Basic and Microsoft Office, and finally switching to Swift programming for Apple products like the Macintosh and iPhone.

When he's not helping people discover the joys of programming, he performs stand-up comedy and appears on two radio shows on KNSJ in San Diego (`http://knsj.org`) called "Notes From the Underground" and "Laugh In Your Face Radio."

He also writes a screenwriting blog called "The 15 Minute Movie Method" (`http://15minutemoviemethod.com`), a blog about the latest cat news on the Internet called "Cat Daily News" (`http://catdailynews.com`), and a blog about the latest trends in technology called "Top Bananas" (`http://www.topbananas.com`).

About the Technical Reviewer

Bruce Wade is a software engineer from British Columbia, Canada. He started software development when he was 16 years old by coding his first web site. He went on to study Computer Information Systems ad DeVry Institute of Technology in Calgary, then to further enhance his skills he studied Visual & Game Programming at The Art Institute Vancouver. Over the years he has worked for large corporations as well as several start-ups. His software experience has led him to utilize many different technologies including C/C++, Python, Objective-C, Swift, Postgres, and JavaScript. In 2012 he started the company Warply Designed to focus on mobile 2D/3D and OS X development. Aside from hacking out new ideas, he enjoys spending time hiking with his Boxer Rasco, working out, and exploring new adventures.

CHAPTER 1

Multithreaded Programming Using Grand Central Dispatch

While the idea of programming multithreaded functions in any environment may seem daunting at first (see Figure 1-1), Apple came up with a new approach that makes multithreaded programming much easier. **Grand Central Dispatch** comprises language features, runtime libraries, and system enhancements that provide systemic, comprehensive improvements to the support for concurrent code execution on multicore hardware in iOS and macOS.

Figure 1-1. *Programming multithreaded applications can seem to be a disheartening experience*

A big challenge facing developers today is writing software able to perform complex actions in response to user input while remaining responsive, so that the user isn't constantly kept waiting while the processor does some behind-the-scenes task. That challenge has been with us all along; and in spite of the advances in computing technology that bring us faster CPUs, the problem persists. Look at the nearest computer screen; chances are that the last time you sat down to work at your computer, at some point, your workflow was interrupted by a spinning mouse cursor of some kind or another.

One of the reasons this has become so problematic is the way software is typically written: as a sequence of events to be performed sequentially. Such software can scale up as CPU speeds increase, but only to a certain point. As soon as the program gets stuck waiting for an external resource, such as a file or a network connection, the entire sequence of events is effectively paused. All modern operating systems now allow the use of multiple threads of execution within a program, so that even if a single thread is stuck waiting for a specific event, the other threads can keep going. Even so, many developers see multithreaded programming as a mystery and shy away from it.

> **Note** A thread is a sequence of instructions managed independently by the operating system.

Apple provides Grand Central Dispatch (GCD) giving the developer an entirely new API for splitting up the work the application needs to do into smaller chunks that can be spread across multiple threads and, with the right hardware, multiple CPUs.

We access this API using Swift closures, providing a convenient way to structure interactions between different objects while keeping related code closer together in our methods.

Creating the SlowWorker Application

As a platform for demonstrating how GCD works, we'll create the SlowWorker application that consists of a simple interface driven by a single button and a text view. Click the button, and a synchronous task is immediately started, locking up the app for about ten seconds. Once the task completes, some text appears in the text view, as shown in Figure 1-2.

CHAPTER 1   MULTITHREADED PROGRAMMING USING GRAND CENTRAL DISPATCH

Figure 1-2. *The SlowWorker application hides its interface behind a single button. Click the button, and the interface hangs for about ten seconds while the application does its work.*

Start by using the Single View Application template to make a new application in Xcode, as you've done many times before. Name this one SlowWorker, set Devices to Universal, click Next to save your project, and so on. Next, make the changes to ViewController.swift, as shown in Listing 1-1.

Listing 1-1. Add These Methods to the ViewController.swift File

```
@IBOutlet var startButton: UIButton!
@IBOutlet var resultsTextView: UITextView!

func fetchSomethingFromServer() -> String {
```

```
    Thread.sleep(forTimeInterval: 1)
    return "Hi there"
}

func processData(_ data: String) -> String {
    Thread.sleep(forTimeInterval: 2)
    return data.uppercased()
}

func calculateFirstResult(_ data: String) -> String {
    Thread.sleep(forTimeInterval: 3)
    return "Number of chars: \(data.characters.count)"
}

func calculateSecondResult(_ data: String) -> String {
    Thread.sleep(forTimeInterval: 4)
    return data.replacingOccurrences(of: "E", with: "e")
}

@IBAction func doWork(_ sender: AnyObject) {
        let startTime = NSDate()
        self.resultsTextView.text = ""
        let fetchedData = self.fetchSomethingFromServer()
        let processedData = self.processData(fetchedData)
        let firstResult = self.calculateFirstResult(processedData)
        let secondResult = self.calculateSecondResult(processedData)
        let resultsSummary =
            "First: [\(firstResult)]\nSecond: [\(secondResult)]"
        self.resultsTextView.text = resultsSummary
        let endTime = NSDate()
        print("Completed in \(endTime.timeIntervalSince(startTime as
        Date)) seconds")
}
```

As you can see, the work of this class (such as it is) is split up into a number of small pieces. This code simulates some slow activities, and none of those methods really do anything time consuming at all. To make things interesting, each method contains a call to the sleep(forTimeInterval:) class method in Thread, which simply makes the program (specifically, the thread from which the method is called) effectively pause and do nothing at all for the given number of seconds. The doWork() method also contains code at the beginning and end to calculate the amount of time it took for all the work to be done.

Now open Main.storyboard and drag a Button and a Text View into the empty View window. Position the controls as shown in Figure 1-3. You'll see some default text. Clear the text in the Text View and change the button's title to Start Working. To set the auto layout constraints, start by selecting the Start Working button, and then click the Align button at the bottom right of the editor area. In the pop-up, check Horizontally in Container and Click Add 1 Constraint. Next, Control-drag from the button to the top of the View window, release the mouse, and select Vertical Spacing to Top Layout Guide. To complete the constraints for this button, Control-drag from the button down to the text view, release the mouse, and select Vertical Spacing. To fix the position and size of the text view, expand the View Controller Scene in the Document Outline and Control-drag from the text view in the storyboard to the View icon in the Document Outline. Release the mouse and, when the pop-up appears, hold down the Shift key and select Leading Space to Container Margin, Trailing Space to Container Margin, and Vertical Spacing to Bottom Layout Guide, and then click return to apply the constraints. That completes the auto layout constraints for this application.

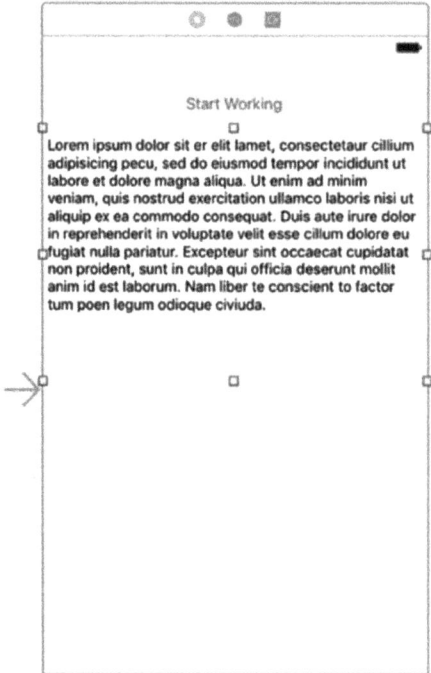

Figure 1-3. *The SlowWorker interface consists of a button and a text view*

Control-drag from the View Controller icon in the Document Outline to connect the view controller's two outlets (i.e., the `startButton` and `resultsTextView` instance variables) to the button and the text view.

Next, Control-drag from the button to the View Controller, release the mouse, and select the `doWork()` method in the pop-up so that it's called when the button is pressed. Finally, select the text view, use the Attributes Inspector to uncheck the Editable check box (it's in the upper-right corner), and delete the default text from the text view.

Save your work, and then select Run. Your app should start up, and pressing the button will make it work for about ten seconds (the sum of all those sleep amounts) before showing you the results. During your wait, you'll see that the Start Working button fades visibly, never turning back to its normal color until the "work" is done. Also, until the work is complete, the application's view is unresponsive. Tapping anywhere on the screen or rotating the device has no effect. In fact, the only way you can interact with your application during this time is by tapping the home button to switch away from it. This is exactly the state of affairs we want to avoid.

Threading Basics

Before we start implementing solutions, let's go over some concurrency basics. This is far from a complete description of threading in iOS or threading in general. I just want to explain enough for you to understand what we're doing in this chapter. Most modern operating systems (including, of course, iOS) support the notion of threads of execution. Each process can contain multiple threads, which all run concurrently. If there's just one processor core, the operating system will switch between all executing threads, much like it switches between all executing processes. If more than one core is available, the threads will be distributed among them, just as processes are.

All threads in a process share the same executable program code and the same global data. Each thread can also have some data that is exclusive to the thread. Threads can make use of a special structure called a **mutex** (short for **mutual exclusion**) or a lock, which can ensure that a particular chunk of code can't be run by multiple threads at once. This is useful for ensuring correct outcomes when multiple threads access the same data simultaneously, by locking out other threads when one thread is updating a value (in what's called a **critical section** of your code).

A common concern when dealing with threads is the idea of code being **thread-safe**. Some software libraries are written with thread concurrency in mind and have all their critical sections properly protected with mutexes. Some code libraries aren't thread-safe. For example, in Cocoa Touch, the Foundation framework is generally considered to be thread-safe. However, the UIKit framework (containing the classes specific to building GUI applications, such as `UIApplication`, `UIView`, and all its subclasses, and so on) is, for the most part, not thread-safe. (Some UIKit functionality such as drawing is considered thread-safe however.) This means that in running an iOS application, all method calls that deal with any `UIKit` objects should be executed from within the same thread, which is commonly known as the **main thread**. If you access `UIKit` objects from another thread, all bets are off. You are likely to encounter seemingly inexplicable bugs (or, even worse, you won't experience any problems, but some of your users will be affected by them after you ship your app).

Tip A lot has been written about thread safety. It's well worth your time to dig in and try to digest as much of it as you can. One great place to start is Apple's own documentation. Take a few minutes and read through this page (it will definitely help):

`https://developer.apple.com/library/ios/documentation/Cocoa/Conceptual/Multithreading/ThreadSafetySummary/ThreadSafetySummary.html`

Units of Work

The problem with the threading model described earlier is that, for the average programmer, writing error-free, multithreaded code is nearly impossible. This is not meant as a critique of our industry or of the average programmer's abilities; it's simply an observation. The complex interactions you must account for in your code when synchronizing data and actions across multiple threads are really just too much for most people to tackle. Imagine that 5% of all people have the capacity to write software at all. Only a small fraction of those 5% are really up to the task of writing heavy-duty multithreaded applications. Even people who have done it successfully will often advise others to not follow their example.

Fortunately, there are alternatives. It is possible to implement some concurrency without too much low-level detailed work. Just as we have the ability to display data on the screen without directly poking bits into video RAM and to read data from disk without interfacing directly with disk controllers, we can also leverage software abstractions that let us run our code on multiple threads without requiring us to do much directly with the threads.

The solutions Apple encourages us to use center around the idea of splitting up long-running tasks into units of work and putting those units into queues for execution. The system manages the queues for us, executing units of work on multiple threads. We don't need to start or manage the background threads directly, and we are freed from much of the bookkeeping that's usually involved in implementing multithreaded applications; the system takes care of that for us.

GCD: Low-Level Queuing

This idea of putting units of work into queues that can be executed in the background, with the system managing the threads for you, provides power and greatly simplifies many development situations where concurrency is needed. GCD made its debut on OS X (now macOS) several years ago, providing the infrastructure to do just that. A couple of years later, this technology came to the iOS platform as well. GCD puts some great concepts — units of work, painless background processing, and automatic thread management — into a C interface that can be used not only with Objective-C, but also with C, C++, and, of course, Swift. To top things off, Apple has made its implementation of GCD open source, so it can be ported to other Unix-like operating systems, as well.

One of the key concepts of GCD is the **queue**. The system provides a number of predefined queues, including a queue that's guaranteed to always do its work on the main thread. It's perfect for the non-thread-safe UIKit. You can also create your own queues — as many as you like. GCD queues are strictly first-in, first-out (FIFO). Units of work added to a GCD queue will always be started in the order they were placed in the queue. That said, they may not always finish in the same order, since a GCD queue will automatically distribute its work among multiple threads, if possible.

GCD accesses a pool of threads that are reused throughout the lifetime of the application. It tries to maintain a number of threads appropriate for the machine's architecture. It automatically takes advantage of a more powerful machine by utilizing more processor cores when it has work to do. Until a few years ago, iOS devices were all single-core, so this wasn't much of an issue. But now that all iOS devices released in the past few years feature multicore processors, GCD has become truly useful.

GCD uses closures to encapsulate the code to be added to a queue. Closures are first-class language citizens in Swift — you can assign a closure to a variable, pass one to a method, or return one as the result of a method call. Closures are the equivalent of Objective-C's blocks and similar features, sometimes referred to using the term **lambdas**, in other programming languages, such as Python. Much like a method or function, a closure can take one or more parameters and specify a return value, although closures used with GCD can neither accept arguments nor return a value. To declare a closure variable, you simply assign to it some code wrapped in curly braces, optionally with arguments:

```
// Declare a closure variable "loggerClosure" with no parameters
// and no return value.
let loggerClosure = {
    print("I'm just glad they didn't call it a lambda")
}
```

You can execute the closure in the same way as you call a function:

```
// Execute the closure, producing some output in the console.
loggerClosure()
```

Improving SlowWorker

To see how to use closures with GCD, let's revisit SlowWorker's doWork() method. It currently looks like this:

```
@IBAction func doWork(_ sender: AnyObject) {
    let startTime = NSDate()
    self.resultsTextView.text = ""
    let fetchedData = self.fetchSomethingFromServer()
    let processedData = self.processData(fetchedData)
    let firstResult = self.calculateFirstResult(processedData)
    let secondResult = self.calculateSecondResult(processedData)
    let resultsSummary =
        "First: [\(firstResult)]\nSecond: [\(secondResult)]"
    self.resultsTextView.text = resultsSummary
```

```
        let endTime = NSDate()
        print("Completed in \(endTime.timeIntervalSince(startTime as
        Date)) seconds")
    }
```

We can make this method run entirely in the background by wrapping all the code in a closure and passing it to a GCD function called `DispatchQueue`. This function takes two parameters: a GCD queue and the closure to assign to the queue. Make the changes in Listing 1-2 to your copy of `doWork()`.

Listing 1-2. Modifications to the doWork Method to Use GCD

```
    @IBAction func doWork(sender: AnyObject) {
        let startTime = NSDate()
        resultsTextView.text = ""
        let queue = DispatchQueue.global(qos: .default)
        queue.async {
            let fetchedData = self.fetchSomethingFromServer()
            let processedData = self.processData(fetchedData)
            let firstResult = self.calculateFirstResult(processedData)
            let secondResult = self.calculateSecondResult(processedData)
            let resultsSummary =
                "First: [\(firstResult)]\nSecond: [\(secondResult)]"
            self.resultsTextView.text = resultsSummary
            let endTime = NSDate()
            print("Completed in \(endTime.timeIntervalSince(startTime as
            Date)) seconds")
        }
    }
```

The first changed line grabs a preexisting global queue that's always available, using the `DispatchQueue.global()` function. That function takes one arguments letting you specify a priority. If you specify a different priority in the argument you will actually get a different global queue, which the system will prioritize differently. For now, we'll stick with the default global queue.

The queue is then passed to the `queue.async()` function, along with the closure. GCD takes the closure and puts it on the queue, from where it will be scheduled to run on a background thread and executed one step at a time, just as when it was running in the main thread.

Note that we defined a variable called `startTime` just before the closure is created, and then use its value at the end of the closure. Intuitively, this doesn't seem to make sense because, by the time the closure is executed, the `doWork()` method has returned, so the `NSDate` instance that the `startTime` variable is pointing to should already be released! This is a crucial point to understand about closures: if a closure accesses any variables from "the outside" during its execution, then some special setup happens when the closure is created, allowing it to continue to access to them. All of this is done automatically by the Swift compiler and runtime — you don't need to do anything special to make it happen.

Don't Forget That Main Thread

Getting back to the project at hand, there's one problem here: UIKit thread safety. Remember that messaging any GUI object from a background thread, including our `resultsTextView`, is a no-no. In fact, if you run the example now, you'll see an exception appear in the Xcode console after about ten seconds, when the closure tries to update the text view. Fortunately, GCD provides a way to deal with this, too. Inside the closure, we can call another dispatching function, passing work back to the main thread. Make one additional change to your version of `doWork()`, as shown in Listing 1-3.

Listing 1-3. *The modified doWork Method*

```swift
@IBAction func doWork(sender: AnyObject) {
    let startTime = NSDate()
    resultsTextView.text = ""
    let queue = DispatchQueue.global(attributes: DispatchQueue.
    GlobalAttributes.qosDefault)
    queue.async {
        let fetchedData = self.fetchSomethingFromServer()
        let processedData = self.processData(fetchedData)
        let firstResult = self.calculateFirstResult(processedData)
        let secondResult = self.calculateSecondResult(processedData)
        let resultsSummary =
            "First: [\(firstResult)]\nSecond: [\(secondResult)]"
```

```
        DispatchQueue.main.async {
            self.resultsTextView.text = resultsSummary
        }
        let endTime = NSDate()
        print("Completed in \(endTime.timeIntervalSince(startTime as
        Date)) seconds")
    }
}
```

Giving Some Feedback

If you build and run your app at this point, you'll see that it now seems to work a bit more smoothly, at least in some sense. The button no longer gets stuck in a highlighted position after you touch it, which perhaps leads you to tap again, and again, and so on. If you look in the Xcode console log, you'll see the result of each of those taps, but only the results of the last tap will be shown in the text view. What we really want to do is enhance the GUI so that, after the user presses the button, the display is immediately updated in a way that indicates that an action is underway. We also want the button to be disabled while the work is in progress so that the user can't keep clicking it to spawn more and more work into background threads. We'll do this by adding a UIActivityIndicatorView to our display. This class provides the sort of spinner seen in many applications and web sites. Start by adding an outlet for it at the top of ViewController.swift:

```
@IBOutlet var spinner : UIActivityIndicatorView!
```

Next, open Main.Storyboard; locate an Activity Indicator View in the library; and drag it into our view, next to the button. You'll need to add layout constraints to fix the activity indicator's position relative to the button. One way to do this is to Control-drag from the button to the activity indicator and select Horizontal Spacing from the pop-up menu to fix the horizontal separation between them, and then Control-drag again and select Center Vertically to make sure that their centers remain vertically aligned.

With the activity indicator spinner selected, use the Attributes Inspector to check the Hides When Stopped check box so that our spinner will appear only when we tell it to start spinning (no one wants an unspinning spinner in their GUI). Next, Control-drag from the View Controller icon to the spinner and connect the spinner outlet. Save your changes.

Now open ViewController.swift. Here, we'll first work on the doWork() method a bit, adding a few lines to manage the appearance of the button and the spinner when the user taps the button and when the work is done. We'll first set the button's enabled property to false, which prevents it from registering any taps and also shows that the button is disabled by making its text gray and somewhat transparent. Next, we get the spinner moving by calling its **startAnimating**() method. At the end of the closure, we re-enable the button and stop the spinner, which causes it to disappear again, as shown in Listing 1-4.

Listing 1-4. Adding the Spinner Functions to our doWork Method

```swift
@IBAction func doWork(sender: AnyObject) {
    let startTime = NSDate()
    resultsTextView.text = ""
    startButton.isEnabled = false
    spinner.startAnimating()
    let queue = DispatchQueue.global(qos: .default)
    queue.async {
        let fetchedData = self.fetchSomethingFromServer()
        let processedData = self.processData(fetchedData)
        let firstResult = self.calculateFirstResult(processedData)
        let secondResult = self.calculateSecondResult(processedData)
        let resultsSummary =
            "First: [\(firstResult)]\nSecond: [\(secondResult)]"
        DispatchQueue.main.async {
            self.resultsTextView.text = resultsSummary
            self.startButton.isEnabled = true
            self.spinner.stopAnimating()
        }
        let endTime = NSDate()
        print("Completed in \(endTime.timeIntervalSince(startTime as Date)) seconds")
    }
}
```

Build and run the app, and press the button. Even though the work being done takes a few seconds, the user isn't just left hanging. The button is disabled and looks the part as well. Also, the animated spinner lets the user know that the app hasn't actually hung up and can be expected to return to normal at some point.

Concurrent Closures

The sharp-eyed among you will notice that, after going through these motions, we still haven't really changed the basic sequential layout of our algorithm (if you can even call this simple list of steps an algorithm). All that we're doing is moving a chunk of this method to a background thread and then finishing up in the main thread. The Xcode console output proves it: this work takes ten seconds to run, just as it did at the outset. The issue is that the `calculateFirstResult()` and `calculateSecondResult()` methods don't depend on each and therefore don't need to be called in sequence. Doing them concurrently gives us a substantial speedup.

Fortunately, GCD has a way to accomplish this by using what's called a **dispatch group**. All closures that are dispatched asynchronously within the context of a group, via the `dispatch_group_async()` function, are set loose to execute as fast as they can, including being distributed to multiple threads for concurrent execution, if possible. We can also use `dispatch_group_notify()` to specify an additional closure that will be executed when all the closures in the group have been run to completion.

Make these final changes to the doWork method, as shown in Listing 1-5.

Listing 1-5. *The Final Version of Our doWork Method*

```swift
@IBAction func doWork(_ sender: AnyObject) {
    let startTime = Date()
    self.resultsTextView.text = ""
    startButton.isEnabled = false
    spinner.startAnimating()
    let queue = DispatchQueue.global(qos: .default)
    queue.async {
        let fetchedData = self.fetchSomethingFromServer()
        let processedData = self.processData(fetchedData)
        var firstResult: String!
        var secondResult: String!
        let group = DispatchGroup()
```

```
            queue.async(group: group) {
                firstResult = self.calculateFirstResult(processedData)
            }
            queue.async(group: group) {
                secondResult = self.calculateSecondResult(processedData)
            }
            group.notify(queue: queue) {
                let resultsSummary = "First: [\(firstResult!)]\nSecond: [\(secondResult!)]"
                DispatchQueue.main.async {
                    self.resultsTextView.text = resultsSummary
                    self.startButton.isEnabled = true
                    self.spinner.stopAnimating()
                }
                let endTime = Date()
                print("Completed in \(endTime.timeIntervalSince(startTime)) seconds")
            }
        }
    }
```

One complication here is that each of the `calculate` methods returns a value that we want to grab, so we need to make sure that the variables `firstResult` and `secondResult` can be assigned from the closures. To do this, we declare them using `var` instead of `let`. However, Swift requires a variable that's referenced from a closure to be initialized, so the following declarations don't work:

```
var firstResult: String
var secondResult: String
```

You can, of course, work around this problem by initializing both variables with an arbitrary value, but it's easier to make them implicitly unwrapped optionals by adding ! to the declaration:

```
var firstResult: String!
var secondResult: String!
```

Now, Swift doesn't require an initialization, but we need to be sure that both variables will have a value when they are eventually read. In this case, we can be sure of that, because the variables are read in the completion closure for the async group, by which time they are certain to have been assigned a value. With this in place, build and run the app again. You'll see that your efforts have paid off. What was once a ten-second operation now takes just seven seconds, thanks to the fact that we're running both of the calculations simultaneously.

Obviously, our contrived example gets the maximum effect because these two "calculations" don't actually do anything but cause the thread they're running on to sleep. In a real application, the speedup would depend on what sort of work is being done and what resources are available. The performance of CPU-intensive calculations is helped by this technique only if multiple CPU cores are available. It will get better almost for free as more cores are added to future iOS devices. Other uses, such as fetching data from multiple network connections at once, would see a speed increase even with just one CPU.

As you can see, GCD is not a panacea. Using GCD won't automatically speed up every application. But by carefully applying these techniques at those points in your app where speed is essential, or where you find that your application feels like it's lagging in its responses to the user, you can easily provide a better user experience, even in situations where you can't improve the real performance.

Background Processing

Another important technology for handling concurrency is background processing. This allows your apps to run in the background — in some circumstances, even after the user has pressed the home button.

This functionality should not be confused with the true multitasking that modern desktop operating systems now feature, where all the programs you launch remain resident in the system RAM until you explicitly quit them (or until the operating system needs to free up some space and starts swapping them to disk). iOS devices still have too little RAM to be able to pull that off very well. Instead, this background processing is meant to allow applications that require specific kinds of system functionality to continue to run in a constrained manner when they are in the background. For instance, if you have an app that plays an audio stream from an Internet radio station, iOS will let that app continue to run, even if the user switches to another app. Beyond that, it will even provide standard pause and volume controls in the iOS control center (the translucent control panel that appears when you swipe up from the bottom of the screen) while your app is playing audio.

Assume you're creating an app that does one of the following things: plays audio even when the user is running another app, requests continuous location updates, responds to a special type of push request telling it to load new data from a server, or implements Voice over IP (VoIP) to let users send and receive phone calls on the Internet. In each of these cases, you can declare this situation in your app's Info.plist file, and the system will treat your app in a special way. This usage, while interesting, is probably not something that most readers of this book will be tackling right away, so we're not going to delve into it here.

Besides running apps in the background, iOS also includes the ability to put an app into a suspended state after the user presses the home button. This state of suspended execution is conceptually similar to putting your Mac into sleep mode. The entire working memory of the application is held in RAM; it just isn't executed while suspended. As a result, switching back to such an application is lightning fast. This isn't limited to special applications. In fact, it is the default behavior of any app you build with Xcode (though this can be disabled by another setting in the Info.plist file). To see this in action, open your device's Mail application and drill down into a message. Next, press the home button, open the Notes application, and select a note. Now double-tap the home button and switch back to Mail. You'll see that there's no perceptible lag; it just slides into place as if it had been running all along.

For most applications, this sort of automatic suspension and resumption is all you're likely to need. However, in some situations, your app may need to know when it's about to be suspended and when it has just been awakened. The system provides ways of notifying an app about changes to its execution state via the `UIApplication` class, which has a number of delegate methods and notifications for just this purpose. I'll show you how to use them later in this chapter.

When your application is about to be suspended, one thing it can do, regardless of whether it's one of the special backgroundable application types, is request a bit of additional time to run in the background. The idea is to make sure your app has enough time to close any open files, network resources, and so on. We'll see an example of this shortly.

Application Life Cycle

Before we get into the specifics of how to deal with changes to your app's execution state, let's talk a bit about the various states in its life cycle:

- **Not Running**: This is the state that all apps are in on a freshly rebooted device. An application that has been launched at any point after the device is turned on will return to this state only under specific conditions:
    - If its Info.plist includes the `UIApplicationExitsOnSuspend` key (with its value set to YES)
    - If it was previously Suspended and the system needs to clear out some memory
    - If it crashes while running
- **Active**: This is the normal running state of an application when it's displayed on the screen. It can receive user input and update the display.
- **Background**: In this state, an app is given some time to execute some code, but it can't directly access the screen or get any user input. All apps enter this state briefly when the user presses the home button; most of them quickly move on to the Suspended state. Apps that want to do any sort of background processing stay in this state until they're made Active again.
- **Suspended**: A Suspended app is frozen. This is what happens to normal apps after their brief stint in the Background state. All the memory the app was using while it was active is held just as it was. If the user brings the app back to the Active state, it will pick up right where it left off. On the other hand, if the system needs more memory for whichever app is currently Active, any Suspended apps may be terminated (and placed back into the Not Running state) and their memory freed for other use.
- **Inactive**: An app enters the Inactive state only as a temporary rest stop between two other states. The only way an app can stay Inactive for any length of time is if the user is dealing with a system prompt (such as those shown for an incoming call or SMS message) or if the user has locked the screen. This state is basically a sort of limbo.

State-Change Notifications

To manage changes between these states, `UIApplication` defines a number of methods that its delegate can implement. In addition to the delegate methods, `UIApplication` also defines a matching set of notification names (see Table 1-1). This allows other objects besides the app delegate to register for notifications when the application's state changes.

Table 1-1. *Delegate Methods for Tracking Your Application's Execution State and Their Corresponding Notification Names*

Delegate Method	Notification Name
`application(_:didFinishLaunchingWithOptions:)`	`UIApplicationDidFinishLaunching`
`applicationWillResignActive()`	`UIApplicationWillResignActive`
`applicationDidBecomeActive()`	`UIApplicationDidBecomeActive`
`applicationDidEnterBackground()`	`UIApplicationDidEnterBackground`
`applicationWillEnterForeground()`	`UIApplicationWillEnterForeground`
`applicationWillTerminate()`	`UIApplicationWillTerminate`

Note that each of these methods is directly related to one of the running states: Active, Inactive, and Background. Each delegate method is called (and each notification posted) in only one of those states. The most important state transitions are between Active and other states. Some transitions, like from Background to Suspended, occur without any notice whatsoever. Let's go through these methods and discuss how they're meant to be used.

The first of these, `application(_:didFinishLaunchingWithOptions:)`, represents the primary way of doing application-level coding directly after the app has launched. There is a similar method called `application(_:willFinishLaunchingWithOptions:)` that's called first and which is intended for applications that use the view controller-based state save and restore feature (which is beyond the scope of this book). That method is not listed here because it's not associated with a state change.

The next two methods, applicationWillResignActive() and applicationDidBecomeActive(), are both used in a number of circumstances. If the user presses the home button, applicationWillResignActive() gets called. If the user later brings the app back to the foreground, applicationDidBecomeActive() is called. The same sequence of events occurs if the user receives a phone call. applicationDidBecomeActive() is also called when the application launches for the first time. In general, this pair of methods brackets the movement of an application from the Active state to the Inactive state. They are good places to enable and disable any animations, in-app audio, or other items that deal with the app's presentation to the user. Because of the multiple situations where applicationDidBecomeActive() is used, you may want to put some of your app initialization code there instead of in application(_:didFinishLaunchingWithOptions:). Note that you should not assume in applicationWillResignActive() that the application is about to be sent to the background; it may just be a temporary change that ends up with a move back to the Active state.

After those methods we see applicationDidEnterBackground() and applicationWillEnterForeground(), which have a slightly different usage area: dealing with an app that is definitely being sent to the background. applicationDidEnterBackground() is where your app should free all resources that can be re-created later, save all user data, close network connections, and so forth. This is also the spot where you can request more time to run in the background if you need it, as we'll see shortly. If you spend too much time doing things in applicationDidEnterBackground() — more than about five seconds — the system will decide that your app is misbehaving and terminate it. You should implement applicationWillEnterForeground() to re-create whatever was torn down in applicationDidEnterBackground(), such as reloading user data, reestablishing network connections, and so on. Note that when applicationDidEnterBackground() is called, you can safely assume that applicationWillResignActive() has also been recently called. Likewise, when applicationWillEnterForeground() gets called, you can assume that applicationDidBecomeActive() will soon be called, as well.

Finally, applicationWillTerminate(), which you'll probably rarely use, if ever, is called only if your application is already in the background and the system decides to skip suspension for some reason and simply terminate the app.

Now that you have a basic theoretical understanding of the states an application transitions between, let's put this knowledge to the test with a simple app that does nothing more than write a message to Xcode's console log each time one of these

CHAPTER 1 ■ MULTITHREADED PROGRAMMING USING GRAND CENTRAL DISPATCH

methods is called. We'll then manipulate the running app in a variety of ways, just as a user might, and see which transitions occur. To get the most out of this example, you'll need an iOS device. If you don't have one, you can use the simulator and skip over the parts that require a device.

Creating State Lab

In Xcode, create a new project based on the Single View Application template and name it State Lab. Initially at least, this app won't display anything but the default white screen it's born with. Later, we'll make it do something more interesting, but for now, all the output it's going to generate will end up in the Xcode console. The AppDelegate.swift file already contains all the methods we're interested in. We just need to add some logging, as shown in bold. Note that we've also removed the comments from these methods, as shown in Listing 1-6, just for the sake of brevity.

Listing 1-6. The AppDelegate.swift Logging Methods

```
func application(_ application: UIApplication,
                 didFinishLaunchingWithOptions launchOptions:
                 [NSObject: AnyObject]?) -> Bool {
    print(#function)
    return true
}
func applicationWillResignActive(_ application: UIApplication) {
    print(#function)
}
func applicationDidEnterBackground(_ application: UIApplication) {
    print(#function)
}
func applicationWillEnterForeground(_ application: UIApplication) {
    print(#function)
}
func applicationDidBecomeActive(_ application: UIApplication) {
    print(#function)
}
```

```
func applicationWillTerminate(_ application: UIApplication) {
    print(#function)
}
```

You may be wondering about the value that's being passed to the `print()` function in each of these methods: the literal expression `#function` evaluates to the name of the method in which it appears. Here, we are using it to get the current method name without needing to retype it or copy and paste it into each of the life cycle methods.

Exploring Execution States

Now build and run the app and take a look at the console (View ➤ Debug Area ➤ Activate Console), where you should see something like this:

```
application(_:didFinishLaunchingWithOptions:)
applicationDidBecomeActive
```

among a number of other messages. You can use the search field below the console output to filter what you observe.

Here, you can see that the application has successfully launched and been moved into the Active state. Now press the home button (if you're using the simulator, you'll have to do this by selecting Hardware ➤ Home from the simulator's menu or Shift + Command + H on the keyboard. You should see the following in the console:

```
applicationWillResignActive
applicationDidEnterBackground
```

These two lines show the app actually transitioning between two states: it first becomes Inactive, and then it goes to Background. What you can't see here is that the app also switches to a third state: Suspended. Remember that you do not get any notification that this has happened; it's completely outside your control. Note that the app is still live in some sense, and Xcode is still connected to it, even though it's not actually getting any CPU time. Verify this by tapping the app's icon to relaunch it, which should produce this output:

```
applicationWillEnterForeground
applicationDidBecomeActive
```

CHAPTER 1 MULTITHREADED PROGRAMMING USING GRAND CENTRAL DISPATCH

There you are, back in business. The app was previously Suspended, is woken up to Inactive, and then ends up Active again. So, what happens when the app is really terminated? Tap the home button again and you'll see this:

```
applicationWillResignActive
applicationDidEnterBackground
```

Now double-tap the home button (or on the simulator, press Shift + Command + H — you need to press the H key twice). The sideways-scrolling screen of apps should appear. Press and swipe upward on the State Lab screenshot until it flies offscreen, killing the application. You should see something like the following:

```
2016-07-21 10:15:40.201746 temp[2825:864732] [Common]
<FBSUIApplicationWorkspaceClient [0x6080000f8700]>: Received exit event
applicationDidEnterBackground
applicationWillTerminate
```

Tip Do not rely on the `applicationWillTerminate()` method being called to save the state of your application – do this in `applicationDidEnterBackground()` instead.

There's one more interesting interaction to examine here. It's what happens when the system shows an alert dialog, temporarily taking over the input stream from the app and putting it into an Inactive state. This state can be readily triggered only when running on a real device instead of the simulator, using the built-in Messages app. Messages, like many other apps, can receive messages from the outside and display them in several ways.

To see how these are set up, run the Settings app on your device, choose Notifications from the list, and then select the Messages app from the list of apps. The hot "new" way to show messages, which debuted way back in iOS 5, is called **Banners**. This works by showing a small banner overlaid at the top of the screen, which doesn't need to interrupt whatever app is currently running. What we want to show is the bad old Alerts method, which makes a modal panel appear in front of the current app, requiring a user action. Under the heading ALERT STYLE WHEN UNLOCKED, select Alerts so that the Messages app turns back into the kind of pushy jerk that users of iOS 4 and earlier always had to deal with.

Now back to your computer. In Xcode, use the pop-up at the upper left to switch from the simulator to your device, and then hit the Run button to build and run the app on your device. Now all you need to do is send a message to your device from the outside. If your device is an iPhone, you can send it an SMS message from another phone. If it's an iPod touch or an iPad, you're limited to Apple's own iMessage communication, which works on all iOS devices, as well as macOS in the Messages app. Figure out what works for your setup, and send your device a message via SMS or iMessage. When your device displays the system alert showing the incoming message, this will appear in the Xcode console:

```
applicationWillResignActive
```

Note that our app didn't get sent to the background. It's in the Inactive state and can still be seen behind the system alert. If this app was a game or had any video, audio, or animations running, this is where we would probably want to pause them.

Press the Close button on the alert, and you'll get this:

```
applicationDidBecomeActive
```

Now let's see what happens if you decide to reply to the message instead. Send another message to your device, generating this:

```
applicationWillResignActive
```

This time, hit Reply, which switches you over to the Messages app. You should see the following flurry of activity:

```
applicationDidBecomeActive
applicationWillResignActive
applicationDidEnterBackground
```

Our app quickly becomes Active, becomes Inactive again, and finally goes to Background (and then, silently, Suspended).

25

Using Execution State Changes

So, what should we make of all this? Based on what was just demonstrated, it seems like there's a clear strategy to follow when dealing with these state changes:

Active ➤ Inactive

Use `applicationWillResignActive()`/`UIApplicationWillResignActive` notification to "pause" your app's display. If your app is a game, you probably already have the ability to pause the gameplay in some way. For other kinds of apps, make sure no time-critical demands for user input are in the works because your app won't be getting any user input for a while.

Inactive ➤ Background

Use `applicationDidEnterBackground()`/`UIApplicationDidEnterBackground` notification to release any resources that don't need to be kept around when the app is backgrounded (such as cached images or other easily reloadable data) or that might not survive backgrounding anyway (such as active network connections). Getting rid of excess memory usage here will make your app's eventual Suspended snapshot smaller, thereby decreasing the risk that your app will be purged from RAM entirely. You should also use this opportunity to save any application data that will help your users pick up where they left off the next time your app is relaunched. If your app comes back to the Active state, normally this won't matter; however, in case it's purged and must be relaunched, your users will appreciate starting off in the same place.

Background ➤ Inactive

Use `applicationWillEnterForeground()`/`UIApplicationWillEnterForeground` notification to undo anything you did when switching from Inactive to Background. For example, here you can reestablish persistent network connections.

Inactive ➤ Active

Use `applicationDidBecomeActive()`/`UIApplicationDidBecomeActive` notification to undo anything you did when switching from Active to Inactive. Note that, if your app is a game, this probably does not mean dropping out of pause straight to the game; you should let your users do that on their own. Also keep in mind that this method and notification are used when an app is freshly launched, so anything you do here must work in that context, as well.

There is one special consideration for the Inactive ➤ Background transition. Not only does it have the longest description in the previous list, but it's also probably the most code- and time-intensive transition in applications because of the amount of bookkeeping you may want your app to do. When this transition is underway, the system won't give you the benefit of an unlimited amount of time to save your changes here. It gives you a few seconds. If your app takes longer than that to return from the delegate method (and handle any notifications you've registered for), then your app will be summarily purged from memory and pushed into the Not Running state. If this seems unfair, don't worry because there is a reprieve available. While handling that delegate method or notification, you can ask the system to perform some additional work for you in a background queue, which buys you some extra time.

Handling the Inactive State

The simplest state change your app is likely to encounter is from Active to Inactive, and then back to Active. You may recall that this is what happens if your iPhone receives an SMS message while your app is running and displays it for the user. In this section, we're going to make State Lab do something visually interesting so that you can see what happens if you ignore that state change. Next, I'll show you how to fix it.

We'll also add a UILabel to our display and make it move using Core Animation, which is a really nice way of animating objects in iOS.

Start by adding a UILabel in ViewController.swift:

```
class ViewController: UIViewController {
    private var label:UILabel!
```

Now let's set up the label when the view loads. Modify the viewDidLoad() method as shown in Listing 1-7.

Listing 1-7. Our Modified viewDidLoad Method

```
    override func viewDidLoad() {
        super.viewDidLoad()
        // Do any additional setup after loading the view, typically from a nib.
        let bounds = view.bounds
```

CHAPTER 1   MULTITHREADED PROGRAMMING USING GRAND CENTRAL DISPATCH

```
    let labelFrame = CGRect(origin: CGPoint(x: bounds.origin.x,
    y: bounds.midY - 50), size: CGSize(width:  bounds.size.width,
    height: 100))
    label = UILabel(frame: labelFrame)
    label.font = UIFont(name: "Helvetica", size:70)
    label.text = "Bazinga!"
    label.textAlignment = NSTextAlignment.center
    label.backgroundColor = UIColor.clear()
    view.addSubview(label)
}
```

This vertically centers the label in its parent view and makes it stretch across the full width of its parent. Next, let's set up some animation. We'll define two methods: one to rotate the label to an upside-down position:

```
func rotateLabelDown() {
    UIView.animate(withDuration: 0.5, animations: {
            self.label.transform = CGAffineTransform(rotationAngle:
            CGFloat(M_PI))
        },
        completion: {(Bool) -> Void in
            self.rotateLabelUp()
        }
    )
}
```

This one rotates it back to normal:

```
func rotateLabelUp() {
    UIView.animate(withDuration: 0.5, animations: {
            self.label.transform = CGAffineTransform(rotationAngle: 0)
        },
        completion: {(Bool) -> Void in
                self.rotateLabelDown()
        }
    )
}
```

This deserves a bit of explanation. `UIView` defines a class method called `animate(withDuration: completion:)`, which sets up an animation. Attributes that can be animated, which we set within the animations closure, don't have an immediate effect on the receiver. Instead, Core Animation will smoothly transition that attribute from its current value to the new value we specify. This is what's called an **implicit animation**, which is one of the main features of Core Animation. The completion closure lets us specify what will happen after the animation is complete. Note carefully the syntax of this closure:

```
completion: {(Bool) -> Void in
    if self.animate {
        self.rotateLabelDown()
    }
}
```

The code in bold is the signature of the closure — it says that the closure is called with a single Boolean argument and returns nothing. The argument has a value of `true` if the animation completed normally, `false` if it was cancelled. In this example, we don't make any use of this argument.

So, each of these methods sets the label's `transform` property to a particular rotation angle, specified in radians, and uses the completion closure to call the other method, so the text will continue to animate back and forth forever.

Finally, we need to set up a way to kick-start the animation. For now, we'll do this by adding this line at the end of `viewDidLoad()`:

```
rotateLabelDown()
```

CHAPTER 1   MULTITHREADED PROGRAMMING USING GRAND CENTRAL DISPATCH

Build and run the app. You should see the Bazinga! label rotate back and forth, as shown in Figure 1-4.

Figure 1-4. *The State Lab application rotating the label*

To test the Active ➤ Inactive transition, you really need to once again run this on an actual iPhone and send an SMS message to it from elsewhere. Build and run the app on an iPhone, and see that the animation is running along. Now send an SMS message to the device. When the system alert comes up to show the message, you'll see that the animation keeps on running. That may be slightly comical, but it's probably irritating for a user. We will use application state transition notifications to stop our animation when this occurs.

Our controller class will need to have some internal state to keep track of whether it should be animating at any given time. For this purpose, let's add a property to the ViewController class:

```
class ViewController: UIViewController {
    private var label:UILabel!
    private var animate = false
```

As you've seen, changes in the application state are notified to the application delegate, but since our class isn't the application delegate, we can't just implement the delegate methods and expect them to work. Instead, we sign up to receive notifications from the application when its execution state changes. Do this by adding the following code to the end of the viewDidLoad method in ViewController.swift:

```
let center = NotificationCenter.default
center.addObserver(self, selector: #selector(ViewController.
applicationWillResignActive),
        name: Notification.Name.UIApplicationWillResignActive,
        object: nil)
 center.addObserver(self, selector: #selector(ViewController.
applicationDidBecomeActive),
        name: NSNotification.Name.UIApplicationDidBecomeActive,
        object: nil)
```

This sets up the notifications so that each will call a method in our class at the appropriate time. Add the following methods to the ViewController class:

```
func applicationWillResignActive() {
    print("VC: \(#function)")
    animate = false
}

func applicationDidBecomeActive() {
    print("VC: \(#function)")
    animate = true
    rotateLabelDown()
}
```

CHAPTER 1   MULTITHREADED PROGRAMMING USING GRAND CENTRAL DISPATCH

These methods include the same method logging as before, just so you can see where the methods occur in the Xcode console. We added the preface "VC: " to distinguish this call from the similar calls in the delegate (VC is for view controller). The first of these methods just turns off the animate flag. The second turns the flag back on, and then actually starts up the animations again. For that first method to have any effect, we need to add some code to check the animate flag and keep on animating only if it's enabled:

```
func rotateLabelUp() {
    UIView.animate(withDuration: 0.5, animations: {
            self.label.transform = CGAffineTransform(rotationAngle: 0)
        },
        completion: {(Bool) -> Void in
            if self.animate {
                self.rotateLabelDown()
            }
        }
    )
}
```

We added this to the completion block of rotateLabelUp(), (and only there) so that our animation will stop only when the text is right-side up. Finally, since we are now starting the animation when the application becomes active, and this happens right after it is launched, we no longer need the call rotateLabelDown() in viewDidLoad(), so delete it:

```
override func viewDidLoad() {
    rotateLabelDown();
    let center = NSNotificationCenter.default
```

Now build and run the app again, and you should see that it's animating as before. Once again, send an SMS message to your iPhone. This time, when the system alert appears, you'll see that the animation in the background stops as soon as the text is right-side up. Tap the Close button, and the animation starts back up.

Now you've seen what to do for the simple case of switching from Active to Inactive and back. The bigger task, and perhaps the more important one, is dealing with a switch to the background and then back to foreground.

32

Handling the Background State

As mentioned earlier, switching to the Background state is pretty important to ensure the best possible user experience. This is the spot where you'll want to discard any resources that can easily be reacquired (or will be lost anyway when your app goes silent) and save information about your app's current state, all without occupying the main thread for more than five seconds.

To demonstrate some of these behaviors, we're going to extend State Lab in a few ways. First, we're going to add an image to the display so that I can later show you how to get rid of the in-memory image. Then I'm going to show you how to save some information about the app's state, so we can easily restore it later. Finally, I'll show you how to make sure these activities aren't taking up too much main thread time by putting all this work into a background queue.

Removing Resources When Entering the Background

Start by adding smiley.png from the 15 - Image folder in the book's source archive to your project's State Lab folder. Be sure to enable the check box that tells Xcode to copy the file to your project directory. Don't add it to the Assets.xcassets asset catalog because that would provide automatic caching, which would interfere with the specific resource management we're going to implement.

Now let's add properties for both the image and an image view to ViewController.swift:

```
class ViewController: UIViewController {
    private var label:UILabel!
    private var smiley:UIImage!
    private var smileyView:UIImageView!
    private var animate = false
```

Next, set up the image view and put it on the screen by modifying the viewDidLoad() method, as shown in Listing 1-8.

Listing 1-8. Modified viewDidLoad Methods

```
    override func viewDidLoad() {
        super.viewDidLoad()
        // Do any additional setup after loading the view, typically from a nib.
```

```swift
let bounds = view.bounds
let labelFrame = CGRect(origin: CGPoint(x: bounds.origin.x, y:
bounds.midY - 50), size: CGSize(width:  bounds.size.width,
height: 100))
label = UILabel(frame:labelFrame)
label.font = UIFont(name:"Helvetica", size:70)
label.text = "Bazinga!"
label.textAlignment = NSTextAlignment.center
label.backgroundColor = UIColor.clear()

// smiley.png is 84 x 84
let smileyFrame = CGRect(x: bounds.midX - 42,
    y: bounds.midY/2 - 42, width: 84, height: 84)

smileyView = UIImageView(frame:smileyFrame)
smileyView.contentMode = UIViewContentMode.center
let smileyPath =
    Bundle.main.pathForResource("smiley", ofType: "png")!
smiley = UIImage(contentsOfFile: smileyPath)
smileyView.image = smiley
view.addSubview(smileyView)

view.addSubview(label)

let center = NotificationCenter.default
center.addObserver(self, selector: #selector(ViewController.
applicationWillResignActive),
        name: NSNotification.Name.UIApplicationWillResignActive,
        object: nil)
center.addObserver(self, selector: #selector(ViewController.
applicationDidBecomeActive),
        name: NSNotification.Name.UIApplicationDidBecomeActive,
        object: nil)
}
```

Build and run the app. You'll see the incredibly happy-looking smiley face toward the top of your screen, as shown in Figure 1-5.

Figure 1-5. *The State Lab application rotating the label with the addition of a smiley icon*

Next, press the home button to switch your app to the background, and then tap its icon to launch it again. You'll see that when the app resumes, the label starts rotating again, as expected. All seems well, but in fact, we're not yet optimizing system resources as well as we could. Remember that the fewer resources we use while our app is suspended, the lower the risk that iOS will terminate our app entirely. By clearing any easily re-created resources from memory when we can, we increase the chance that our app will stick around and therefore relaunch super quickly.

CHAPTER 1 MULTITHREADED PROGRAMMING USING GRAND CENTRAL DISPATCH

Let's see what we can do about that smiley face. We would really like to free up that image when going to the Background state and re-create it when coming back from the Background state. To do that, we'll need to add two more notification registrations inside `viewDidLoad()`:

```
center.addObserver(self, selector: #selector(ViewController.
applicationDidEnterBackground),
        name: NSNotification.Name.UIApplicationDidEnter
        Background, object: nil)
center.addObserver(self, selector: #selector(ViewController.
applicationWillEnterForeground),
        name: NSNotification.Name.UIApplicationWillEnter
        Foreground, object: nil)
```

And we want to implement the two new methods:

```
func applicationDidEnterBackground() {
    print("VC: \(#function)")
    self.smiley = nil;
    self.smileyView.image = nil;
}
func applicationWillEnterForeground() {
    print("VC: \(__FUNCTION__)")
    let smileyPath =
        Bundle.main.path(forResource:"smiley", ofType:"png")!
    smiley = UIImage(contentsOfFile: smileyPath)
    smileyView.image = smiley
}
```

Build and run the app, and repeat the same steps of backgrounding your app and switching back to it. You should see that, from the user's standpoint, the behavior appears to be about the same. If you want to verify for yourself that this is really happening, comment out the contents of the `applicationWillEnterForeground()` method, and then build and run the app again. You'll see that the image really does disappear.

Saving State When Entering the Background

Now that you've seen an example of how to free up some resources when entering the Background state, it's time to think about saving state. Remember that the idea is to save information relevant to what the user is doing, so that if your application is later dumped from memory, users can still pick up right where they left off the next time they return.

The kind of state we're talking about here is really application specific, not view specific. Do not confuse this with saving and restoring the locations of views or which screen of your application the user was looking at when it was last active — for that, iOS provides the state saving and restoration mechanism, which you can read about in the *iOS App Programming Guide* on Apple's web site (`https://developer.apple.com/library/ios/documentation/iPhone/Conceptual/iPhoneOSProgrammingGuide/StrategiesforImplementingYourApp/StrategiesforImplementingYourApp.html`). Here, we're thinking about things like user preferences in applications for which you do not want to implement a separate settings bundle. Using the same `UserDefaults` API that we will introduce to you to in Chapter 12, you can quickly and easily save preferences from within the application and read them back later. Of course, if your application is not visually complex or you don't want to use the state-saving and restoration mechanism, you can save information that will allow you to restore its visual state in the user preferences, too.

The State Lab example is too simple to have real user preferences, so let's take a shortcut and add some application-specific state to its one and only view controller. Add a property called `index` in ViewController.swift, along with a segmented control:

```
class ViewController: UIViewController {
    private var label:UILabel!
    private var smiley:UIImage!
    private var smileyView:UIImageView!
    private var segmentedControl:UISegmentedControl!
    private var index = 0
    private var animate = false
```

We're going to allow the user to set the value of this property using a segmented control and we're going to save it in the user defaults. We're then going to terminate and relaunch the application, to demonstrate that we can recover the value of the property.

CHAPTER 1   MULTITHREADED PROGRAMMING USING GRAND CENTRAL DISPATCH

Next, move to the middle of the `viewDidLoad()` method, where you'll create the segmented control, and add it to the view:

```
smileyView.image = smiley
segmentedControl =
    UISegmentedControl(items: ["One","Two", "Three", "Four"])
segmentedControl.frame = CGRect(x: bounds.origin.x + 20, y: 50,
    width: bounds.size.width - 40, height: 30)
segmentedControl.addTarget(self, action: #selector(ViewController.
selectionChanged(_:)),
    for: UIControlEvents.valueChanged)

view.addSubview(segmentedControl)
view.addSubview(smileyView)
```

We also used the `addTarget(_:action:forControlEvents)` method to connect the segmented control to the `selectionChanged()` method, which we need to have called when the selected segment changes. Add the implementation of this method anywhere in the implementation of the `ViewController` class:

```
func selectionChanged(_ sender:UISegmentedControl) {
        index = segmentedControl.selectedSegmentIndex
}
```

Now whenever the user changes the selected segment, the value of the `index` property will be updated.

Build and run the app. You should see the segmented control and be able to click its segments to select them one at a time. As you do so, the value of the `index` property will change, although you can't actually see this happening. Background your app again by clicking the home button, bring up the task manager (by double-clicking the home button) and kill your app, and then relaunch it. When the application restarts, the `index` property will have a value of zero again and there will be no selected segment. That's what we need to fix next.

Saving the value of the `index` property is simple enough; we just need one line of code to the end of the `applicationDidEnterBackground()` method in ViewController.swift:

```
func applicationDidEnterBackground() {
    print("VC: \(#function)")
    self.smiley = nil;
    self.smileyView.image = nil;
    UserDefaults.standard.set(self.index,
        forKey:"index")
}
```

But where should we restore the property value and use it to configure the segmented control? The inverse of this method, `applicationWillEnterForeground()`, isn't what we want. When that method is called, the app has already been running, and the setting is still intact. Instead, we need to access this when things are being set up after a new launch, which brings us back to the `viewDidLoad()` method. Add the bold lines shown here to that method:

```
        view.addSubview(label)

        index = UserDefaults.standard.integer(forKey: "index")
        segmentedControl.selectedSegmentIndex = index
```

When the application is being launched for the first time, there will not be a value saved in the user defaults. In this case, the `integerForKey()` method returns the value zero, which happens to be the correct initial value for the `index` property. If you wanted to use a different initial value, you could do so by registering it as the default value for the `index` key, as described in "Registering Default Values" in Chapter 12.

Now build and run the app. You'll notice a difference immediately — the first segment in the segmented control is preselected, because its selected segment index was set in the `viewDidLoad()` method. Now touch a segment, and then do the full background-kill-restart dance. There it is — the index value has been restored and, as a result, the correct segment in the segmented control is now selected.

Obviously, what we've shown here is pretty minimal, but the concept can be extended to all kinds of application states. It's up to you to decide how far you want to take it in order to maintain the illusion for the users that your app was always there, just waiting for them to come back.

CHAPTER 1 MULTITHREADED PROGRAMMING USING GRAND CENTRAL DISPATCH

Requesting More Backgrounding Time

Earlier, I mentioned the possibility of your app being dumped from memory if moving to the Background state takes too much time. For example, your app may be in the middle of doing a file transfer that it would really be a shame not to finish; however, trying to hijack the `applicationDidEnterBackground()` method to make it complete the work there, before the application is really backgrounded, isn't really an option. Instead, you should use `applicationDidEnterBackground()` as a point for telling the system that you have some extra work you would like to do, and then start up a block to actually do it. Assuming that the system has enough available RAM to keep your app in memory while the user does something else, the system will oblige you and keep your app running for a while.

Let's demonstrate this, not with an actual file transfer, but with a simple sleep call. Once again, we'll be using our new acquaintances GCD to make the contents of our `applicationDidEnterBackground()` method run in a separate queue.

In ViewController.swift, modify the `applicationDidEnterBackground()` method as shown in Listing 1-9.

Listing 1-9. *The Updated applicationDidEnterBackground Method*

```swift
func applicationDidEnterBackground() {
    print("VC: \(#function)")
    UserDefaults.standard.set(self.index,
        forKey:"index")
    
    let app = UIApplication.shared()
    var taskId = UIBackgroundTaskInvalid
    let id = app.beginBackgroundTask() {
        print("Background task ran out of time and was terminated.")
        app.endBackgroundTask(taskId)
    }
    taskId = id
    
    if taskId == UIBackgroundTaskInvalid {
        print("Failed to start background task!")
        return
    }
```

CHAPTER 1   MULTITHREADED PROGRAMMING USING GRAND CENTRAL DISPATCH

```
    DispatchQueue.global(qos: .default).async {
        print("Starting background task with " +
            "\(app.backgroundTimeRemaining) seconds remaining")

        self.smiley = nil
        self.smileyView.image = nil

        // simulate a lengthy (25 seconds) procedure
        Thread.sleep(forTimeInterval: 25)

        print("Finishing background task with " +
            "\(app.backgroundTimeRemaining) seconds remaining")
        app.endBackgroundTask(taskId)
    });
}
```

Let's look through this code piece by piece. First, we grab the shared UIApplication instance, since we'll be using it several times in this method. And then comes this:

```
var taskId = UIBackgroundTaskInvalid
let id = app.beginBackgroundTask() {
    print("Background task ran out of time and was terminated.")
    app.endBackgroundTask(taskId)
}
taskId = id
```

With the call to app.beginBackgroundTask(), we're basically telling the system that we need more time to accomplish something, and we promise to let it know when we're finished. The closure we give as a parameter may be called if the system decides that we've been going way too long anyway and decides to stop our background task. The call to app.beginBackgroundTask() returns an identifier that we save in the local variable taskId (if it better suits your class design, you could also store this value in a property of the view controller class).

Note that the closure ends with a call to endBackgroundTask(), passing along taskId. That tells the system that we're finished with the work for which we previously requested extra time. It's important to balance each call to app.beginBackgroundTask() with a matching call to endBackgroundTask() so that the system knows when we've completed the work.

41

Note Depending on your computing background, the use of the word **task** here may evoke associations with what we usually call a **process**, consisting of a running program that may contain multiple threads, and so on. In this case, try to put that out of your mind. The use of task in this context really just means "something that needs to get done." Any task you create here is running within your still-executing app.

Next, we do this:

```
if taskId == UIBackgroundTaskInvalid {
    print("Failed to start background task!")
    return
}
```

If our earlier call to app.beginBackgroundTask() returned the special value UIBackgroundTaskInvalid, which means the system is refusing to grant us any additional time. In that case, you could try to do the quickest part of whatever needs doing anyway and hope that it completes quickly enough that your app won't be terminated before it's finished. This was more likely to be an issue when running on older devices, such as the iPhone 3G, that didn't support multitasking. In this example, however, we're just letting it slide. Next comes the interesting part where the work itself is actually done:

```
DispatchQueue.global(qos: .default).async {
    print("Starting background task with " +
        "\(app.backgroundTimeRemaining) seconds remaining")

    self.smiley = nil;
    self.smileyView.image = nil

    // simulate a lengthy (25 seconds) procedure
    Thread.sleep(forTimeInterval: 25)

    print("Finishing background task with " +
        "\(app.backgroundTimeRemaining) seconds remaining")
    app.endBackgroundTask(taskId)
});
```

All this does is take the same work our method was doing in the first place and place it in a background queue. Notice, though, that the code that uses UserDefaults to save state has not been moved into this closure. That's because it's important to save that state whether or not iOS grants the application additional time to run when it moves into the background. At the end of the closure, we call `endBackgroundTask()` to let the system know that we're finished.

With that in place, build and run the app, and then background your app by pressing the home button. Watch the Xcode console and after 25 seconds, you will see the final log in your output. A complete run of the app up to this point should give you console output along these lines:

```
application(_:didFinishLaunchingWithOptions:)
applicationDidBecomeActive
VC: applicationDidBecomeActive()
applicationWillResignActive
VC: applicationWillResignActive()
applicationDidEnterBackground
VC: applicationDidEnterBackground()
Starting background task with 179.808078499991 seconds remaining
Finishing background task with 154.796897583336 seconds remaining
```

As you can see, the system is much more generous with time when doing things in the background than it is in the main thread of your app — in this example, it should give you a couple of minutes to complete whatever you need to get done in the background. Following this procedure can really help you out if you have any ongoing tasks to deal with.

Note that we used only a single background task, but in practice, you can use as many as you need. For example, if you have multiple network transfers happening at Background time and you need to complete them, you can create a background task for each and allow them to continue running in a background queue. So, you can easily allow multiple operations to run in parallel during the available time.

Summary

This has been a pretty intense chapter, with a lot of new concepts thrown your way. You've discovered a new conceptual paradigm for dealing with concurrency without worrying about threads. Techniques for making sure your apps play nicely in the multitasking world of iOS were also demonstrated. Now that we've gotten some of this heavy stuff out of the way, let's move on to the next chapter, which focuses on drawing.

CHAPTER 2

Simple Games Using SpriteKit

In iOS 7, Apple introduced SpriteKit, a framework for the high-performance rendering of 2D graphics. Unlike Core Graphics (which is focused on drawing graphics using a painter's model) or Core Animation (which is focused on animating attributes of GUI elements), SpriteKit focuses on a different area entirely — video games — and it is Apple's first foray into the graphical side of game programming in the iOS era. It was released for iOS 7 and OS X 10.9 (Mavericks) at the same time, providing the same API on both platforms, so that apps written for one can be easily ported to the other. Although Apple has never before supplied a framework quite like SpriteKit, it has clear similarities to various open source libraries such as Cocos2D. If you've used Cocos2D or something similar in the past, you'll feel right at home.

SpriteKit does not implement a flexible, general-purpose drawing system like Core Graphics — there are no methods for drawing paths, gradients, or filling spaces with color. Instead, what you get is a **scene graph** (analogous to UIKit's view hierarchy); the ability to transform each graph node's position, scale, and rotation; and the ability for each node to draw itself. Most drawing occurs in an instance of the SKSprite class (or one of its subclasses), which represents a single graphical image ready for putting on the screen.

In this chapter, we're going to use SpriteKit to build a simple shooting game called **TextShooter**. Instead of using premade graphics, we're going to build our game objects with pieces of text, using a subclass of SKSprite that is specialized for just this purpose. Using this approach, you won't need to pull graphics out of a project library or anything like that. The app we'll make will be simple in appearance, but easy to modify and use.

Creating the TextShooter App

In Xcode, press ⌘N or select File ➤ New ➤ Project… and choose the Game template from the iOS section. Press Next, name your project **TextShooter**, set Devices to Universal, set Game Technology to SpriteKit, and create the project. While you're here, it's worth looking briefly at the other available technology choices. OpenGL ES and Metal (the latter of which is new in iOS 8) are low-level graphics APIs that give you almost total control over the graphics hardware, but are much more difficult to use than SpriteKit. Also, don't select Integrate GamePlayKit, because we won't be working with that feature here. Whereas SpriteKit is a 2D API, SceneKit (which was also introduced in iOS 8) is a toolkit that you can use to build 3D graphics applications. After you've read this chapter, it's worth checking out the SceneKit documentation at `https://developer.apple.com/library/prerelease/ios/documentation/SceneKit/Reference/SceneKit_Framework/index.html` if you have any interest in 3D game programming.

If you run the TextShooter project now, you'll see the default SpriteKit application, which is shown in Figure 2-1. Initially, you'll just see the "Hello, World" text. If you click or tap on any portion of the screen, you'll see the text fade and a rotating shape appear for a few seconds. Over the course of this chapter, we'll replace everything in this template and progressively build up a simple application of our own.

CHAPTER 2 SIMPLE GAMES USING SPRITEKIT

Figure 2-1. *The default SpriteKit app in action showing some text displayed in the center of the screen*

Now let's take a look at the project that Xcode created. You'll see it has a standard `AppDelegate` class and a small view controller class called `GameViewController` that does some initial configuration of an `SKView` object. This object, which is loaded from the application's storyboard, is the view that will display all our SpriteKit content. Here's the code from the `GameViewController` `viewDidLoad()` method that initializes the `SKView`:

```
override func viewDidLoad() {
    super.viewDidLoad()
    
    if let view = self.view as! SKView? {
        // Load the SKScene from 'GameScene.sks'
        if let scene = SKScene(fileNamed: "GameScene") {
            // Set the scale mode to scale to fit the window
            scene.scaleMode = .aspectFill
```

47

CHAPTER 2   SIMPLE GAMES USING SPRITEKIT

```
            // Present the scene
            view.presentScene(scene)
        }

        view.ignoresSiblingOrder = true

        view.showsFPS = true
        view.showsNodeCount = true
    }
}
```

This code gets the `SKView` instance from the storyboard and configures it to show some performance-related values while the game is running. SpriteKit applications are constructed as a set of **scenes**, represented by the `SKScene` class. When developing with SpriteKit, you'll probably make a new `SKScene` subclass for each visually distinct portion of your app. A scene can represent a fast-paced game display with dozens of objects animating around the screen, or something as simple as a start menu. We'll see multiple uses of `SKScene` in this chapter. The template generates an initially empty scene in the shape of a class called `GameScene`.

The relationship between `SKView` and `SKScene` has some parallels to the `UIViewController` classes we've been using throughout this book. The `SKView` class acts a bit like `UINavigationController`, in the sense that it is sort of a blank slate that simply manages access to the display for other controllers. At this point, things start to diverge, however. Unlike `UINavigationController`, the top-level objects managed by `SKView` aren't `UIViewController` subclasses. Instead, they're subclasses of `SKScene`, which knows how to manage a graph of objects that can be displayed, acted upon by the physics engine, and so on.

This method creates the initial scene:

```
            if let scene = SKScene(fileNamed: "GameScene") {
```

There are two ways to create a scene — you can allocate and initialize an instance programmatically, or you can load one from a SpriteKit scene file. The Xcode template takes the latter approach — it generates a SpriteKit scene file called **GameScene.sks** containing an archived copy of an `SKScene` object. SKScene, like most of the other SpriteKit classes, conforms to the `NSCoder` protocol, which we will discuss in Chapter 13. The GameScene.sks file is just a standard archive, which you can read and write using

CHAPTER 2 ■ SIMPLE GAMES USING SPRITEKIT

the `NSKeyedUnarchiver` and `NSKeyedArchiver` classes. Usually, though, you'll use the `SKScene(fileNamed:) initializer`, which loads the `SKScene` from the archive for you and initializes it as an instance of the concrete subclass on which it is invoked — in this case, the archived `SKScene` data is used to initialize the `GameScene` object.

You may be wondering why the template code goes to the trouble of loading an empty scene object from the scene file when it could have just created one. The reason is the Xcode **SpriteKit Level Designer**, which lets you design a scene much like you construct a user interface in Interface Builder. Having designed your scene, you save it to the scene file and run your application again. This time, of course, the scene is not empty and you should see the design that you created in the Level Designer. Having loaded the initial scene, you are at liberty to programmatically add additional elements to it. We'll be doing a lot of that in this chapter. Alternatively, if you don't find the Level Designer useful, you can build all your scenes completely in code.

If you select the GameScene.sks file in the Project Navigator, Xcode opens it in the Level Designer, as shown in Figure 2-2.

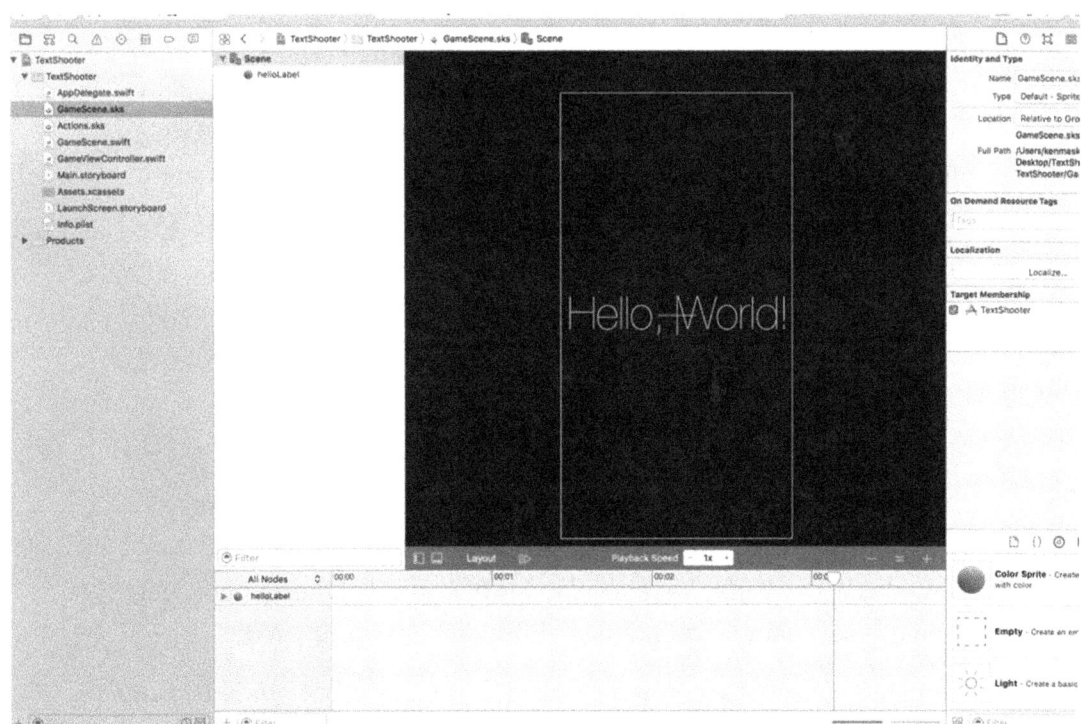

Figure 2-2. *The Xcode SpriteKit Level Designer showing the initial GameScene with the label*

49

The scene is displayed in the editor area. To the right of it is the **SKNode Inspector**, which you can use to set properties of the node that's selected in the editor. SpriteKit scene elements are all nodes — instances of the SKNode class. SKScene itself is a subclass of SKNode. Here, the SKScene node is selected, so the SKNode Inspector is displaying its properties. Below the inspector, in the bottom right, is the usual Xcode Object Library, which is automatically filtered to show only the types of objects you can add to a SpriteKit scene. You design your scene by dragging objects from here and dropping them onto the editor.

Now let's go back and finish discussing the viewDidLoad method.

```
// Set the scale mode to scale to fit the window
scene.scaleMode = .aspectFill
```

This is the scene's scaleMode property, which we've set to .aspectFill, scaling each dimension so that the larger of the two (width, height) is chosen. We can also select .fill, .aspectFit, and .resizeFill. These have the following characteristics:

- SKSceneScaleMode.aspectFill resizes the scene so that it fills the screen while preserving its aspect (width-to-height ratio). This mode ensures that every pixel of the SKView is covered, but loses part of the scene – in this case, the scene has been cropped on the left and right. The content of the scene is also scaled, so the text is smaller than in the original scene, but its position relative to the scene is preserved.

- SKSceneScaleMode.aspectFit also preserves the scene's aspect ratio, but ensures that the whole scene is visible. The result is a letter-box view, with parts of the SKView visible above and below the scene content.

- SKSceneScaleMode.fill scales the scene along both axes so that it exactly fits the view. This ensures that everything in the scene is visible, but since the aspect ratio of the original scene is not preserved, there may be unacceptable distortion of the content. Here, you can see that the text has been horizontally compressed.

- Finally, SKSceneScaleMode.resizeFill places the bottom-left corner of the scene in the bottom-left corner of the view and leaves it at its original size.

CHAPTER 2 SIMPLE GAMES USING SPRITEKIT

This tells our rendering that we don't really care about parent-child scene relationships when the scenes are displayed:

```
view.ignoresSiblingOrder = true
```

Depending on how your game works, you may want to set this so the appropriate stacking order of elements is followed. This line animates the scene change:

```
view.presentScene(scene)
```

Calling this method when there's already a presented scene causes the new scene to immediately replace the old one. You'll see examples of this later in the chapter. In this case, since we are making the initial scene visible, there is nothing to transition from, so it's acceptable to use the presentScene() method.

```
view.showsFPS = true
view.showsNodeCount = true
```

These last two lines just display some information about the animation shown on the bottom of the display, as shown in Figure 2-3.

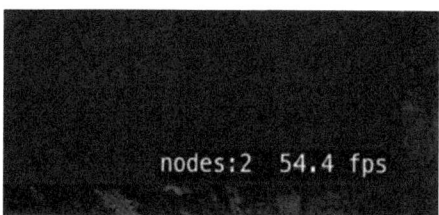

Figure 2-3. *Additional information about the animation shown in the view*

Initial Scene Customization

Select the GameScene class. We don't need most of the code that the Xcode template generated for us, so let's remove it. First, delete the entire didMoveToView() method. This method is called whenever the scene is presented in an SKView and it is typically used to make last-minute changes to the scene before it becomes visible. Next, change the touchesBegan(_:withEvent:) method, leaving just the for loop and the first line of code.

51

CHAPTER 2 SIMPLE GAMES USING SPRITEKIT

```
override func touchesBegan(_ touches: Set<UITouch>, with event: UIEvent?) {
    /* Called when a touch begins */

    for touch in touches {
        let location = touch.location(in: self)
    }
}
```

Since we're not going to load our scene from GameScene.sks, we need a method that will create a scene for us, with some initial content. We'll also need to add properties for the current game-level number, the number of lives the player has, and a flag to let us know whether the level is finished. Modify the GameScene.swift file, as shown in Listing 2-1.

Listing 2-1. Our First Modifications to GameScene.swift

```
class GameScene: SKScene {

    private var levelNumber: Int
    private var playerLives: Int
    private var finished = false

    @objc class func scene(size:CGSize, levelNumber:Int) -> GameScene {
        return GameScene(size: size, levelNumber: levelNumber)
    }

    override convenience init(size:CGSize) {
        self.init(size: size, levelNumber: 1)
    }

    @objc init(size:CGSize, levelNumber:Int) {
        self.levelNumber = levelNumber
        self.playerLives = 5
        super.init(size: size)

        backgroundColor = SKColor.lightGray()

        let lives = SKLabelNode(fontNamed: "Courier")
        lives.fontSize = 16
        lives.fontColor = SKColor.black()
```

```
        lives.name = "LivesLabel"
        lives.text = "Lives: \(playerLives)"
        lives.verticalAlignmentMode = .top
        lives.horizontalAlignmentMode = .right
        lives.position = CGPoint(x: frame.size.width,
                                 y: frame.size.height)
        addChild(lives)

        let level = SKLabelNode(fontNamed: "Courier")
        level.fontSize = 16
        level.fontColor = SKColor.black()
        level.name = "LevelLabel"
        level.text = "Level \(levelNumber)"
        level.verticalAlignmentMode = .top
        level.horizontalAlignmentMode = .left
        level.position = CGPoint(x: 0, y: frame.height)
        addChild(level)
    }

    required init?(coder aDecoder: NSCoder) {
        levelNumber = aDecoder.decodeInteger(forKey: "level")
        playerLives = aDecoder.decodeInteger(forKey: "playerLives")
        super.init(coder: aDecoder)
    }

    override func encode(with aCoder: NSCoder) {
        aCoder.encode(Int(levelNumber), forKey: "level")
        aCoder.encode(playerLives, forKey: "playerLives")
    }
}
```

The first method, `scene(size:levelNumber:)`, gives us a factory method that will work as a shorthand for creating a level and setting its level number at once. In the second method, `init()`, we override the class's default initializer, passing control to the third method (and passing along a default value for the level number). That third method in turn calls the designated initializer from its superclass's implementation, after setting the initial values of `levelNumber` and `playerLives` properties. This may seem like a roundabout way of doing things, but it's a common pattern when you want to add new initializers to a class while still using the class's designated initializer. After calling the superclass initializer, we set the scene's background color. Note that we're using a class called SKColor instead of UIColor here. In fact, SKColor isn't really a class at all; it's a type alias that is mapped to UIColor for an iOS app and NSColor for an macOS app. This allows us to port games between iOS and macOS a little more easily.

Note We use the @objc keyword on variables that need to be exposed to the Objective-C runtime.

After that, we create two instances of a class called SKLabelNode. This is a handy class that works somewhat like a UILabel, allowing us to add some text to the scene and letting us choose a font, set a text value, and specify some alignments. We create one label for displaying the number of lives at the upper right of the screen and another that will show the level number at the upper left of the screen. Look closely at the code that we use to position these labels. Here is the code that sets the position of the lives label:

```
lives.position = CGPoint(x: frame.size.width,
                         y: frame.size.height)
```

If you think about the points we're passing in as the position for this label, you may be surprised to see that we're passing in the scene's height. In UIKit, positioning anything at the height of a UIView would put it at the bottom of that view; but in Scene Kit, the y-axis is flipped — the coordinate origin is at the bottom left of the scene and the y-axis points upward. As a result, the maximum value of the scene's height is a position at the top of the screen instead. What about the label's x coordinate? We're setting that to be the width of the view. If you did that with a UIView, the view would be positioned just off the right side of the screen. That doesn't happen here, because we also did this:

```
lives.horizontalAlignmentMode = .right
```

Setting the horizontalAlignmentMode property of the SKLabelNode to SKLabelHorizontalAlignmentMode.right moves the point of the label node that's used to position it (it's actually a property called position) to the right of the text. Since we want the text to be right justified on the screen, we therefore need to set the x coordinate of the position property to be the width of the scene. By contrast, the text in the

CHAPTER 2 ■ SIMPLE GAMES USING SPRITEKIT

level label is left-aligned and we position it at the left edge of the scene by setting its x coordinate to zero:

```
level.horizontalAlignmentMode = .left
level.position = CGPoint(x: 0, y: frame.height)
```

You'll also see that we gave each label a name. This works similarly to a tag or identifier in other parts of UIKit, and it will let us retrieve those labels later by asking for them by name.

We added the `init(coder:)` and `encode(with aCoder:)` methods because all SpriteKit nodes, including `SKScene`, conform to the `NSCoding` protocol. This requires us to override `init(coder:)`, so we also implement `encode(with aCoder:)` for the sake of consistency, even though we won't be archiving the scene object in this application. You'll see the same pattern in all of the `SKNode` subclasses that we create, although we won't implement the `encode(with aCoder:)` method when the subclass has no additional state of its own, since the base class version does everything that we need in that case.

Now select **GameViewController.swift** and make the following changes to the `viewDidLoad` method:

```
override func viewDidLoad() {
    super.viewDidLoad()
    
    let scene = GameScene(size: view.frame.size, levelNumber: 1)
    
    // Configure the view.
    let skView = self.view as! SKView
    skView.showsFPS = true
    skView.showsNodeCount = true
    
    /* Sprite Kit applies additional optimizations to improve rendering
    performance */
    skView.ignoresSiblingOrder = true
    
    /* Set the scale mode to scale to fit the window */
    scene.scaleMode = .aspectFill
    
    skView.presentScene(scene)
}
```

CHAPTER 2 SIMPLE GAMES USING SPRITEKIT

Instead of loading the scene from the scene file, we're using the `scene(size:levelNumber:)` method that we just added to `GameScene` to create and initialize the scene and make it the same size as the `SKView`. Since the view and scene are the same size, there is no longer any need to set the scene's `scaleMode` property, so you can go ahead and remove the line of code that does that. Near the end of **GameViewController.swift**, you'll find the following method:

```
override func prefersStatusBarHidden() -> Bool {
    return true
}
```

This code makes the iOS status bar disappear while our game is running. The Xcode template includes this method because hiding the status bar is usually what you want for action games like this. Now run the game. You'll see that we have a very basic structure in place, as shown in Figure 2-4.

Figure 2-4. *Our game doesn't have much fun factor right now, but at least it has a high frame rate*

> **Tip** The node count and frame rate at the bottom right of the scene are useful for debugging, but you don't want them to be there when you release your game. You can switch them off by setting the `showsFPS` and `showsNodeCount` properties of the `SKView` to `false` in the `viewDidLoad` method of `GameViewController`. There are some other `SKView` properties that let you get more debugging information – refer to the API documentation for the details.

Player Movement

Now it's time to add a little interactivity. We're going to make a new class that represents a player. It will know how to draw itself as well as how to move to a new location in a nicely animated way. Next, we'll insert an instance of the new class into the scene and write some code to let the player move the object around by touching the screen. Every object that's going to be part of our scene must be a subclass of SKNode, so use Xcode's File menu to create a new Cocoa Touch class named `PlayerNode` that's a subclass of SKNode. In the nearly empty **PlayerNode.swift** file that's created, import the SpriteKit framework and add the following code:

```
import SpriteKit

class PlayerNode: SKNode {
    override init() {
        super.init()
        name = "Player \(self)"
        initNodeGraph()
    }

    required init?(coder aDecoder: NSCoder) {
        super.init(coder: aDecoder)
    }
```

```
    private func initNodeGraph() {
        let label = SKLabelNode(fontNamed: "Courier")
        label.fontColor = SKColor.darkGray()
        label.fontSize = 40
        label.text = "v"
        label.zRotation = CGFloat(MDouble.pi)
        label.name = "label"
        self.addChild(label)
    }
}
```

Our `PlayerNode` doesn't display anything itself, because a plain `SKNode` has no way to do any drawing of its own. Instead, the `init()` method sets up a subnode that will do the actual drawing. This subnode is another instance of `SKLabelNode`, just like the one we created for displaying the level number and the number of lives remaining. `SKLabelNode` is a subclass of `SKNode` that *does* know how to draw itself. Another such subclass is `SKSpriteNode`. We're not setting a position for the label, which means that its position is coordinate (0, 0). Just like views, each `SKNode` lives in a coordinate system that is inherited from its parent object. Giving this node a zero position means that it will appear onscreen at the `PlayerNode` instance's position. A non-zero value would effectively be an offset from that point.

We also set a rotation value for the label, so that the lowercase letter "v" that it contains will be shown upside-down. The name of the rotation property, `zRotation`, may seem a bit surprising; however, it simply refers to the z-axis of the coordinate space in use with SpriteKit. You only see the x and y axes on screen, but the z-axis is useful for ordering items for display purposes, as well as for rotating things around. The values assigned to `zRotation` need to be in radians instead of degrees, so we assign the value `Double.pi`, which is a constant that is approximately equal to π. Since π radians are equal to 180°, this is just what we want.

Adding the Player to the Scene

Now switch back to **GameScene.swift**. Here, we're going to add an instance of `PlayerNode` to the scene. Start off by adding a property to represent the player node:

```
    private let playerNode: PlayerNode = PlayerNode()
```

CHAPTER 2 ■ SIMPLE GAMES USING SPRITEKIT

Continue by adding the following bold code at the end of the init(size:levelNumber:) method:

```
level.position = CGPoint(x: 0, y: frame.height)
addChild(level)

playerNode.position = CGPoint(x: frame.midX,
                              y: frame.height * 0.1)
addChild(playerNode)
```

If you build and run the app now, you should see that the player appears near the lower middle of the screen, as shown in Figure 2-5.

Figure 2-5. *Added an upside-down V as our player*

59

CHAPTER 2 SIMPLE GAMES USING SPRITEKIT

Handling Touches: Player Movement

Next, we're going to put some logic back into the touchesBegan(_:withEvent:) method, which we earlier left nearly empty. Insert the bold lines shown here in **GameScene.swift** (you'll get a compiler error when you add this code — we'll fix it shortly):

```swift
override func touchesBegan(_ touches: Set<UITouch>, with event:
UIEvent?) {
    /* Called when a touch begins */
    
    for touch in touches {
        let location = touch.location(in: self)
        if location.y < frame.height * 0.2 {
            let target = CGPoint(x: location.x, y: playerNode.
            position.y)
            playerNode.moveToward(target)
        }
    }
}
```

The preceding code segment uses any touch location in the lower fifth of the screen as the basis of a new location toward which you want the player node to move. It also tells the player node to move toward it. The compiler complains because we haven't defined the player node's moveToward() method yet. So switch over to **PlayerNode.swift** and add the implementation of that method:

```swift
@objc func moveToward(_ location: CGPoint) {
    removeAction(forKey: "movement")
    
    let distance = pointDistance(position, location)
    let screenWidth = UIScreen.main.bounds.size.width
    let duration = TimeInterval(2 * distance/screenWidth)
    
    run(SKAction.move(to: location, duration: duration),
        withKey:"movement")
}
```

We'll skip the first line for now, returning to it shortly. This method compares the new location to the current position and figures out the distance and the number of pixels to move. Next, it figures out how much time the movement should take, using a numeric constant to set the speed of the overall movement. Finally, it creates an SKAction to make the move happen. SKAction is a part of SpriteKit that knows how to make changes to nodes over time, letting you easily animate a node's position, size, rotation, transparency, and more. In this case, we are creating an action that animates a simple movement action over a particular duration, and then assigning that action to the player node, using the key "movement." As you see, this key is the same as the key used in the first line of this method to remove an action. We started off this method by removing any existing action with the same key, so that the user can tap several locations in quick succession without spawning a lot of competing actions trying to move in different ways.

Geometry Calculations

Now you'll notice that we've introduced another problem, because Xcode can't find any function called pointDistance(). This is one of several simple geometric functions that our app will use to perform calculations using points, vectors, and floats. Let's put this in place now. Use Xcode to create a new Swift file called **Geometry.swift** and give it the following content:

```
import UIKit

// Takes a CGVector and a CGFloat.
// Returns a new CGFloat where each component of v has been multiplied by m.
func vectorMultiply(_ v: CGVector, _ m: CGFloat) -> CGVector {
    return CGVector(dx: v.dx * m, dy: v.dy * m)
}

// Takes two CGPoints.
// Returns a CGVector representing a direction from p1 to p2.
func vectorBetweenPoints(_ p1: CGPoint, _ p2: CGPoint) -> CGVector {
    return CGVector(dx: p2.x - p1.x, dy: p2.y - p1.y)
}
```

CHAPTER 2 SIMPLE GAMES USING SPRITEKIT

```swift
// Takes a CGVector.
// Returns a CGFloat containing the length of the vector, calculated using
// Pythagoras' theorem.
func vectorLength(_ v: CGVector) -> CGFloat {
    return CGFloat(sqrtf(powf(Float(v.dx), 2) + powf(Float(v.dy), 2)))
}

// Takes two CGPoints. Returns a CGFloat containing the distance between them,
// calculated with Pythagoras' theorem.
func pointDistance(_ p1: CGPoint, _ p2: CGPoint) -> CGFloat {
    return CGFloat(
    sqrtf(powf(Float(p2.x - p1.x), 2) + powf(Float(p2.y - p1.y), 2)))
}
```

These are simple implementations of some common operations that are useful in many games: multiplying vectors, creating vectors pointing from one point to another, and calculating distances. Now build and run the app. After the player's "ship" appears, tap anywhere in the bottom portion of the screen to see that the ship slides left or right to reach the point you tapped. You can tap again before the ship reaches its destination, and it will immediately begin a new animation to move toward the new spot. That's fine, but wouldn't it be nice if the player's ship were a bit livelier in its motion?

Making It Wobble

Let's give the ship a bit of a wobble as it moves by adding another animation. Add the bold lines to PlayerNode's moveToward: method.

```swift
    @objc func moveToward(_ location: CGPoint) {
        removeAction(forKey: "movement")
        removeAction(forKey: "wobbling")
        
        let distance = pointDistance(position, location)
        let screenWidth = UIScreen.main.bounds.size.width
        let duration = TimeInterval(2 * distance/screenWidth)
        
        run(SKAction.move(to: location, duration: duration),
                            withKey:"movement")
```

```
        let wobbleTime = 0.3
        let halfWobbleTime = wobbleTime/2
        let wobbling = SKAction.sequence([
                SKAction.scaleX(to: 0.2, duration: halfWobbleTime),
                SKAction.scaleX(to: 1.0, duration: halfWobbleTime)
        ])
        let wobbleCount = Int(duration/wobbleTime)
        run(SKAction.repeat(wobbling, count: wobbleCount),
                                    withKey:"wobbling")
    }
```

What we just did is similar to the movement action we created earlier, but it differs in some important ways. For the basic movement, we simply calculated the movement duration, and then created and ran a movement action in a single step. This time, it's a little more complicated. First, we define the time for a single "wobble" (the ship may wobble multiple times while moving, but will wobble at a consistent rate throughout). The wobble itself consists of first scaling the ship along the x-axis (i.e., its width) to 2/10ths of its normal size, and then scaling it back to its full size. Each of these is a single action that is packed together into another kind of action called a **sequence**, which performs all the actions it contains one after another. Next, we figure out how many times this wobble can happen during the duration of the ship's travel and wrap the `wobbling` sequence inside a repeat action, telling it how many complete wobble cycles it should execute. And, as before, we start the method by canceling any previous wobbling action, since we wouldn't want competing wobblers.

Now run the app. You'll see that the ship wobbles pleasantly when moving back and forth. It kind of looks like it's walking.

Creating Your Enemies

So far so good, but this game is going to need some enemies for our players to shoot at. Use Xcode to make a new Cocoa Touch class called `EnemyNode`, using `SKNode` as the parent class. We're not going to give the enemy class any real behavior just yet, but we will give it an appearance. We'll use the same technique that we used for the player, using text to build the enemy's body. Surely, there's no text character more intimidating

CHAPTER 2 SIMPLE GAMES USING SPRITEKIT

than the letter X, so our enemy will be a letter X… made of lowercase Xs. Add this code to **EnemyNode.swift**:

```
import SpriteKit

class EnemyNode: SKNode {
    override init() {
        super.init()
        name = "Enemy \(self)"
        initNodeGraph()
    }

    required init?(coder aDecoder: NSCoder) {
        super.init(coder: aDecoder)
    }
    private func initNodeGraph() {
        let topRow = SKLabelNode(fontNamed: "Courier-Bold")
        topRow.fontColor = SKColor.brown()
        topRow.fontSize = 20
        topRow.text = "x x"
        topRow.position = CGPoint(x: 0, y: 15)
        addChild(topRow)

        let middleRow = SKLabelNode(fontNamed: "Courier-Bold")
        middleRow.fontColor = SKColor.brown()
        middleRow.fontSize = 20
        middleRow.text = "x"
        addChild(middleRow)

        let bottomRow = SKLabelNode(fontNamed: "Courier-Bold")
        bottomRow.fontColor = SKColor.brown()
        bottomRow.fontSize = 20
        bottomRow.text = "x x"
        bottomRow.position = CGPoint(x: 0, y: -15)
        addChild(bottomRow)
    }
}
```

CHAPTER 2   SIMPLE GAMES USING SPRITEKIT

There's nothing much new there; we're just adding multiple "rows" of text by shifting the y value for each of their positions.

Putting Enemies in the Scene

Now let's make some enemies appear in the scene by making some changes to **GameScene.swift**. First, add a new property to hold the enemies that will be added to this level:

```
private let enemies = SKNode()
```

You might think that we'd use an `Array<SKNode>` for this, but it turns out that using a plain SKNode is perfect for the job. SKNode can hold any number of child nodes. And since we need to add all the enemies to the scene anyway, we may as well hold them all in an SKNode for easy access. The next step is to add the `spawnEnemies()` method, as shown here:

```
private func spawnEnemies() {
    let count = Int(log(Float(levelNumber))) + levelNumber
    for _ in 0..<count {
        let enemy = EnemyNode()
        let size = frame.size;
        let x = arc4random_uniform(UInt32(size.width * 0.8))
                    + UInt32(size.width * 0.1)
        let y = arc4random_uniform(UInt32(size.height * 0.5))
                    + UInt32(size.height * 0.5)
        enemy.position = CGPoint(x: CGFloat(x), y: CGFloat(y))
        enemies.addChild(enemy)
    }
}
```

Add these lines near the end of the init(`size:levelNumber:`) method to add the enemies node to the scene, and then call the `spawnEnemies` method:

```
addChild(playerNode)
addChild(enemies)
spawnEnemies()
```

Since we added the enemies node to the scene, any child enemy nodes we add to the enemies node will also appear in the scene. Notice that we're using the

65

CHAPTER 2 SIMPLE GAMES USING SPRITEKIT

arc4random_uniform() function to get random values for the x and y coordinates of our enemy nodes. We'll get random numbers that are less predictable if we "stir" the random number generator before using it. To do that, open **AppDelegate.swift** and add the following line in bold to the application(_:didFinishLaunchingWithOptions:) method:

```
func application(application: UIApplication,
   didFinishLaunchingWithOptions launchOptions: [NSObject: AnyObject]?) ->
   Bool {
   // Override point for customization after application launch.
   arc4random_stir()
   return true
}
```

Now build and run the app. You'll see a dreadful enemy placed randomly in the upper portion of the screen, as shown in Figure 2-6. Don't you wish you could shoot it?

Figure 2-6. *I'm sure you'll agree that the X made of Xs just needs to be shot*

Start Shooting

It's time to implement the next logical step in the development of this game: letting the player attack the enemies. We want the player to be able to tap anywhere in the upper 80% of the screen to shoot a bullet at the enemies. We're going to use the **physics engine** included in SpriteKit both to move our player's bullets and to let us know when a bullet collides with an enemy.

But first, what is this thing we call a physics engine? Basically, a physics engine is a software component that keeps track of multiple physical objects (commonly referred to as **physics bodies**) in a world, along with the forces that are acting upon them. It also makes sure that everything moves in a realistic way. It can take into account the force of gravity, handle collisions between objects (so that objects don't occupy the same space simultaneously), and even simulate physical characteristics like friction and bounciness. It's important to understand that a physics engine is usually separate from a graphics engine. Apple provides convenient APIs to let us work with both, but they are essentially separate. It's common to have objects in your display, such as our labels that show the current level number and remaining lives, which are completely separate from the physics engine. And it's possible to create objects that have a physics body, but don't actually display anything at all.

Defining Your Physics Categories

One of the things that the SpriteKit physics engine lets us do is to assign objects to several distinct **physics categories**. A physics category is a way to group related objects so that the physics engine can handle collisions between them in different ways. In this game, for example, we'll create three categories: one for enemies, one for the player, and one for player missiles. We definitely want the physics engine to concern itself with collisions between enemies and player missiles, but we probably want it to ignore collisions between player missiles and the player itself. This is easy to set up using physics categories. So, let's create the categories we're going to need. Press ⌘N to bring up the new file assistant, choose Swift File from the iOS Source section, and press Next. Give the new file the name **PhysicsCategories.swift** and save it, and then add the following code to it:

```swift
import Foundation

let PlayerCategory: UInt32 = 1 << 1
let EnemyCategory: UInt32 = 1 << 2
let PlayerMissileCategory: UInt32 = 1 << 3
```

Here we declared three category constants. Note that the categories work as a bitmask, so each of them must be a power of two. We can easily do this by bit-shifting. These are set up as a bitmask in order to simplify the physics engine's API a little bit. With bitmasks, we can logically OR several values together. This enables us to use a single API call to tell the physics engine how to deal with collisions between many different pairs of nodes. We'll see this in action soon.

Creating the BulletNode Class

Now that we've laid some groundwork, let's create some bullets so we can start shooting. Create a new Cocoa Touch class called `BulletNode`, once again using `SKNode` as its superclass. Start by importing the SpriteKit framework and adding a property to hold this bullet's thrust vector:

```
import SpriteKit

class BulletNode: SKNode {
    @objc var thrust: CGVector = CGVector(dx: 0, dy: 0)

}
```

Next, we implement the `init()` method. Like the other `init()` methods in this application, this is where we create the object graph for our bullet. This will consist of a single dot. While we're at it, let's also configure physics for this class by creating and configuring an `SKPhysicsBody` instance and attaching it to `self`. In the process, we tell the new body what category it belongs to and which categories should be checked for collisions with this object:

```
    override init() {
        super.init()

        let dot = SKLabelNode(fontNamed: "Courier")
        dot.fontColor = SKColor.black()
        dot.fontSize = 40
        dot.text = "."
        addChild(dot)

        let body = SKPhysicsBody(circleOfRadius: 1)
        body.isDynamic = true
```

CHAPTER 2 SIMPLE GAMES USING SPRITEKIT

```
    body.categoryBitMask = PlayerMissileCategory
    body.contactTestBitMask = EnemyCategory
    body.collisionBitMask = EnemyCategory
    body.fieldBitMask = GravityFieldCategory
    body.mass = 0.01

    physicsBody = body
    name = "Bullet \(self)"
}
```

We'll also add the init(coder aDecoder:) and encode(with aCoder:) methods:

```
required init?(coder aDecoder: NSCoder) {
    super.init(coder: aDecoder)
    let dx = aDecoder.decodeFloat(forKey: "thrustX")
    let dy = aDecoder.decodeFloat(forKey: "thrustY")
    thrust = CGVector(dx: CGFloat(dx), dy: CGFloat(dy))
}

override func encode(with aCoder: NSCoder) {
    super.encode(with: aCoder)
    aCoder.encode(Float(thrust.dx), forKey: "thrustX")
    aCoder.encode(Float(thrust.dy), forKey: "thrustY")
}
```

Applying Physics

Next, we'll add the factory method that creates a new bullet and gives it a thrust vector that the physics engine will use to propel the bullet toward its target:

```
@objc class func bullet(from start: CGPoint, toward destination: CGPoint) -> BulletNode {
    let bullet = BulletNode()
    bullet.position = start
    let movement = vectorBetweenPoints(start, destination)
    let magnitude = vectorLength(movement)
    let scaledMovement = vectorMultiply(movement, 1/magnitude)
    let thrustMagnitude = CGFloat(100.0)
```

```
        bullet.thrust = vectorMultiply(scaledMovement, thrustMagnitude)
        bullet.run(SKAction.playSoundFileNamed("shoot.wav",
                                            waitForCompletion: false))
        return bullet
    }
```

The basic calculations are pretty simple. We first determine a movement vector that points from the start location to the destination, and then we determine its magnitude (length). Dividing the movement vector by its magnitude produces a normalized **unit vector**, a vector that points in the same direction as the original but is exactly one unit long (a unit, in this case, is the same as a "point" on the screen — for example, two pixels on a Retina device, one pixel on older devices). Creating a unit vector is very useful because we can multiply that by a fixed magnitude (in this case, 100) to determine a uniformly powerful thrust vector, no matter how far away the user tapped the screen. The final piece of code we need to add to this class is this method, which applies thrust to the physics body. We'll call this once per frame, from inside the scene:

```
@objc func applyRecurringForce() {
    physicsBody!.applyForce(thrust)
}
```

Adding Bullets to the Scene

Now switch over to **GameScene.swift** to add bullets to the scene itself. For starters, add another property to contain all bullets in a single SKNode, just as you did earlier for enemies:

```
private let playerBullets = SKNode()
```

Find the section of the init(size:levelNumber:) method where you previously added the enemies. That's the place to set up the playerBullets node, too.

```
    addChild(enemies)
    spawnEnemies()

    addChild(playerBullets)
}
```

Now we're ready to code the actual missile launches. Add this `else` clause to the `touchesBegan(_:withEvent:)` method, so that all taps in the upper part of the screen shoot a bullet instead of moving the ship:

```
    } else {
        let bullet = BulletNode.bullet(from: playerNode.position,
            toward: location)
        playerBullets.addChild(bullet)
    }
```

That adds the bullet, but none of the bullets we add will actually move unless we tell them to by applying thrust every frame. Our scene already contains an empty method called `update()` that was added as part of the project template. If the `update()` method is not present, add it as shown in the following. SpriteKit calls this method every frame and it's the perfect place to do any game logic that needs to occur in each frame. Rather than updating all our bullets right in that method, however, we put that code in a separate method that we call from the `update()` method:

```
override func update(_ currentTime: TimeInterval) {
    /* Called before each frame is rendered */
    updateBullets()
 }
private func updateBullets() {
    var bulletsToRemove:[BulletNode] = []
    for bullet in playerBullets.children as! [BulletNode] {
        // Remove any bullets that have moved off-screen
        if !frame.contains(bullet.position) {
            // Mark bullet for removal
            bulletsToRemove.append(bullet)
            continue
        }

        // Apply thrust to remaining bullets
        bullet.applyRecurringForce()
    }

    playerBullets.removeChildren(in: bulletsToRemove)
 }
```

Before telling each bullet to apply its recurring force, we also check whether it is still onscreen. Any bullet that's gone offscreen is put into a temporary array; and then, at the end, those are swept out of the `playerBullets` node. Note that this two-stage process is necessary because the `for` loop at work in this method is iterating over all children in the `playerBullets` node. Making changes to a collection while you're iterating over it is never a good idea, and it can easily lead to a crash. Now build and run the app. You'll see that, in addition to moving the player's ship, you can make it shoot missiles upward by tapping on the screen (see Figure 2-7).

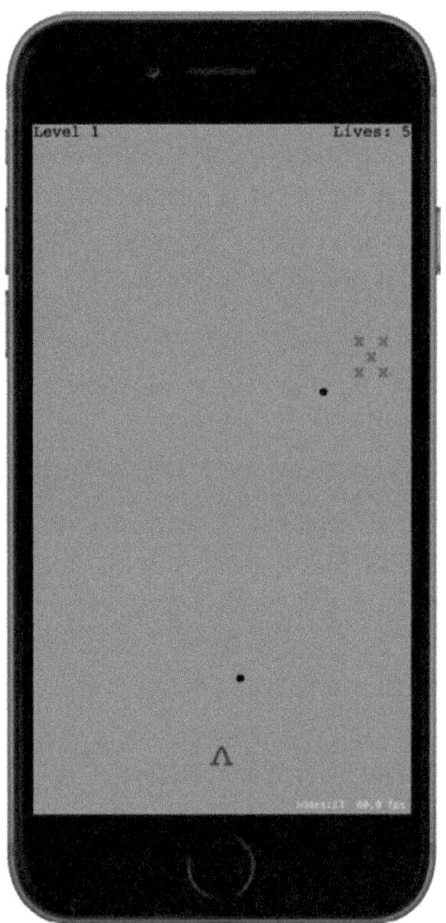

Figure 2-7. Firing bullets

Attacking Enemies with Physics

A couple of important gameplay elements are still missing from our game. The enemies never attack us, and we can't yet get rid of the enemies by shooting them. Let's take care of the latter right now. We're going to set things up so that shooting an enemy has the effect of dislodging it from the spot where it's currently fixed on the screen. This feature will use the physics engine for most of the work, and involves making changes to PlayerNode, EnemyNode, and GameScene.

For starters, let's add physics bodies to our nodes that don't already have them. Start with **EnemyNode.swift**. Add the following line to the init() method:

```
initPhysicsBody()
```

Now add the code to really set up the physics body. This is pretty similar to what you did earlier for the PlayerBullet class:

```
private func initPhysicsBody() {
    let body = SKPhysicsBody(rectangleOf: CGSize(width: 40, height: 40))
    body.affectedByGravity = false
    body.categoryBitMask = EnemyCategory
    body.contactTestBitMask = PlayerCategory | EnemyCategory
    body.mass = 0.2
    body.angularDamping = 0
    body.linearDamping = 0
    body.fieldBitMask = 0
    physicsBody = body
}
```

Then select **PlayerNode.swift**, where you're going to do a pretty similar set of things. First, add the line shown here to the init() method:

initPhysicsBody()

Finally, add the new initPhysicsBody() method:

```
private func initPhysicsBody() {
    let body = SKPhysicsBody(rectangleOf: CGSize(width: 20, height: 20))
    body.affectedByGravity = false
    body.categoryBitMask = PlayerCategory
    body.contactTestBitMask = EnemyCategory
```

```
        body.collisionBitMask = 0
        body.fieldBitMask = 0
        physicsBody = body
    }
```

At this point, you can run the app and see that your bullets now have the ability to knock enemies into space. However, you'll also see there's a problem here. When you start the game and then send the lone enemy hurtling into space, you're stuck so it's probably a good time to add level management to the game.

Finishing Levels

Begin by adding this `updateEnemies()` method to **GameScene.swift**. It works a lot like the `updateBullets()` method added earlier:

```
    private func updateEnemies() {
        var enemiesToRemove:[EnemyNode] = []
        for node in enemies.children as! [EnemyNode] {
            if !frame.contains(node.position) {
                // Mark enemy for removal
                enemiesToRemove.append(node)
            }
        }
        enemies.removeChildren(in: enemiesToRemove)
    }
```

That takes care of removing each enemy from the level's `enemies` array each time one goes offscreen. Now let's modify the `update()` method, telling it to call `updateEnemies()`, as well as a new method we haven't yet implemented:

```
override func update(currentTime: CFTimeInterval) {
    if finished {
        return
    }
    updateBullets()
    updateEnemies()
    checkForNextLevel()
}
```

We started out that method by checking the `finished` property. Since we're about to add code that can officially end a level, we want to be sure that we don't keep doing additional processing after the level is complete. Then, just as we're checking each frame to see if any bullets or enemies have gone offscreen, we're going to call `checkForNextLevel` each frame to see if the current level is complete. Let's add this method:

```
private func checkForNextLevel() {
    if enemies.children.isEmpty {
        goToNextLevel()
    }
}
```

Transitioning to the Next Level

The `checkForNextLevel()` method in turn calls another method we haven't yet implemented. The `goToNextLevel()` method marks this level as finished, displays some text on the screen to let the player know, and then starts the next level:

```
private func goToNextLevel() {
    finished = true

    let label = SKLabelNode(fontNamed: "Courier")
    label.text = "Level Complete!"
    label.fontColor = SKColor.blue()
    label.fontSize = 32
    label.position = CGPoint(x: frame.size.width * 0.5,
                             y: frame.size.height * 0.5)
    addChild(label)

    let nextLevel = GameScene(size: frame.size, levelNumber:
        levelNumber + 1)
    nextLevel.playerLives = playerLives
    view!.presentScene(nextLevel, transition:
        SKTransition.flipHorizontal(withDuration: 1.0))
}
```

CHAPTER 2   SIMPLE GAMES USING SPRITEKIT

The second half of the `goToNextLevel()` method creates a new instance of `GameScene` and gives it all the start values it needs. It then tells the view to present the new scene, using a transition to smooth things over. The `SKTransition` class lets us pick from a variety of transition styles. Run the app and complete a level to see what this one looks like, as shown in Figure 2-8.

Figure 2-8. *The end-of-level screen-flipping transition*

The transition in use here makes it looks like we're flipping a card over its horizontal axis, but there are plenty more to choose from. See the documentation for `SKTransition` to view more possibilities.

Customizing Collisions

Now we've got a game that you can really play. You can clear level after level by knocking enemies upward off the screen. That's OK, but there's really not much challenge. I mentioned earlier that having enemies attack the player is one piece of missing gameplay, and now it's time to make that happen. We're going to make things a little harder by making the enemies fall down when they're bumped, either from being hit by a bullet or from being touched by another enemy. We also want to make it so that being hit by a falling enemy takes a life away from the player. You also may have noticed that after a bullet hits an enemy, the bullet squiggles its way around the enemy and continues on its upward trajectory, which is pretty weird. We're going to tackle all these things by implementing a collision-handling method in **GameScene.swift**.

The method for handling detected collisions is a delegate method for the `SKPhysicsWorld` class. Our scene has a physics world by default, but we need to set it up a little bit before it will tell us anything. For starters, it's good to let the compiler know that we're going to implement a delegate protocol, so let's add this declaration to the `GameScene` class:

```
class GameScene: SKScene, SKPhysicsContactDelegate {
```

We still need to configure the world a bit (giving it a slightly less cruel amount of gravity) and tell it who its delegate is. To do so, we add these bold lines near the end of the `init(size:levelNumber:)` method:

```
physicsWorld.gravity = CGVector(dx: 0, dy: -1)
physicsWorld.contactDelegate = self
```

Now that we've set the physics world's `contactDelegate` to be the `GameScene`, we can implement the relevant delegate method. The core of the method looks like this:

```
func didBegin(_ contact: SKPhysicsContact) {
    if contact.bodyA.categoryBitMask == contact.bodyB.categoryBitMask {
        // Both bodies are in the same category
        let nodeA = contact.bodyA.node!
        let nodeB = contact.bodyB.node!
```

```
            // What do we do with these nodes?
    } else {
        var attacker: SKNode
        var attackee: SKNode

        if contact.bodyA.categoryBitMask
                > contact.bodyB.categoryBitMask {
            // Body A is attacking Body B
            attacker = contact.bodyA.node!
            attackee = contact.bodyB.node!
        } else {
            // Body B is attacking Body A
            attacker = contact.bodyB.node!
            attackee = contact.bodyA.node!
        }

        if attackee is PlayerNode {
            playerLives -= 1
        }

        // What do we do with the attacker and the attackee?
    }
}
```

Go ahead and add that method, but if you look at it right now, you'll see that it doesn't really do much yet. In fact, the only concrete result of that method would be to reduce the number of player lives each time a falling enemy hits the player's ship. But the enemies aren't falling yet.

The idea behind this implementation is to look at the two colliding objects and to figure out whether they are of the same category (in which case, they are "friends" to one another) or if they are of different categories. If they are of different categories, we have to determine who is attacking whom. If you look at the order of the categories declared in **PhysicsCategories.swift**, you'll see that they are specified in order of increased "attackyness": Player nodes can be attacked by Enemy nodes, which in turn can be attacked by nodes that have the PlayerMissile category (i.e., BulletNodes). That means that we can use a simple greater-than comparison to figure out who is the "attacker" in this scenario.

For the sake of simplicity and modularity, we don't really want the scene to decide how each object should react to being attacked by an enemy or bumped by another object. It's much better to build those details into the affected node classes themselves. But, as you see in the method we've got, the only thing we're sure of is that each side has an SKNode instance. Rather than coding up a big chain of `if-else` statements to ask each node which SKNode subclass it belongs to, we can use regular polymorphism to let each of our node classes handle things in its own way. In order for that to work, we have to add methods to SKNode, with default implementations that do nothing, and let our subclasses override them where appropriate. This calls for a class extension.

Adding a Class Extension to SKNode

To add an extension to SKNode, right-click the TextShooter folder in the Xcode Project Navigator and choose New File… from the pop-up menu. From the assistant's iOS Source section, choose Swift File, and then click Next. Name the file **SKNode+Extra.swift**, and press Create. Open the file in the editor and add the code shown here:

```swift
import SpriteKit

extension SKNode {
    func receiveAttacker(_ attacker: SKNode, contact: SKPhysicsContact) {
        // Default implementation does nothing
    }
    func friendlyBumpFrom(_ node: SKNode) {
        // Default implementation does nothing
    }
}
```

Now head back over to **GameScene.swift** to finish up its part of the collision handling. Go back to the `didBegin(_ contact: )` method, where you'll add the bits that actually do some work:

```swift
func didBegin(_ contact: SKPhysicsContact) {
    if contact.bodyA.categoryBitMask == contact.bodyB.categoryBitMask {
        // Both bodies are in the same category
        let nodeA = contact.bodyA.node!
        let nodeB = contact.bodyB.node!
```

```
        // What do we do with these nodes?
        nodeA.friendlyBumpFrom(nodeB)
        nodeB.friendlyBumpFrom(nodeA)
    } else {
        var attacker: SKNode
        var attackee: SKNode

        if contact.bodyA.categoryBitMask
                > contact.bodyB.categoryBitMask {
            // Body A is attacking Body B
            attacker = contact.bodyA.node!
            attackee = contact.bodyB.node!
        } else {
            // Body B is attacking Body A
            attacker = contact.bodyB.node!
            attackee = contact.bodyA.node!
        }

        if attackee is PlayerNode {
            playerLives -= 1
        }

        // What do we do with the attacker and the attackee?
        attackee.receiveAttacker(attacker, contact: contact)
        playerBullets.removeChildren(in: [attacker])
        enemies.removeChildren(in: [attacker])
    }
}
```

All we added here were a few calls to our new methods. If the collision is "friendly fire," such as two enemies bumping into each other, we'll tell each of them that it received a friendly bump from the other. Otherwise, after figuring out who attacked whom, we tell the attackee that it's come under attack from another object. Finally, we remove the attacker from both the `playerBullets` node and the `enemies` node. We tell each of those nodes to remove the attacker, even though it can only be in one of them, but that's OK. Telling a node to remove a child it doesn't have isn't an error — it just has no effect.

Adding Custom Collision Behavior to Enemies

Now that all that is in place, we can implement some specific behaviors for our nodes by overriding the extension methods we added to SKNode. Select **EnemyNode.swift** and add the following two overrides:

```
override func friendlyBumpFrom(_ node: SKNode) {
    physicsBody!.affectedByGravity = true
}
override func receiveAttacker(_ attacker: SKNode, contact:
SKPhysicsContact) {
    physicsBody!.affectedByGravity = true
    let force = vectorMultiply(attacker.physicsBody!.velocity,
                               contact.collisionImpulse)
    let myContact =
        scene!.convert(contact.contactPoint, to: self)
    physicsBody!.applyForce(force, at: myContact)
}
```

The first of those methods, `friendlyBumpFrom()`, simply turns on gravity for the affected enemy. So, if one enemy is in motion and bumps into another, the second enemy will suddenly notice gravity and start falling downward.

The `receiveAttacker(_:contact:)` method, which is called if the enemy is hit by a bullet, first turns on gravity for the enemy. However, it also uses the contact data that was passed in to figure out just where the contact occurred and applies a force to that point, giving it an extra push in the direction that the bullet was fired.

Showing Accurate Player Lives

Run the game again. You'll see that you can shoot at enemies to knock them down. You'll also see that any other enemies bumped into by a falling enemy will fall, as well.

> **Note** At the start of each level, the game world performs one step of its physics simulation to make sure that there aren't physics bodies overlapping each other. This will produce an interesting side effect at higher levels, since there will be an increasing chance that multiple randomly placed enemies will occupy overlapping spaces. Whenever that happens, the enemies will be immediately shifted so they no longer overlap, and our collision-handling code will be triggered, which subsequently turns on gravity and lets them fall! This behavior wasn't anything we planned on when we started building this game, but it turns out to be a happy accident that makes higher levels progressively more difficult, so we're letting physics run its course.

If you let enemies hit you as they fall, the number of player lives decreases, but... hey wait, it just shows 5 all the time! The Lives display is set up when the level is created, but it's never updated after that. Fortunately, this is easily fixed by adding a property observer to the `playerLives` property in **GameScene.swift**, like this:

```swift
private var playerLives: Int {
    didSet {
        let lives = childNode(withName: "LivesLabel") as! SKLabelNode
        lives.text = "Lives: \(playerLives)"
    }
}
```

The preceding snippet uses the name we previously associated with the label (in the `init(size:levelNumber:)` method) to find the label again and set a new text value. Play the game again, and you'll see that, as you let enemies rain down on your player, the number of lives will decrease to zero. And then the game doesn't end. After several hits, you end up with negative number of lives, as you can see in Figure 2-9.

CHAPTER 2 SIMPLE GAMES USING SPRITEKIT

Figure 2-9. *Since we don't have a way to end the game, we can end up with a negative number of lives*

The reason this problem appears is because we haven't written any code to detect the end of the game; that is, the point in time when the number of player lives hits zero. We'll do that soon, but first let's make our onscreen collisions a bit more stimulating.

Spicing Things Up with Particles

One of the nice features of SpriteKit is the inclusion of a particle system. Particle systems are used in games to create visual effects simulating smoke, fire, explosions, and more. Right now, whenever our bullets hit an enemy or an enemy hits the player, the attacking object simply blinks out of existence. Let's make a couple of particle systems to improve this situation.

83

CHAPTER 2 SIMPLE GAMES USING SPRITEKIT

Start out by pressing ⌘N to bring up the new file assistant. Select the iOS Resource section on the left, and then choose SpriteKit Particle File on the right. Click Next, and on the following screen choose the `SparkKit particle file`. Click Next again and name this file MissileExplosion.sks.

Your First Particle

You'll see that Xcode creates the particle file and also adds a new resource called **spark.png** to the project. At the same time, the entire Xcode editing area switches over to the new particle file, showing you a huge, animated exploding thing. We don't want something quite this extravagant and enormous when our bullets hit enemies, so let's reconfigure this thing. All the properties that define this particle's animation are available in the SKNode Inspector, which you can bring up by pressing Opt-Cmd-7. Figure 2-10 shows both the massive explosion and the inspector.

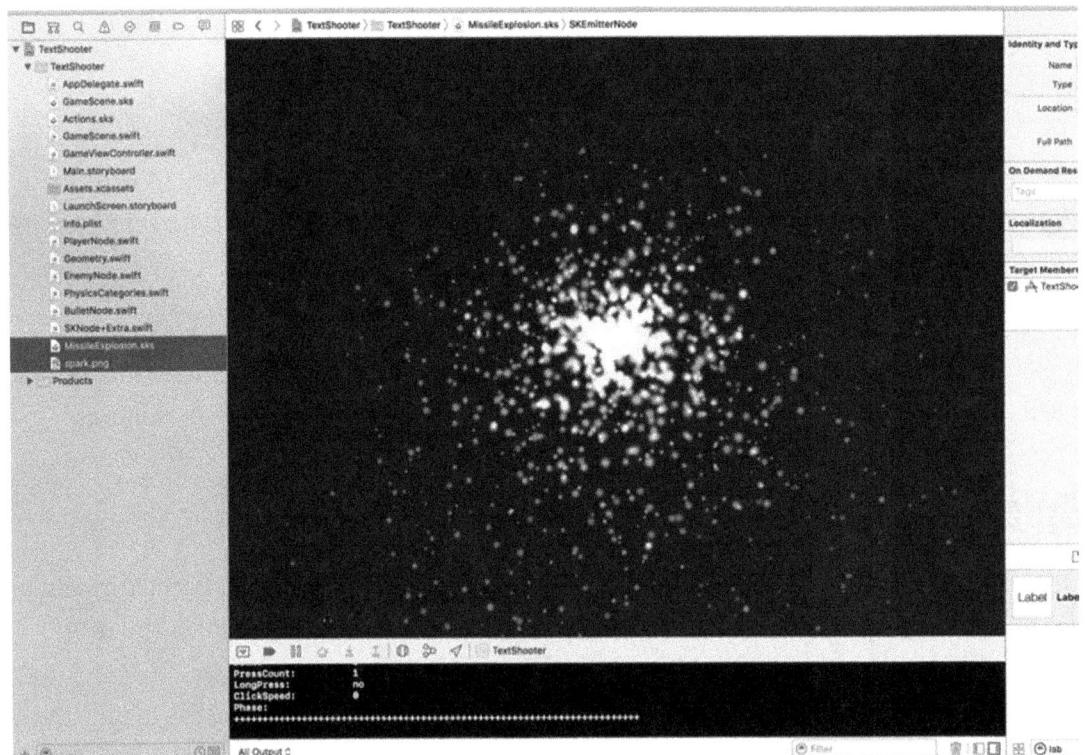

Figure 2-10. *The parameters shown on the right define how the default particle looks*

84

CHAPTER 2 SIMPLE GAMES USING SPRITEKIT

Now, for our bullet hit, let's make it a much smaller explosion. It will have a whole different set of parameters, all of which you configure right in the inspector. First, fix the colors to match what our game looks like by clicking the small color well in the Color Ramp at the bottom and setting it to black. Next, change the Background color to white and change the Blend Mode to Alpha. Now you'll see that the flaming fountain has turned all inky. The rest of the parameters are all numeric. Change them one at a time, setting them all, as shown in Figure 2-11. At each step of the way, you'll see the particle effect change until it eventually reaches its target appearance.

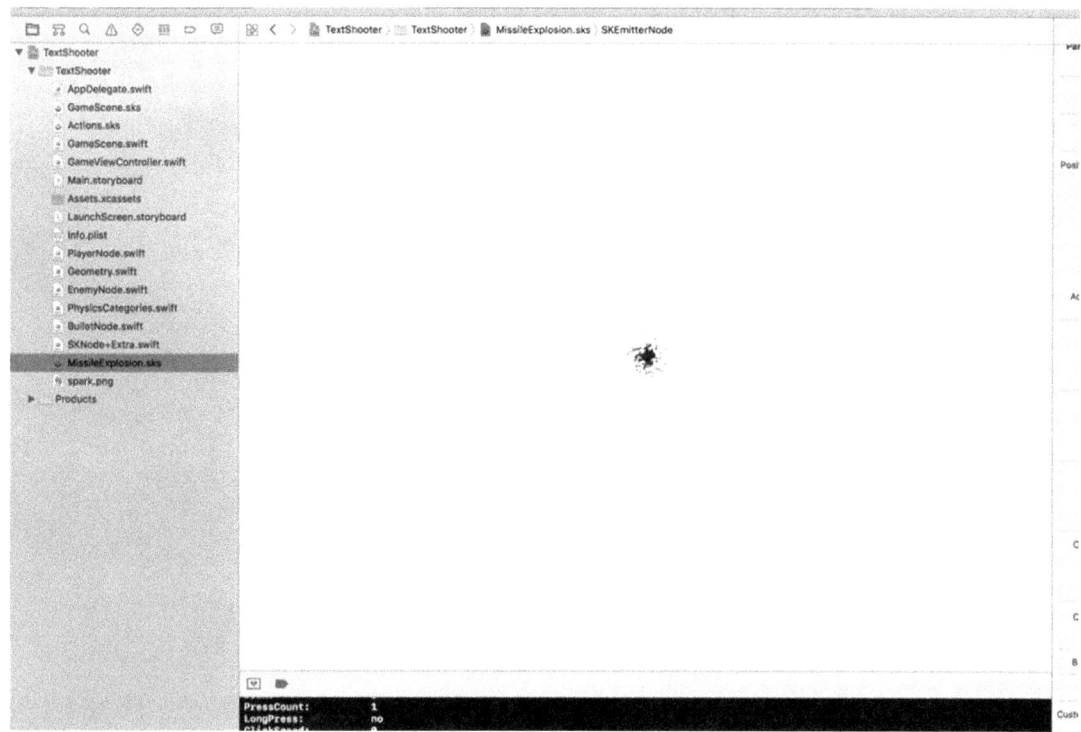

Figure 2-11. *This is the final missile explosion particle effect we want*

Now make another particle system, once again using the Spark template. Name this one EnemyExplosion.sks and set its parameters, as shown in Figure 2-12.

85

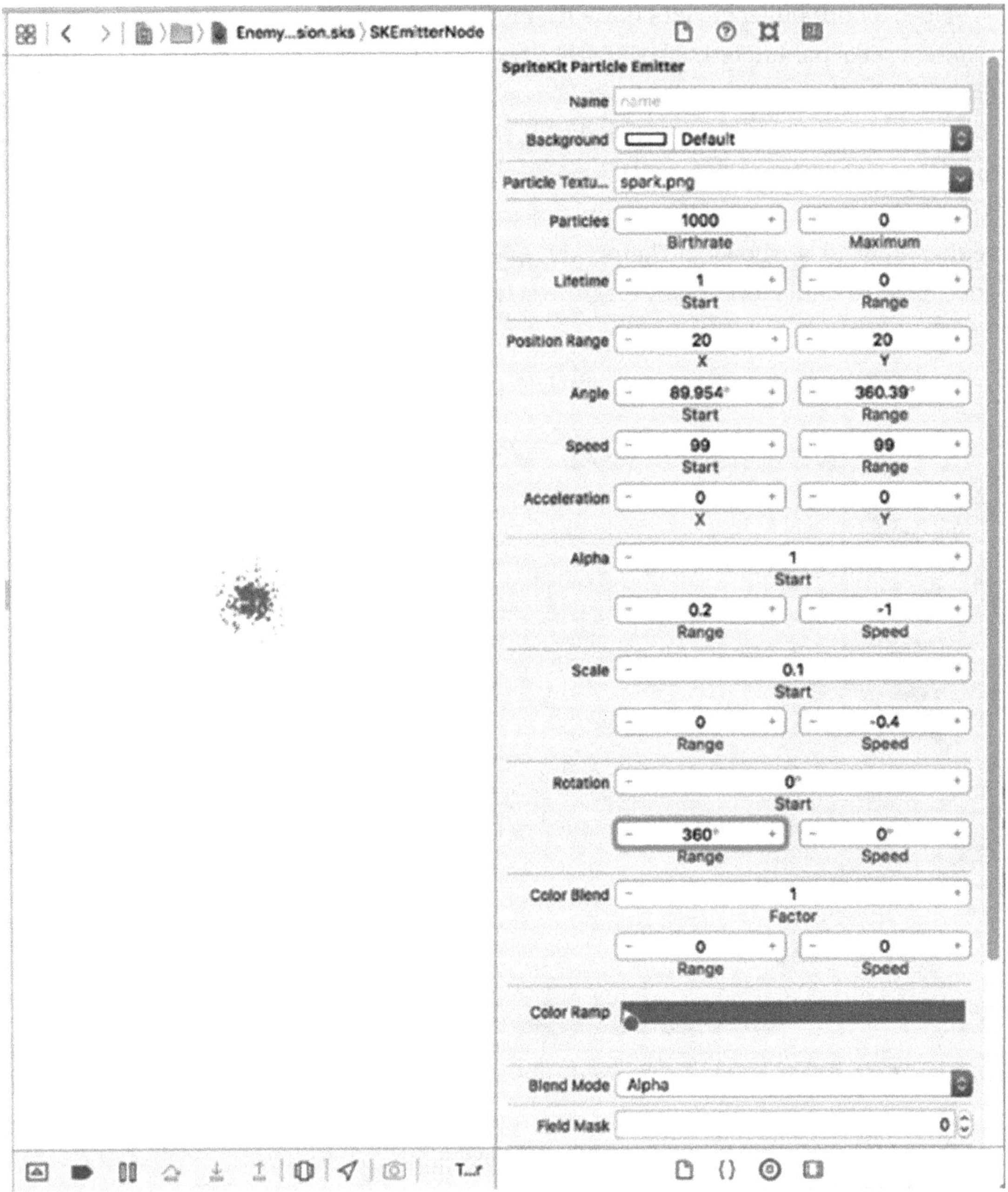

CHAPTER 2 SIMPLE GAMES USING SPRITEKIT

Figure 2-12. *Here's the enemy explosion we want to create. In case you're seeing this book in black and white, the color we've chosen in the Color Ramp at the bottom is deep red.*

Putting Particles into the Scene

Now let's start putting these particles to use. Switch over to **EnemyNode.swift** and add the bold code shown here to the bottom of the receiveAttacker(_:contact:) method:

```
override func receiveAttacker(_ attacker: SKNode, contact:
SKPhysicsContact) {
    physicsBody!.affectedByGravity = true
    let force = vectorMultiply(attacker.physicsBody!.velocity,
                                contact.collisionImpulse)
    let myContact =
        scene!.convert(contact.contactPoint, to: self)
    physicsBody!.applyForce(force, at: myContact)
    let path = Bundle.main.path(forResource: "MissileExplosion",
                                                ofType: "sks")
    let explosion = NSKeyedUnarchiver.unarchiveObject(withFile: path!)
        as! SKEmitterNode
    explosion.numParticlesToEmit = 20
    explosion.position = contact.contactPoint
    scene!.addChild(explosion)
}
```

Run the game and shoot some enemies. You'll see a nice little explosion where each bullet hits an enemy, as shown in Figure 2-13.

CHAPTER 2   SIMPLE GAMES USING SPRITEKIT

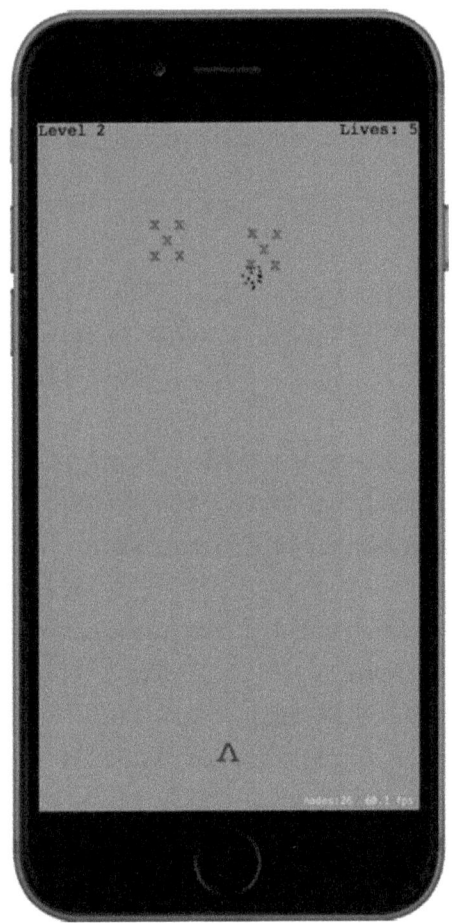

Figure 2-13. *Bullet explosions after impact*

Now let's do something similar for those times an enemy smashes into a player's ship. Select **PlayerNode.swift** and add this method:

```
override func receiveAttacker(_ attacker: SKNode, contact: 
SKPhysicsContact) {
    let path = Bundle.main.path (forResource: "EnemyExplosion",
                                            ofType: "sks")
    let explosion = NSKeyedUnarchiver.unarchiveObject(withFile: path!)
        as! SKEmitterNode
    explosion.numParticlesToEmit = 50
    explosion.position = contact.contactPoint
    scene!.addChild(explosion)
}
```

CHAPTER 2 SIMPLE GAMES USING SPRITEKIT

Play it again. You'll see a nice red splat every time an enemy hits the player, as shown in Figure 2-14.

Figure 2-14. *The explosion when an enemy ship hits the player*

These changes are pretty simple, but they improve the feel of the game substantially. Now when things collide, you have visual consequences and can see that something happened.

Ending the Game

As mentioned before, we currently have a small problem in the game. When the number of lives hits zero, we need to end the game. What we'll do is create a new scene class to transition to when the game is over. You've seen us do a scene transition before, when

CHAPTER 2 SIMPLE GAMES USING SPRITEKIT

moving from one level to the next. This will be similar, but with a new class. So, create a new iOS/Cocoa Touch class. Use SKScene as the parent class and name the new class GameOverScene. We'll start with a very simple implementation that just displays "Game Over" text and does nothing more. We'll accomplish this by adding this code to **GameOverScene.swift**:

```swift
import SpriteKit

class GameOverScene: SKScene {
    override init(size: CGSize) {
        super.init(size: size)
        backgroundColor = SKColor.purple
        let text = SKLabelNode(fontNamed: "Courier")
        text.text = "Game Over"
        text.fontColor = SKColor.white
        text.fontSize = 50
        text.position = CGPoint(x: frame.size.width/2, y: frame.size.height/2)
        addChild(text)
    }

    required init?(coder aDecoder: NSCoder) {
        super.init(coder: aDecoder)
    }
}
```

Now let's switch back to **GameScene.swift**. The basic action of what to do when the game ends is defined by a new method called `triggerGameOver()`. Here, we show both an extra explosion and kick off a transition to the new scene we just created:

```swift
private func triggerGameOver() {
    finished = true

    let path = Bundle.main.path(forResource:"EnemyExplosion",
                                ofType: "sks")
    let explosion = NSKeyedUnarchiver.unarchiveObject(withFile: path!)
        as! SKEmitterNode
```

CHAPTER 2   SIMPLE GAMES USING SPRITEKIT

```
        explosion.numParticlesToEmit = 200
        explosion.position = playerNode.position
        scene!.addChild(explosion)
        playerNode.removeFromParent()

        let transition = SKTransition.doorsOpenVertical(withDuration: 1)
        let gameOver = GameOverScene(size: frame.size)
        view!.presentScene(gameOver, transition: transition)
    }
```

Next, create this new method that will check for the end of the game, call `triggerGameOver()` if it's time, and return either `true` to indicate the game ended or `false` to indicate that it's still on:

```
    private func checkForGameOver() -> Bool {
        if playerLives == 0 {
            triggerGameOver()
            return true
        }
        return false
    }
```

Finally, make the following change shown in bold to the existing `update()` method. It checks for the game-over state and only looks for a potential next-level transition if the game is still going. Otherwise, there's a risk that the final enemy on a level could take the player's final life and trigger two scene transitions at once.

```
    override func update(_ currentTime: TimeInterval) {
        /* Called before each frame is rendered */
        if finished {
            return
        }
        updateBullets()

        updateEnemies()
        if (!checkForGameOver()) {
            checkForNextLevel()
        }
    }
```

91

Chapter 2 Simple Games Using SpriteKit

Now run the game again, and let falling enemies damage your ship five times. You'll see the Game Over screen, as shown in Figure 2-15.

Figure 2-15. *The Game Over screen*

Create a StartScene

This leads us to another problem: what do we do after the game is over? We could allow the player to tap to restart the game; but while thinking of that, a thought crossed my mind. Shouldn't this game have some sort of start screen, so the player isn't immediately thrust into a game at launch time? And shouldn't the game-over screen lead you back there? Of course, the answer to both questions is yes. Go ahead and create another new iOS/Cocoa Touch class, once again using SKScene as the superclass, and this time naming it StartScene. We're going to make a super-simple start scene here. All it will do

CHAPTER 2 SIMPLE GAMES USING SPRITEKIT

is display some text and start the game when the user taps anywhere. Add all the code shown here to **StartScene.swift** to complete this class:

```swift
import SpriteKit

class StartScene: SKScene {

    override init(size: CGSize) {
        super.init(size: size)
        backgroundColor = SKColor.green()

        let topLabel = SKLabelNode(fontNamed: "Courier")
        topLabel.text = "TextShooter"
        topLabel.fontColor = SKColor.black()
        topLabel.fontSize = 48
        topLabel.position = CGPoint(x: frame.size.width/2,
                                    y: frame.size.height * 0.7)
        addChild(topLabel)

        let bottomLabel = SKLabelNode(fontNamed: "Courier")
        bottomLabel.text = "Touch anywhere to start"
        bottomLabel.fontColor = SKColor.black()
        bottomLabel.fontSize = 20
        bottomLabel.position = CGPoint(x: frame.size.width/2,
                                       y: frame.size.height * 0.3)
        addChild(bottomLabel)
    }

    required init?(coder aDecoder: NSCoder) {
        super.init(coder: aDecoder)
    }

    override func touchesBegan(_ touches: Set<UITouch>, with event: UIEvent?) {
        let transition = SKTransition.doorway(withDuration: 1.0)
        let game = GameScene(size:frame.size)
        view!.presentScene(game, transition: transition)
    }
}
```

Now go back to **GameOverScene.swift**, so we can make the game-over scene perform a transition to the start scene. Add the following code:

```
override func didMove(to view: SKView) {
    DispatchQueue.main.after(
        when: DispatchTime.now() + Double(3 * Int64(NSEC_PER_SEC))
        / Double(NSEC_PER_SEC)) {
            let transition = SKTransition.flipVertical(withDuration: 1)
            let start = StartScene(size: self.frame.size)
            view.presentScene(start, transition: transition)
    }
}
```

As you saw earlier, the `didMoveToView()` method is called on any scene after it's been put in place in a view. Here, we simply trigger a three-second pause, followed by a transition back to the start scene. There's just one more piece of the puzzle to make all our scenes transition to each other as they should. We need to change the app startup procedure so that, instead of jumping right into the game, it shows us the start screen instead. This takes us back to **GameViewController.swift**. In the `viewDidLoad()` method, we just replace the code to create one scene class with another:

```
/* Pick a size for the scene */
let scene = GameScene(size: view.frame.size, levelNumber: 1)
let scene = StartScene(size: view.frame.size)
```

Now give it a try. Launch the app and you'll be greeted by the start scene. Touch the screen, play the game, die a lot, and you'll eventually get to the game-over scene. Wait a few seconds and you're back to the start screen, as shown in Figure 2-16.

CHAPTER 2 ■ SIMPLE GAMES USING SPRITEKIT

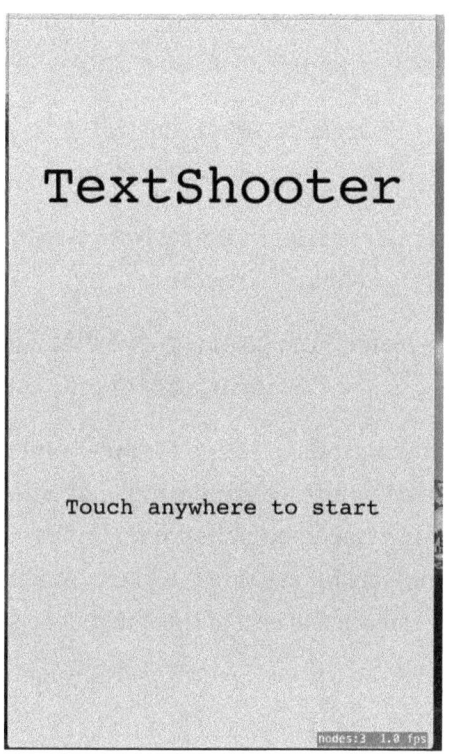

Figure 2-16. *The game's start screen*

Adding Sound Effects

We've been working on a video game, and video games are known for being noisy, but ours is completely silent. Fortunately, SpriteKit contains audio playback code that's extremely easy to use. In the 17 – Sound Effects folder in the source code for this chapter, you'll find the prepared audio files: enemyHit.wav, gameOver.wav, gameStart.wav, playerHit.wav, and shoot.wav. Drag all of them into the Xcode Project Navigator.

Now we'll bake in easy playback for each of these sound effects. Starting with **BulletNode.swift**, add the bold code to the end of the bullet(from:toward:) method, just before the return line:

```
bullet.run(SKAction.playSoundFileNamed("shoot.wav",
                          waitForCompletion: false))
```

95

Next, switch over to **EnemyNode.swift**, adding these lines to the end of the `receiveAttacker(_:contact:)` method:

```
run(SKAction.playSoundFileNamed("enemyHit.wav",
                    waitForCompletion: false))
```

Now do something extremely similar in **PlayerNode.swift**, adding these lines to the end of the `receiveAttacker(_:contact:)` method:

```
run(SKAction.playSoundFileNamed("playerHit.wav",
                    waitForCompletion: false))
```

Those are enough in-game sounds to satisfy for the moment. Go ahead and run the game at this point to try them out. We think you'll agree that the simple addition of particles and sounds gives the game a much better feel.

Now let's just add some effects for starting the game and ending the game. In **StartScene.swift**, add these lines at the end of the `touchesBegan(_:withEvent:)` method:

```
run(SKAction.playSoundFileNamed("gameStart.wav",
                    waitForCompletion: false))
```

And finally, add these lines to the end of the `triggerGameOver()` method in **GameScene.swift**:

```
run(SKAction.playSoundFileNamed("gameOver.wav",
                    waitForCompletion: false))
```

Making the Game a Little Harder: Force Fields

One of the most interesting features of SpriteKit is the ability to place force fields in a scene. A force field has a type, a location, a region in which it takes effect, and several other properties that specify how it behaves. The idea is that the field perturbs the motion of objects as they move through its sphere of influence, which is defined by its `region` property. There are various standard force fields that you can use, just by creating and configuring an instance and adding it to a scene. If you are feeling ambitious, you can even create custom force fields. For a list of the standard force fields and their behaviors, which include gravity fields, electric and magnetic fields, and turbulence, look at the API documentation for the `SKFieldNode` class.

CHAPTER 2 SIMPLE GAMES USING SPRITEKIT

To make our game a little more challenging, we're going to add some **radial gravity fields** to the scene. Radial gravity fields act like a large mass concentrated at a point. As an object moves through the region of a radial gravity field, it will be deflected toward it (or away from it, if you want to configure it that way), much like a meteor passing close enough to the Earth would be as it flies past. We're going to arrange for our gravity fields to act on missiles, so that you won't always be able to directly aim at an enemy and be sure of hitting it. Let's get started.

First, we need to add a new category to **PhysicsCategories.swift**. Make the following change in that file:

```
let GravityFieldCategory: UInt32 = 1 << 4
```

A field acts on a node if the `fieldBitMask` in the node's physics body has any category in common with the field's `categoryBitMask`. By default, a physics body's `fieldBitMask` has all categories set, which means it will be affected by any field that it comes within range of. We don't want the player or enemies to be affected by the gravity field, so we need to clear their `fieldBitMask` by adding the following code in **EnemyNode.swift**:

```
    private func initPhysicsBody() {
        let body = SKPhysicsBody(rectangleOf: CGSize(width: 40, height: 40))
        body.affectedByGravity = false
        body.categoryBitMask = EnemyCategory
        body.contactTestBitMask = PlayerCategory | EnemyCategory
        body.mass = 0.2
        body.angularDamping = 0
        body.linearDamping = 0
        body.fieldBitMask = 0
        physicsBody = body
    }
```

Make a similar change in **PlayerNode.swift**:

```
    private func initPhysicsBody() {
        let body = SKPhysicsBody(rectangleOf: CGSize(width: 20, height: 20))
        body.affectedByGravity = false
        body.categoryBitMask = PlayerCategory
        body.contactTestBitMask = EnemyCategory
```

CHAPTER 2   SIMPLE GAMES USING SPRITEKIT

```
        body.collisionBitMask = 0
        body.fieldBitMask = 0
        physicsBody = body
    }
```

The missile nodes will respond to the gravity field even if we don't do anything, since their physics nodes have all field categories set by default, but it's cleaner if we make this explicit, so make the following change in **BulletNode.swift**:

```
    override init() {
        super.init()

        let dot = SKLabelNode(fontNamed: "Courier")
        dot.fontColor = SKColor.black()
        dot.fontSize = 40
        dot.text = "."
        addChild(dot)

        let body = SKPhysicsBody(circleOfRadius: 1)
        body.isDynamic = true
        body.categoryBitMask = PlayerMissileCategory
        body.contactTestBitMask = EnemyCategory
        body.collisionBitMask = EnemyCategory
        body.fieldBitMask = GravityFieldCategory
        body.mass = 0.01

        physicsBody = body
        name = "Bullet \(self)"
    }
```

The rest of the changes are going to be in the file GameScene.swift. We're going to add three gravity fields centered at random points just below the center of the scene. As we did with the missiles and enemies, we'll add the force field nodes to a parent node that we'll then add to the scene. Add the definition of the parent node as a new property:

```
class GameScene: SKScene, SKPhysicsContactDelegate {
    private var levelNumber: Int
    private var playerLives: Int {
```

CHAPTER 2   SIMPLE GAMES USING SPRITEKIT

```swift
        didSet {
            let lives = childNode(withName: "LivesLabel") as! SKLabelNode
            lives.text = "Lives: \(playerLives)"
        }
    }
    private var finished = false
    private let playerNode: PlayerNode = PlayerNode()
    private let enemies = SKNode()
    private let playerBullets = SKNode()
    private let forceFields = SKNode()
```

At the end of the init(size:levelNumber:) method, add code to add the forceFields node to the scene and create the actual force field nodes:

```swift
        addChild(forceFields)
        createForceFields()
        
        physicsWorld.gravity = CGVector(dx: 0, dy: -1)
        physicsWorld.contactDelegate = self
    }
```

Finally, add the implementation of the createForceFields() method:

```swift
    private func createForceFields() {
        let fieldCount = 3
        let size = frame.size
        let sectionWidth = Int(size.width)/fieldCount
        for i in 0..<fieldCount {
            let x = CGFloat(UInt32(i * sectionWidth) +
                            arc4random_uniform(UInt32(sectionWidth)))
            let y = CGFloat(arc4random_uniform(UInt32(size.height * 0.25))
                            + UInt32(size.height * 0.25))
            
            let gravityField = SKFieldNode.radialGravityField()
            gravityField.position = CGPoint(x: x, y: y)
            gravityField.categoryBitMask = GravityFieldCategory
            gravityField.strength = 4
```

```
                gravityField.falloff = 2
                gravityField.region = SKRegion(size: CGSize(width:
                size.width * 0.3,
                height: size.height * 0.1))
                forceFields.addChild(gravityField)

                let fieldLocationNode = SKLabelNode(fontNamed: "Courier")
                fieldLocationNode.fontSize = 16
                fieldLocationNode.fontColor = SKColor.red()
                fieldLocationNode.name = "GravityField"
                fieldLocationNode.text = "*"
                fieldLocationNode.position = CGPoint(x: x, y: y)
                forceFields.addChild(fieldLocationNode)
            }
        }
```

All force fields are represented by instances of the `SKFieldNode` class. For each type of field, the `SKFieldNode` class has a factory method that lets you create a node of that field's type. Here, we use the `radialGravityField()` method to create three instances of a radial gravity field. We place them in a band just below the center of the scene. The `strength` and `falloff` properties control how strong the gravity field is and how rapidly it diminishes with the distance from the field node. A falloff value of 2 makes the force proportional to the inverse square of the distance between the field node and the affected object, just like in the real world. A positive force makes the field node attract the other object. Experiment with different `strength` values, including negative ones, to see how the effect varies. We also create three `SKLabelNodes` at the same positions as the gravity force fields, so that the player can see where they are. That's all we need to do. Build and run the app and watch what happens when your bullets fly close to one of the red asterisks in the scene.

Summary

Although TextShooter may be simple in appearance, the techniques we've covered in this chapter form the basis for all sorts of game development using SpriteKit. You've learned how to organize your code across multiple node classes, group objects together using the node graph, and more. You've also been given a taste of what it's like to build this sort of game one feature at a time, discovering each step along the way. Of course, we're not showing you all of our own missteps made along the way — this book is already over 500 pages long without that — but even counting those, this app really was built from scratch, in roughly the order shown in this chapter, in just a few short hours.

Once you get going, SpriteKit allows you to build up a lot of structure in a short amount of time. As you've seen, you can use text-based sprites if you don't have images handy. And if you want to swap them out for real graphics later, it's no problem. One early reader even pointed out a middle path: "Instead of plain old ASCII text in the strings in your source code, you can insert emoji characters by using Apple's Character Viewer input source." Accomplishing this is left as an exercise to the reader.

CHAPTER 3

Taps, Touches, and Gestures

The screens of the iPhone, iPod touch, and iPad — with their crisp, bright, touch-sensitive display — represent masterpieces of engineering. The multitouch screen common to all iOS devices provides one of the key factors in the platform's tremendous usability. Because the screen can detect multiple touches at the same time and track them independently, applications are able to detect a wide range of gestures, giving the user power that goes beyond the interface.

Suppose you are in the Mail application staring at a long list of junk e-mail that you want to delete. You can tap each one individually to read it; tap the trash icon to delete it; and then wait for the next message to download, deleting each one in turn. This method is best if you want to read each message before you delete it. If you have an iPhone 6s or iPhone 6s Plus, you can even take advantage of its 3D Touch feature to preview an e-mail without actually opening it. Alternatively, from the list of messages, you can tap the Edit button in the upper-right corner, tap each e-mail row to mark it, and then hit the Trash button to delete all marked messages. This method is best if you don't need to read each message before deleting it. Another alternative is to swipe across a message in the list from right to left. That gesture produces a More button and a Trash button for that message. Tap the Trash button, and the message is deleted.

This example is just one of the many gestures that are made possible by the multitouch display. You can pinch your fingers together to zoom out while viewing a picture or reverse-pinch to zoom in. On the home screen, you can long-press an icon to turn on "jiggly mode," allowing you to delete applications from your iOS device; on the iPhone 6s and iPhone 6s, you can summon a list of shortcuts for an application that supports 3D Touch. In this chapter, we're going to look at the underlying architecture that lets you detect gestures. You'll learn how to detect the most common gestures, as well as how to create and detect a completely new gesture.

CHAPTER 3   TAPS, TOUCHES, AND GESTURES

Multitouch Terminology

Before we dive into the architecture, let's cover some basic vocabulary. First, a **gesture** is any sequence of events that happens from the time you touch the screen with one or more fingers until you lift your fingers off the screen. No matter how long it takes, as long as one or more fingers remain against the screen, you are still within a gesture (unless a system event, such as an incoming phone call, interrupts it). In some sense, a gesture is a verb, and a running app can watch the user input stream to see if one is happening. A gesture is passed through the system inside a series of events. Events are generated when you interact with the device's multitouch screen. They contain information about the touch or touches that occurred.

The term **touch** refers to a finger being placed on the screen, dragging across the screen, or being lifted from the screen. The number of touches involved in a gesture is equal to the number of fingers on the screen at the same time. You can actually put all five fingers on the screen, and as long as they aren't too close to each other, iOS recognizes and tracks them all. Experimentation has shown that the iPad can handle up to 11 simultaneous touches! This may seem excessive, but could be useful if you're working on a multiplayer game, in which several players are interacting with the screen at the same time. The newest iOS devices can report how hard the user is pressing on the screen, making it possible for you to implement gestures that depend on that information.

A **tap** happens when you touch the screen with a finger and then immediately lift your finger off the screen without moving it around. The iOS device keeps track of the number of taps and can tell you if the user double-tapped, triple-tapped, or even 20-tapped. It handles all the timing and other work necessary to differentiate between two single-taps and a double-tap, for example.

A **gesture recognizer** object knows how to watch the stream of events generated by a user and recognize when the user is touching and dragging in a way that matches a predefined gesture. The `UIGestureRecognizer` class and its various subclasses can help take a lot of work off your hands when you want to watch for common gestures. This class encapsulates the work of looking for a gesture and can be easily applied to any view in your application.

In the first part of this chapter, we'll see the events that are reported when the user touches the screen with one or more fingers, and how to track the movement of fingers on the screen. We can use these events to handle gestures in a custom view or in our application delegate. Next, we'll look at some of the gesture recognizers that come with the iOS SDK, and finally, you'll see how to build your own gesture recognizer.

The Responder Chain

Since gestures are passed through the system inside events, and events are passed through the **responder chain**, you need to have an understanding of how the responder chain works in order to handle gestures properly. If you've worked with Cocoa for macOS (or previously OS X), you're probably familiar with the concept of a responder chain, as the same basic mechanism is used in both Cocoa and Cocoa Touch. If this is new material, don't worry; we'll explain how it works.

Responding to Events

The first responder is usually the object with which the user is currently interacting. The first responder is the start of the responder chain, but it's not alone. There are always other responders in the chain as well. In a running application, the responder chain is a changing set of objects that are able to respond to user events. Any class that has `UIResponder` as one of its superclasses is a **responder**. `UIView` is a subclass of `UIResponder`, and `UIControl` is a subclass of `UIView`, so all views and all controls are responders. `UIViewController` is also a subclass of `UIResponder`, meaning that it is a responder, as are all of its subclasses, such as `UINavigationController` and `UITabBarController`. Responders, then, are so named because they respond to system-generated events, such as screen touches.

If a responder doesn't handle a particular event, such as a gesture, it usually passes that event up the responder chain. If the next object in the chain responds to that particular event, it will usually consume the event, which stops the event's progression through the responder chain. In some cases, if a responder only partially handles an event, that responder will take an action and forward the event to the next responder in the chain. That's not usually what happens, though. Normally, when an object responds to an event, that's the end of the line for the event. If the event goes through the entire responder chain and no object handles the event, the event is then discarded.

Let's take a more specific look at the responder chain. An event first gets delivered to the `UIApplication` object, which in turn passes it to the application's `UIWindow`. The `UIWindow` handles the event by selecting an initial responder. The initial responder is chosen as follows:

- In the case of a touch event, the `UIWindow` object determines the view that the user touched, and then offers the event to any gesture recognizers that are registered for that view or any view higher up in the view hierarchy. If any gesture recognizer handles the event, it goes no further. If not, the initial responder is the touched view and the event will be delivered to it.

- For an event generated by the user shaking the device or from a remote control device, the event is delivered to the first responder.

If the initial responder doesn't handle the event, it passes the event to its parent view, if there is one, or to the view controller if the view is the view controller's view. If the view controller doesn't handle the event, it continues up the responder chain through the view hierarchy of its parent view controller, if it has one.

If the event makes it all the way up through the view hierarchy without being handled by a view or a controller, the event is passed to the application's window. If the window doesn't handle the event, the `UIApplication` object will pass it to the application delegate, if the delegate is a subclass of `UIResponder` (which it normally is if you create your project from one of Apple's application templates). Finally, if the app delegate isn't a subclass of `UIResponder` or doesn't handle the event, then the event goes gently into the good night.

This process is important for a number of reasons. First, it controls the way gestures can be handled. Let's say a user is looking at a table and swipes a finger across a row of that table. What object handles that gesture? If the swipe is within a view or control that's a subview of the table view cell, that view or control will get a chance to respond. If it doesn't respond, the table view cell gets a chance. In an application like Mail, in which a swipe can be used to delete a message, the table view cell probably needs to look at that event to see if it contains a swipe gesture. Most table view cells don't respond to gestures, however. If they don't respond, the event proceeds up to the table view, and then up the rest of the responder chain until something responds to that event or it reaches the end of the line.

Forwarding an Event: Keeping the Responder Chain Alive

Let's consider that table view cell in the Mail application. We don't know the internal details of the Apple Mail application; however, let's assume that the table view cell handles the delete swipe and only the delete swipe. That table view cell must implement the methods related to receiving touch events (discussed shortly) so that it can check to see if that event could be interpreted as part of a swipe gesture. If the event matches a swipe that the table view is looking for, then the table view cell takes an action, and that's that; the event goes no further.

If the event doesn't match the table view cell's swipe gesture, the table view cell takes the responsibility for forwarding that event to the next object in the responder chain. If it doesn't do its forwarding job, the table and other objects up the chain will never get a chance to respond, and the application may not function as the user expects. That table view cell could prevent other views from recognizing a gesture.

Whenever you respond to a touch event, you need to keep in mind that your code doesn't work in a vacuum. If an object intercepts an event that it doesn't handle, it needs to pass it along manually. One way to do this is to call the same method on the next responder. We see an example of this in Listing 3-1.

Listing 3-1. Passing Along a Gesture to Be Handled Elsewhere

```
func respondToFictionalEvent(event: UIEvent) {
    if shouldHandleEvent(event) {
        handleEvent(event)
    } else {
        nextResponder().respondToFictionalEvent(event)
    }
}
```

Notice that we call the same method on the next responder. That's how to implement a good responder-chain process. Fortunately, most of the time, methods that respond to an event also consume the event. However, it's important to know that if that's not the case, you need to make sure the event is passed along to the next link in the responder chain.

CHAPTER 3 TAPS, TOUCHES, AND GESTURES

The Multitouch Architecture

Now that we've talked a little about the responder chain, let's look at the process of handling touches. As we've indicated, touches are passed along the responder chain, embedded in events. This means that the code to handle any kind of interaction with the multitouch screen needs to be contained in an object in the responder chain. Generally, that means we can choose to either embed that code in a subclass of `UIView` or embed the code in a `UIViewController`. So, does this code belong in the view or in the view controller?

If the view needs to do something to itself based on the user's touches, the code probably belongs in the class that defines that view. For example, many control classes, such as `UISwitch` and `UISlider`, respond to touch-related events. A `UISwitch` might want to turn itself on or off based on a touch. The folks who created the `UISwitch` class embedded gesture-handling code in the class so the `UISwitch` can respond to a touch. Often, however, when the gesture being processed affects more than the object being touched, the gesture code really belongs in the relevant view controller class. For example, if the user makes a gesture touching one row that indicates that all rows should be deleted, the gesture should be handled by code in the view controller. The way you respond to touches and gestures in both situations is exactly the same, regardless of the class to which the code belongs.

The Four Touch Notification Methods

Four methods are used to notify a responder about touches. When the user first touches the screen, the system looks for a responder that has a method called `touchesBegan(_:withEvent:)`. To find out when the user first begins a gesture or taps the screen, implement this method in your view or your view controller. An example of what that method might look like can be seen in Listing 3-2.

Listing 3-2. Discover When the Gesture or Tap Began

```
override func touchesBegan(touches: Set<UITouch>, withEvent event: UIEvent?) {
    if let touch = touches.first {
        let numTaps = touch.tapCount
        let numTouches = event?.allTouches()?.count
    }
    // Do something here
}
```

Each time a finger touches the screen for the first time, a new `UITouch` object is allocated to represent that finger and added to the set that is delivered with each `UIEvent` and can be retrieved by calling its `allTouches()` method. All future events that report activity for that same finger will contain *the same UITouch instance* in the `allTouches()` set (and it will also appear in the `touches` set if there is new activity to report for the corresponding finger) until that finger is removed from the screen. Thus, to track the activity of any given finger, you need to monitor its `UITouch` object.

You can determine the number of fingers currently pressed against the screen by getting a count of the objects returned by `allTouches()`. If the event reports a touch that is part of a series of taps by any given finger, you can get the tap count from the `tapCount` property of the `UITouch` object for that finger. If there's only one finger touching the screen, or if you don't care which finger you ask about, you can quickly get a `UITouch` object to query by using the `first` property of the Set structure. In the preceding example, a `numTaps` value of 2 tells you that the screen was tapped twice in quick succession by at least one finger. Similarly, a `numTouches` value of 2 tells you the user has two fingers touching the screen.

Not all of the objects in `touches` or the `allTouches()` set may be relevant to the view or view controller in which you've implemented this method. A table view cell, for example, probably doesn't care about touches that are in other rows or that are in the navigation bar. You can get the set of touches that falls within a particular view from the event using `let myTouches = event?.touchesForView(self.view)`.

Every `UITouch` represents a different finger, and each finger is located at a different position on the screen. You can find out the position of a specific finger using the `UITouch` object. It will even translate the point into the view's local coordinate system using `let point = touch.locationInView(self.view)   // point is of type CGPoint`.

You can get notified while the user is moving fingers across the screen by implementing `touchesMoved(_:withEvent:)`. This method gets called multiple times during a long drag, and each time, you will get another set of touches and another event. In addition to being able to find out each finger's current position from the `UITouch` objects, you can also discover the previous location of that touch, which is the finger's position the last time either `touchesMoved(_:withEvent:)` or `touchesBegan(_:withEvent:)` was called.

When any of the user's fingers is removed from the screen, another method, `touchesEnded(_:withEvent:)`, is invoked. When this method is called, you know that the user is finished with some interaction using the affected finger.

There's one final touch-related method that responders might implement: `touchesCancelled(_:withEvent:)`. It is called if the user is in the middle of a sequence of operations when something happens to interrupt it, like the phone ringing. This is where you can do any cleanup you might need so you can start fresh with a new gesture. When this method is called, `touchesEnded(_:withEvent:)` will not be called for the current set of touches.

Creating the TouchExplorer Application

We're going to build a little application that will give you a better feel for when the four touch-related responder methods are called. In Xcode, create a new project using the Single View Application template. Enter **TouchExplorer** as the Product Name. TouchExplorer prints messages to the screen that indicate the touch and tap count every time a touch-related method is called. On devices that support 3D Touch, it will also show the force applied by the finger that caused the most recent touch event, as shown in Figure 3-1.

CHAPTER 3 ■ TAPS, TOUCHES, AND GESTURES

Figure 3-1. *The TouchExplorer application*

Note Although the applications in this chapter will run on the simulator, you won't be able to see all the available multitouch or 3D Touch functionality unless you run them on a real iOS device. 3D Touch requires an iPhone 6s or iPhone 6s Plus.

We need four labels for this application: one to indicate which method was last called, another to report the current tap count, a third to report the number of touches, and a fourth for the 3D Touch force value. Single-click ViewController.swift and add four outlets to the view controller class:

```
class ViewController: UIViewController {
    @IBOutlet var messageLabel: UILabel!
```

```
@IBOutlet var tapsLabel: UILabel!
@IBOutlet var touchesLabel: UILabel!
@IBOutlet var forceLabel: UILabel!
```

Now select Main.storyboard to create the user interface. You'll see the usual empty view contained in all new projects of this kind. Drag a label onto the view, using the blue guidelines to place the label toward the upper-left corner of the view. Hold down the Option key and drag three more labels out from the original, spacing them one below the other. This leaves you with four labels (see Figure 3-1). Feel free to play with the fonts and colors if you're feeling a bit creative. When you're done, select the bottom label and use the Attributes Inspector to set its `Lines` property to 0, because we're going to use it to show more than one line of text.

Now we need to set the auto layout constraints for the labels. In the Document Outline, Control-drag from the first label to the main view and release the mouse. Hold down the Shift key and select Vertical Spacing to Top Layout Guide and Leading Space to Container Margin, and then click Return. Do the same for the other three labels. The next step is to connect the labels to their outlets. Control-drag from the View Controller icon to each of the four labels, connecting the top one to the `messageLabel` outlet, the second one to the `tapsLabel` outlet, the third one to the `touchesLabel` outlet, and the bottom one to the `forceLabel` outlet. Finally, double-click each label and press the Delete key to get rid of its text.

Next, single-click either the background of the main view or the View icon in the Document Outline, and then bring up the Attributes Inspector (see Figure 3-2). In the Inspector, go to the View section and make sure that both User Interaction Enabled and Multiple Touch are checked. If Multiple Touch is not checked, your controller class's touch methods will always receive one and only one touch, no matter how many fingers are actually touching the phone's screen.

CHAPTER 3 TAPS, TOUCHES, AND GESTURES

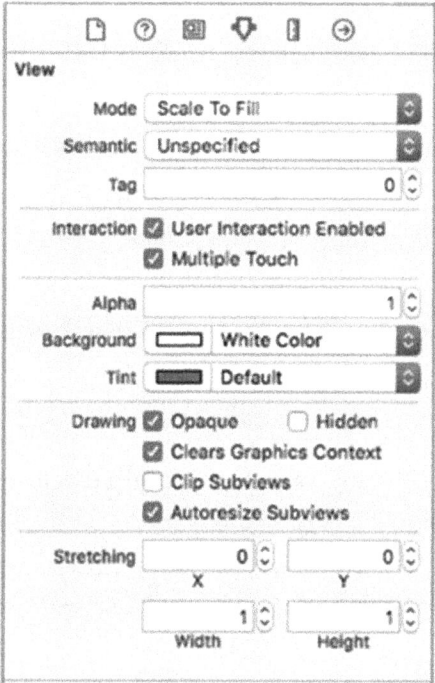

Figure 3-2. *In the View attributes, both User Interaction Enabled and Multiple Touch are checked*

When you're finished, switch back to ViewController.swift and make the changes, as shown in Listing 3-3.

Listing 3-3. *The ViewController.swift file to Support TouchExplorer*

```
override func viewDidLoad() {
    super.viewDidLoad()
    // Do any additional setup after loading the view, typically from a nib.
}

private func updateLabelsFromTouches(_ touch: UITouch?, allTouches:
Set<UITouch>?) {
    let numTaps = touch?.tapCount ?? 0
    let tapsMessage = "\(numTaps) taps detected"
    tapsLabel.text = tapsMessage
```

```
        let numTouches = allTouches?.count ?? 0
        let touchMsg = "\(numTouches) touches detected"
        touchesLabel.text = touchMsg

        if traitCollection.forceTouchCapability == .available {
            forceLabel.text = "Force: \(touch?.force ?? 0)\nMax force:
            \(touch?.maximumPossibleForce ?? 0)"
        } else {
            forceLabel.text = "3D Touch not available"
        }
    }

    override func touchesBegan(_ touches: Set<UITouch>, with event: UIEvent?) {
        messageLabel.text = "Touches Began"
        updateLabelsFromTouches(touches.first, allTouches: event?.allTouches())
    }

    override func touchesCancelled(_ touches: Set<UITouch>, with event:
    UIEvent?) {
        messageLabel.text = "Touches Cancelled"
        updateLabelsFromTouches(touches.first, allTouches: event?.allTouches())
    }

    override func touchesEnded(_ touches: Set<UITouch>, with event: UIEvent?) {
        messageLabel.text = "Touches Ended"
        updateLabelsFromTouches(touches.first, allTouches: event?.allTouches())
    }

    override func touchesMoved(_ touches: Set<UITouch>, with event: UIEvent?) {
        messageLabel.text = "Drag Detected"
        updateLabelsFromTouches(touches.first, allTouches: event?.allTouches())
    }
```

In this controller class, we implement all four of the touch-related methods we discussed earlier. Each one sets `messageLabel` so the user can see when each method has been called. Next, all four of them call `updateLabelsFromTouches()` to update the other three labels. The `updateLabelsFromTouches()` method gets the tap count from the current touch, figures out the number of fingers touching the screen by looking at the count property of the set of touches that it receives (which is taken from the `UIEvent` object), and updates the labels with that information. It also obtains and displays force information. Let's take a close look at that part of the code:

```
if traitCollection.forceTouchCapability == .available {
    forceLabel.text = "Force: \(touch?.force ?? 0)\nMax force:
        \(touch?.maximumPossibleForce ?? 0)"
} else {
    forceLabel.text = "3D Touch not available"
}
```

3D Touch is not available on all devices, so the first line of code uses the `forceTouchCapability` property of the `UITraitCollection` class to check whether it is. Every view controller has a trait collection and here we use the trait collection of the application's only view controller to make the check. If 3D Touch is supported, we use the `force` property of `UITouch` to find out how hard the user is currently pressing on the screen and the `maximumPossibleForce` property to get the largest possible force value. If 3D touch is not available, we simply say so.

Build and run the application. If you're running in the simulator, try repeatedly clicking the screen to drive up the tap count. You should also try clicking and holding down the mouse button while dragging around the view to simulate a touch and drag. If you have a device that supports 3D Touch, try pressing with varying amounts of force to see the measurements that are reported.

You can emulate a two-finger pinch in the iOS simulator by holding down the Option key while you click with the mouse and drag. You can also simulate two-finger swipes by first holding down the Option key to simulate a pinch, moving the mouse so the two dots representing virtual fingers are next to each other, and then holding down the Shift key (while still holding down the Option key). Pressing the Shift key will lock the position of the two fingers relative to each other, enabling you to do swipes and other two-finger gestures. You won't be able to do gestures that require three or more fingers, but you can do most two-finger gestures on the simulator using combinations of the Option and Shift keys.

If you're able to run this program on a device, see how many touches you can get to register at the same time. Try dragging with one finger, followed by two fingers, and then three. Try double- and triple-tapping the screen, and see if you can get the tap count to go up by tapping with two fingers.

CHAPTER 3 TAPS, TOUCHES, AND GESTURES

Play around with the TouchExplorer application until you feel comfortable with what's happening and with the way that the four touch methods work. When you're ready, continue on to see how to detect one of the most common gestures: the swipe.

Creating the Swipes Application

The application we're about to build does nothing more than detect swipes, both horizontal and vertical. If you swipe your finger across the screen from left to right, right to left, top to bottom, or bottom to top, the app will display a message across the top of the screen for a few seconds, informing you that a swipe was detected (see Figure 3-3).

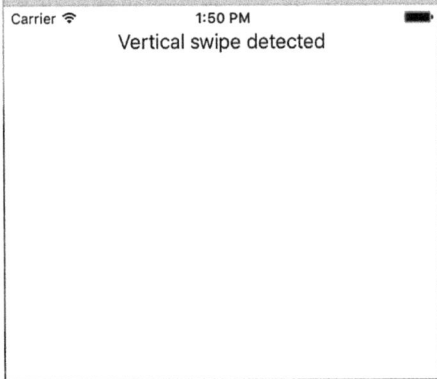

Figure 3-3. *The Swipes application detects both vertical and horizontal swipes*

Using Touch Events to Detect Swipes

Detecting swipes is relatively easy. We'll define a minimum gesture length in pixels, which is how far the user needs to swipe before the gesture counts as a swipe. We'll also define a variance, which is how far from a straight line our user can veer and still have the gesture count as a horizontal or vertical swipe. A diagonal line generally won't count as a swipe, but one that's just a little off from horizontal or vertical will.

When the user touches the screen, we'll save the location of the first touch in a variable. We'll then check as the user's finger moves across the screen to see if it reaches a point where it has gone far enough and straight enough to count as a swipe. There's actually a built-in gesture recognizer that does exactly this, but we're going to use what we've learned about touch events to make one of our own. Let's build it. Create a new project in Xcode

CHAPTER 3 TAPS, TOUCHES, AND GESTURES

using the Single View Application template, set Devices to Universal, and name the project **Swipes**. Single-click ViewController.swift and add the following code to class:

```swift
class ViewController: UIViewController {
    @IBOutlet var label: UILabel!
    private var gestureStartPoint: CGPoint!
```

This code declares an outlet for our label and a variable to hold the first spot the user touches.

Select Main.storyboard to open it for editing. Make sure that the view controller's view is set so User Interaction Enabled and Multiple Touch are both checked using the Attributes Inspector, and drag a label from the library and drop it in the upper portion of the View window. Set the text alignment to center and feel free to play with the other text attributes to make the label easier to read. In the Document Outline, Control-drag from the label to its parent view, release the mouse, hold down Shift and select Vertical Spacing to Top Layout Guide and Center Horizontally in Container, and then press Return. Control-drag from the View Controller icon to the label and connect it to the label outlet. Finally, double-click the label and delete its text. Now switch over to ViewController.swift and update it to that shown in Listing 3-4.

Listing 3-4. Updates to ViewController.swift File for the Touches App

```swift
class ViewController: UIViewController {
    @IBOutlet var label: UILabel!
    private var gestureStartPoint: CGPoint!
    private static let minimumGestureLength = Float(25.0)
    private static let maximumVariance = Float(5)

    override func viewDidLoad() {
        super.viewDidLoad()
        // Do any additional setup after loading the view, typically from a nib.
    }

    override func touchesBegan(_ touches: Set<UITouch>, with event: UIEvent?) {
        if let touch = touches.first {
            gestureStartPoint = touch.location(in: self.view)
        }
    }
```

CHAPTER 3 TAPS, TOUCHES, AND GESTURES

```
override func touchesMoved(_ touches: Set<UITouch>, with event: UIEvent?) {
    if let touch = touches.first, gestureStartPoint = self.
    gestureStartPoint {
        let currentPosition = touch.location(in: self.view)

        let deltaX = fabsf(Float(gestureStartPoint.x - currentPosition.x))
        let deltaY = fabsf(Float(gestureStartPoint.y - currentPosition.y))

        if deltaX >= ViewController.minimumGestureLength
                    && deltaY <= ViewController.maximumVariance {
            label.text = "Horizontal swipe detected"
            DispatchQueue.main.after(when: DispatchTime.now() +
            Double(Int64(2 * NSEC_PER_SEC)) / Double(NSEC_PER_SEC)) {
                self.label.text = ""
            }
        } else if deltaY >= ViewController.minimumGestureLength
                    && deltaX <= ViewController.maximumVariance {
            label.text = "Vertical swipe detected"
            DispatchQueue.main.after(when: DispatchTime.now() +
            Double(Int64(2 * NSEC_PER_SEC)) / Double(NSEC_PER_SEC)) {
                self.label.text = ""
            }
        }
    }
}
```

Let's start with the `touchesBegan(_:withEvent:)` method. All we do there is grab a touch from the `touches` set and store its touch point. We're primarily interested in single-finger swipes right now, so we don't worry about how many touches there are; we just grab the first one in the set:

```
if let touch = touches.first {
    gestureStartPoint = touch.location(in: self.view)
}
```

We're using the `UITouch` objects in the `touches` argument instead of the ones in the `UIEvent` because we're interested in tracking changes as they happen, not in the overall

CHAPTER 3 TAPS, TOUCHES, AND GESTURES

state of all of the active touches. In the next method, `touchesMoved(_:withEvent:)`, we do the real work. First, we get the current position of the user's finger:

```
if let touch = touches.first, gestureStartPoint = self.gestureStartPoint {
    let currentPosition = touch.location(in: self.view)
```

Here, we're using a form of the `if let` statement that lets us check more than one condition — we're ensuring both that there is a current touch and that we have previously stored a gesture start point. In practice, both of these conditions should always be met, but the fact that the `touches.first` property, which we use both here and in the `touchesBegan(_:withEvent:)` method, returns an optional value means that we should make these checks to be sure that we don't crash our application by trying to unwrap a `nil` optional value in the event that something unexpected happens.

Next, we calculate how far the user's finger has moved both horizontally and vertically from its starting position. `fabsf()` is a function from the standard C math library that returns the absolute value of a `float`. This allows us to subtract one from the other without needing to worry about which is the higher value:

```
let deltaX = fabsf(Float(gestureStartPoint.x - currentPosition.x))
let deltaY = fabsf(Float(gestureStartPoint.y - currentPosition.y))
```

Once we have the two deltas, we check to see if the user has moved far enough in one direction without having moved too far in the other to constitute a swipe. If that's true, we set the label's text to indicate whether a horizontal or vertical swipe was detected. We also use the GCD `DispatchQueue.main.after()` function to erase the text after it has been on the screen for two seconds. That way, the user can practice multiple swipes without needing to worry whether the label is referring to an earlier attempt or the most recent one:

```
if deltaX >= ViewController.minimumGestureLength
            && deltaY <= ViewController.maximumVariance {
    label.text = "Horizontal swipe detected"
    DispatchQueue.main.after(when: DispatchTime.now() +
            Double(Int64(2 * NSEC_PER_SEC)) / Double
            (NSEC_PER_SEC)) {
        self.label.text = ""
} else if deltaY >= ViewController.minimumGestureLength
            && deltaX <= ViewController.maximumVariance {
```

119

```
            label.text = "Vertical swipe detected"
            DispatchQueue.main.after(when: DispatchTime.now() +
                    Double(Int64(2 * NSEC_PER_SEC)) / Double
                    (NSEC_PER_SEC)) {
                self.label.text = ""
            }
        }
```

Build and run the application. If you find yourself clicking and dragging with no visible results, be patient. Click and drag straight down or straight across until you get the hang of swiping.

Automatic Gesture Recognition

The procedure we just used for detecting a swipe wasn't too bad. All the complexity is in the touchesMoved(_:withEvent:) method, and even that wasn't all that complicated. But there's an even easier way to do this. iOS includes a class called UIGestureRecognizer, which eliminates the need for watching all the events to see how fingers are moving. You don't use UIGestureRecognizer directly, but instead create an instance of one of its subclasses, each of which is designed to look for a particular type of gesture, such as a swipe, pinch, double-tap, triple-tap, and so on. Let's see how to modify the Swipes app to use a gesture recognizer instead of our hand-rolled procedure. As always, you might want to make a copy of your Swipes project folder and start from there. In the example source code archive, you'll find the completed version of this application in the Swipes 2 folder.

Start by selecting ViewController.swift and deleting both the touchesBegan(_:withEvent:) and touchesMoved(_:withEvent:) methods because you won't need them and add a couple of new methods in their place:

```
func reportHorizontalSwipe(_ recognizer:UIGestureRecognizer) {
    label.text = "Horizontal swipe detected"
    DispatchQueue.main.after(when: DispatchTime.now() +
            Double(Int64(2 * NSEC_PER_SEC)) / Double(NSEC_PER_SEC)) {
        self.label.text = ""
    }
}
```

```
    func reportVerticalSwipe(_ recognizer:UIGestureRecognizer) {
        label.text = "Vertical swipe detected"
            DispatchQueue.main.after(when: DispatchTime.now() +
                Double(Int64(2 * NSEC_PER_SEC)) / Double(NSEC_PER_SEC)) {
            self.label.text = ""
        }
    }
```

These methods implement the actual functionality (if you can call it that) that's provided by the swipe gestures, just as the touchesMoved(_:withEvent:) did previously, except that there is no longer any code to detect the actual swipes. Now add the new code shown here to the viewDidLoad method:

```
super.viewDidLoad()
// Do any additional setup after loading the view, typically from a nib.

let vertical = UISwipeGestureRecognizer(target: self, action:
"reportVerticalSwipe:")
vertical.direction = [.up, .down]
view.addGestureRecognizer(vertical)

let horizontal = UISwipeGestureRecognizer(target: self,
        action: "reportHorizontalSwipe:")
horizontal.direction = [.left, .right]
view.addGestureRecognizer(horizontal)
```

All we're doing here is creating two gesture recognizers — one that will detect vertical movement and another to detect horizontal movement. When one of them recognizes its configured gesture, it will call either the reportVerticalSwipe() or the reportHorizontalSwipe() method and sets the label's text appropriately. To sanitize things even further, you can also delete the declaration of the gestureStartPoint property and the two constant values from ViewController.swift. Now build and run the application to try out the new gesture recognizers.

In terms of total lines of code, there's not much difference between these two approaches for a simple case like this. But the code that uses gesture recognizers is undeniably simpler to understand and easier to write. You don't need to give even a moment's thought to the issue of calculating a finger's movement over time because that's done for you by the UISwipeGestureRecognizer. And better yet, Apple's gesture recognition system is extendable, which means that if your application requires really complex gestures that aren't covered by any of Apple's recognizers, you can make your own, and keep the complex code (along the lines of what we saw earlier) tucked away in the recognizer class instead of polluting your view controller code. We'll build an example of just such a thing later in this chapter. Meanwhile, run the application and you'll see that it behaves just like the previous version.

Implementing Multiple Swipes

In the Swipes application, we worried about only single-finger swipes, so we just grabbed the first object in the `touches` set to figure out where the user's finger was during the swipe. This approach is fine if you're interested in only single-finger swipes, the most common type of swipe used. But what if you want to handle two- or three-finger swipes? In the earliest versions of this book, we dedicated about 50 lines of code, and a fair amount of explanation, to achieving this by tracking multiple `UITouch` instances across multiple touch events. Now that we have gesture recognizers, this is a solved problem. A `UISwipeGestureRecognizer` can be configured to recognize any number of simultaneous touches. By default, each instance expects a single finger, but you can configure it to look for any number of fingers pressing the screen at once. Each instance responds only to the exact number of touches you specify, so what we'll do is create a whole bunch of gesture recognizers in a loop.

Make another copy of your Swipes project folder to experiment with this — you'll find the completed version in the Swipes 3 folder of the example source code archive. Edit ViewController.swift and modify the `viewDidLoad` method, replacing it with the one shown here:

```swift
    override func viewDidLoad() {
        super.viewDidLoad()
        // Do any additional setup after loading the view, typically from a nib.

        for touchCount in 0..<5 {
            let vertical = UISwipeGestureRecognizer(target: self,
                action: #selector(ViewController.reportVerticalSwipe(_:)))
            vertical.direction = [.up, .down]
            vertical.numberOfTouchesRequired = touchCount
            view.addGestureRecognizer(vertical)
```

```
        let horizontal = UISwipeGestureRecognizer(target: self,
            action: #selector(ViewController.reportHorizontalSwipe(_:)))
        horizontal.direction = [.left, .right]
        horizontal.numberOfTouchesRequired = touchCount
        view.addGestureRecognizer(horizontal)
    }
}
```

What we're doing here is adding ten different gesture recognizers to the view — the first one recognizes a vertical swipe with one finger, the second a vertical swipe with two fingers, and so on. All of them call the `reportVerticalSwipe()` method when they recognize their gesture. The second set of recognizers handles horizontal swipes and call the `reportHorizontalSwipe()` method instead. Note that in a real application, you might want different numbers of fingers swiping across the screen to trigger different behaviors. You can easily do that using gesture recognizers, simply by having each of them call a different action method.

Now all we need to do is change the logging by adding a method that gives us a handy description of the number of touches, and then using that in the reporting methods, as shown here. Add this method toward the bottom of the `ViewController` class, just above the two swipe-reporting methods:

```
@objc func descriptionForTouchCount(_ touchCount:Int) -> String {
    switch touchCount {
    case 1:
        return "Single"
    case 2:
        return "Double"
    case 3:
        return "Triple"
    case 4:
        return "Quadruple"
    case 5:
        return "Quintuple"
    default:
        return ""
    }
}
```

Next, modify the two swipe-reporting methods as shown:

```
@objc func reportHorizontalSwipe(_ recognizer:UIGestureRecognizer) {
    label.text = "Horizontal swipe detected"
    let count = descriptionForTouchCount(recognizer.numberOfTouches())
    label.text = "\(count)-finger horizontal swipe detected"
    DispatchQueue.main.after(when: DispatchTime.now() +
            Double(Int64(2 * NSEC_PER_SEC)) / Double(NSEC_PER_SEC)) {
        self.label.text = ""
    }
}

@objc func reportVerticalSwipe(_ recognizer:UIGestureRecognizer) {
    label.text = "Vertical swipe detected"
    let count = descriptionForTouchCount(recognizer.numberOfTouches())
    label.text = "\(count)-finger vertical swipe detected"
    DispatchQueue.main.after(when: DispatchTime.now() +
            Double(Int64(2 * NSEC_PER_SEC)) / Double(NSEC_PER_SEC)) {
        self.label.text = ""
    }
}
```

Build and run the app. You should be able to trigger double- and triple-swipes in both directions, yet still be able to trigger single-swipes. If you have small fingers, you might even be able to trigger a quadruple- or quintuple-swipe.

Tip In the simulator, if you hold down the Option key, a pair of dots, representing a pair of fingers, will appear. Get them close together, and then hold down the Shift key. This will keep the dots in the same position relative to each other, allowing you to move the pair of fingers around the screen. Now click and drag down the screen to simulate a double-swipe.

With a multiple-finger swipe, one thing to be careful of is that your fingers aren't too close to each other. If two fingers are very close to each other, they may register as only a single touch. Because of this, you shouldn't rely on quadruple- or quintuple-swipes for any important gestures because many people will have fingers that are too big to do those swipes effectively. Also, on the iPad some four- and five-finger gestures are turned on by default at the system level for switching between apps and going to the home screen. These can be turned off in the Settings app, but you're probably better off just not using such gestures in your own apps.

Detecting Multiple Taps

In the TouchExplorer application, we printed the tap count to the screen, so you've already seen how easy it is to detect multiple taps. It's not quite as straightforward as it seems, however, because often you will want to take different actions based on the number of taps. If the user triple-taps, you get notified three separate times. You get a single-tap, a double-tap, and finally a triple-tap. If you want to do something on a double-tap but something completely different on a triple-tap, having three separate notifications could cause a problem, since you will first receive notification of a double-tap, and then a triple-tap. Unless you write your own clever code to take this into account, you'll wind up doing both actions. Fortunately, Apple anticipated this situation, and provided a mechanism to let multiple gesture recognizers work nicely together, even when they're faced with ambiguous inputs that could seemingly trigger any of them. The basic idea is that you place a restriction on a gesture recognizer, telling it to not trigger its associated method unless some other gesture recognizer fails to trigger its own method.

That seems a bit abstract, so let's make it real. Tap gestures are recognized by the `UITapGestureRecognizer` class. A tap recognizer can be configured to do its thing when a particular number of taps occur. Imagine that we have a view for which we want to define distinct actions that occur when the user taps once or double-taps. You might start off with something like the following:

```
let singleTap = UITapGestureRecognizer(target: self,
    action: #selector(ViewController.singleTap))
singleTap.numberOfTapsRequired = 1
singleTap.numberOfTouchesRequired = 1
view.addGestureRecognizer(singleTap)

let doubleTap = UITapGestureRecognizer(target: self,
    action: #selector(ViewController.doubleTap))
doubleTap.numberOfTapsRequired = 2
doubleTap.numberOfTouchesRequired = 1
view.addGestureRecognizer(doubleTap)
```

The problem with this piece of code is that the two recognizers are unaware of each other, and they have no way of knowing that the user's actions may be better suited to another recognizer. If the user double-taps the view in the preceding code, the doDoubleTap() method will be called, but the doSingleMethod() will also be called — twice! — once for each tap.

The way around this is to create a failure requirement. We tell singleTap that it should trigger its action only if doubleTap doesn't recognize and respond to the user input by adding this single line:

```
singleTap.require(toFail: doubleTap)
```

This means that, when the user taps once, singleTap doesn't do its work immediately. Instead, singleTap waits until it knows that doubleTap has decided to stop paying attention to the current gesture (that is, the user didn't tap twice). We're going to build on this further with our next project.

In Xcode, create a new project with the Single View Application template. Call this new project Taps and use the Devices pop-up to choose Universal. This application will have four labels: one each that informs us when it has detected a single-tap, double-tap, triple-tap, and quadruple-tap (see Figure 3-4).

CHAPTER 3   TAPS, TOUCHES, AND GESTURES

Figure 3-4. *The Taps application detects up to four sequential taps*

We need outlets for the four labels and we also need separate methods for each tap scenario to simulate what we would have in a real application. We'll also include a method for erasing the text fields. Open ViewController.swift and add the label outlets to the class:

```
class ViewController: UIViewController {
    @IBOutlet var singleLabel:UILabel!
    @IBOutlet var doubleLabel:UILabel!
    @IBOutlet var tripleLabel:UILabel!
    @IBOutlet var quadrupleLabel:UILabel!
```

Save the file and select Main.storyboard to edit the GUI. Once you're there, add four labels to the view from the library and arrange them one above the other. In the Attributes Inspector, set the text alignment for each label to Center. In the Document Outline, Control-drag from the top label to its parent view and release the mouse. Hold down Shift and select Vertical Spacing to Top Layout Guide and Center Horizontally in Container, and then press Return. Do the same for the other three labels to set their auto layout constraints. When you're finished, Control-drag from the View Controller icon to each label and connect each one to singleLabel, doubleLabel, tripleLabel, and quadrupleLabel, respectively. Finally, make sure you double-click each label and press the delete key to get rid of any text. Now select ViewController.swift and make the code changes shown in Listing 3-5.

Listing 3-5. The Taps App Changes to the ViewController.swift File

```
override func viewDidLoad() {
    super.viewDidLoad()
    // Do any additional setup after loading the view, typically from a nib.
    
    let singleTap = UITapGestureRecognizer(target: self,
            action: #selector(ViewController.singleTap))
    singleTap.numberOfTapsRequired = 1
    singleTap.numberOfTouchesRequired = 1
    view.addGestureRecognizer(singleTap)
    
    let doubleTap = UITapGestureRecognizer(target: self,
            action: #selector(ViewController.doubleTap))
    doubleTap.numberOfTapsRequired = 2
    doubleTap.numberOfTouchesRequired = 1
    view.addGestureRecognizer(doubleTap)
    singleTap.require(toFail: doubleTap)
    
    let tripleTap = UITapGestureRecognizer(target: self,
            action: #selector(ViewController.tripleTap))
    tripleTap.numberOfTapsRequired = 3
```

```swift
    tripleTap.numberOfTouchesRequired = 1
    view.addGestureRecognizer(tripleTap)
    doubleTap.require(toFail: tripleTap)

    let quadrupleTap = UITapGestureRecognizer(target: self,
            action: #selector(ViewController.quadrupleTap))
    quadrupleTap.numberOfTapsRequired = 4
    quadrupleTap.numberOfTouchesRequired = 1
    view.addGestureRecognizer(quadrupleTap)
    tripleTap.require(toFail: quadrupleTap)
}
@objc func singleTap() {
    showText("Single Tap Detected", inLabel: singleLabel)
}

@objc func doubleTap() {
    showText("Double Tap Detected", inLabel: doubleLabel)
}

@objc func tripleTap() {
    showText("Triple Tap Detected", inLabel: tripleLabel)
}

@objc func quadrupleTap() {
    showText("Quadruple Tap Detected", inLabel: quadrupleLabel)
}

private func showText(_ text: String, inLabel label: UILabel) {
    label.text = text
    DispatchQueue.main.after(when: DispatchTime.now() +
            Double(Int64(2 * NSEC_PER_SEC)) / Double(NSEC_PER_SEC)) {
            label.text = ""
    }
}
```

CHAPTER 3   TAPS, TOUCHES, AND GESTURES

The four tap methods do nothing more in this application than set one of the four labels and use `DispatchQueue.main.after()` to erase that same label after two seconds. The interesting part of this is what occurs in the `viewDidLoad` method. We start off simply enough, by setting up a tap gesture recognizer and attaching it to our view:

```
let singleTap = UITapGestureRecognizer(target: self,
        action: #selector(ViewController.singleTap))
singleTap.numberOfTapsRequired = 1
singleTap.numberOfTouchesRequired = 1
view.addGestureRecognizer(singleTap)
```

Note that we set both the number of taps (touches in the same position, one after another) required to trigger the action and touches (number of fingers touching the screen at the same time) to 1. After that, we set another tap gesture recognizer to handle a double-tap:

```
let doubleTap = UITapGestureRecognizer(target: self,
        action: #selector(ViewController.doubleTap))
doubleTap.numberOfTapsRequired = 2
doubleTap.numberOfTouchesRequired = 1
view.addGestureRecognizer(doubleTap)
singleTap.require(toFail: doubleTap)
```

This is pretty similar to the previous code, right up until that last line, in which we give `singleTap` some additional context. We are effectively telling `singleTap` that it should trigger its action only in case some other gesture recognizer — in this case, `doubleTap` — decides that the current user input isn't what it's looking for.

Let's think about what this means. With those two tap gesture recognizers in place, a single tap in the view will immediately make `singleTap` think, "Hey, this looks like it's for me." At the same time, `doubleTap` will think, "Hey, this looks like it *might* be for me, but I'll need to wait for one more tap." Because `singleTap` is set to wait for `doubleTap`'s "failure," it doesn't trigger its action method right away; instead, it waits to see what happens with `doubleTap`.

After that first tap, if another tap occurs immediately, `doubleTap` says, "Hey, that's mine all right," and it fires its action. At that point, `singleTap` will realize what happened and give up on that gesture. On the other hand, if a particular amount of time goes by (the amount of time that the system considers to be the maximum length of time between taps in a double-tap), `doubleTap` will give up, and `singleTap` will see the failure and finally trigger its event. The rest of the method goes on to define gesture recognizers for three and four taps, and at each point it configures one gesture to be dependent on the failure of the next:

```
let tripleTap = UITapGestureRecognizer(target: self,
        action: #selector(ViewController.tripleTap))
tripleTap.numberOfTapsRequired = 3
tripleTap.numberOfTouchesRequired = 1
view.addGestureRecognizer(tripleTap)
doubleTap.require(toFail: tripleTap)

let quadrupleTap = UITapGestureRecognizer(target: self,
        action: #selector(ViewController.quadrupleTap))
quadrupleTap.numberOfTapsRequired = 4
quadrupleTap.numberOfTouchesRequired = 1
view.addGestureRecognizer(quadrupleTap)
tripleTap.require(toFail: quadrupleTap)
```

Note that we don't need to explicitly configure every gesture to be dependent on the failure of each of the higher tap-numbered gestures. That multiple dependency comes about naturally as a result of the chain of failure established in our code. Since `singleTap` requires the failure of `doubleTap`, `doubleTap` requires the failure of `tripleTap`, and `tripleTap` requires the failure of `quadrupleTap`. By extension, `singleTap` requires that all of the others fail.

Build and run the app. Whether you single-, double-, triple-, or quadruple-tap, you should see only one label displayed at the end of the sequence. After about a second and a half, the label will clear itself and you can try again.

Detecting Pinch and Rotation Gestures

Another common gesture is the two-finger pinch. It's used in a number of applications (e.g., Mobile Safari, Mail, and Photos) to let you zoom in (if you pinch apart) or zoom out (if you pinch together). Detecting pinches is really easy, thanks to `UIPinchGestureRecognizer`. This one is referred to as a **continuous gesture recognizer** because it calls its action method over and over again during the pinch. While the gesture is underway, the recognizer goes through a number of states. When the gesture is recognized, the recognizer is in state `UIGestureRecognizerState.began` and its scale property is set to an initial value of 1.0; for the rest of the gesture, the state is UIGestureRecognizerState.changed and the scale value goes up and down, relative to how far the user's fingers move from the start. We're going to use the scale value to resize an image. Finally, the state changes to UIGestureRecognizerState.ended.

Another common gesture is the two-finger rotation. This is also a continuous gesture recognizer and is named UIRotationGestureRecognizer. It has a rotation property that is 0.0 by default when the gesture begins, and then changes from 0.0 to 2.0*PI as the user rotates her fingers. In the next example, we'll use both pinch and rotation gestures. Create a new project in Xcode, again using the Single View Application template, and call this one **PinchMe**. First, drag and drop the beautiful yosemite-meadows.png image from the 18 - Image folder in the example source code archive (or some other favorite photo of yours) into your project's Assets.xcassets. Now make the changes in Listing 3-6 to the ViewController.swift file.

Listing 3-6. Updated ViewController.swift File for the PinchMe App Modifications

```swift
class ViewController: UIViewController, UIGestureRecognizerDelegate {
    private var imageView:UIImageView!
    private var scale = CGFloat(1)
    private var previousScale = CGFloat(1)
    private var rotation = CGFloat(0)
    private var previousRotation = CGFloat(0)

    override func viewDidLoad() {
        super.viewDidLoad()
        // Do any additional setup after loading the view, typically from a nib.

        let image = UIImage(named: "yosemite-meadows")
        imageView = UIImageView(image: image)
        imageView.isUserInteractionEnabled = true
        imageView.center = view.center
        view.addSubview(imageView)

        let pinchGesture = UIPinchGestureRecognizer(target: self,
                action: #selector(ViewController.doPinch(_:)))
        pinchGesture.delegate = self
        imageView.addGestureRecognizer(pinchGesture)
```

```swift
        let rotationGesture = UIRotationGestureRecognizer(target: self,
                action: #selector(ViewController.doRotate(_:)))
        rotationGesture.delegate = self
        imageView.addGestureRecognizer(rotationGesture)
    }

    func gestureRecognizer(_ gestureRecognizer: UIGestureRecognizer,
                shouldRecognizeSimultaneouslyWith
                    otherGestureRecognizer: UIGestureRecognizer) -> Bool {
        return true
    }

    @objc func transformImageView() {
        var t = CGAffineTransform(scaleX: scale * previousScale, y: scale *
        previousScale)
        t = t.rotate(rotation + previousRotation)
        imageView.transform = t
    }

    @objc func doPinch(_ gesture:UIPinchGestureRecognizer) {
        scale = gesture.scale
        transformImageView()
        if gesture.state == .ended {
            previousScale = scale * previousScale
            scale = 1
        }
    }

    @objc func doRotate(_ gesture:UIRotationGestureRecognizer) {
        rotation = gesture.rotation
        transformImageView()
        if gesture.state == .ended {
            previousRotation = rotation + previousRotation
            rotation = 0
        }
    }
}
```

CHAPTER 3   TAPS, TOUCHES, AND GESTURES

First, we define four instance variables for the current and previous scale and rotation. The previous values are the values from a previously triggered and ended gesture recognizer; we need to keep track of these values as well because the `UIPinchGestureRecognizer` for scaling and `UIRotationGestureRecognizer` for rotation will always start at the default positions of 1.0 scale and 0.0 rotation. Next, in `viewDidLoad()`, we begin by creating a `UIImageView` to pinch and rotate, load our Yosemite image into it, and center it in the main view. We must remember to enable user interaction on the image view because `UIImageView` is one of the few UIKit classes that have user interaction disabled by default.

```swift
let image = UIImage(named: "yosemite-meadows")
imageView = UIImageView(image: image)
imageView.isUserInteractionEnabled = true
imageView.center = view.center
view.addSubview(imageView)
```

Next, we set up a pinch gesture recognizer and a rotation gesture recognizer. We tell them to notify us when their gestures are recognized via the `doPinch()` and `doRotation()` methods, respectively. We tell both to use `self` as their delegate:

```swift
let pinchGesture = UIPinchGestureRecognizer(target: self,
        action: #selector(ViewController.doPinch(_:)))
pinchGesture.delegate = self
imageView.addGestureRecognizer(pinchGesture)

let rotationGesture = UIRotationGestureRecognizer(target: self,
        action: #selector(ViewController.doRotate(_:)))
rotationGesture.delegate = self
imageView.addGestureRecognizer(rotationGesture)
```

In the `gestureRecognizer(_:shouldRecognizeSimultaneoslyWithGestureRecognizer:)` method (which is the only method from the `UIGestureRecognizerDelegate` protocol that we need to implement), we always return `true` to allow our pinch and rotation gestures to work together; otherwise, the gesture recognizer that starts first would always block the other:

```swift
func gestureRecognizer(_ gestureRecognizer: UIGestureRecognizer,
        shouldRecognizeSimultaneouslyWith
```

CHAPTER 3 TAPS, TOUCHES, AND GESTURES

```
        otherGestureRecognizer: UIGestureRecognizer) -> Bool {
    return true
}
```

Next, we implement a helper method for transforming the image view according to the current scaling and rotation from the gesture recognizers. Notice that we multiply the scale by the previous scale. We also add to the rotation with the previous rotation. This allows us to adjust for pinch and rotation that has been done previously when a new gesture starts from the default 1.0 scale and 0.0 rotation.

```
func transformImageView() {
    var t = CGAffineTransform(scaleX: scale * previousScale, y: scale * previousScale)
    t = t.rotate(rotation + previousRotation)
    imageView.transform = t
}
```

Finally we implement the action methods that take the input from the gesture recognizers, and update the transformation of the image view. In both doPinch() and doRotate(), we first extract the new scale or rotation values. Next, we update the transformation for the image view. And finally, if the gesture recognizer reports that its gesture has ended by having a state equal to UIGestureRecognizerState.Ended, we store the current correct scale or rotation values, and then reset the current scale or rotation values to the default 1.0 scale or 0.0 rotation:

```
func doPinch(_ gesture:UIPinchGestureRecognizer) {
    scale = gesture.scale
    transformImageView()
    if gesture.state == .ended {
        previousScale = scale * previousScale
        scale = 1
    }
}

func doRotate(_ gesture:UIRotationGestureRecognizer) {
    rotation = gesture.rotation
    transformImageView()
```

```
    if gesture.state == .ended {
        previousRotation = rotation + previousRotation
        rotation = 0
    }
}
```

And that's all there is to pinch and rotation detection. Build and run the app to give it a try. As you do some pinching and rotation, you'll see the image change in response (see Figure 3-5). If you're on the simulator, remember that you can simulate a pinch by holding down the Option key and clicking and dragging in the simulator window using your mouse.

Figure 3-5. *The PinchMe application detects the pinch and rotation gesture*

Summary

You should now understand the mechanism that iOS uses to tell your application about touches, taps, and gestures. You also learned how to detect the most commonly used iOS gestures. We also saw a couple of basic examples of the use of the new 3D Touch feature. There's quite a bit more to this than we were able to cover here — for the full details, refer to Apple's document on the subject, which you can find at `https://developer.apple.com/library/ios/documentation/UserExperience/Conceptual/Adopting3DTouchOniPhone/`.

The iOS user interface relies on gestures for much of its ease of use, so you'll want to have these techniques ready for most of your iOS development. In the next chapter we'll tell you how to figure out where in the world you are by using Core Location.

CHAPTER 4

Determining Location

Every iOS device has the ability to determine where in the world it is, using a framework called **Core Location**. iOS also includes the **Map Kit** framework, which lets you easily create a live interactive map that shows any locations you like, including, of course, the user's location. In this chapter, we'll work with both of these frameworks. Core Location can actually leverage three technologies to do this: GPS, cell ID location, and Wi-Fi Positioning Service (WPS). GPS provides the most accurate positioning of the three technologies, but it is not available on first-generation iPhones, iPod touches, or Wi-Fi-only iPads. In short, any device with at least a 3G data connection also contains a GPS unit. GPS reads microwave signals from multiple satellites to determine the current location.

Note Apple uses a version of GPS called **Assisted GPS**, also known as A-GPS. A-GPS uses network resources to help improve the performance of stand-alone GPS. The basic idea is that the telephony provider deploys services on its network that mobile devices will automatically find and collect some data from. This allows a mobile device to determine its starting location much more quickly than if it was relying on the GPS satellites alone.

Cell ID location lookup gives a rough approximation of the current location based on the physical location of the cellular base station that the device is currently in contact with. Since each base station can cover a fairly large area, there is a fairly large margin of error here. Cell ID location lookup requires a cell radio connection, so it works only on the iPhone (all models, including the very first) and any iPad with a 3G data connection. The WPS option uses the media access control (MAC) addresses from nearby Wi-Fi access points to make a guess at your location by referencing a large database of known service providers and the areas they service, but can have a mile or more inaccuracy.

All three methods significantly drain the battery, so keep that in mind when using Core Location. Your application shouldn't poll for location any more often than is absolutely necessary. When using Core Location, you have the option of specifying a desired accuracy. By carefully specifying the absolute minimum accuracy level you need, you can prevent unnecessary battery drain. The technologies that Core Location depends on are hidden from your application. We don't tell Core Location whether to use GPS, triangulation, or WPS. We just tell it how accurate we would like it to be, and it will decide from the technologies available to it which is best for fulfilling our request.

The Location Manager

Apple provides a fairly easy-to-use Core Location API. The main class we'll work with is `CLLocationManager`, usually referred to as the location manager. To interact with Core Location, you need to create an instance of the location manager:

```
let locationManager = CLLocationManager()
```

This creates an instance of the location manager, but it doesn't actually start polling for your location. You must create an object that conforms to the `CLLocationManagerDelegate` protocol and assign it as the location manager's delegate. The location manager will call delegate methods when location information becomes available or changes. The process of determining location may take some time — even a few seconds.

Setting the Desired Accuracy

After you set the delegate, you also want to set the desired accuracy. As mentioned, don't specify a degree of accuracy any greater than you absolutely need. If you're writing an application that just needs to know which state or country the phone is in, don't specify a high level of precision. Remember that the more accuracy you demand of Core Location, the more power you're likely to use. Also, keep in mind that there is no guarantee that you will get the level of accuracy you have requested. Listing 4-1 shows an example of setting the delegate and requesting a specific accuracy.

Listing 4-1. Setting the Delegate and Desired Accuracy

```
locationManager.delegate = self
locationManager.desiredAccuracy = kCLLocationAccuracyBest
```

The accuracy is set using a CLLocationAccuracy value, a type that's defined as a Double. The value is in meters, so if you specify a desiredAccuracy of 10, you're telling Core Location that you want it to try to determine the current location within 10 meters, if possible. Specifying kCLLocationAccuracyBest (as we did previously) or specifying kCLLocationAccuracyBestForNavigation (where it uses other sensor data as well) tells Core Location to use the most accurate method that's currently available. In addition, you can also use: kCLLocationAccuracyNearestTenMeters, kCLLocationAccuracyHundredMeters, kCLLocationAccuracyKilometer, and kCLLocationAccuracyThreeKilometers.

Setting the Distance Filter

By default, the location manager will notify the delegate of any detected change in the device's location. By specifying a distance filter, you are telling the location manager not to notify you of every change, but instead to notify you only when the location changes by more than a certain amount. Setting up a distance filter can reduce the amount of polling your application does. Distance filters are also set in meters. Specifying a distance filter of 1000 tells the location manager not to notify its delegate until the iPhone has moved at least 1000 meters from its previously reported position as in locationManager.distanceFilter = 1000.

If you ever want to return the location manager to the default setting, which applies no filter, you can use the constant kCLDistanceFilterNone, like this:

```
locationManager.distanceFilter = kCLDistanceFilterNone.
```

Just as when specifying the desired accuracy, you should take care to avoid getting updates any more frequently than you really need them; otherwise, you waste battery power. A speedometer app that's calculating the user's velocity based on location changes will probably want to have updates as quickly as possible, but an app that's going to show the nearest fast food restaurant can get by with a lot fewer updates.

Getting Permission to Use Location Services

Before your application can use location services, you need to get the user's permission to do so. Core Location offers several different services, some of which can be used when your application is in the background — in fact, you can even request to have your application launched when certain events happen while it is not running. Depending on your application's functionality, it may be enough to request permission to access location services only while the user is using your application, or it might need to always be able to use the service. When writing an application, you need to decide which type of permission you require and make the request before initiating the services that you need. You'll see how to do this in the course of creating the example application for this chapter.

Starting the Location Manager

When you're ready to start polling for location, and after you request from the user to access location services, you tell the location manager to start. It will go off and do its thing, and then call a delegate method when it has determined the current location. Until you tell it to stop, it will continue to call your delegate method whenever it senses a change that exceeds the current distance filter. Here's how you start the location manager:

```
locationManager.startUpdatingLocation()
```

Using the Location Manager Wisely

If you need to determine the current location only and you don't need continuous updates, you can use the requestLocation() method instead of startUpdatingLocation(). This method automatically stops location polling as soon as the user's position has been determined. On the other hand, if you need to poll, make sure you stop polling as soon as you possibly can. Remember that as long as you are getting updates from the location manager, you are putting a strain on the user's battery. To tell the location manager to stop sending updates to its delegate, call stopUpdatingLocation(), like this:

```
locationManager.stopUpdatingLocation()
```

It's not necessary to call this method if you use requestLocation() instead of startUpdatingLocation().

The Location Manager Delegate

The location manager delegate must conform to the `CLLocationManagerDelegate` protocol, which defines several methods, all of them optional. One of these methods is called by the location manager when the availability of user authorization to use location services changes, another when it has determined the current location or when it detects a change in location. Yet another method gets called when the location manager encounters an error. We'll implement all of these delegate methods in this chapter's project.

Getting Location Updates

When the location manager wants to inform its delegate of the current location, it calls the `locationManager(_:didUpdateLocations:)` method. This method takes two parameters:

- The first parameter references the location manager that called the method.

- The second parameter contains an array of `CLLocation` objects representing the current location of the device and perhaps a few previous locations. If several location updates occur in a short period of time, they may be reported all at once with a single call to this method. In any case, the most recent location is always the last item in this array.

Getting Latitude and Longitude Using CLLocation

Location information gets passed from the location manager using instances of the `CLLocation` class. This class provides seven properties that might be of interest to your application:

- `coordinate`
- `horizontalAccuracy`
- `altitude`
- `verticalAccuracy`

- floor
- timestamp
- description

The latitude and longitude are stored in a property called `coordinate`. To get the latitude and longitude in degrees, use the code in Listing 4-2.

Listing 4-2. Getting Latitude and Longitude

```
let latitude = theLocation.coordinate.latitude
let longitude = theLocation.coordinate.longitude
```

The latitude and longitude variables will be inferred to be of type `CLLocationDegrees`. The `CLLocation` object can also tell you how confident the location manager is in its latitude and longitude calculations. The `horizontalAccuracy` property describes the radius of a circle (in meters, like all Core Location measurements) with the `coordinate` as its center. The larger the value in `horizontalAccuracy`, the less certain Core Location is of the location. A very small radius indicates a high level of confidence in the determined location.

You can see a graphic representation of `horizontalAccuracy` in the Maps application, as shown in Figure 4-1. The circle shown in Maps uses `horizontalAccuracy` for its radius when it detects your location. The location manager thinks you are at the center of that circle. If you're not, you're almost certainly somewhere inside the circle. A negative value in `horizontalAccuracy` is an indication that you cannot rely on the values in the `coordinate` for some reason.

CHAPTER 4 DETERMINING LOCATION

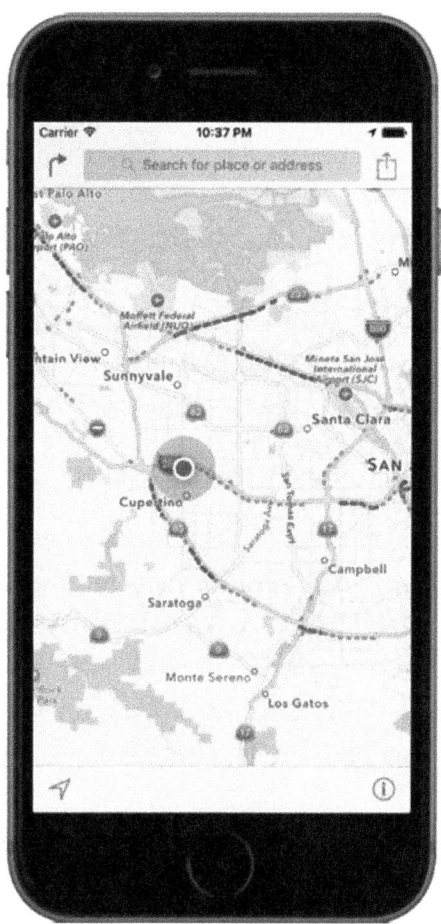

Figure 4-1. *The Maps application uses Core Location to determine your current position. The outer circle is a visual representation of the horizontal accuracy.*

The CLLocation object also has a property called altitude, of type CLLocationDistance, which tells you how many meters above (or below) sea level you are:

```
let altitude = theLocation.altitude
```

Each CLLocation object maintains a property called verticalAccuracy that is an indication of how confident Core Location is in its determination of altitude. The value in altitude could be off by as many meters as the value in verticalAccuracy. If the verticalAccuracy value is negative, Core Location is telling you it could not determine a valid altitude.

145

The `floor` property gives the floor within the building in which the user is located. This value is only valid in buildings that are able to provide the information, so you should not rely on its availability.

`CLLocation` objects include a `timestamp` that tells when the location manager made the location determination.

In addition to these properties, `CLLocation` has a useful instance method that will let you determine the distance between two `CLLocation` objects. The method is called `distanceFromLocation()` and it returns a value of type `CLLocationDistance`, which is just a `Double`, so you can use it in arithmetic calculations, as you'll see in the application we're about to create. Here's how you use this method:

```
let distance = fromLocation.distanceFromLocation(toLocation)
```

The preceding line of code returns the distance between two `CLLocation` objects: `fromLocation` and `toLocation`. This `distance` value returned contains the result of a great-circle distance calculation that ignores the `altitude` property and calculates the distance as if both points were at sea level. For most purposes, a great-circle calculation provides more than sufficient information; however, if you do want to take altitude into account when calculating distances, you'll need to write your own code to do it.

Note If you're not sure what's meant by *great-circle distance*, the idea is that the shortest distance between any two points on the earth's surface will be found along a path that would, if extended, go the entire way around the earth: a "great circle." The most obvious great circles are perhaps the ones you've seen on maps: the equator and the longitudinal lines. However, such a circle can be found for any two points on the surface of the earth. The calculation performed by `CLLocation` determines the distance between two points along such a route, taking the curvature of the earth into account. Without accounting for that curvature, you would end up with the length of a straight line connecting the two points, which isn't much use, since that line would invariably go straight through some amount of the earth.

Error Notifications

If Core Location needs to report an error to your application, it will call a delegate method named `locationManager(_:didFailWithError:)`. One possible cause of an error is that the user denied access to location services, in which case the method will be called with the error code `CLError.Denied`. Another commonly encountered error code supported by the location manager is `CLError.LocationUnknown`, which indicates that Core Location was unable to determine the location but that it will keep trying. While a `CLError.LocationUnknown` error indicates a problem that may be temporary, `CLError.Denied` and other errors may indicate that your application will not be able to access Core Location any time during the remainder of the current session.

Note The simulator has no way to determine your current location, but you can choose one (such as Apple's HQ, which is the default) or set your own, from the simulator's Debug ➤ Location menu.

Creating the WhereAmI Application

Let's build a small application to detect your device's current location and the total distance traveled while the program has been running. You can see what the first version of our application will look like the one in Figure 4-2.

CHAPTER 4   DETERMINING LOCATION

Figure 4-2. *The WhereAmI application in action*

In Xcode, create a new project using the Single View Application template and call it **WhereAmI**. When the project window opens, select ViewController.swift, and make the following changes:

import UIKit

import CoreLocation
import MapKit

class ViewController: UIViewController**, CLLocationManagerDelegate** {

CHAPTER 4 DETERMINING LOCATION

First, notice that we've imported the Core Location framework. Core Location is not part of either UIKit or Foundation, so we need to import it manually. Next, we conform this class to the `CLLocationManagerDelegate` method, so that we can receive location information from the location manager.

Now add these property declarations:

```
private let locationManager = CLLocationManager()
private var previousPoint: CLLocation?
private var totalMovementDistance = CLLocationDistance(0)

@IBOutlet var latitudeLabel: UILabel!
@IBOutlet var longitudeLabel: UILabel!
@IBOutlet var horizontalAccuracyLabel: UILabel!
@IBOutlet var altitudeLabel: UILabel!
@IBOutlet var verticalAccuracyLabel: UILabel!
@IBOutlet var distanceTraveledLabel: UILabel!
@IBOutlet var mapView:MKMapView!
```

The `locationManager` property holds the reference to the `CLLocationManager` instance that we'll be using. The `previousPoint` property will keep track of the location from the last update we received from the location manager. This way, each time the user moves far enough to trigger an update, we'll be able to add the latest movement distance to our running total, which we'll keep in the `totalMovementDistance` property. The remaining properties are outlets that will be used to update labels on the user interface.

Now select Main.storyboard and let's start creating the user interface. First, expand the view controller hierarchy in the Document Outline, select the View item, and in the Attributes Inspector, change its background color to light gray. Next, drag a `UIView` from the object library, drop it onto the existing view, and then position and size it so that it covers the bottom part of the Main View. Make sure that the bottom, left, and right sides of the view exactly match those of the gray view. You are aiming to create something like the arrangement shown in Figure 4-2, where the view that you just dropped is the one at the bottom of the figure with the white background.

In the Document Outline, select the view that you just added, Control-drag from it to its parent view, and release the mouse. In the pop-up menu that appears, hold down the Shift key and click Leading Space to Container Margin, Trailing Space to Container Margin, and Vertical Spacing to Bottom Layout Guide. This pins the view in place, but does not yet set its height. To fix that, with the view still selected in the Document Outline, click the Pin button. In the pop-up, select the Height check box, set the height to **166**, set Update Frames to Items of New Constraint, and then press Add 1 Constraint to set the height. That should do the job.

Next, we'll create the rightmost column of labels shown in Figure 4-2. Drag a label from the object library and drop it a little way below the top of the white view. Resize it to a width of about **80** points and move it so that it is close to the right edge of the view. Option-drag a copy of this label downward five times to create a stack of labels, as shown in Figure 4-2. Now let's fix the labels' sizes and positions relative to their parent view.

Starting with the topmost label in the Document Outline, Control-drag from the label to its parent view. Release the mouse. Hold down the Shift key, select Top Space to Container and Trailing Space to Container, and then press Return. To set the label's size, click the Pin button to open the Add New Constraints pop-up menu, click the Width and Height check boxes to select them, enter **80** as the width and **21** as the height (if they are not already set), and click Add 2 Constraints. You have now fixed the size and position of the top label. Repeat the same procedure for the other five labels.

Next, we'll add the second column of labels. Drag a label from the object library and place it to the left of the topmost label, leaving a small horizontal gap between them. Drag the left side of the label so that it almost reaches the left edge of the white view, and then in the Attributes Inspector, set the Alignment so that the label text is right-aligned. Make five copies of this label by Option-dragging downward, aligning each of them with the corresponding label on the right, to make the arrangement in Figure 4-3.

CHAPTER 4 DETERMINING LOCATION

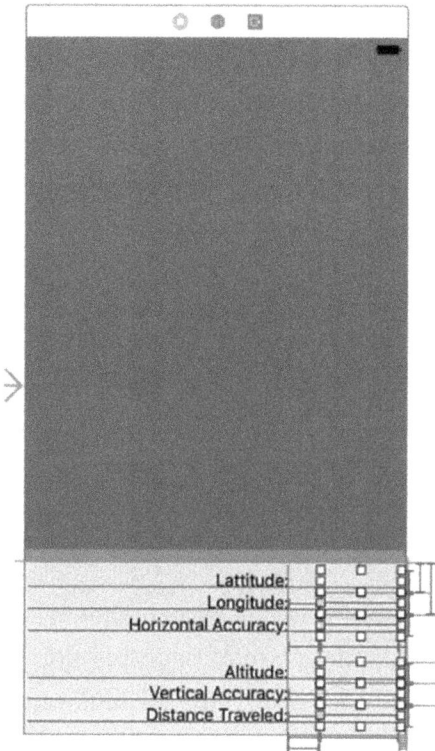

Figure 4-3. *Our UI layout goal*

Select the top label in the left column and Control-drag from its left side to the left side of the white view. Release the mouse and, in the context menu, select Leading Space to Container. Next, Control-drag from the same label to the matching label in the right-hand column. Release the mouse to open the context menu, hold down the Shift key, select Horizontal Spacing and Baseline, and press Return. Do the same for the other five labels in the left column. Finally, select the View Controller icon in the Document Outline, click the Resolve Auto Layout Issues button, and select Update Frames, if it's enabled.

We are almost there. We now need to connect the labels in the right column to the outlets in the view controller. Control-drag from the yellow view controller icon in the Document Outline to the top label in the right column and release the mouse. In the pop-up that appears, select `latitudeLabel`. Control-drag from the view controller icon to the second label to connect it to the `longitudeLabel` outlet, to the third label to connect it to `horizontalAccuracyLabel`, to the fourth to connect it to `altitudeLabel`, to the fifth to connect it to `verticalAccuracyLabel`, and to the bottom label to connect it to the `distanceTraveledLabel` outlet. You have now connected all six outlets.

151

Finally, clear the text from all of the labels in the right column, and change the text of the labels in the left column to match that shown in Figure 4-3; the top label's text should be Latitude:, the next one down should be Longitude:, and so on.

Now let's write the code to display some useful information in all those labels. Select ViewController.swift and insert the following lines in `viewDidLoad()` to configure the location manager:

```swift
override func viewDidLoad() {
    super.viewDidLoad()
    // Do any additional setup after loading the view, typically
    from a nib.
    locationManager.delegate = self
    locationManager.desiredAccuracy = kCLLocationAccuracyBest
    locationManager.requestWhenInUseAuthorization()
```

We assign our controller class as the location manager's delegate, set the desired accuracy to the best available, and then request permission to use the location service while the user is using our application. This is sufficient authorization for the purposes of this example. To use some of the more advanced features of Core Location, which are beyond the scope of this book, you will probably need to request permission to use Core Location at any time by calling the `requestAlwaysAuthorization()` method instead.

Note In this simple example, the request for authorization is made as the application starts up, but Apple recommends that, in a real application, you should delay making the request until you actually need to use location services. The reason for this is that the user is more likely to agree if it's obvious why you need access to the device's location, based on operation that has been requested, than if an application, probably one that the user has just installed, requests permission as soon as it launches.

The first time this application runs, iOS will display an alert asking the user whether your application should be allowed to use your location. You need to supply a short piece of text that iOS will include in the alert pop-up, explaining why your application needs to know the user's location. Open the Info.plist file and add the text you'd like to have displayed under the key `NSLocationWhenInUseUsageDescription` (if you need to request

CHAPTER 4 DETERMINING LOCATION

permission to use location services even when the application is not actively being used, the text should be added under the key `NSLocationWhenInUseUsageDescription` instead). For the purposes of this example, use something like "This application needs to know your location to update your position on a map."

Caution   In some earlier versions of iOS, supplying text to qualify the permission request was optional. Beginning with iOS 8, it became mandatory. If you don't supply any text, the permission request will not be made.

If you run the application now, you'll see that iOS uses your text in the permission request, as shown in Figure 4-4. If the prompt does not appear, make sure that you have spelled the name of the key in Info.plist properly. Because we haven't completed our app yet at this point in time, you won't see the map yet in the background. But Figure 4-4 gives you an idea of where we are headed.

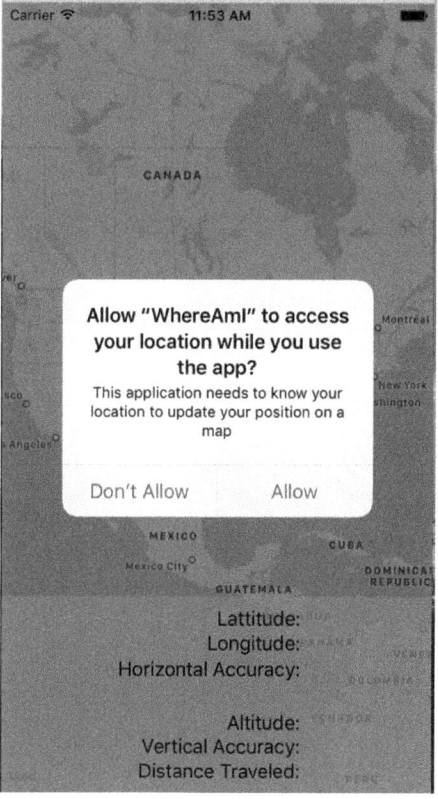

Figure 4-4. *Prompting the user for permission to use location services*

153

CHAPTER 4 DETERMINING LOCATION

This prompt appears only once in the lifetime of the application. Whether or not the user allows your application to use location services, this request will never be made again, no matter how many times the application is run. That's not to say that the user can't change his mind about this, of course. We'll say more about that in the upcoming "Changing Location Service Permissions" section. As far as testing is concerned, rerunning the application from Xcode has no effect on the user's saved response — to get a clean state for testing, you have to delete the application from the simulator or device. If you do that, iOS will prompt for permission again when you reinstall and relaunch the application. For now, reply "Allow" to the prompt and let's continue writing our application.

You probably noticed that the `viewDidLoad()` method did not call the location manager's `startUpdatingLocation()` method immediately after calling `requestWhenInUseAuthorization()`. There is, in fact, no point in doing so, because the authorization process does not take place immediately. At some point after `viewDidLoad()` returns, the location manager delegate's `locationManager(_:didChangeAuthorizationStatus:)` method will be called with the application's authorization status. This may be the result of the user's reply to the permission request pop-up, or it may be the saved authorization state from when the application last executed. Either way, this method is an ideal place to start listening for location updates or request the user's location, assuming you are authorized to. Add the following implementation of this method to the *ViewController.swift* file:

```swift
func locationManager(_ manager: CLLocationManager,
            didChangeAuthorization status: CLAuthorizationStatus) {
    print("Authorization status changed to \(status.rawValue)")
    switch status {
    case .authorizedAlways, .authorizedWhenInUse:
        locationManager.startUpdatingLocation()

    default:
        locationManager.stopUpdatingLocation()
    }
}
```

This code starts by listening for location updates if authorization was granted, and stops listening if it was not. Since we don't start listening unless we have authorization, what's the point of calling stopUpdatingLocation() if we didn't get permission? That's a good question. The reason this code is required is because the user can give your application permission to use Core Location and then later revoke it. In that case, we need to stop listening for updates. For more on this, see "Changing Location Service Permissions" later in this chapter.

If your application tries to use location services when it doesn't have permission to do so, or if an error occurs at any time, the location manager calls its delegate's locationManager(_:didFailWithError:) method. Let's add an implementation of that method to the view controller:

```swift
func locationManager(_ manager: CLLocationManager,
            didFailWithError error: NSError) {
    let errorType = error.code == CLError.denied.rawValue
                ? "Access Denied": "Error \(error.code)"
    let alertController = UIAlertController(title: "Location
    Manager Error",
                    message: errorType, preferredStyle: .alert)
    let okAction = UIAlertAction(title: "OK", style: .cancel,
                    handler: { action in })
    alertController.addAction(okAction)
    present(alertController, animated: true,
                    completion: nil)
}
```

For the purposes of this example, when an error occurs, we just alert the user. In a real application, you would use a more meaningful error message and clean up the application state as required.

Using Location Manager Updates

Now that we've dealt with getting permission to use the user's location, let's do something with that information. Insert this implementation (see Listing 4-3), of the delegate's locationManager(_:didUpdateLocations:) method in ViewController.swift.

CHAPTER 4 DETERMINING LOCATION

Listing 4-3. Our didUpateLocations Location Manager Delegate Method

```
func locationManager(_ manager: CLLocationManager, didUpdateLocations
                    locations: [CLLocation]) {
    if let newLocation = locations.last {
        let latitudeString = String(format: "%g\u{00B0}",
                        newLocation.coordinate.latitude)
        latitudeLabel.text = latitudeString

        let longitudeString = String(format: "%g\u{00B0}",
                        newLocation.coordinate.longitude)
        longitudeLabel.text = longitudeString

        let horizontalAccuracyString = String(format:"%gm",
                        newLocation.horizontalAccuracy)
        horizontalAccuracyLabel.text = horizontalAccuracyString

        let altitudeString = String(format:"%gm", newLocation.altitude)
        altitudeLabel.text = altitudeString

        let verticalAccuracyString = String(format:"%gm",
                        newLocation.verticalAccuracy)
        verticalAccuracyLabel.text = verticalAccuracyString

        if newLocation.horizontalAccuracy < 0 {
            // invalid accuracy
            return
        }

        if newLocation.horizontalAccuracy > 100 ||
                newLocation.verticalAccuracy > 50 {
            // accuracy radius is so large, we don't want to use it
            return
        }

        if previousPoint == nil {
            totalMovementDistance = 0
        } else {
```

CHAPTER 4 DETERMINING LOCATION

```
        print("movement distance: " +
            "\(newLocation.distance(from: previousPoint!))")
        totalMovementDistance +=
            newLocation.distance(from: previousPoint!)
    }
    previousPoint = newLocation

    let distanceString = String(format:"%gm", totalMovementDistance)
    distanceTraveledLabel.text = distanceString
  }
}
```

The first thing we do in the delegate method is to update the first five labels in the second column of Figure 4-3 with values from the `CLLocation` objects passed in the `locations` argument. The array could contain more than one location update, but we always use the last entry, which represents the most recent information.

Note Both the longitude and latitude are displayed in formatting strings containing the cryptic-looking \u{00B0}. This is the hexadecimal value of the Unicode representation of the degree symbol (°). It's never a good idea to put anything other than ASCII characters directly in a source code file, but including the hex value in a string is just fine, and that's what we've done here.

Next, we check the accuracy of the values that the location manager gives us. High accuracy values indicate that the location manager isn't quite sure about the location, while negative accuracy values indicate that the location is actually invalid. Some devices do not have the hardware required to determine vertical position. On these devices, and on the simulator, the `verticalAccuracy` property will always be –1, so we don't exclude position reports that have this value. The accuracy values are in meters and indicate the radius of a circle from the location we're given, meaning that the true location could be anywhere in that circle. Our code checks to see whether these values

157

are acceptably accurate; if not, it simply returns from this method rather than doing anything more with garbage data:

```
if newLocation.horizontalAccuracy < 0 {
    // invalid accuracy
    return
}
if newLocation.horizontalAccuracy > 100 ||
        newLocation.verticalAccuracy > 50 {
    // accuracy radius is so large, we don't want to use it
    return
}
```

Next, we check whether `previousPoint` is `nil`. If it is, then this update is the first valid one we've gotten from the location manager, so we zero out the `distanceFromStart` property. Otherwise, we add the latest location's distance from the previous point to the total distance. In either case, we update `previousPoint` to contain the current location:

```
if previousPoint == nil {
    totalMovementDistance = 0
} else {
    print("movement distance: " +
        "\(newLocation.distance(from: previousPoint!))")
    totalMovementDistance +=
        newLocation.distance(from: previousPoint!)
}
previousPoint = newLocation
```

After that, we populate the final label with the total distance that we've traveled from the start point. While this application runs, if the user moves far enough for the location manager to detect the change, the Distance Traveled: field will be continually updated with the distance the user has moved since the application started:

```
let distanceString = String(format:"%gm", totalMovementDistance)
distanceTraveledLabel.text = distanceString
```

CHAPTER 4   DETERMINING LOCATION

And there you have it. Core Location is fairly straightforward and easy to use. Compile and run the application, and then try it. If you have the ability to run the application on your iPhone or iPad, try going for a drive, having someone else doing the driving, with the application running and watch the values change as you move around.

Visualizing Your Movement on a Map

What we've done so far is pretty interesting, but wouldn't it be nice if we could visualize our travel on a map? Fortunately, iOS includes the Map Kit framework to help us out here. Map Kit utilizes the same back-end services that Apple's Maps app uses, which means it's fairly robust and improving all the time. It contains a view class that presents a map, which responds to user gestures just as you'd expect of any modern mapping app. This view also lets us insert annotations for any locations we want to show up on our map, which by default show up as "pins" that can be touched to reveal some more info. We're going to extend our WhereAmI app to display the user's starting position and current position on a map.

Select ViewController.swift and add the following line to import the Map Kit framework:

```
import UIKit
import CoreLocation
import MapKit
```

Now add a new property declaration for the Map View that will display the user's location:

Now select Main.storyboard to edit the view. Drag a Map View from the object library and drop it onto the top half of the user interface. Resize the Map View so that it covers the whole screen, including the view that we added earlier and all of its labels, and then choose Editor ➤ Arrange ➤ Send to Back to move the Map View behind the other view.

Tip   If the Send to Back option is not enabled, you can get the same effect by dragging the Map View in the Document Outline upward, so that it appears before the view that contains the labels in its parent's child list.

In the Document Outline, Control-drag from the Map View to its parent view and, in the context menu, hold down the Shift key and select Leading Space to Container Margin, Trailing Space to Container Margin, Vertical Spacing to Top Layout Guide, and Vertical Spacing to Bottom Layout Guide, and then press the Return key.

The Map View is now locked in place, but the bottom part of it is obscured. We can fix that by making the view at the bottom partly transparent. To do that, select it in the Document Outline; open the Attributes Inspector; click the Background color editor, and, in the pop-up that appears, choose Other… to open a color chooser. Select a white background and move the Opacity slider to about 70%. Finally, Control-drag from the view controller icon in the Document Outline to the Map View and select `mapView` in the pop-up that appears to connect the map to its outlet.

Now that these preliminaries are in place, it's time to write a little code that will make the map do some work for us. Before dealing with the code required in the view controller, we need to set up a sort of model class to represent our starting point. MKMapView is built as the View part of an MVC (Model-View-Controller) architecture. It works best if we have distinct classes to represent markers on the map. We can pass model objects off to the map view and it will query them for coordinates, a title, and so on, using a protocol defined in the Map Kit framework.

Press ⌘N to bring up the new file assistant, and in the iOS Source section, choose Cocoa Touch Class. Name the class `Place` and make it a subclass of `NSObject`. Open Place.swift and modify it as shown next. You need to import the Map Kit framework, specify a protocol that the new class conforms to, and specify the properties as shown in Listing 4-4.

Listing 4-4. Our New Place Class in the Place.swift File

```
import UIKit
import MapKit

class Place: NSObject, MKAnnotation {
    let title: String?
    let subtitle: String?
    var coordinate: CLLocationCoordinate2D
```

```
    @objc init(title:String, subtitle:String, coordinate:CLLocation
    Coordinate2D) {
        self.title = title
        self.subtitle = subtitle
        self.coordinate = coordinate
    }
}
```

This is a fairly "dumb" class that acts solely as a holder for these properties. In a real-world example, you may have real model classes that need to be shown on a map as an annotation, and the `MKAnnotation` protocol lets you add this capability to any class of your own without messing up any existing class hierarchies. Select ViewController.swift and add the two bold lines to the `locationManager(_:didChangeAuthorizationStatus:)` method:

```
    func locationManager(_ manager: CLLocationManager,
                    didChangeAuthorization status: CLAuthorizationStatus) {
        print("Authorization status changed to \(status.rawValue)")
        switch status {
        case .authorizedAlways, .authorizedWhenInUse:
            locationManager.startUpdatingLocation()
            mapView.showsUserLocation = true

        default:
            locationManager.stopUpdatingLocation()
            mapView.showsUserLocation = false
        }
    }
```

The Map View's `showsUserLocation` property does just what you probably imagine: it saves us the hassle of manually moving a marker around as the user moves by automatically drawing one for us. It uses Core Location to get the user's location and it works only if your application is authorized for that; so we enable the property when we are told that we have permission to use Core Location and then disable it again if we lose permission.

CHAPTER 4 DETERMINING LOCATION

Now let's revisit the `locationManager(_:didUpdateLocations:)` method. We've already gotten some code in there that notices the first valid location data we receive and establishes our start point. We're also going to allocate a new instance of our `Place` class. We set its properties, giving it a location. We also add a title and subtitle that we want to appear when a marker for this location is displayed. Finally, we pass this object off to the map view. We also create an instance of `MKCoordinateRegion`, a `struct` included in Map Kit that lets us tell the view which section of the map we want it to display. `MKCoordinateRegion` uses our new location's coordinates and a pair of distances in meters (100, 100) that specify how wide and tall the displayed map portion should be. We pass this off to the map view as well, telling it to animate the change. All of this is done by adding the bold lines shown here:

```
if previousPoint == nil {
   totalMovementDistance = 0
   let start = Place(title:"Start Point",
             subtitle:"This is where we started",
             coordinate:newLocation.coordinate)
   mapView.addAnnotation(start)
   let region = MKCoordinateRegionMakeWithDistance(newLocation.coordinate,
                100, 100)
    mapView.setRegion(region, animated: true)
    } else {
        print("movement distance: " +
          "\(newLocation.distance(from: previousPoint!))")
        totalMovementDistance +=
        newLocation.distance(from: previousPoint!)
}
```

So now we've told the map view that we have an annotation (i.e., a visible placemark) that we want the user to see. But how should it be displayed? Well, the map view figures out what sort of view to display for each annotation by asking its delegate. In a more complex app, that would work for us. But in this example we haven't made ourselves a delegate, simply because it's not necessary for our simple use case. Unlike `UITableView`, which requires its data source to supply cells for display, `MKMapView` has a different strategy: if it's not provided with annotation views by a delegate, it simply displays a default sort of view represented by a red "pin" on the map that reveals some more information when touched.

CHAPTER 4   DETERMINING LOCATION

There's one final thing you need to do — enable your application to use Map Kit. To do this, select the project in the Project Navigator and then select the WhereAmI target. At the top of editor area, select Capabilities, locate the Maps section, and move the selector switch on the right from OFF to ON. Now build and run your app, and you'll see the map view load. As soon as it gets valid position data, you'll see it scroll to the right location, drop a pin at your starting point, and mark your current location with a glowing blue dot (see Figure 4-5). Not bad for a few dozen lines of code.

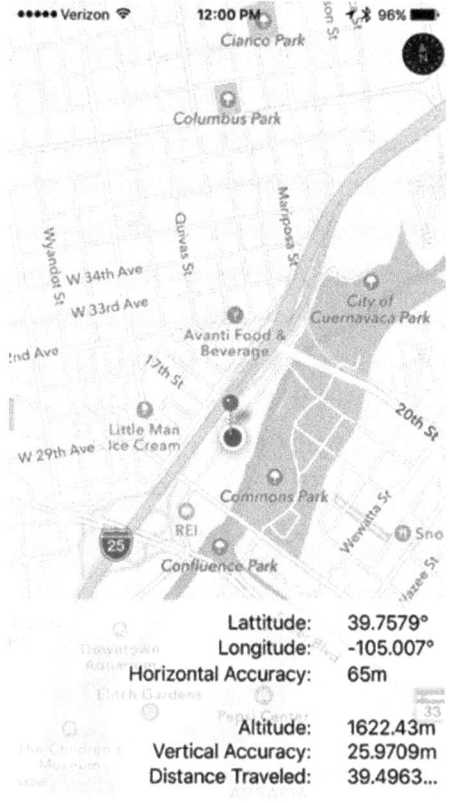

Figure 4-5. The red pin marks our starting location, and the blue dot shows how far we've gotten — in this case, no distance at all

---

Tip   If you are using a real device and the map does not zoom to show your current position, it's because Core Location can't figure out where you are to within 100 meters. You might be able to help it out by enabling Wi-Fi, which can sometimes improve Core Location's accuracy.

163

Changing Location Service Permissions

When your application runs for the first time, you hope the user will give it permission to use location services. Whether you get permission or not, you can't assume that nothing changes. The user can grant or revoke location permission via the Settings app. You can test this on the simulator. Launch the app and grant yourself permission to use Core Location (if you've previously denied permission, you'll need to remove and reinstall the app first). You should see your location on the map. Now go to the Settings app and choose Privacy ➤ Location Services. At the top of the screen is a switch that turns location services on or off. Turn the switch to OFF and go back to your application. You'll see that the map no longer shows your position. That's because the location manager called the `locationManager(_:didChangeAuthorizationStatus:)` method with authorization code `CLAuthorizationStatus.denied`, in response to which the application stops receiving position updates and tells Map Kit to stop tracking the user's position. Now go back to the Settings app, re-enable Core Location in Locations Services, and come back to your application; you'll find that it's tracking your position again.

Switching Location Services off is not the only way for the user to change your app's ability to use Core Location. Go back to the Settings app. Below the switch that enables Location Services, you'll see a list of all the apps that are using it, including WhereAmI, as shown on the left in Figure 4-6. Clicking the application name takes you to another page where you can allow or deny access to your application, which you can see on the right in Figure 4-6. At the moment, the application can use location services while the user is using the app. If you click Never, that permission is revoked, as you can prove by returning to the application again. This demonstrates that it's important to code the application so that it can detect and respond properly to changes in its authorization status.

CHAPTER 4 DETERMINING LOCATION

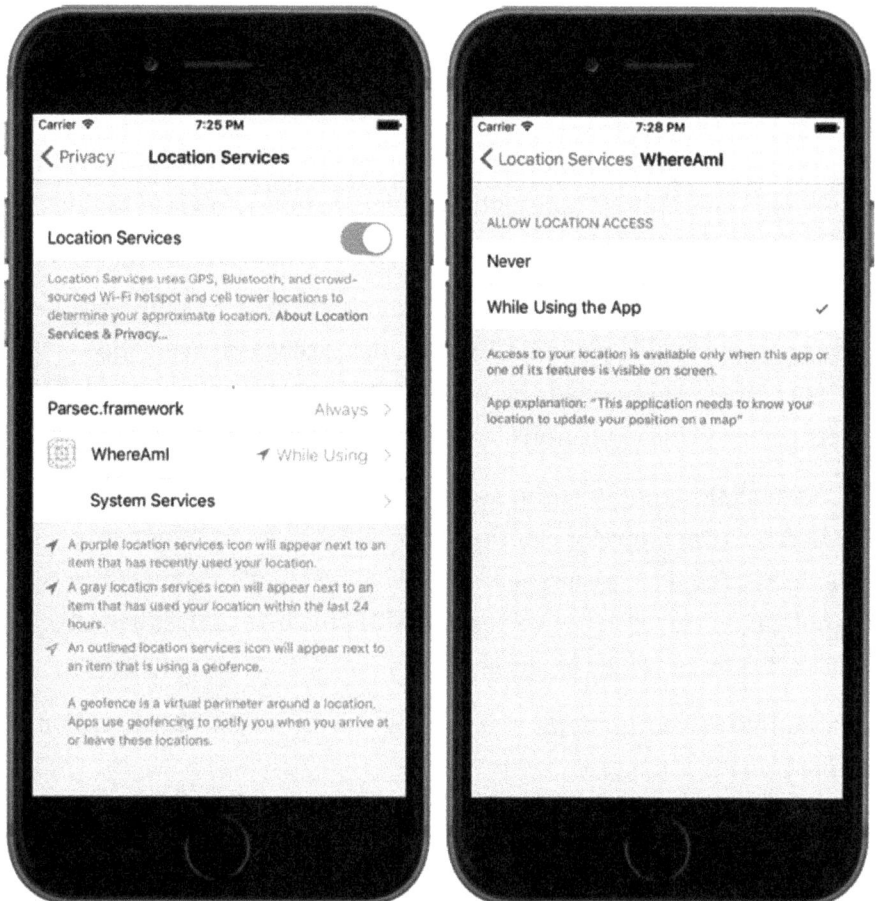

Figure 4-6. Changing Core Location access permission for the WhereAmI app

Summary

That's the end of our introduction to Core Location and Map Kit. There is quite a lot more to be discovered about both of these frameworks. Here are just a few of the highlights:

- Instead of closely tracking the user's location using the startUpdatingLocation() method, applications that need less positional accuracy and/or less frequent updates, such as Weather apps, can use the Significant Location Updates service. You should use this service if at all possible, because it can significantly reduce power consumption.

- On devices that have a magnetometer, Core Location can report the user's heading. If the device also has a GPS, it can report the direction in which the user is moving.

- Core Location can report when the user enters or leaves application-defined geographical regions (defined as a circle of a given radius and center) or when the application is in the vicinity of an iBeacon.

- You can convert between the coordinates reported by Core Location and a user-friendly placemark object and vice versa, using the Geocoding service. In addition to this, Map Kit includes an API that lets you search for locations by name or address.

- Core Location monitors the user's movement and can determine when the user stops for a period of time at a location. When this happens, the user is assumed to be "visiting" that location. Your application can receive notification when the user arrives at and departs from a visited location.

The best source of information for all of these features is Apple's *Location and Maps Programming Guide*.

Although the underlying technologies are quite complex, Apple has provided simple interfaces that hide most of the complexity, making it quite easy to add location-related and mapping features to your applications so that you can tell where the users are, notice when they move, and mark their location (and any other locations) on a map. And speaking of moving, in the next chapter we'll explore the iPhone's built-in accelerometer.

CHAPTER 5

Device Orientation and Motion

The iPhone, iPad, and iPod touch all include a built-in accelerometer — the tiny device that lets iOS know how the device is being held and if it's being moved. iOS uses the accelerometer to handle autorotation, and many games use it as a control mechanism. The accelerometer can also be used to detect shakes and other sudden movement. This capability was extended even further with the introduction of the iPhone 4, which was the first iPhone to include a built-in gyroscope to let developers determine the angle at which the device is positioned around each axis. The gyro and accelerometer are now standard on all new iPads and iPod touches. In this chapter, we'll explore using the Core Motion framework to access the gyro and accelerometer values in your application.

Accelerometer Physics

An **accelerometer** measures both acceleration and gravity by sensing the amount of inertial force in a given direction. The accelerometer inside your iOS device is a three-axis component. This means that it is capable of detecting either movement or the pull of gravity in three-dimensional space. In other words, you can use the accelerometer to discover not only how the device is currently being held (as autorotation does), but also to learn if it's laying on a table and even whether it's face down or face up. Accelerometers give measurements in g-forces (**g** for gravity), so a value of 1.0 returned by the accelerometer means that 1g is sensed in a particular direction, as in these examples:

- If the device is being held still with no movement, there will be approximately 1 g of force exerted on it by the pull of the earth.

CHAPTER 5 DEVICE ORIENTATION AND MOTION

- If the device is being held perfectly upright, in portrait orientation, it will detect and report about 1 g of force exerted on its y axis.

- If the device is being held at an angle, that 1 g of force will be distributed along different axes depending on how it is being held. When held at a 45-degree angle, the 1 g of force will be split roughly equally between two of the axes.

Sudden movement can be detected by looking for accelerometer values considerably larger than 1 g. In normal usage, the accelerometer does not detect significantly more than 1 g on any axis. If you shake, drop, or throw your device, the accelerometer will detect a greater amount of force on one or more axes.

Figure 5-1 shows a graphic representation of the three axes used by the accelerometer. Notice that the accelerometer uses the more standard convention for the y coordinate, with increases in y indicating upward force, which is the opposite of Quartz 2D's coordinate system (discussed in Chapter 16). When you are using the accelerometer as a control mechanism with Quartz 2D, you need to translate the y coordinate. When working with Sprite Kit, which is more likely when you are using the accelerometer to control animation, no translation is required.

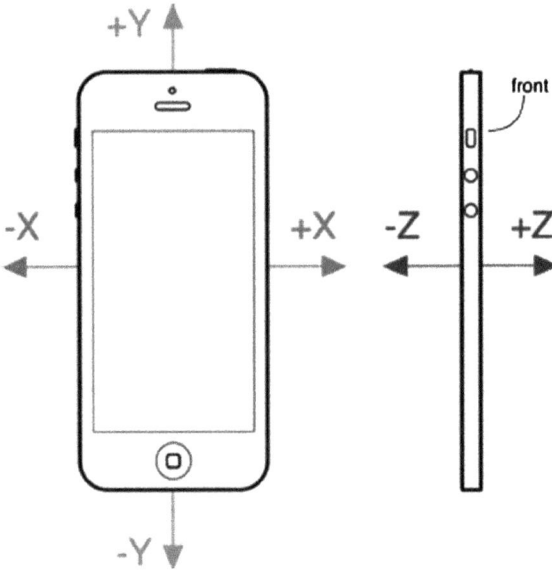

Figure 5-1. *The iPhone accelerometer's axes in three dimensions. The front view of an iPhone on the left shows the x and y axes. The side view on the right shows the z-axis.*

Rotation Detection Using the Gyroscope

I mentioned earlier that all current devices include a gyroscope sensor, allowing you to read values describing the device's rotation around its axes. If the difference between the gyroscope and the accelerometer seems unclear, consider an iPhone lying flat on a table. If you begin to turn the phone around while it's lying flat, the accelerometer values won't change. That's because the forces bent on moving the phone — in this case, just the force of gravity pulling straight down the z-axis — aren't changing. (In reality, things are a bit fuzzier than that, and the action of your hand bumping the phone will surely trigger a small amount of accelerometer action.) During that same movement, however, the device's rotation values will change — particularly the z-axis rotation value. Turning the device clockwise will generate a negative value, and turning it counterclockwise gives a positive value. Stop turning, and the z-axis rotation value will go back to zero. Rather than registering an absolute rotation value, the gyroscope tells you about changes to the device's rotation as they happen. You'll see how this works in this chapter's first example.

Core Motion and the Motion Manager

We'll access accelerometer and gyroscope values using the Core Motion framework. This framework provides, among other things, the `CMMotionManager` class, which acts as a gateway for all the values describing how the device is being moved by its user. An application creates an instance of `CMMotionManager` and then puts it to use in one of two modes:

- It can execute some code for you whenever motion occurs.

- It can hang on to a perpetually updated structure that lets you access the latest values at any time.

The latter method provides an ideal solution for games and other highly interactive applications that need to be able to poll the device's current state during each pass through the game loop. I'll show you how to implement both approaches. Note that the `CMMotionManager` class isn't actually a singleton, but your application should treat it like one and you should create only one of these per app. So, if you need to access the motion manager from several places in your app, you should probably create it in your application delegate and provide access to it from there.

Besides the `CMMotionManager` class, Core Motion also provides a few other classes, such as `CMAccelerometerData` and `CMGyroData`, which are simple containers through which your application can access raw accelerometer and gyroscope information; and `CMDeviceMotion`, a class that combines accelerometer and gyroscope measurements together with attitude information — that is, whether the device is lying flat, tilting upward or to the left, and so on. We'll be using the `CMDeviceMotion` class in the examples in this chapter.

Creating the MotionMonitor Application

I mentioned that the motion manager can operate in a mode where it executes some code for you each time the motion data changes. Most other Cocoa Touch classes offer this sort of functionality by letting you connect to a delegate that gets a message when the time comes, but Core Motion does things a little differently. Instead of using a set of delegate methods to let us know what happens, `CMMotionManager` lets you pass in a closure to execute whenever motion occurs. We've already used closures a couple of times in this book, and now you're going to see another application of this technique.

Use Xcode to create a new Single View Application project named MotionMonitor. This will be a simple app that reads both accelerometer data, gyroscope data (if available), and attitude information, and then it displays the information on the screen.

> **Note** The applications in this chapter do not function on the simulator because the simulator has no accelerometer.

Now select the ViewController.swift file and make the following changes:

```
class ViewController: UIViewController {
    @IBOutlet var gyroscopeLabel: UILabel!
    @IBOutlet var accelerometerLabel: UILabel!
    @IBOutlet var attitudeLabel: UILabel!
```

This provides us with outlets to three labels where we'll display the information. Nothing much needs to be explained here, so just go ahead and save your changes. Next, open Main.storyboard in Interface Builder. Now drag out a `Label` from the library into the view. Resize the label to make it run from the left side of the screen to the right, resize it to be about one-third the height of the entire view, and then align the top of the label to the top blue guideline. Now open the Attributes Inspector and change the Lines field from 1 to 0. The Lines attribute is used to specify the number of lines of text that may appear in the label, and it provides a hard upper limit. If you set it to 0, no limit is applied, and the label can contain as many lines as you like.

Next, drag a second label from the library and drop it directly below the first one. Align its top with the bottom of the first label and align its sides with the left and right edges of the screen. Resize it to be about the same height as the first label. You don't need to be too exact with this since we will be using auto layout to control the final height of the labels. Drag out a third label, placing it with its top edge along the bottom edge of the second label, and then resize it so that its bottom edge is along the bottom edge of the screen, and align its sides to the left and right edges of the screen. Set the Lines attribute for both labels to 0.

Now let's fix the positions and sizes of the three labels. In the Document Overview, Control-drag from the top label to its parent view and release the mouse. In the pop-up menu, hold down the Shift key and select Leading Space to Container Margin, Vertical Spacing to Top Layout Guide, and Trailing Space to Container Margin, and then press Return. Control-drag from the second label to the parent view. In the pop-up menu, hold down Shift and select Leading Space to Container Margin and Trailing Space to Container Margin, and press Return. Control-drag from the third label to Main View, and this time, holding down Shift, select Leading Space to Container Margin, Vertical Spacing to Bottom Layout Guide, and Trailing Space to Container Margin.

Now that all three labels are pinned to the edges of their parent view, let's link them to each other. Control-drag from the second label to the first label and select Vertical Spacing from the pop-up menu. Control-drag from the second label to the third label and do the same. Finally, we need to ensure that the labels have the same height. To do this, hold down the Shift key and click all three labels so that they are all selected. Click the Pin button. In the pop-up, click the Equal Heights check box and press Add 2 Constraints. Click the Resolve Auto Layout Issues button and then click Update All Frames in View Controller. If this item is not available, select the View Controller icon in the Document Outline and try again.

That completes the layout; now let's connect the labels to their outlets. Control-drag from the view controller icon in the Document Outline the top label, release the mouse and select `gyroscopeLabel` from the pop-up menu to connect the label to its outlet. Do the same with the second label, connecting it to `accelerometerLabel` and the third label, which should be linked to `attitudeLabel`. Finally, double-click each of the labels and delete the existing text. This simple GUI is complete, so save your work and get ready for some coding.

CHAPTER 5 DEVICE ORIENTATION AND MOTION

Next, select ViewController.swift. Now comes the interesting part. Add the code in Listing 5-1 to the ViewController.swift file.

Listing 5-1. Add the Following Code to the ViewController.swift File

```
private let motionManager = CMMotionManager()
private let queue = OperationQueue()

override func viewDidLoad() {
    super.viewDidLoad()
    // Do any additional setup after loading the view, typically from a nib.

    if motionManager.isDeviceMotionAvailable {
        motionManager.deviceMotionUpdateInterval = 0.1
        motionManager.startDeviceMotionUpdates(to: queue) {
                (motion:CMDeviceMotion?, error:NSError?) -> Void in
            if let motion = motion {
                let rotationRate = motion.rotationRate
                let gravity = motion.gravity
                let userAcc = motion.userAcceleration
                let attitude = motion.attitude

                let gyroscopeText =
                    String(format: "Rotation Rate:\n----------------\n" +
                                "x: %+.2f\ny: %+.2f\nz: %+.2f\n",
                            rotationRate.x, rotationRate.y, rotationRate.z)
                let acceleratorText =
                    String(format: "Acceleration:\n---------------\n" +
                                "Gravity x: %+.2f\t\tUser x: %+.2f\n" +
                                "Gravity y: %+.2f\t\tUser y: %+.2f\n" +
                                "Gravity z: %+.2f\t\tUser z: %+.2f\n",
                            gravity.x, userAcc.x, gravity.y,
                            userAcc.y, gravity.z,userAcc.z)
                let attitudeText =
                    String(format: "Attitude:\n----------\n" +
                                "Roll: %+.2f\nPitch: %+.2f\nYaw: %+.2f\n",
                            attitude.roll, attitude.pitch, attitude.yaw)
```

CHAPTER 5 DEVICE ORIENTATION AND MOTION

```
            DispatchQueue.main.async {
                self.gyroscopeLabel.text = gyroscopeText
                self.accelerometerLabel.text = acceleratorText
                self.attitudeLabel.text = attitudeText
            }
        }
    }
  }
}
```

First, we import the Core Motion framework and add two additional properties to the class:

```
import UIKit
import CoreMotion
class ViewController: UIViewController {
    @IBOutlet var gyroscopeLabel: UILabel!
    @IBOutlet var accelerometerLabel: UILabel!
    @IBOutlet var attitudeLabel: UILabel!
    private let motionManager = CMMotionManager()
    private let queue = OperationQueue()
```

This code first creates an instance of `CMMotionManager`, which we'll use to monitor motion events. The code then creates an operation queue, which is simply a container for a work that needs to be done.

Caution The motion manager wants to have a queue in which it will put the bits of work to be done, as specified by the closure you will give it, each time an event occurs. It would be tempting to use the system's default queue for this purpose, but the documentation for `CMMotionManager` explicitly warns not to do this. The concern is that the default queue could end up chock-full of these events and have a hard time processing other crucial system events as a result.

173

Next, in the `viewDidLoad` method, we add the code to request device motion updates and update the labels with the gyroscope, accelerometer, and attitude readings as we get them. We first check to make sure the device actually has the required equipment to provide motion information. All handheld iOS devices released so far do, but it's worth checking in case some future device doesn't. Next, we set the time interval we want between updates, specified in seconds. Here, we're asking for a tenth of a second. Note that setting this doesn't guarantee that we'll receive updates at precisely that speed. In fact, that setting is really a cap, specifying the best rate the motion manager will be allowed to give us. In reality, it may update less frequently than that:

```
if motionManager.isDeviceMotionAvailable {
    motionManager.deviceMotionUpdateInterval = 0.1
```

Next, we tell the motion manager to start reporting device motion updates. We pass in the closure that defines the work that will be done each time an update occurs and the queue where the closure will be queued for execution. In this case, the closure receives a `CMDeviceMotion` object that contains the most recent motion data and possibly an `NSError` object if an error occurs while acquiring the data:

```
motionManager.startDeviceMotionUpdates(to: queue) {
        (motion:CMDeviceMotion?, error:NSError?) -> Void in
```

What follows is the closure itself. It creates strings based on the current motion values and pushes them into the labels. We can't do that directly here because UIKit classes like `UILabel` usually work well only when accessed from the main thread. Due to the way this code will be executed, from within an `NSOperationQueue`, we simply don't know the specific thread in which we'll be executing. So, we use the `DispatchQueue.main.async` function to pass control to the main thread before setting the labels' `text` properties.

The gyroscope values are accessed through the `rotationRate` property of the `CMDeviceMotion` object that was passed into the closure. The `rotationRate` property is of type `RotationRate`, which is just a simple `struct` containing three `Float` values that represent the rotation rates around the x, y, and z axes. The accelerometer data is a little more complex, since Core Motion reports two different values — the acceleration due to gravity and any additional acceleration caused by forces applied by the user. You get these values from the `gravity` and `userAcceleration` properties, which are both of type `CMAcceleration`. `CMAcceleration` is another simple `struct` that holds the accelerations along the x, y, and z axes. Finally, the device attitude is reported in the

CHAPTER 5 DEVICE ORIENTATION AND MOTION

`attitude` property, which is of type `CMAttitude`. We'll discuss this further when we run the application.

Before trying out the application, there is one more thing to do. We are going to be moving and rotating the device in various ways to see how the values in the `CMDeviceMotion` structure correlate to what's happening to the device. While we're doing this, we don't want autorotation to kick in. To prevent this, select the project in the Project Navigator, select the MotionMonitor target, and then the General tab. In the Device Orientation section under Deployment Info, select Portrait and make sure that the other three orientations are not selected. This locks the application to Portrait orientation only. Now build and run your app on whatever iOS device you have, and then try it, as shown in Figure 5-2.

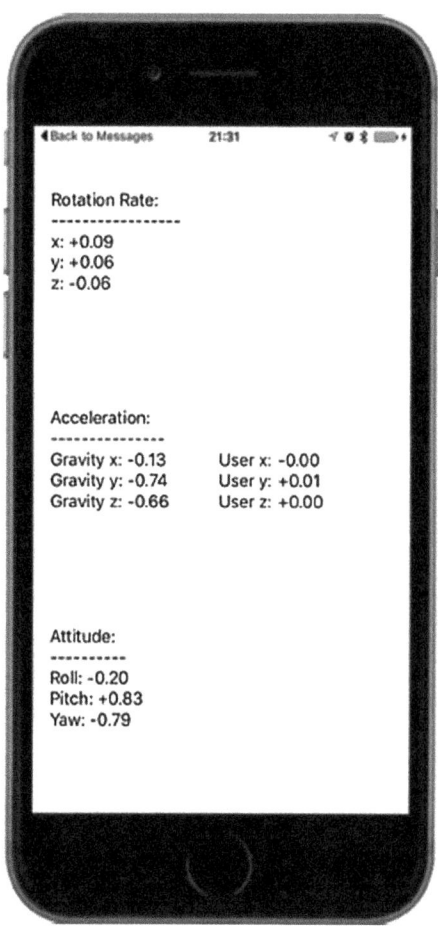

Figure 5-2. *MotionMonitor running on an iPhone. Unfortunately, you'll get no useful information if you run this app in the simulator.*

175

As you tilt your device around in different ways, you'll see how the rotation rate, accelerometer, and attitude values adjust to each new position and will hold steady as long as you hold the device steady. Whenever the device is standing still, no matter which orientation it is in, the rotation values will hover around zero. As you rotate the device, you'll see that the rotation values change, depending on how you turn it around its various axes. The values will always move back to zero when you stop moving the device. We'll look more closely at all of the results shortly.

Proactive Motion Access

You've seen how to access motion data by passing `CMMotionManager` closures to be called as motion occurs. This kind of event-driven motion handling can work well enough for the average Cocoa app, but sometimes it doesn't quite fit an application's particular needs. Interactive games, for example, typically have a perpetually running loop that processes user input, updates the state of the game, and redraws the screen. In such a case, the event-driven approach isn't such a good fit, since you would need to implement an object that waits for motion events, remembers the latest positions from each sensor as they're reported, and is ready to report the data back to the main game loop when necessary. Fortunately, `CMMotionManager` has a built-in solution. Instead of passing in closures, we can just tell it to activate the sensors using the `startDeviceMotionUpdates()` method. Once we do so, we can simply read the values any time we want, directly from the motion manager.

Let's change our MotionMonitor app to use this approach, just so you can see how it works. Start by making a copy of your MotionMonitor project folder or compressing it as we did in earlier examples.

Note You'll find a completed version of this project in the MonitorMotion2 folder in the example source code.

Close the open Xcode project and open the one from the new copy instead, heading straight to ViewController.swift. The first step is to remove the queue property and add a new property, a pointer to an `NSTimer` that will trigger all our display updates:

```
class ViewController: UIViewController {
    @IBOutlet var gyroscopeLabel: UILabel!
```

```
@IBOutlet var accelerometerLabel: UILabel!
@IBOutlet var attitudeLabel: UILabel!
private let motionManager = CMMotionManager()
private var updateTimer: Timer!
```

Next, delete the `viewDidLoad()` method because we are not going to need it. We'll use a timer to collect motion data directly from the motion manager every tenth of a second instead of having it delivered to a closure. We want our timer—and the motion manager itself — to be active only while the application's view is actually being displayed. That way, we keep the usage of our main game loop to a bare minimum. We can accomplish this by implementing the `viewWillAppear()` and `viewDidDisappear()` methods, as shown in Listing 5-2.

Listing 5-2. *Our viewWillAppear and viewDidDisappear Methods for Proactive Motion Access*

```swift
override func viewWillAppear(_ animated: Bool) {
    super.viewWillAppear(animated)
    if motionManager.isDeviceMotionAvailable {
        motionManager.deviceMotionUpdateInterval = 0.1
        motionManager.startDeviceMotionUpdates()
        updateTimer =
            Timer.scheduledTimer(timeInterval: 0.1, target: self,
                    selector: #selector(ViewController.updateDisplay),
                    userInfo: nil, repeats: true)
    }
}

override func viewDidDisappear(_ animated: Bool) {
    super.viewDidDisappear(animated)
    if motionManager.isDeviceMotionAvailable {
        motionManager.stopDeviceMotionUpdates()
        updateTimer.invalidate()
        updateTimer = nil
    }
}
```

CHAPTER 5   DEVICE ORIENTATION AND MOTION

The code in viewWillAppear() calls the motion manager's startDeviceMotionUpdates() method to start it off device motion information, and then creates a new timer and schedules it to fire once every tenth of a second, calling the updateDisplay() method, which we haven't created yet. Add the method in Listing 5-3 just below viewDidDisappear().

Listing 5-3. The updateDisplay Method Goes in the ViewController.swift File

```swift
@objc func updateDisplay() {
    if let motion = motionManager.deviceMotion {
        let rotationRate = motion.rotationRate
        let gravity = motion.gravity
        let userAcc = motion.userAcceleration
        let attitude = motion.attitude
        
        let gyroscopeText =
            String(format: "Rotation Rate:\n-----------------\n" +
                           "x: %+.2f\ny: %+.2f\nz: %+.2f\n",
                    rotationRate.x, rotationRate.y, rotationRate.z)
        let acceleratorText =
            String(format: "Acceleration:\n---------------\n" +
                           "Gravity x: %+.2f\t\tUser x: %+.2f\n" +
                           "Gravity y: %+.2f\t\tUser y: %+.2f\n" +
                           "Gravity z: %+.2f\t\tUser z: %+.2f\n",
                    gravity.x, userAcc.x, gravity.y,
                    userAcc.y, gravity.z,userAcc.z)
        let attitudeText =
            String(format: "Attitude:\n----------\n" +
                           "Roll: %+.2f\nPitch: %+.2f\nYaw: %+.2f\n",
                    attitude.roll, attitude.pitch, attitude.yaw)
        
        DispatchQueue.main.async {
            self.gyroscopeLabel.text = gyroscopeText
            self.accelerometerLabel.text = acceleratorText
            self.attitudeLabel.text = attitudeText
        }
    }
}
```

This is a copy of the code from the closure in the previous version of this example, except that the `CMDeviceMotion` object is obtained directly from the motion manager. Notice the `if let` expression that ensures that the `CMDeviceMotion` value returned by the motion manager is not `nil`; this is required because the timer may fire before the motion manager has acquired its first data sample. Build and run the app on your device, and you should see that it behaves exactly like the first version. Now you've seen two ways of accessing motion data. Use whichever suits your application best.

Gyroscope and Attitude Results

The gyroscope measures the rate at which the device is rotating about the x, y, and z axes. Refer to Figure 5-1 to see how the axes relate to the body of the device. First, lay the device flat on a table. While it's not moving, all three rotation rates will be close to zero and you'll see that the roll, pitch, and yaw values are also close to zero. Now gently rotate the device clockwise. As you do, you'll see that the rotation rate around the z-axis becomes negative. The faster you rotate the device, the larger the absolute value of the rotation rate will be.

When you stop rotating, the rotation rate will return to zero, but the yaw does not. The yaw represents the angle through which the device has been rotated about the z-axis from its initial rest position. If you rotate the device clockwise, the yaw will decrease through negative values until the device is 180° from its rest position, when its value will be around –3. If you continue to rotate the device clockwise, the yaw will jump to a value slightly larger than +3 and then decrease to zero as you rotate it back to its initial position. If you start by rotating counterclockwise, the same thing happens, except that the yaw is initially positive. The yaw angle is actually measured in radians, not degrees. A rotation of 180° is the same as a rotation by π radians, which is why the maximum yaw value is about 3 (since π is a little larger than 3.14).

With the device flat on the table again, hold the top edge and rotate it upward, leaving the base on the table. This is a rotation around the x-axis, so you'll see the x rotation rate increase through positive values until you hold the device steady, at which point it returns to zero. Now look at the pitch value. It has increased by an amount that depends on the angle through which you have lifted the top edge of the device. If you lift the device all the way to the vertical, the pitch value will be around 1.5. Like yaw, pitch is measured in radians, so when the device is vertical, it has rotated through 90°, or π/2 radians, which is a little over 1.5. If you lay the device flat again and repeat — but this time lift the bottom edge and leave the top on the table, you are performing a counterclockwise rotation about the x-axis and you'll see a negative rotation rate and a negative pitch.

Finally, with the device flat on the table again, lift its left edge, leaving the right edge on the table. This is a rotation about the y-axis and you'll see this reflect in the y-axis rotation rate. You can get the total rotation angle at any point from the roll value. It will be about 1.5 (actually π/2) radians when the device is standing upright on its right edge and it will increase all the way to π radians if you turn it on its face; although, of course, you'll need a glass table to be able to see this.

In summary, use the rotation rates to see how fast the device is rotating about each axis and the yaw, pitch, and roll values to get its current total rotation about these axes, relative to its starting orientation.

Accelerometer Results

I mentioned earlier that the iPhone's accelerometer detects acceleration along three axes; it provides this information using two `CMAcceleration` structs. Each `CMAcceleration` has an x, y, and z field, each of which holds a floating-point value. A value of 0 means that the accelerometer detects no movement on that particular axis. A positive or negative value indicates force in one direction. For example, a negative value for y indicates that a downward pull is sensed, which is probably an indication that the phone is being held upright in portrait orientation. A positive value for y indicates some force is being exerted in the opposite direction, which could mean the phone is being held upside down or that the phone is being moved in a downward direction. The `CMDeviceMotion` object separately reports the acceleration along each axis due to gravity and any additional forces caused by the user.

For example, if you hold the device flat, you'll see that gravity value is close to –1 along the z axis and the user acceleration components are all close to zero. Now if you quickly raise the device, keeping it level, you'll see that the gravity values remain about the same, but there is positive user acceleration along the z-axis. For some applications, it is useful to have separate gravity and user acceleration values, while for others, you need the total acceleration, which you can get by adding together the components of the `gravity` and `userAcceleration` properties of the `CMDeviceMotion` object.

Keeping the diagram in Figure 5-1 in mind, let's look at some accelerometer results in Figure 5-3. This figure shows the reported acceleration due to gravity while the device is in a given attitude and not moving. Note that in real life you will almost never get values this precise, as the accelerometer is sensitive enough to sense even tiny amounts of motion, and you will usually pick up at least some tiny amount of force on all three axes. This is real-world physics, not high school physics.

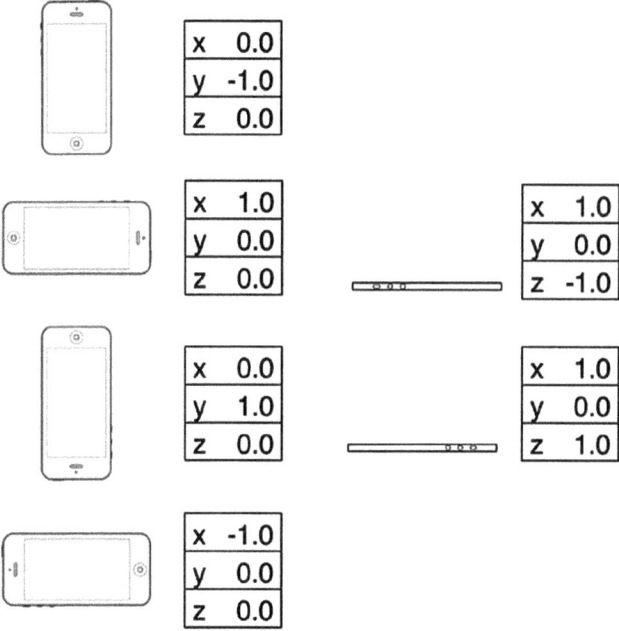

Figure 5-3. *Idealized gravity acceleration values for different device orientations*

Probably the most common usage of the accelerometer in third-party applications is as a controller for games. We'll create a program that uses the accelerometer for input a little later in the chapter, but first we'll look at another common accelerometer use: detecting shakes.

181

CHAPTER 5 DEVICE ORIENTATION AND MOTION

Detecting Shakes

Like a gesture, a shake can be used as a form of input to your application. For example, the drawing program GLPaint, which is one of Apple's iOS sample code projects, lets users erase drawings by shaking their iOS device, sort of like an Etch A Sketch. Detecting shakes is relatively trivial. All it requires is checking for an absolute value of user acceleration on one of the axes that is greater than a set threshold. During normal usage, it's not uncommon for one of the three axes to register values up to around 1.3g, but getting values much higher than that generally requires intentional force. The accelerometer seems to be unable to register values higher than around 2.3g (at least in our experience), so you might not want to set your threshold any higher than that.

To detect a shake, you could check for an absolute value greater than 1.5 for a slight shake and 2.0 for a strong shake, by adding code like this to the motion manager closure in the MotionMonitor example:

```
let userAcc = motion.userAcceleration
if fabsf(Float(userAcc.x)) > 2.0
      || fabsf(Float(userAcc.y)) > 2.0
      || fabsf(Float(userAcc.z)) > 2.0 {
    // Do something here...
}
```

This code would detect any movement on any axis that exceeded two g-forces.

Baked-In Shaking

There's actually another, much simpler way to check for shakes — one that's baked right into the responder chain. Similar where we implemented methods like `touchesBegan(_:withEvent:)` to get touches, iOS also provides three similar responder methods for detecting motion:

- When motion begins, the `motionBegan(_:withEvent:)` method is called on the first responder and then on through the responder chain, as discussed in Chapter 18.

CHAPTER 5 DEVICE ORIENTATION AND MOTION

- When the motion ends, the motionEnded(_:withEvent:) method is called.

- If the phone rings, or some other interrupting action happens during the shake, the motionCancelled(_:withEvent:) method is called.

The first argument to each of these methods is an event subtype, one of which is UIEventSubtype.motionShake. This means that you can actually detect a shake without using CMMotionManager directly. All you need to do is override the appropriate motion-sensing methods in your view or view controller, and they will be called automatically when the user shakes the phone. Unless you specifically need more control over the shake gesture, you should use the baked-in motion detection rather than the manual method described previously. However, I thought we would show you the basics of the manual method in case you ever need more control.

The Shake and Break Application

For this project we'll write an application that detects shakes, and then makes your phone look and sound as if it broke as a result of the shake. When you launch the application, the program will display a picture that looks like the iPhone home screen shown in Figure 5-4. Shake the phone hard enough, though, and your poor phone will make a sound that you never want to hear coming out of a consumer electronics device. What's more, your screen will look like the one shown in Figure 5-5. Don't worry. You can reset the iPhone to its previously pristine state by touching the screen.

CHAPTER 5 DEVICE ORIENTATION AND MOTION

Figure 5-4. *The ShakeAndBreak application looks innocuous enough*

CHAPTER 5   DEVICE ORIENTATION AND MOTION

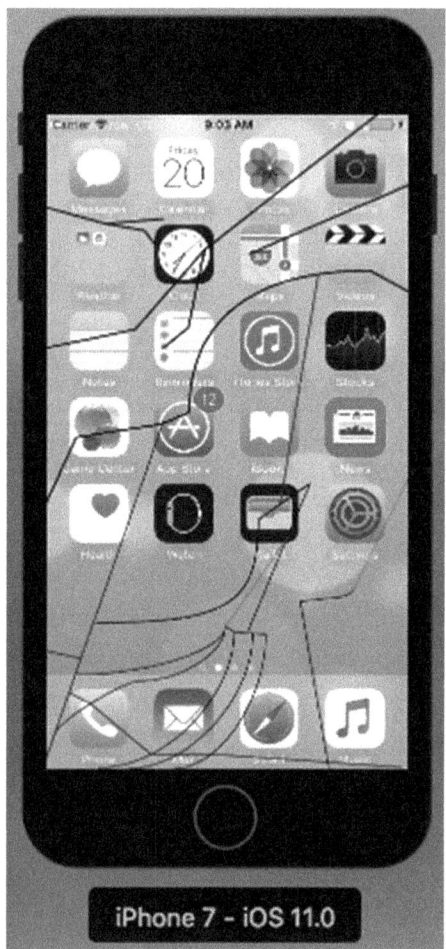

Figure 5-5. *Shake it and it will simulate a broken iPhone screen*

Create a new project in Xcode using the Single View Application template. Make sure that the device type is set to iPhone — unlike most of the other examples in this book, this one only works on iPhone because the images are of the correct size for an iPhone 6/6s screen (and they should scale reasonably well if you have an iPhone 6/6s Plus). Of course, it's easy to extend this project to iPad if you create additional images. Call the new project ShakeAndBreak. In the Images and Sounds folder of the example source code, we've provided the two images and the sound file you need for this application. Select Assets.xcassets in the Project Navigator and drag the images Home.png and BrokenHome.png into it. Drag glass.wav into the Project Navigator.

CHAPTER 5 DEVICE ORIENTATION AND MOTION

Now let's start creating our view controller. We're going to need to create an outlet to point to an image view so that we can change the displayed image. Single-click ViewController.swift and add the following property to it:

```
class ViewController: UIViewController {
    @IBOutlet var imageView: UIImageView!
```

Save the file. Now select Main.storyboard to edit the file in Interface Builder. Drag an Image View over from the library to the view in the layout area and resize it so that it fills its parent view. In the Document Overview, Control-drag from the Image View to its parent View, hold down Shift, and in the context menu, select Leading Space to Container Margin, Trailing Space to Container Margin, Vertical Spacing to Top Layout Guide, and Vertical Spacing to Bottom Layout Guide, and press Return to lock the size and position of the image view. Finally, Control-drag from the View Controller icon to the image view and select the imageView outlet, and then save the storyboard.

Next, go back to the ViewController.swift file. We're going to add some additional properties for both of the images we're going to display, to track whether we're showing the broken image. We're also adding an audio player object that we'll use to play our breaking glass sound. The following bold lines go near the top of the file:

```
import UIKit
import AVFoundation

class ViewController: UIViewController {
    @IBOutlet var imageView: UIImageView!
    private var fixed: UIImage!
    private var broken: UIImage!
    private var brokenScreenShowing = false
    private var crashPlayer: AVAudioPlayer?
```

Add the following code to the viewDidLoad() method:

```
        if let url = url = Bundle(for: type(of: self)).
        url(forResource:"glass", withExtension:"wav"){
            do {
                crashPlayer = try AVAudioPlayer(contentsOf: url,
                    fileTypeHint: AVFileTypeWAVE)
            } catch let error as NSError {
```

CHAPTER 5 DEVICE ORIENTATION AND MOTION

```
            print("Audio error! \(error.localizedDescription)")
        }
    }
    fixed = UIImage(named: "Home")
    broken = UIImage(named: "HomeBroken")
    imageView.image = fixed
```

At this point, we've initialized the URL variable to point to our sound file and initialized an instance of `AVAudioPlayer`, a class that will simply play the sound. Then we loaded both images we need to use and put the first one in place. Next, add the following new method:

```
override func motionEnded(_ motion: UIEventSubtype, with event: UIEvent?) {
    if !brokenScreenShowing && motion == .motionShake {
        imageView.image = broken;
        crashPlayer?.play()
        brokenScreenShowing = true;
    }
}
```

This overrides the `UIResponder` `motionEnded(_:withEvent:)` method, which is called whenever a shake happens. After checking to make sure the broken screen isn't already showing and that the event we're looking at really is a shake event, the method shows the broken image and plays our shattering noise.

The last method is one you should already be familiar with by now. It's called when the screen is touched. All we need to do in that method is set the image back to the unbroken screen and set `brokenScreenShowing` back to `false`:

```
override func touchesBegan(_ touches: Set<UITouch>, with event: UIEvent?) {
    imageView.image = fixed
    brokenScreenShowing = false
}
```

Build and run the application, and try shaking your device. For those of you who don't have the ability to run this application on your iOS device, you can still give this a try. The simulator does not simulate the accelerometer hardware, but it does include a menu item that simulates the shake event, so this will work with the simulator, too. Go have some fun with it. When you're finished, we'll see how to use the accelerometer as a controller for games and other programs.

Accelerometer as a Directional Controller

Instead of using buttons to control the movement of a character or object in a game, developers often use an accelerometer to accomplish this task. In a car-racing game, for example, twisting the iOS device like a steering wheel might steer your car, while tipping it forward might accelerate, and tipping it back might activate the brakes. Exactly how you use the accelerometer as a controller will vary greatly, depending on the specific mechanics of the game. In the simplest cases, you might just take the value from one of the axes, multiply it by a number, and add that to one of the coordinates of the controlled objects. In more complex games where physics are modeled more realistically, you would need to make adjustments to the velocity of the controlled object based on the values returned from the accelerometer.

The one tricky aspect of using the accelerometer as a controller is that the delegate method is not guaranteed to call back at the interval you specify. If you tell the motion manager to read the accelerometer 60 times a second, all that you can say for sure is that it won't update more than 60 times a second. You're not guaranteed to get 60 evenly spaced updates every second. So, if you're doing animation based on input from the accelerometer, you must keep track of the time that passes between updates and factor that into your equations to determine how far objects have moved.

The Ball Application

For our next project, we're going to move a sprite around the iPhone's screen by tilting the phone. This is a very simple example of using the accelerometer to receive input. We'll use Quartz 2D to handle our animation.

> **Note** As a general rule, when you're working with games and other programs that need smooth animation, you'll probably want to use Sprite Kit, OpenGL ES, or Metal. We're using Quartz 2D in this application for the sake of simplicity and to reduce the amount of code that's unrelated to using the accelerometer.

In this application, as you tilt your iPhone, the marble will roll around as if it were on the surface of a table, as shown in Figure 5-6. Tip it to the left, and the ball will roll to the left. Tip it farther, and it will move faster. Tip it back, and it will slow down, and then start going in the other direction.

CHAPTER 5   DEVICE ORIENTATION AND MOTION

Figure 5-6. *The Ball application lets you roll a marble around the screen*

In Xcode, create a new project using the Single View Application template. Set the device type to Universal and call the project Ball. In the Images and Sounds folder in the example source code, you'll find an image called ball.png. Using the Project Navigator, drag ball.png into Assets.xcassets.

Next, select the Ball project in the Project Navigator followed by the General tab of the Ball target. In the Device Orientation section under Deployment Info, select Portrait and deselect all of the other check boxes, as you did for the MotionMonitor application earlier in this chapter. This disables the default interface orientation changes; we want to roll our ball and not change interface orientation as we move our device around.

189

CHAPTER 5 DEVICE ORIENTATION AND MOTION

Now single-click the Ball folder and select File ➤ New ➤ File.... Select Cocoa Touch Class from the iOS Source section, and click Next. Make the new class a subclass of UIView and name it BallView, and then click Create. We'll get back to editing this class a little later. Select Main.storyboard to edit the file in Interface Builder. Single-click the View icon in the Document Outline and use the identity inspector to change the view's class from UIView to BallView. Next, switch to the Attributes Inspector and change the view's Background to Light Gray Color. Finally, save the storyboard.

Now it's time to edit ViewController.swift. Add the lines in Listing 5-4 to the top of the file.

Listing 5-4. Modify the ViewController.swift and the viewDidLoad Method As Shown

```swift
import UIKit
import CoreMotion

class ViewController: UIViewController {
    private static let updateInterval = 1.0/60.0
    private let motionManager = CMMotionManager()
    private let queue = OperationQueue()

    override func viewDidLoad() {
        super.viewDidLoad()
        // Do any additional setup after loading the view, typically from a nib.

        motionManager.startDeviceMotionUpdates(to: queue) {
                (motionData: CMDeviceMotion?, error: NSError?) -> Void in
            let ballView = self.view as! BallView
            ballView.acceleration = motionData!.gravity
            DispatchQueue.main.async {
                ballView.update()
            }
        }
    }
}
```

Note After entering this code, you will see errors as a result of `BallView` not being complete. We're doing the bulk of our work in the `BallView` class.

The `viewDidLoad()` method here is similar to some of what we've done elsewhere in this chapter. The main difference is that we are using a much higher update interval of 60 times per second. In the closure where we tell the motion manager to execute when there are accelerometer updates to report, we pass the acceleration object along to our view. We then call a method named `update`, which updates the position of the ball in the view based on acceleration and the amount of time that has passed since the last update. Since that closure can be executed on any thread, and the methods belonging to UIKit objects (including UIView) can be safely used only from the main thread, we once again force the `update` method to be called in the main thread.

Writing the Ball View

Select BallView.swift. Here, we'll need to import the Core Motion framework and add the property that our controller will use to pass along an acceleration value and five other properties that we'll use in the class implementation:

```
import UIKit
```
`import CoreMotion`
```
class BallView: UIView {
    @objc var acceleration = CMAcceleration(x: 0, y: 0, z: 0)
    private let image = UIImage(named : "ball")!
    @objc var currentPoint : CGPoint = CGPoint.zero
    private var ballXVelocity = 0.0
    private var ballYVelocity = 0.0
    private var lastUpdateTime = Date()
```

Let's look at the properties and talk about what we're doing with each of them. The `acceleration` property will hold the most recent acceleration values, which the controller gets from a device motion update. Next is a `UIImage` that points to the sprite that we'll be moving around the screen:

```
    private let image = UIImage(named : "ball")!
```

CHAPTER 5 DEVICE ORIENTATION AND MOTION

The `currentPoint` property will hold the current position of the ball. We'll use this value, together with its previous value (which Swift gives us for free) so that we can build an update rectangle that encompasses both the new and old positions of the ball, so that it is drawn at the new spot and erased at the old one:

```
private var currentPoint : CGPoint = CGPoint.zero
```

We also have two variables to keep track of the ball's current velocity in two dimensions. Although this isn't going to be a very complex simulation, we do want the ball to move in a manner similar to a real ball. We'll calculate the ball movement in the next section. We'll get acceleration from the accelerometer and keep track of velocity on two axes with these variables.

```
private var ballXVelocity = 0.0
private var ballYVelocity = 0.0
```

Finally, the `lastUpdateTime` property is set each time we update the ball's position. We'll use it to calculate speed changes based on the time between updates and the ball's acceleration.

Now let's write the code to draw and move the ball around the screen. First, add the methods shown in Listing 5-5 to the BallView.swift file.

Listing 5-5. Add init Methods for the BallView Class

```
override init(frame: CGRect) {
    super.init(frame: frame)
    commonInit()
}

required init?(coder aDecoder: NSCoder) {
    super.init(coder: aDecoder)
    commonInit()
}

private func commonInit() -> Void {
    currentPoint = CGPoint(x: (bounds.size.width / 2.0) +
                              (image.size.width / 2.0),
                           y: (bounds.size.height / 2.0) +
                              (image.size.height / 2.0))
}
```

Both the `init?(coder: )` and the `init(frame:)` methods call our `commonInit()` method. Our view that is created in a storyboard file will be initialized with the `initWithCoder()` method. We call the `commonInit()` method from both initializer methods so that our view class can safely be created both from code and from a nib file. This is a nice thing to do for any view class that may be reused, such as this fancy ball rolling view. Now uncomment the commented-out `drawRect:` method and give it this simple implementation to draw the ball image at `currentPoint`:

```swift
override func draw(_ rect: CGRect) {
    // Drawing code
    image.draw(at: currentPoint)
}
```

Next, add our `update()` method to the end of the class, as shown in Listing 5-6.

Listing 5-6. *The BallClass Update Method*

```swift
func update() -> Void {
    let now = Date()
    let secondsSinceLastDraw = now.timeIntervalSince(lastUpdateTime)
    ballXVelocity =
            ballXVelocity + (acceleration.x * secondsSinceLastDraw)
    ballYVelocity =
            ballYVelocity - (acceleration.y * secondsSinceLastDraw)

    let xDelta = secondsSinceLastDraw * ballXVelocity * 500
    let yDelta = secondsSinceLastDraw * ballYVelocity * 500
    currentPoint = CGPoint(x: currentPoint.x + CGFloat(xDelta),
    y: currentPoint.y + CGFloat(yDelta))
    lastUpdateTime = now
}
```

CHAPTER 5 DEVICE ORIENTATION AND MOTION

Finally, add the property observer in Listing 5-7 to the currentPoint property.

Listing 5-7. The currentProperty Observer

```
var currentPoint : CGPoint = CGPoint.zero {
    didSet {
        var newX = currentPoint.x
        var newY = currentPoint.y
        if newX < 0 {
            newX = 0
            ballXVelocity = 0
        } else if newX > bounds.size.width - image.size.width {
            newX = bounds.size.width - image.size.width
            ballXVelocity = 0
        }
        if newY < 0 {
            newY = 0
            ballYVelocity = 0
        } else if newY > bounds.size.height - image.size.height {
            newY = bounds.size.height - image.size.height
            ballYVelocity = 0
        }
        currentPoint = CGPoint(x: newX, y: newY)
        let currentRect = CGRect(x: newX, y: newY,
                                 width: newX + image.size.width,
                                 height: newY + image.size.height)
        let prevRect = CGRect(x: oldValue.x, y: oldValue.y,
                              width: oldValue.x + image.size.width,
                              height: oldValue.y + image.size.height)
        setNeedsDisplay(currentRect.union(prevRect))
    }
}
```

Calculating Ball Movement

Our `drawRect()` method couldn't be much simpler. We just draw the ball image at the position stored in `currentPoint`. The property observer for `currentPoint` is another story, however. When a new position is set (from the `update()` method, which you'll see shortly), we need to check whether the ball has hit the edges of the screen and, if so, stop its motion along either the x- or y-axis. We do that by implementing a property observer from which we can access the new value of the property and modify it without causing the property observer to be called again (which would be infinite recursion).

The first thing we do is get the current x and y coordinates of the ball and do a boundary check. If either the x or y position of the ball is less than 0 or greater than the width or height of the screen (accounting for the width and height of the image), then the acceleration in that direction is stopped and we change the ball's coordinate so that it appears at the edge of the screen:

```
var newX = currentPoint.x
var newY = currentPoint.y
if newX < 0 {
    newX = 0
    ballXVelocity = 0
} else if newX > bounds.size.width - image.size.width {
    newX = bounds.size.width - image.size.width
    ballXVelocity = 0
}
if newY < 0 {
    newY = 0
    ballYVelocity = 0
} else if newY > bounds.size.height - image.size.height {
    newY = bounds.size.height - image.size.height
    ballYVelocity = 0
}
```

Tip Do you want to make the ball bounce off the walls more naturally, instead of just stopping? It's easy enough to do. Just change the two lines in setCurrentPoint: that currently read ballXVelocity = 0 to **ballXVelocity = -(ballXVelocity / 2.0)**. And change the two lines that currently read ballYVelocity = 0 to **ballYVelocity = -(ballYVelocity / 2.0)**. With these changes, instead of killing the ball's velocity, we reduce it in half and set it to the inverse. Now the ball has half the velocity in the opposite direction.

Throughout this code, we keep the ball's coordinates in local variables called newX, newY. Once we've modified its position, if necessary, we use these values to create and store the updated value back in the property:

```
currentPoint = CGPoint(x: newX, y: newY)
```

After that, we calculate two CGRects based on the size of the image. One rectangle encompasses the area where the new image will be drawn, and the other encompasses the area where it was last drawn. We calculate the second of these rectangles using the previous value of the ball's location, which Swift stores for us in a constant variable called oldValue. We'll use these two rectangles to ensure that the old ball is erased at the same time the new one is drawn:

```
let currentRect = CGRect(x: newX, y: newY,
                         width: newX + image.size.width,
                         height: newY + image.size.height)
let prevRect = CGRect(x: oldValue.x, y: oldValue.y,
                      width: oldValue.x + image.size.width,
                      height: oldValue.y + image.size.height)
```

Finally, we create a new rectangle that is the union of the two rectangles we just calculated and feed that to setNeedsDisplay(currentRect:) to indicate the part of our view that needs to be redrawn:

```
setNeedsDisplay(currentRect.union(prevRect))
```

The last substantive method in our class is `update()`, which is used to figure out the correct new location of the ball. This method is called from the accelerometer method of its controller class after it feeds the view to the new acceleration object. First, we calculate how long it has been since the last time this method was called. The `NSDate` instance returned by `Date()` represents the current time. By asking it for the time interval since `lastUpdateTime`, we get a number representing the number of seconds between now and the last time this method was called:

```
let now = Date()
let secondsSinceLastDraw = now.timeIntervalSince(lastUpdateTime)
```

Next, we calculate the new velocity in both directions by adding the current acceleration to the current velocity. We multiply acceleration by `secondsSinceLastDraw` so that our acceleration is consistent across time. Tipping the phone at the same angle will always cause the same amount of acceleration:

```
ballXVelocity =
        ballXVelocity + (acceleration.x * secondsSinceLastDraw)
ballYVelocity =
        ballYVelocity - (acceleration.y * secondsSinceLastDraw)
```

After that, we figure out the actual change in pixels since the last time the method was called based on the velocity. The product of velocity and elapsed time is multiplied by 500 to create movement that looks natural. If we didn't multiply it by some value, the acceleration would be extraordinarily slow, as if the ball were stuck in molasses:

```
let xDelta = secondsSinceLastDraw * ballXVelocity * 500
let yDelta = secondsSinceLastDraw * ballYVelocity * 500
```

Once we know the change in pixels, we create a new point by adding the current location to the calculated acceleration and assign that to `currentPoint`:

```
currentPoint = CGPoint(x: currentPoint.x + CGFloat(xDelta),
                       y: currentPoint.y + CGFloat(yDelta))
```

That ends our calculations, so all that's left is to update `lastUpdateTime` with the current time:

```
lastUpdateTime = now
```

Now build and run the app. If all went well, the application will launch, and you should be able to control the movement of the ball by tilting the phone. When the ball gets to an edge of the screen, it should stop. Tip the phone back the other way, and it should start rolling in the other direction.

Summary

Well, we've certainly seen some interesting things in this chapter with physics and the iOS accelerometer and gyroscope. We created a prank app to "break" a phone and we saw the basics of using the accelerometer as a control device. The possibilities for applications with the accelerometer and gyro are wide and varied. In the next chapter we're going to get into using another bit of iOS hardware: the built-in camera.

CHAPTER 6

Using the Camera and Accessing Photos

It should come as no surprise that the iPhone, iPad, and iPod touch contain a built-in camera with the Photos application to help you manage the pictures and videos you've taken (see Figure 6-1). What you may not know is that your programs can use the built-in camera to take pictures. Your applications can also allow the user to select from among and view the media already stored on the device. We'll look at both of these abilities in this chapter.

Figure 6-1. *In this chapter, we'll explore accessing the iPhone camera and photo library in our own application*

Using the Image Picker and UIImagePickerController

Because of the way iOS applications are sandboxed, ordinarily they can't get access to photographs or other data that live outside their own sandboxes. Fortunately, both the camera and the media library are made available to your application by way of an image picker.

Using the Image Picker Controller

As the name implies, an image picker provides the mechanism allowing you to select an image from a specified source. When this class first appeared in iOS, it was used only for images. Nowadays, you can use it to capture video as well. Typically, an image picker uses a list of images and/or videos as its source, as shown in Figure 6-2 (left side). You can, however, specify that the picker use the camera as its source, as shown in Figure 6-2 (right side).

CHAPTER 6 USING THE CAMERA AND ACCESSING PHOTOS

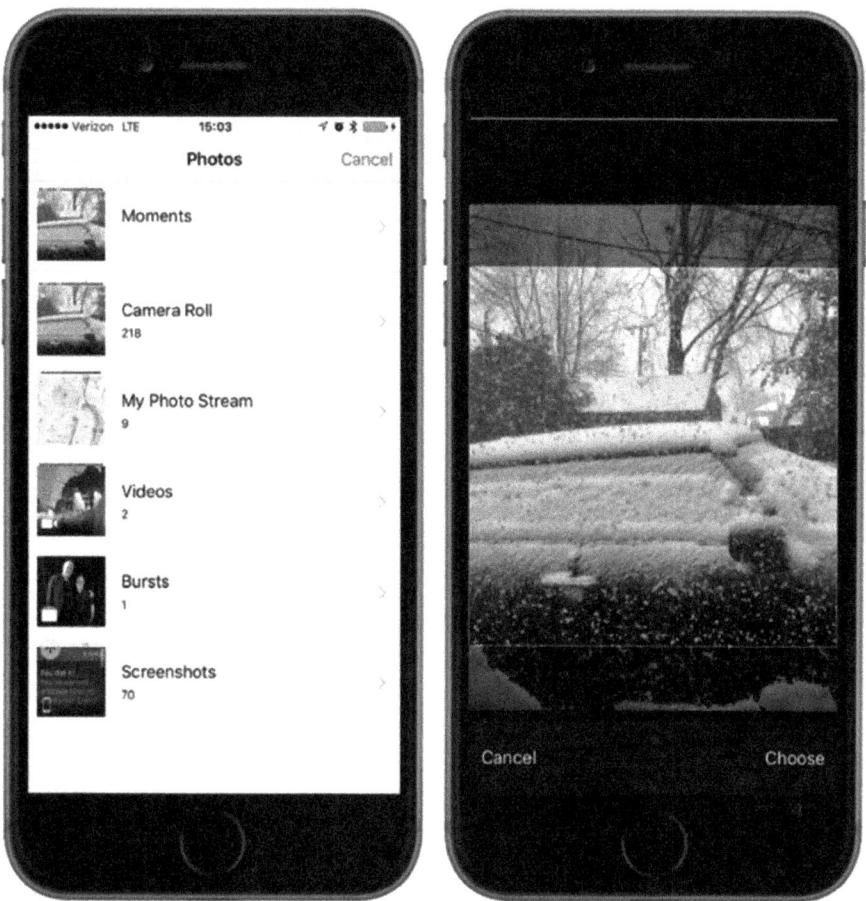

Figure 6-2. *An image picker presents users with a list of their pictures (left), allowing one to be moved and scaled (right) after selection*

We implement the image picker interface using a controller class called `UIImagePickerController`. We create an instance of this class, specify a delegate, specify its image source and whether you want the user to pick an image or a video, and then present it. The image picker takes control of the device allowing the user to select a picture or video from the existing media library. Or the user can take a new picture or video with the camera. Once the user makes a selection, we can give her an opportunity to do some basic editing, such as scaling or cropping an image, or trimming away a bit of a video clip. All of that behavior gets implemented by the `UIImagePickerController`, so our effort becomes minimized.

Assuming the user doesn't press Cancel, the image or video that the user either captures or selects from the library passes to your delegate. Regardless of whether the

CHAPTER 6 USING THE CAMERA AND ACCESSING PHOTOS

user selects a media file or cancels, your delegate becomes responsible for dismissing the UIImagePickerController so that the user can return to your application.

Creating a UIImagePickerController is extremely straightforward. You just create an instance the way you would with most classes. There is one catch, however: not every iOS device has a camera, so before you create an instance of UIImagePickerController, you need to check to see whether the device your app is currently running on supports the image source you want to use. For example, before letting the user take a picture with the camera, you should make sure the program is running on a device that has a camera. You can check that by using a class method on UIImagePickerController, like this:

```
if UIImagePickerController.isSourceTypeAvailable(.Camera) {
```

In this example, we're passing UIImagePickerControllerSourceType.Camera to indicate that we want to let the user take a picture or shoot a video using the built-in camera. The method isSourceTypeAvailable() returns true if the specified source is currently available. We can specify two other values in addition to UIImagePickerControllerSourceType.camera:

- UIImagePickerControllerSourceType.PhotoLibrary specifies that the user should pick an image or video from the existing media library. That image will be returned to your delegate.

- UIImagePickerControllerSourceType.SavedPhotosAlbum specifies that the user will select the image from the library of existing photographs, but that the selection will be limited to the camera roll. This option will run on a device without a camera, where it is less useful but still allows you to select any screenshots you have taken.

After making sure that the device your program is running on supports the image source you want to use, launching the image picker is shown in Listing 6-1.

Listing 6-1. Launching the Image Picker from Inside a View Controller

```
let picker = UIImagePickerController()
picker.delegate = self
picker.sourceType = UIImagePickerControllerSourceType.camera
picker.cameraDevice = UIImagePickerControllerCameraDevice.front
self.present (picker, animated:true, completion: nil)
```

Tip On a device that has more than one camera, you can select which one to use by setting the `cameraDevice` property to `UIImagePickerControllerCameraDevice.front` or `UIImagePickerControllerCameraDevice.rear`. To find out whether a front or rear camera is available, use the same constants with the `isCameraDeviceAvailable()` method.

After we have created and configured the `UIImagePickerController`, we use a method that our class inherited from `UIView` called `self.present(_:animated:completion:)` to present the image picker to the user, called as a method of the view controller, which we refer to here using self.

Implementing the Image Picker Controller Delegate

To find out when the user has finished using the image picker, you need to implement the `UIImagePickerControllerDelegate` protocol. This protocol defines two methods: imagePickerController (`_:didFinishPickingMediaWithInfo:`) and imagePickerControllerDidCancel().

The imagePickerController(`_:didFinishPickingMediaWithInfo:`) method gets called when the user has successfully captured a photo or video, or selected an item from the media library. The first argument is a pointer to the `UIImagePickerController` that you created earlier. The second argument returns a dictionary that contains the chosen photo or the URL of the chosen video, as well as optional editing information if you enabled editing in the image picker controller (and if the user actually did some editing). That dictionary contains the original, unedited image stored under the key `UIImagePickerControllerOriginalImage`. Listing 6-2 shows an example of a delegate method that retrieves the original image.

Listing 6-2. Delegate Method for Retrieving an Image

```
func imagePickerController(picker: UIImagePickerController,
                           didFinishPickingMediaWithInfo info: [String :
                           AnyObject]) {
   let selectedImage: UIImage? =
       info[UIImagePickerControllerEditedImage] as? UIImage
   let originalImage: UIImage? =
```

```
    info[UIImagePickerControllerOriginalImage] as? UIImage

  // do something with selectedImage and originalImage

  picker.dismiss(animated: true, completion:nil)
}
```

The editingInfo dictionary will also tell you which portion of the entire image was chosen during editing by way of an NSValue object stored under the key UIImagePickerControllerCropRect. You can convert this NSValue instance into a CGRect, as shown in Listing 6-3.

Listing 6-3. Converting an NSValue into a CGRect

```
let cropValue:NSValue? = info[UIImagePickerControllerCropRect] as? NSValue
let cropRect:CGRect? = cropValue?.cgRectValue()
```

After this conversion, cropRect specifies the portion of the original image selected during the editing process. If you do not need this information, just ignore it.

Caution If the image returned to your delegate comes from the camera, that image will **not** automatically be stored in the photo library. It is your application's responsibility to save the image, if necessary.

The other delegate method, imagePickerControllerDidCancel(), gets called if the user decides to cancel the process without capturing or selecting any media. When the image picker calls this delegate method, it's just notifying you that the user is finished with the picker and didn't choose anything.

Both of the methods in the UIImagePickerControllerDelegate protocol are marked as optional, but they really aren't, and here is why: modal views like the image picker must be told to dismiss themselves. As a result, even if you don't need to take any application-specific actions when the user cancels an image picker, you still need to dismiss the picker. At a bare minimum, your imagePickerControllerDidCancel() method will need to look like this for your program to function correctly:

```
func imagePickerControllerDidCancel(picker: UIImagePickerController) {
    picker.dismiss(true, completion:nil)
}
```

CHAPTER 6 USING THE CAMERA AND ACCESSING PHOTOS

In this chapter, we're going to build an application that lets the user take a picture or shoot some video with the camera. Or the user can select something from the photo library, and then display the selection on the screen, as shown in Figure 6-3. If the user is on a device without a camera, we will hide the New Photo or Video button and allow selection only from the photo library.

Figure 6-3. *Our Camera application in action*

Creating the Camera Interface

Create a new project in Xcode using the Single View Application template, naming the application **Camera**. The first order of business is to add a couple of outlets to this application's view controller. We need one to point to the image view so that we can update it with the image returned from the image picker. We'll also need an outlet to

205

point to the New Photo or Video button so that we can hide the button if the device doesn't have a camera. We also need two action methods: one for the New Photo or Video button and one that lets the user select an existing picture from the photo library.

```
class ViewController: UIViewController, UIImagePickerControllerDelegate,
                                        UINavigationControllerDelegate {
    @IBOutlet var imageView: UIImageView!
    @IBOutlet var takePictureButton: UIButton!
```

The first thing you might notice is that we've actually conformed our class to two different protocols: `UIImagePickerControllerDelegate` and `UINavigationControllerDelegate`. Because `UIImagePickerController` is a subclass of `UINavigationController`, we must conform our class to both of these protocols. The methods in `UINavigationControllerDelegate` are optional. We don't need either of them to use the image picker; however, we do need to conform to the protocol, or the compiler will give us an error later on.

The other thing you might notice is that, while we added a property of type `UIImageView` for displaying a chosen image, we didn't add anything similar for displaying a chosen video. UIKit doesn't include any publicly available class like `UIImageView` that works for showing video content, so we'll have to show video using another technique instead. When we get to that point, we will use an instance of `AVPlayerViewController`, grabbing its `view` property and inserting it into our view hierarchy. This is a highly unusual way of using any view controller, but it's actually an Apple-approved technique to show video inside a view hierarchy.

We're also going to add two action methods that we want to connect our buttons to. For now, we'll just create empty implementations so that Interface Builder can see them. We'll fill in the actual code later:

```
@IBAction func shootPictureOrVideo(sender: UIButton) {
}

@IBAction func selectExistingPictureOrVideo(sender: UIButton) {
}
```

The layout we're going to build for this application is very simple — just an image view and two buttons. The finished layout is shown in Figure 6-4. Use this as a guide as you work.

CHAPTER 6 USING THE CAMERA AND ACCESSING PHOTOS

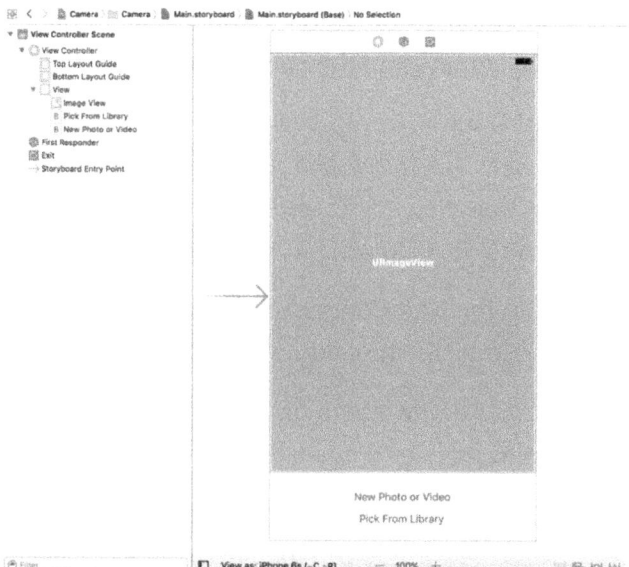

Figure 6-4. *The storyboard layout for our Camera application*

Drag two Buttons from the library and drop them onto the view in the storyboard. Place them one above the other, aligning the bottom button with the bottom blue guideline. Double-click the top button and give it a title of New Photo or Video. Now double-click the bottom button and give it a title of Pick from Library. Next, drag an Image View from the library and place it above the buttons. Expand the image view to take up the entire space of the view above the buttons, as shown earlier in Figure 6-3. In the Attributes Inspector, change the image view's background to black and set its Mode to Aspect Fit, which will cause it to resize images so that they fit within its bounds, but maintain their original aspect ratio.

Now Control-drag from the View Controller icon to the image view and select the `imageView` outlet. Drag again from View Controller to the New Photo or Video button and select the `takePictureButton` outlet. Next, select the New Photo or Video button and bring up the connections inspector. Drag from the Touch Up Inside event to View Controller icon, and then select the `shootPictureOrVideo:` action. Now click the Pick from Library button, drag from the Touch Up Inside event in the connections inspector to the View Controller icon, and select the `selectExistingPictureOrVideo:` action.

207

The final step, as usual, is to add auto layout constraints. Start by expanding the view controller in the Document Outline and then add constraints as follows:

1. In the Document Outline, Control-drag from the Pick from Library button to its parent view, and then release the mouse. When the pop-up appears, hold down Shift and select Center Horizontally in Container and Vertical Spacing to Bottom Layout Guide.

2. Control-drag from the New Photo or Video button to the Pick from Library button, release the mouse, and select Vertical Spacing.

3. Control-drag from the New Photo or Video button to its parent view, release the mouse, hold down the Shift key, and select Center Horizontally in Container.

4. Control-drag from New Photo or Video to the image view and select Vertical Spacing.

5. Control-drag from the image view to its parent view and use the Shift key to select Leading Space to Container Margin, Trailing Space to Container Margin, and Vertical Spacing to Top Layout Guide.

All of the layout constraints should now be in place, so save your changes.

Privacy Options

Because we're planning on using the camera, and that bit of hardware is protected by iOS, we'll have to ask the user's permission to do so. Similarly, because we plan on taking video, we'll want to have access to the microphone… unless we're only interested in silent movies. And we'll also want to access the photo library. Fortunately, iOS handles much of this for us as long as we properly request what we need. To do so requires adding a couple of lines to the Info.plist file.

Since we've accessed our property list a few times before, simply add the three bottom entries as shown in Figure 6-5. The text in the rightmost column is what will be displayed to the user as additional information about the request to use a specific resource. As such, it helps to be clear and succinct.

CHAPTER 6   USING THE CAMERA AND ACCESSING PHOTOS

▶ Supported interface orientations	Array	(3 items)
▶ Supported interface orientations (i...	Array	(4 items)
Privacy - Camera Usage Description	String	My App Would Like to access the camera
Privacy - Microphone Usage Desc...	String	My App would also like to use the mic
Privacy - Photo Library Usage Des...	String	My App would like to look at your pictures

Figure 6-5. *Add the privacy options for the camera and microphone to the Info.plist file*

When the app needs to access one of the three resources, the user is presented a message like that shown in Figure 6-6.

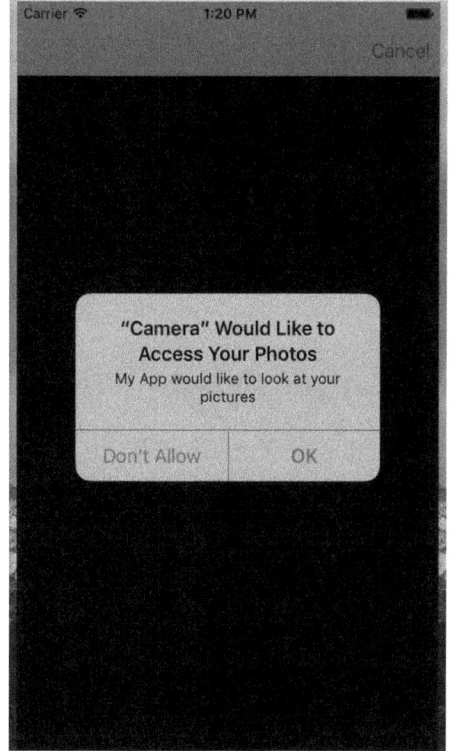

Figure 6-6. *iOS will take care of making requests to the user, but you'll want to make it clear as to why your app is needing a specific resource*

CHAPTER 6   USING THE CAMERA AND ACCESSING PHOTOS

Implementing the Camera View Controller

Select ViewController.swift, where we have some more changes to make. Since we're going to allow users to optionally capture a video, we need a property for an `AVPlayerViewController` instance. Two more properties keep track of the last selected image and video, along with a string to determine whether a video or image was the last thing chosen. We also need to import a few additional frameworks to make this all work. Add the bold lines shown here:

import UIKit
import AVKit
import AVFoundation
import MobileCoreServices

```
class ViewController: UIViewController, UIImagePickerControllerDelegate,
                                        UINavigationControllerDelegate {

    @IBOutlet var imageView: UIImageView!
    @IBOutlet var takePictureButton: UIButton!
    @objc var avPlayerViewController: AVPlayerViewController!
    @objc var image: UIImage?
    @objc var movieURL: URL?
    @objc var lastChosenMediaType: String?
```

Now let's enhance the `viewDidLoad()` method, hiding the New Photo or Video button if the device we're running on does not have a camera. We also implement the `viewDidAppear()` method, having it call the `updateDisplay()` method, which we'll implement soon. First, change the viewDidLoad and viewDidAppear methods as shown in Listing 6-4 in ViewController.swift file.

Listing 6-4. Updated viewDidLoad and viewDidAppear Methods

```
    override func viewDidLoad() {
        super.viewDidLoad()
        // Do any additional setup after loading the view, typically from a nib.

        if !UIImagePickerController.isSourceTypeAvailable(
            UIImagePickerControllerSourceType.camera) {
```

CHAPTER 6 USING THE CAMERA AND ACCESSING PHOTOS

```
            takePictureButton.isHidden = true
        }
    }

    override func viewDidAppear(_ animated: Bool) {
        super.viewDidAppear(animated)
        updateDisplay()
    }
```

It's important to understand the distinction between the `viewDidLoad()` and `viewDidAppear()` methods. The former is called only when the view has just been loaded into memory. The latter is called every time the view is displayed, which happens both at launch and whenever we return to our controller after showing another full-screen view, such as the image picker.

Next up are three utility methods, the first of which is the `updateDisplay()` method. It is called from the `viewDidAppear()` method, which is called both when the view is first created and again after the user picks an image or video and dismisses the image picker. Because of this dual usage, it needs to make a few checks to see what's what and set up the GUI accordingly. Add the code in Listing 6-5 toward the bottom of the ViewController.swift file.

Listing 6-5. The updateDisplay Method

```
    @objc func updateDisplay() {
        if let mediaType = lastChosenMediaType {
            if mediaType == kUTTypeImage as NSString {
                imageView.image = image!
                imageView.isHidden = false
                if avPlayerViewController != nil {
                    avPlayerViewController!.view.isHidden = true
                }
            } else if mediaType == kUTTypeMovie as NSString {
                if avPlayerViewController == nil {
                    avPlayerViewController = AVPlayerViewController()
                    let avPlayerView = avPlayerViewController!.view
                    avPlayerView?.frame = imageView.frame
                    avPlayerView?.clipsToBounds = true
```

211

CHAPTER 6   USING THE CAMERA AND ACCESSING PHOTOS

```
            view.addSubview(avPlayerView!)
            setAVPlayerViewLayoutConstraints()
        }

        if let url = movieURL {
            imageView.isHidden = true
            avPlayerViewController.player = AVPlayer(url: url)
            avPlayerViewController!.view.isHidden = false
            avPlayerViewController!.player!.play()
        }
      }
    }
}
```

This method shows the correct view based on the type of media that the user selected — the image view for a photograph and the AV player for a movie. The image view is always present, but the AV player is created and added to the user interface only when the user picks a movie for the first time. Each time a movie is chosen, we create an `AVPlayer` instance initialized with the movie file's URL and attach it to the `AVPlayerViewController` via its `player` property, and then use the player's `play()` method to start playback.

When we add the AV player, we need to ensure that it occupies the same space as the image view and we need to add layout constraints that ensure that remains the case even if the device is rotated. Here's the code that adds the layout constraints, as shown in Listing 6-6.

Listing 6-6. Setting the AV Player's Layout Constraints in the ViewController.swift File

```
@objc func setAVPlayerViewLayoutConstraints() {
    let avPlayerView = avPlayerViewController!.view
    avPlayerView?.translatesAutoresizingMaskIntoConstraints = false
    let views = ["avPlayerView": avPlayerView!,
                 "takePictureButton": takePictureButton!]
    view.addConstraints(NSLayoutConstraint.constraints(
            withVisualFormat: "H:|[avPlayerView]|", options:
            .alignAllLeft,
```

```
                metrics:nil, views:views))
    view.addConstraints(NSLayoutConstraint.constraints(
                withVisualFormat: "V:|[avPlayerView]-0-
                [takePictureButton]",
                options: .alignAllLeft, metrics:nil, views:views))
}
```

The horizontal constraints tie the movie player to the left and right sides of the main view, and the vertical constraints link it to the top of the main view and the top of the New Photo or Video button.

The final utility method, `pickMediaFromSource()`, is the one that both of our action methods call. This method is pretty simple. It just creates and configures an image picker, using the passed-in `sourceType` to determine whether to bring up the camera or the media library. We do so by adding the code in Listing 6-7 to the bottom of the ViewController.swift file.

Listing 6-7. The pickMediaFromSource Method in the ViewController.swift File

```
@objc func pickMediaFromSource(_ sourceType:UIImagePickerControllerSourceType) {
    let mediaTypes =
            UIImagePickerController.availableMediaTypes(for: sourceType)!
    if UIImagePickerController.isSourceTypeAvailable(sourceType)
                && mediaTypes.count > 0 {
        let picker = UIImagePickerController()
        picker.mediaTypes = mediaTypes
        picker.delegate = self
        picker.allowsEditing = true
        picker.sourceType = sourceType
        present(picker, animated: true, completion: nil)
    } else {
        let alertController = UIAlertController(title:"Error accessing media",
                        message: "Unsupported media source.",
                        preferredStyle: UIAlertControllerStyle.alert)
        let okAction = UIAlertAction(title: "OK",
                        style: UIAlertActionStyle.cancel, handler: nil)
                        alertController.addAction(okAction)
```

CHAPTER 6　USING THE CAMERA AND ACCESSING PHOTOS

```
            present(alertController, animated: true, completion: nil)
    }
}
```

Next, implement the action methods that are linked to the buttons:

```
@IBAction func shootPictureOrVideo(_ sender: UIButton) {
    pickMediaFromSource(UIImagePickerControllerSourceType.camera)
}

@IBAction func selectExistingPictureOrVideo(_ sender: UIButton) {
    pickMediaFromSource(UIImagePickerControllerSourceType.photoLibrary)
}
```

Each of these simply calls out to the `pickMediaFromSource()` method, passing in a constant defined by `UIImagePickerController` to specify where the picture or video should come from.

Now it's finally time to implement the delegate methods for the picker view, as shown in Listing 6-8.

Listing 6-8. *Our Picker View's Delegate Methods*

```
func imagePickerController(_ picker: UIImagePickerController,
            didFinishPickingMediaWithInfo info: [String : AnyObject]) {
    lastChosenMediaType = info[UIImagePickerControllerMediaType] as? String
    if let mediaType = lastChosenMediaType {
        if mediaType == kUTTypeImage as NSString {
            image = info[UIImagePickerControllerEditedImage] as? UIImage
        } else if mediaType == kUTTypeMovie as NSString {
            movieURL = info[UIImagePickerControllerMediaURL] as? URL
        }
    }
    picker.dismiss(animated: true, completion: nil)
}

func imagePickerControllerDidCancel(_ picker: UIImagePickerController) {
    picker.dismiss(animated: true, completion:nil)
}
```

The first delegate method uses the values passed in the `info` dictionary to check whether a picture or video was chosen, makes note of the selection, and then dismisses the modal image picker. If the image is larger than the available space on the screen, it will be resized by the image view when it's displayed, because we set the image view's content mode to Aspect Fit when we created it. The second delegate method is called when the user cancels the image picking process and just dismisses the image picker.

That's all you need to do. Compile and run the app. If you're running on the simulator, you won't have the option to take a new picture, but will only be able to choose from the photo library — as if you had any photos in your simulator's photo library! If you have the opportunity to run the application on a real device, go ahead and try it. You should be able to take a new picture or movie, and zoom in and out of the picture using the pinch gestures. The first time the app needs to access the user's photos on iOS, the user will be asked to allow this access; this is a privacy feature that was added back in iOS 6 to make sure that apps aren't sneakily grabbing photos without users' consent.

After choosing or taking a photo, if you zoom in and pan around before hitting the Use Photo button, the cropped image will be the one returned to the application in the delegate method.

Summary

Believe it or not, that's all there is to letting your users take pictures with the camera so that the pictures can be used by your application. You can even let the user do a small amount of editing on that image if you so choose.

In the next chapter, we're going to look at reaching a larger audience for your iOS applications by making them oh-so-easy to translate into other languages.

CHAPTER 7

Translating Apps Using Localization

At the time of this writing, you'll find iOS devices available in about half the world's countries, with that number continuing to increase over time (see Figure 7-1). Available on every continent except Antarctica, the iPad and iPod touch continue to sell all over the world and are nearly as ubiquitous as the iPhone. If you plan on releasing applications through the App Store, think about more than just people in your own country who speak your own language. Fortunately, iOS provides a robust **localization** architecture letting you easily translate your application (or have it translated by others) into, not only multiple languages, but even into multiple dialects of the same language. Providing different terminology to English speakers in the United Kingdom as opposed to the United States no longer represents a problem.

Figure 7-1. *With iOS devices available in over half the world, developing for multiple languages puts your app in a more favorable position to be the success you want it to be*

Localization presents minimal issues if you've written your code correctly whereas retrofitting an existing application to support localization increases the amount of work needed to get it right. In this chapter, I'll show you how to write your code so it is easy to localize, and then we'll go about localizing a sample application.

Localization Architecture

When an application that has not been configured for localization executes, all of its text gets presented in the developer's own language, also known as the **development base language**. When developers decide to localize their applications, they create a subdirectory in their application bundle for each supported language. Each language's subdirectory contains a subset of the application's resources that were translated into that language. Each subdirectory is called a **localization project**, or **localization folder**. Localization folder names always end with the .lproj extension.

In the iOS Settings application, the user has the ability to set the device's preferred language and region format. For example, if the user's language is English, available regions might be the United States, Australia, and Hong Kong — all regions where English is spoken.

When a localized application needs to load a resource — such as an image, property list, or nib — the application checks the user's language and region, and then looks for a localization folder that matches that setting. If it finds one, it loads the localized version of the resource instead of the base version. For users who select French as their iOS language and Switzerland as their region, the application will look first for a localization folder named fr-CH.lproj. The first two letters of the folder name are the ISO country code that represents the French language. The two letters following the hyphen are the ISO code that represents Switzerland.

If the application cannot find a match using the two-letter code, it will look for a match using the language's three-letter ISO code. In our example, if the application is unable to find a folder named fr-CH.lproj, it looks for a folder named fre-CH or fra-CH.

All languages have at least one three-letter code. Some have two three-letter codes: one for the English spelling of the language and another for the native spelling. Some languages have only two-letter codes but when a language has both a two-letter code and a three-letter code, the two-letter code is preferred.

> **Note** You can find a list of the current ISO country codes on the ISO web site www.iso.org/iso/country_codes.htm. Both the two- and three-letter codes are part of the ISO 3166 standard.

If the application cannot find a folder with an exact match, it looks for a localization folder in the application bundle matching just the language code without the region code. So, staying with French, the application next looks for a localization folder called fr.lproj. If it doesn't find a language folder with that name, it will look for fre.lproj and then fra.lproj. If none of those are found, it checks for French.lproj. The last construct exists to support legacy Mac OS X applications; generally speaking, you should avoid it.

If the application doesn't find a matching folder for either the language/region combination or just the language, it uses the resources from the development base language. If it does find an appropriate localization folder, it then always looks there first for any resources that it needs. If you load a UIImage using imageNamed(), for example, the application will look first for an image with the specified name in the localization folder. If it finds one, it will use that image. If it doesn't, it falls back to the base language resource.

If an application has more than one localization folder that matches — for example, a folder called fr-CH.lproj and one called fr.lproj—it searches first in the more specific match, fr-CH.lproj, if the user has selected Swiss French as their preferred language. If it doesn't find the resource there, it looks in fr.lproj. This gives you the ability to provide resources common to all speakers of a language in one folder, localizing only those resources impacted by differences in dialect or geographic region.

You should choose to localize only those resources affected by language or country. For example, if an image in your application has no words and its meaning is universal, there's no need to localize that image.

Strings Files

What do you do about string literals and string constants in your source code? Consider the source code as shown in Listing 7-1.

Listing 7-1. Example of String Literals and Constants

```
let alertController = UIAlertController(title: "Location Manager Error",
                            message: errorType, preferredStyle: .alert)
let okAction = UIAlertAction(title: "OK", style: .cancel,
                            handler: nil)
alertController.addAction(okAction)
self.presentViewController(alertController, animated: true,
                            completion: nil)
```

If you've gone through the effort of localizing your application for a particular audience, you certainly don't want to be presenting alerts written in the development base language. The answer is to store these strings in special text files called **strings files**.

The Strings File

Strings files are nothing more than Unicode text files that contain a list of string pairs, each identified by a comment. Listing 7-2 shows an example of what a strings file might look like in your application.

Listing 7-2. Example Strings File

```
/* Used to ask the user his/her first name */
"LABEL_FIRST_NAME" = "First Name";

/* Used to get the user's last name */
"LABEL_LAST_NAME" = "Last Name";

/* Used to ask the user's birth date */
"LABEL_BIRTHDAY" = "Birthday";
```

The values between the /* and the */ characters are comments for the translator. They are not used in the application; you could skip adding them, although they are a good idea. The comments give context, showing how a particular string is being used in the application. You'll notice that each line is in two parts, separated by an equals sign. The string on the left side of the equal sign acts as a key, and it will always contain the same value, regardless of language. The value on the right side of the equal sign is the one that is translated to the local language. So, the preceding strings file, localized into French, might look like Listing 7-3.

Listing 7-3. A French Version of the Strings File

```
/* Used to ask the user his/her first name */
"LABEL_FIRST_NAME " = "Prénom";

/* Used to get the user's last name */
"LABEL_LAST_NAME" = "Nom de famille";

/* Used to ask the user's birth date */
"LABEL_BIRTHDAY" = "Anniversaire";
```

The Localized String Function

At runtime, you'll get the localized versions of the strings that you need by using the `NSLocalizedString()` function. Once your source code is final and ready for localization, Xcode searches all your code files for occurrences of this function, pulls out all the unique strings, and embeds them into a file that you send to a translator, or you can add the translations yourself. Once that's completed, you'll have Xcode import the updated file and use its content to create the localized string files for the languages for which you have provided translations. Let's see how the first part of this process works. First, here's a traditional string declaration: `let myString = "First Name"`.

To make this string localizable:

```
let myString = NSLocalizedString("LABEL_FIRST_NAME",
                    comment: "Used to ask the user his/her first name")
```

The `NSLocalizedString()` macro takes five parameters, but three of them have defaults, good enough in most cases, so usually you only need to provide two:

- The first parameter is a key that will be used to look for the localized string. If there is no localization that contains text for the key, the application will use the key itself as the localized text.

- The second parameter is used as a comment to explain how the text is being used. The comment will appear in the file sent to the translator and in the localized strings file after import.

NSLocalizedString() searches in the application bundle within the appropriate localization folder for a strings file named Localizable.strings. If it does not find the file, it returns its first parameter, which is the key for the text that was required. If NSLocalizedString() finds the strings file, it searches the file for a line that matches its first parameter. In the preceding example, NSLocalizedString() will search the strings file for the string "LABEL_FIRST_NAME". If it doesn't find a match in the localization folder that matches the user's language settings, it will then look for a strings file in the base language and use the value there. If there is no strings file, it will just use the first parameter you passed to the NSLocalizedString() function.

You could use the base language text as the key for the NSLocalizedString() function because it returns the key if no matching localized text can be found. This would make the preceding example look like the following:

```
let myString = NSLocalizedString("First Name",
                comment: "Used to ask the user his/her first name")
```

We don't recommend this approach for two reasons. First, you most likely won't come up with the perfect keys on the first attempt, having to go back and change them in in the strings files, a cumbersome and error-prone effort, still ending up with keys that do not match what is used in the app. The second reason is that, by clearly using uppercase keys, you can immediately notice if you have forgotten to localize any text when you run the app just by looking at it.

Now that you have an idea of how the localization architecture and the strings file work, let's take a look at localization in action.

Creating the LocalizeMe App

We'll create a small application that displays the user's current **locale**. A locale (an instance of NSLocale) represents both the user's language and region. The system uses the locale to determine which language to use when interacting with the user, as well as how to display dates, currency, and time information, among other things. After creating the application, we'll localize it into other languages, learning how to localize storyboard files, strings files, images, and even the application's display name.

Figure 7-2 depicts what our app will look like showing the name across the top that comes from the user's locale. The ordinals down the left side of the view are static labels, and their values will be set by localizing the storyboard file. The words down the right side, and the flag image at the bottom of the screen, will all be chosen in our app's code at runtime based on the user's preferred language.

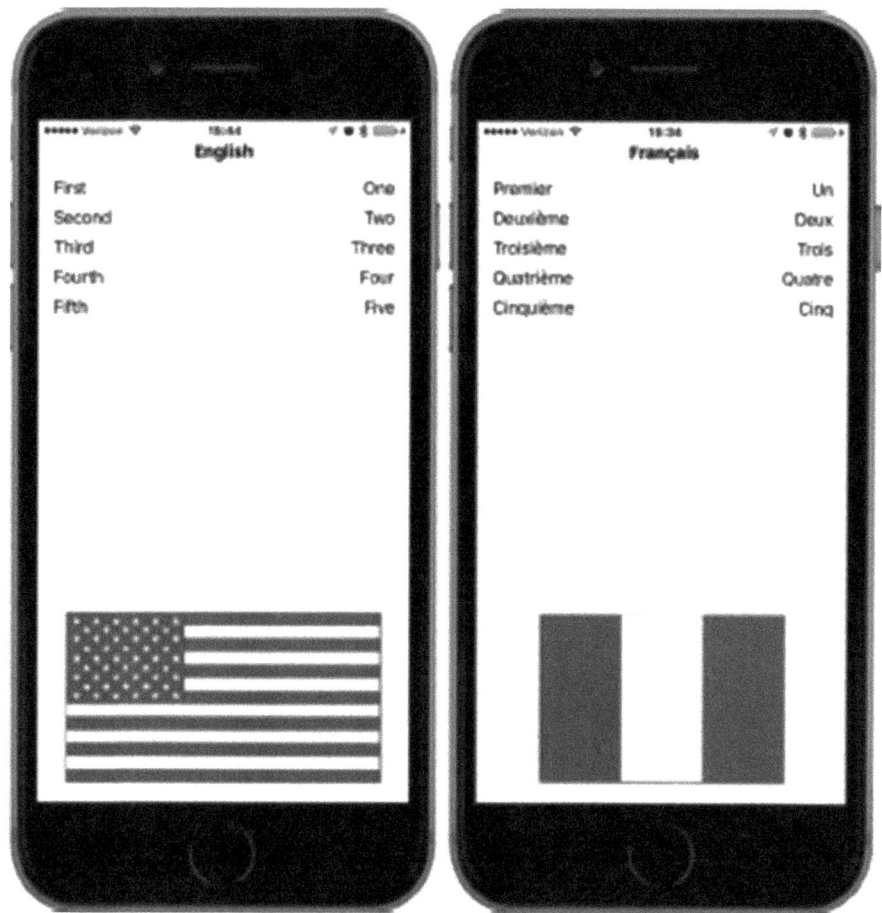

Figure 7-2. *The LocalizeMe application shown with two different language settings*

Create a new project in Xcode using the Single View Application template and call it LocalizeMe. If you look in the folder 22 - Images in the example source code, you'll find a pair of images named flag_usa.png and flag_france.png. In Xcode, select the Assets.xcassets item, and then drag both flag_usa.png and flag_france.png into it. Now let's add some label outlets to the project's view controller. We need to create one outlet for the label across the top of the view, another for the image view that will show a flag, and an outlet collection for all the words down the right-hand side (see Figure 7-2). Select ViewController.swift and make the following changes:

```
class ViewController: UIViewController {
    @IBOutlet var localeLabel : UILabel!
    @IBOutlet var flagImageView : UIImageView!
    @IBOutlet var labels : [UILabel]!
```

Select Main.storyboard to edit the GUI in Interface Builder. Drag a label from the library, dropping it at the top of the main view, aligned with the top blue guideline. Resize the label so that it takes the entire width of the view, from the left margin guideline to the right margin guideline. With the label selected, open the Attributes Inspector. Look for the Font control and click the small T icon it contains to bring up a small font-selection pop-up. Click the Style selector and change it to Bold to make the title label stand out a bit from the rest. Next, use the Attributes Inspector to set the text alignment to centered. You can also use the font selector to make the font size larger if you wish. As long as Autoshrink is set to Minimum Font Size in the object Attributes Inspector, the text will be resized if it gets too long to fit. With your label in place, Control-drag from the View Controller icon in the Document Outline (or the one in the storyboard) to this new label, and then select the `localeLabel` outlet.

Next, drag five more labels from the library and put them against the left margin using the blue guideline, one above the other (again, see Figure 7-2). Double-click the top one and change its text from Label to First. Repeat this procedure with the other four labels, changing the text to the words Second, Third, Fourth, and Fifth. Make sure that all five labels are aligned to the left margin guideline.

Drag another five labels from the library, this time placing them against the right margin. Change the text alignment using the object Attributes Inspector so that they are right-aligned. Control-drag from View Controller to each of the five new labels, connecting each one to the labels outlet collection, and making sure to connect them in the right order from top to bottom.

Drag an Image View from the library over to the bottom part of the view, so that it touches the bottom and left blue guidelines. In the Attributes Inspector, select `flag_usa` for the view's `Image` attribute and resize the image horizontally to stretch from blue guideline to blue guideline, and vertically so that it is about a third of the height of the user interface. In the Attributes Inspector, change the `Mode` attribute from its current value to Aspect Fit. Not all flags have the same aspect ratio, and we want to make sure the

CHAPTER 7 TRANSLATING APPS USING LOCALIZATION

localized versions of the image look right. Selecting this option will cause the image view to resize any images that it displays so they fit, but it will also maintain the correct aspect ratio (height to width). Now Control-drag from the view controller to this image view and select the `flagImageView` outlet.

To complete the user interface, we need to set the auto layout constraints. Starting with the label at the top, Control-drag from it to its parent view in the Document Outline, press the Shift key, select Leading Space to Container Margin, Trailing Space to Container Margin, and Vertical Spacing to Top Layout Guide, and press Return.

Next, we'll fix the positions of each of the five rows of labels. Control-drag from the label with the text First to its parent view in the Document Outline, select both Leading Space to Container Margin and Vertical Spacing to Top Layout Guide, and press Return. Control-drag from the label to the label on the same row to its right and select Baseline, and then Control-drag from the label on the right to its parent view in the Document Outline and select Trailing Space to Container Margin.

We've now positioned the top row of labels. Let's do exactly the same thing for the other four rows. Next, select all of the five labels on the right by holding down the Shift key while clicking them with the mouse, and then Editor ➤ Size to Fit Content. Finally, clear the text from all of these labels because we will be setting it from our code.

To fix the position and size of the flag, Control-drag from the flag label to its parent view in the Document Outline, select Leading Space to Container Margin, Trailing Space to Container Margin, and Vertical Spacing to Bottom Layout Guide, and press Return. With the flag label still selected, click the Pin button, check the Height check box in the pop-up, and press Add 1 Constraint. You have now added all of the auto layout constraints that we need.

Save your storyboard, and then switch to ViewController.swift and add the code from Listing 7-4 to the `viewDidLoad()` method.

Listing 7-4. Modify the viewDidLoad Method As Shown

```
override func viewDidLoad() {
    super.viewDidLoad()
    // Do any additional setup after loading the view, typically from a nib.
    let locale = Locale.current
    let currentLangID = Locale.preferredLanguages[0]
    let displayLang = locale.displayName(forKey: Locale.Key.languageCode, value: currentLangID)
```

```
        let capitalized = displayLang?.capitalized(with: locale)
        localeLabel.text = capitalized

        labels[0].text = NSLocalizedString("LABEL_ONE", comment:
        "The number 1")
        labels[1].text = NSLocalizedString("LABEL_TWO", comment:
        "The number 2")
        labels[2].text = NSLocalizedString("LABEL_THREE", comment:
        "The number 3")
        labels[3].text = NSLocalizedString("LABEL_FOUR", comment:
        "The number 4")
        labels[4].text = NSLocalizedString("LABEL_FIVE", comment:
        "The number 5")

        let flagFile = NSLocalizedString("FLAG_FILE", comment: "Name of
        the flag")
        flagImageView.image = UIImage(named: flagFile)
    }
```

The first thing we do in this code is get an NSLocale instance (remembering that the new version of Xcode and Swift supports much more user-friendly names such as Locale though technically, it's still an NSLocale) that represents the user's current locale. This instance tells us both the user's language and region preferences, as set in the device's Settings application:

```
        let locale = Locale.current
```

Next, we grab the user's preferred language. This gives us a two-character code, such as "en" or "fr," or a string like "fr_CH" for a regional language variant:

```
        let currentLangID = Locale.preferredLanguages[0]
```

The next line of code might need a bit of explanation:

```
        let displayLang = locale.displayName(forKey: Locale.Key.
        languageCode, value: currentLangID)
```

NSLocale works somewhat like a dictionary. It can give you a whole bunch of information about the current user's locale, including the name of the currency and the expected date format. You can find a complete list of the information that you can retrieve in the NSLocale API reference. Here, we're using a method called displayName(forKey value:) to retrieve the actual name of the chosen language, translated into the language of the current locale itself. The purpose of this method is to return the value of the item we've requested in a specific language.

The display name for the French language, for example, is *français* in French, but French in English. This method gives you the ability to retrieve data about any locale, so that it can be displayed appropriately for all users. In this case, we want the display name of the user's preferred language in the language currently being used, which is why we pass currentLangID as the second argument. This string is a two-letter language code, similar to the one we used earlier to create our language projects. For an English speaker, it would be en; and for a French speaker, it would be fr.

The name we get back from this call is going to be something like "English" or "français" — and it will only be capitalized if language names are always capitalized in the user's preferred language. That's the case in English, but not so in French. We want the name capitalized for displaying as a title, however. Fortunately, NSString has methods for capitalizing strings, including one that will capitalize a string according to the rules of a given locale! Let's use that to turn *français* into *Français*:

```
let capitalized = displayLang?.capitalized(with: locale)
```

Here, we are using the fact that the Objective-C class NSString and Swift's String are transparently bridged to call the capitalizedStringWithLocale() method of NSString on our String instance. Once we have the display name, we use it to set the top label in the view:

```
localeLabel.text = capitalized
```

Next, we set the five other labels to the numbers 1 through 5, spelled out in our development base language. We use the NSLocalizedString() function to get the text for these labels, passing it the key and a comment indicating what each word is. You can just pass an empty string for the comment if the words are obvious, as they are here; however, any string you pass in the second argument will be turned into a comment in the strings file, so you can use this comment to communicate with the person doing your translations:

```
labels[0].text = NSLocalizedString("LABEL_ONE", comment:
"The number 1")
labels[1].text = NSLocalizedString("LABEL_TWO", comment:
"The number 2")
labels[2].text = NSLocalizedString("LABEL_THREE", comment:
"The number 3")
labels[3].text = NSLocalizedString("LABEL_FOUR", comment:
"The number 4")
labels[4].text = NSLocalizedString("LABEL_FIVE", comment:
"The number 5")
```

Finally, we do another string lookup to find the name of the flag image to use and populate our image view with the named image:

```
let flagFile = NSLocalizedString("FLAG_FILE", comment: "Name of
the flag")
flagImageView.image = UIImage(named: flagFile)
```

Build and run the application and it should appear similar to Figure 7-3 providing your base language is English.

CHAPTER 7 TRANSLATING APPS USING LOCALIZATION

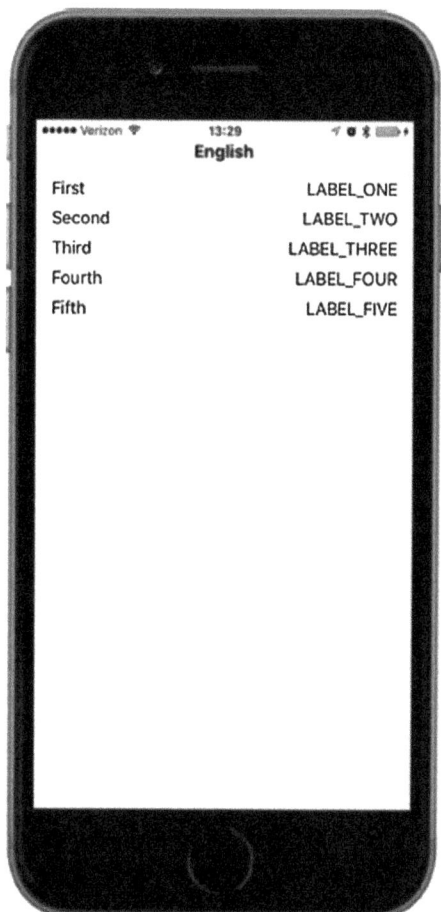

Figure 7-3. *The language running under the authors' base language. The application is set up for localization, but it is not yet localized.*

Because we used the `NSLocalizedString()` function instead of static strings, we are now ready for localization. However, we are not localized yet, as is glaringly obvious from the uppercase labels in the right column and the lack of a flag image at the bottom. If you use the Settings application on the simulator or on your iOS device to change to another language or region, the results look essentially the same, except for the label at the top of the view, as shown in Figure 7-4. If you're not sure how to change the language, hold off for now and we'll get to that shortly.

229

CHAPTER 7 TRANSLATING APPS USING LOCALIZATION

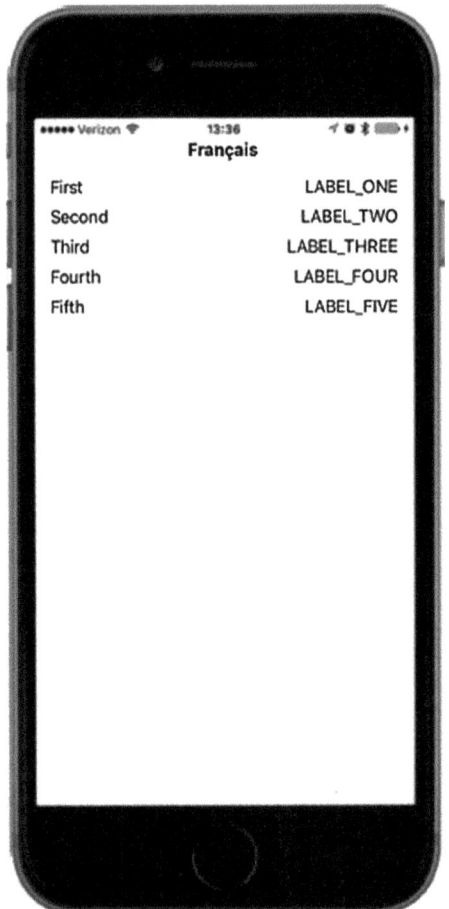

Figure 7-4. *The nonlocalized application running on an iPhone and set to use the French language*

Localizing the Project

Now let's localize the project. In the Xcode Project Navigator, single-click LocalizeMe, click the LocalizeMe project (not one of the targets) in the editing area, and then select the Info tab for the project. Look for the Localizations section in the Info tab. You'll see that it shows one localization, which is for your development language — in my case, that's English. This localization is usually referred to as the base localization and it's added automatically when Xcode creates a project. We want to add French, so click the plus (+) button at the bottom of the Localizations section and select French (fr) from the pop-up list that appears (see Figure 7-5).

CHAPTER 7   TRANSLATING APPS USING LOCALIZATION

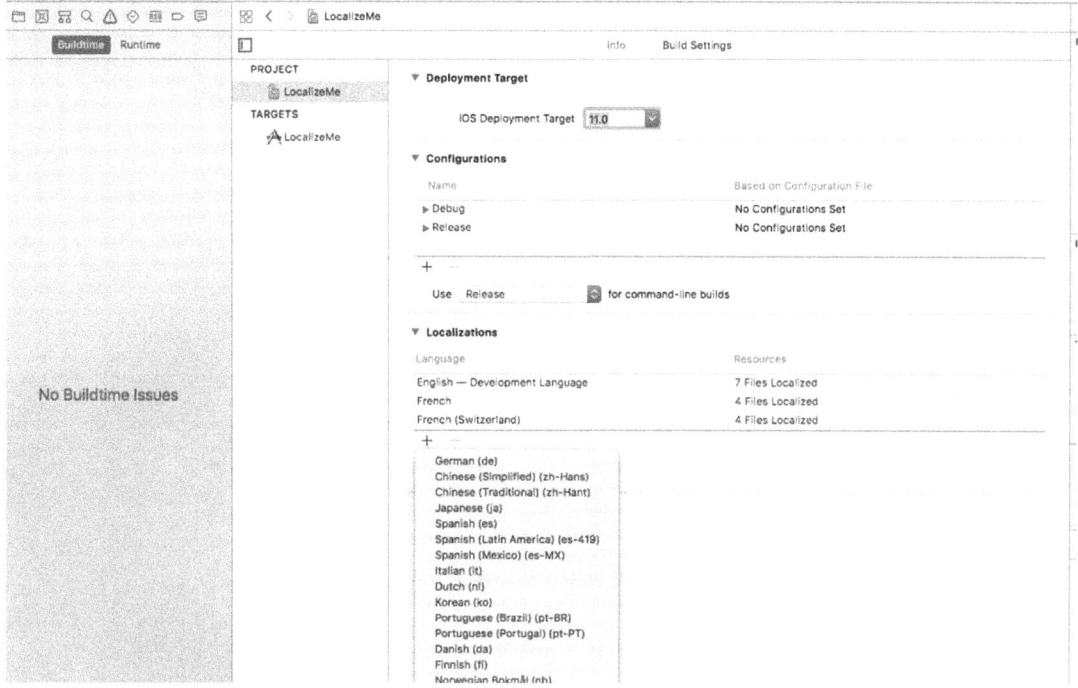

Figure 7-5. *The project info settings showing localizations and other information*

Next, you will be asked to choose all existing localizable files that you want to localize and which existing localization you want the new French localization to start from (see Figure 7-6). Sometimes when you add a new language, it is advantageous to start with the files for the new language based on those of another one for which you already have a localization: for example, to create a Swiss French localization in a project that's already been translated into French (as we will, later in this chapter), you would almost certainly prefer to use the existing French localization as the start point instead of your base language. You would do this by selecting French as the Reference Language when you add the Swiss French localization. Right now, though, there are only two files to be localized and one choice of starting point language (your base language), so just leave everything as it is and click Finish.

231

CHAPTER 7 TRANSLATING APPS USING LOCALIZATION

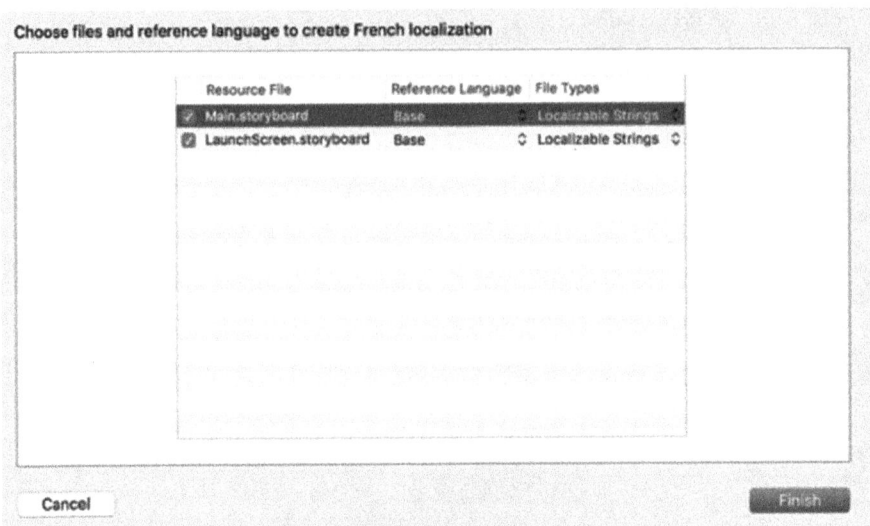

Figure 7-6. *Choosing the files for localization*

Now that you've added a French localization, take a look at the Project Navigator. Notice that the Main.storyboard and Launch.storyboard files now have a disclosure triangle next to them, as if they were a group or folder. Expand them and take a look, as shown in Figure 7-7.

CHAPTER 7 TRANSLATING APPS USING LOCALIZATION

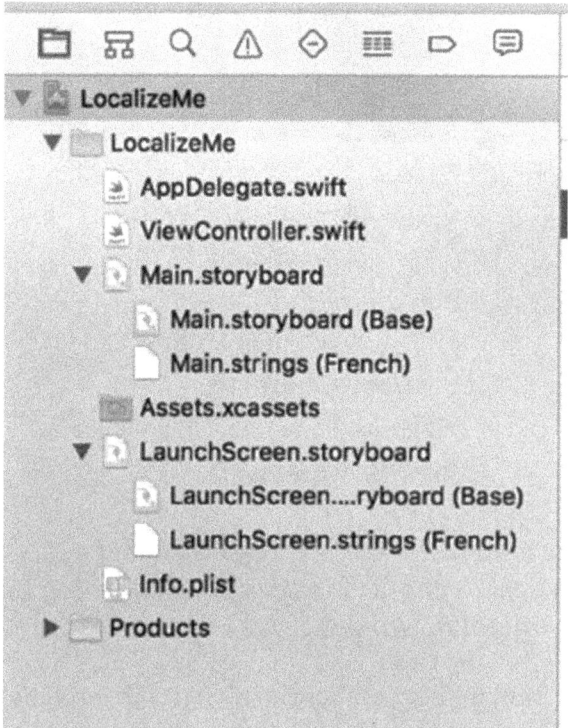

Figure 7-7. *Localizable files have a disclosure triangle and a child value for each language or region you add*

In our project, Main.storyboard is now shown as a group containing two children. The first is called Main.Storyboard and tagged as Base; the second is called Main.strings and tagged as French. The Base version was created automatically when you created the project, and it represents your development base language. The same applies to the LaunchScreen.storyboard file. These files actually live in two different folders: one called Base.lproj and one called fr.lproj. Go to the Finder and open the LocalizeMe folder within your LocalizeMe project folder. In addition to all your project files, you should see folders named Base.lproj and fr.lproj, as shown in Figure 7-8.

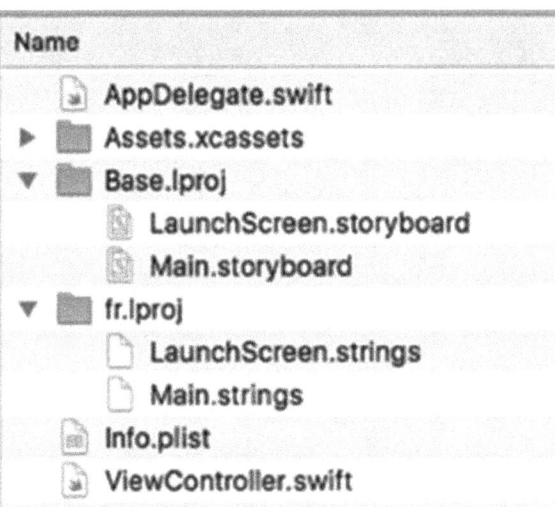

Figure 7-8. *From the outset, our Xcode project included a Base language project folder (Base.lproj). When we chose to make a file localizable, Xcode created a language folder (fr.lproj) for the language we selected.*

Note that the Base.lproj folder was there all along, with its copies of Main.storyboard and LaunchScreen.storyboard inside it. When Xcode finds a resource that has exactly one localized version, it displays it as a single item. As soon as a file has two or more localized versions, Xcode displays them as a group. When you asked Xcode to create the French localization, it created a new localization folder in your project called fr.lproj and placed in it strings files that contain values extracted from Base.lproj/Main.storyboard and Base.lproj/LaunchScreen.storyboard. Instead of duplicating both files, Xcode just extracts every text string from them and creates strings files ready for localization. When the app is built and run, the values in the localized strings files get pulled in to replace the values in the storyboard and launch screen.

Localizing the Storyboard

In the Xcode Project Navigator, select Main.strings (French) to open the French strings file, the contents of which will be injected into the storyboard shown to French speakers. You'll see something like the following text:

```
/* Class = "UILabel"; text = "Fifth"; ObjectID = "5tN-O9-txB"; */
"5tN-O9-txB.text" = "Fifth";

/* Class = "UILabel"; text = "Third"; ObjectID = "GO5-hd-zou"; */
"GO5-hd-zou.text" = "Third";

/* Class = "UILabel"; text = "Second"; ObjectID = "NCJ-hT-XgS"; */
"NCJ-hT-XgS.text" = "Second";

/* Class = "UILabel"; text = "Fourth"; ObjectID = "Z6w-bO-UO6"; */
"Z6w-bO-UO6.text" = "Fourth";

/* Class = "UILabel"; text = "First"; ObjectID = "kS9-Wx-xgy"; */
"kS9-Wx-xgy.text" = "First";

/* Class = "UILabel"; text = "Label"; ObjectID = "yGf-tY-SVz"; */
"yGf-tY-SVz.text" = "Label";
```

Each of the pairs of lines represents a string that was found in the storyboard. The comment tells you the class of the object that contained the string, the original string itself, and a unique identifier for each object (which will probably be different in your copy of this file). The line after the comment is where you actually want to add the translated string on the right-hand side of the equals sign. You'll see that some of these are ordinals such as First; those come from the labels on the left of Figure 7-4, all of which were given names in the storyboard. The entry with the name Label is for the title label, which we set programmatically, so you don't need to localize it.

Prior to iOS 8, the usual practice was to localize the storyboard by directly editing this file. With iOS 8, you can still do that if you choose, but if you plan to use a professional translator, it's likely to be more convenient to have them translate the storyboard text and the strings in your code at the same time. For that reason, Apple has made it possible to collect all of the strings that need to be translated into one file per language that you can send to your translator. If you plan to use that approach, you would leave the storyboard strings file alone and proceed to the next step, which is described in the next section. It's still possible to modify the storyboard strings file and, if you do so, those changes would not be lost should you need to have your translator make changes or localize additional text. So, just on this occasion, let's localize the storyboard strings in the old-fashioned way. To do so, locate the text for the First, Second, Third, Fourth, and Fifth labels, and then change the string to the right of the equal sign to Premier, Deuxième, Troisième, Quatrième, and Cinquième, respectively (similar to):

```
/* Class = "UILabel"; text = "Fifth"; ObjectID = "5tN-O9-txB"; */
"5tN-O9-txB.text" = "Cinquième";

/* Class = "UILabel"; text = "Third"; ObjectID = "GO5-hd-zou"; */
"GO5-hd-zou.text" = "Troisième";

/* Class = "UILabel"; text = "Second"; ObjectID = "NCJ-hT-XgS"; */
"NCJ-hT-XgS.text" = "Deuxième";

/* Class = "UILabel"; text = "Fourth"; ObjectID = "Z6w-bO-U06"; */
"Z6w-bO-U06.text" = "Quatrième";

/* Class = "UILabel"; text = "First"; ObjectID = "kS9-Wx-xgy"; */
"kS9-Wx-xgy.text" = "Premier";

/* Class = "UILabel"; text = "Label"; ObjectID = "yGf-tY-SVz"; */
"yGf-tY-SVz.text" = "Label";
```

Finally, save the file. Our storyboard is now localized in French. There are three ways to see the effects of this localization on your application — you can preview it in Xcode, use a customized scheme to launch it, or change the active language on the simulator or a real device. Let's look at these options in turn, starting with getting a preview.

Using the Assistant Editor to Preview Localizations

Select Main.storyboard in the Project Navigator and open the Assistant Editor. In the Assistant Editor's jump bar, select Preview ➤ Main.storyboard and you'll see the application as it appears in the base development language, as shown on the left in Figure 7-9.

CHAPTER 7 TRANSLATING APPS USING LOCALIZATION

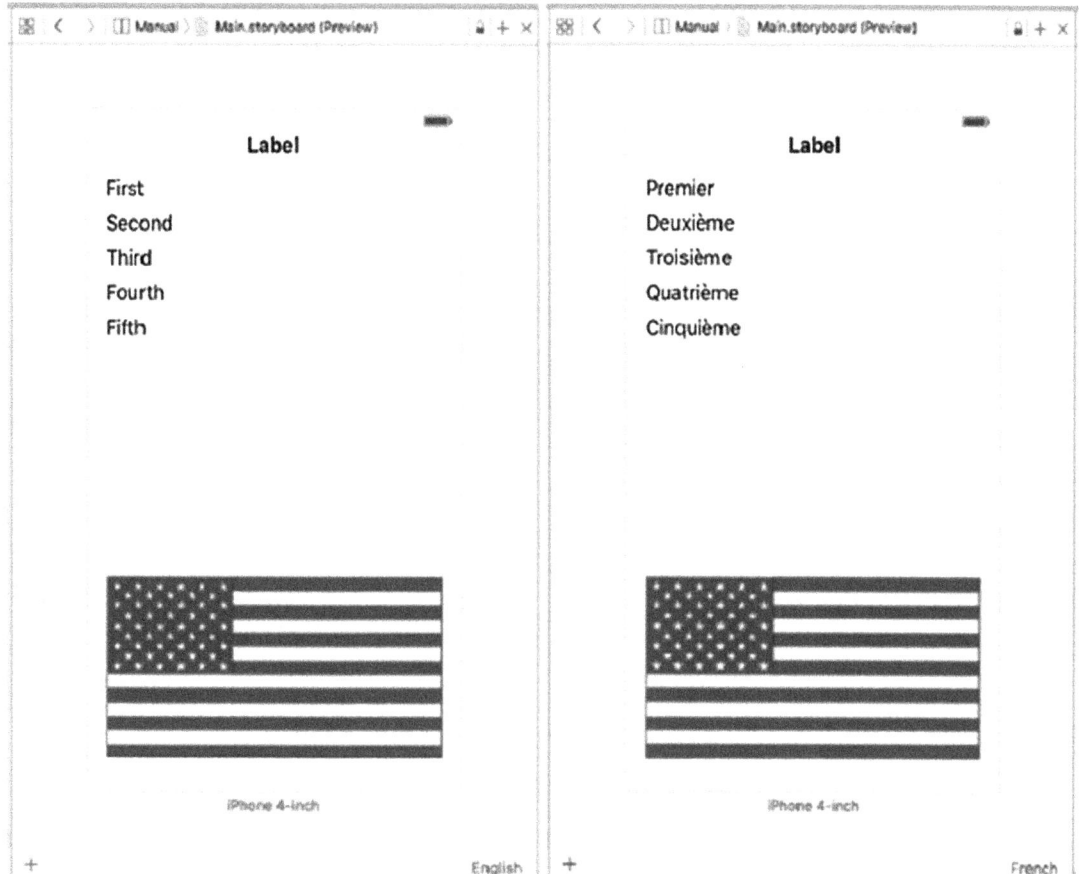

Figure 7-9. *Previewing the application in the base language and in French*

At the bottom right of the Assistant Editor, you'll see that the current language (English) is displayed. Click here to open a pop-up that lists all of the localizations in your project and select French. The preview updates to show how the application appears to a French user, as shown on the right in Figure 7-9, except that the flag is not correct. That's because the preview considers only what's in the localized version of the storyboard, whereas we are actually setting the flag image in code. If you're using code to install localized resources, you'll need to choose one of the other options to get an accurate view.

237

CHAPTER 7 TRANSLATING APPS USING LOCALIZATION

Using a Custom Scheme to Change Language and Region Settings

Creating a customized scheme gives you a quick way to see a localized version of your application running on the simulator or on a real device. Unlike preview, this options lets you see localizations made in code as well as in the storyboard. Start by clicking on the left side of the Scheme selector in Xcode — you'll find it in the top bar, next to the Run and Stop buttons. Currently, the selector should be displaying the text LocalizeMe, which is the name of the current Scheme, and the currently selected device or simulator. When you click LocalizeMe, Xcode opens a pop-up with several options. Choose Manage Schemes... to open the Scheme dialog, as shown in Figure 7-10.

Figure 7-10. The Scheme dialog lets you view, add, and remove schemes

Currently, there is only one scheme. Click the + icon below the scheme list to open another window that allows you to choose a name for your new scheme. Call it `LocalizeMe_fr` and press OK. Back in the Scheme dialog, select your newly created scheme and click Edit... to open the Scheme editor (see Figure 7-11).

238

CHAPTER 7 ■ TRANSLATING APPS USING LOCALIZATION

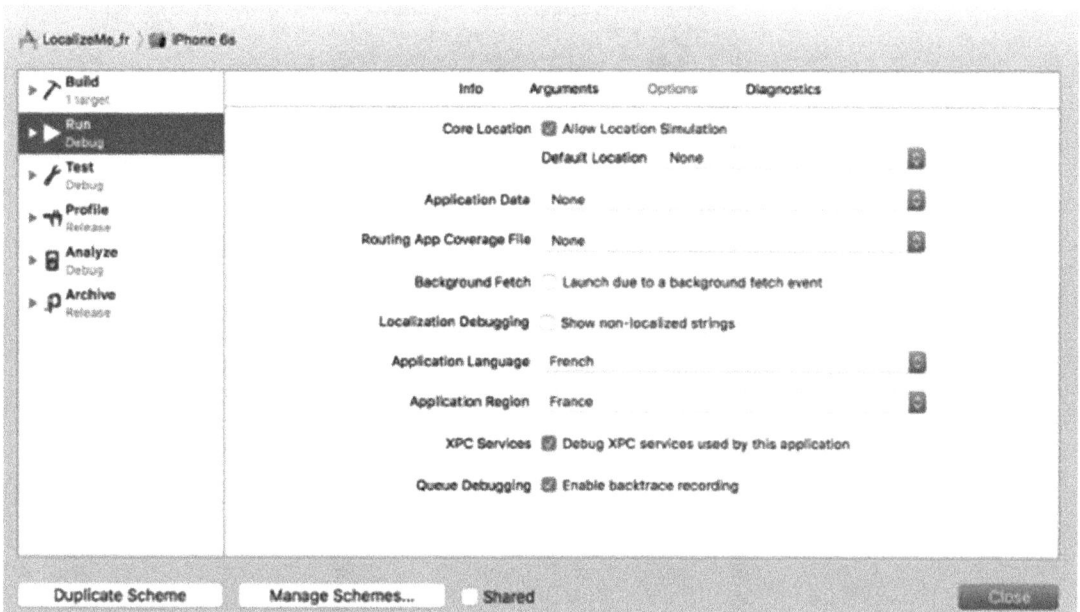

Figure 7-11. *The Scheme editor, with French selected as the Application Language and France as the Application Region*

Make sure that Run is selected in the left column, and then turn your attention to the Application Language and Application Region selectors in the main body of the editor. Here, you can choose the language and region to be used when the application is launched with your custom scheme. Choose French as the language and France as the region, and then click Close. Back in the Xcode main window, you'll see that your new scheme is now selected. Go ahead and run the application and you'll see that the French localization is active, as shown in Figure 7-12.

239

CHAPTER 7　TRANSLATING APPS USING LOCALIZATION

Figure 7-12. *Viewing the current state of the application in French*

As you can see, the flag is missing. Of course, that's because we're installing the flag image in code and we haven't completed the French localization yet. To revert to the base language view, just switch back to the original LocalizeMe scheme and run the application again.

Switching the Language and Region Settings on a Device or Simulator

The final way to see how the application looks in a different language or with different regional settings is to switch those settings in the simulator or on your device. This takes a little more time than either of the other two options, so it's probably better to do this only at the end of the testing cycle, when you are pretty sure that everything works. Here's how to make French the primary language for your device (or simulator).

CHAPTER 7 TRANSLATING APPS USING LOCALIZATION

Go to the Settings application, select the General row, and then select the row labeled Language and Region. From here, you'll be able to change your language and region preferences, as shown in Figure 7-13.

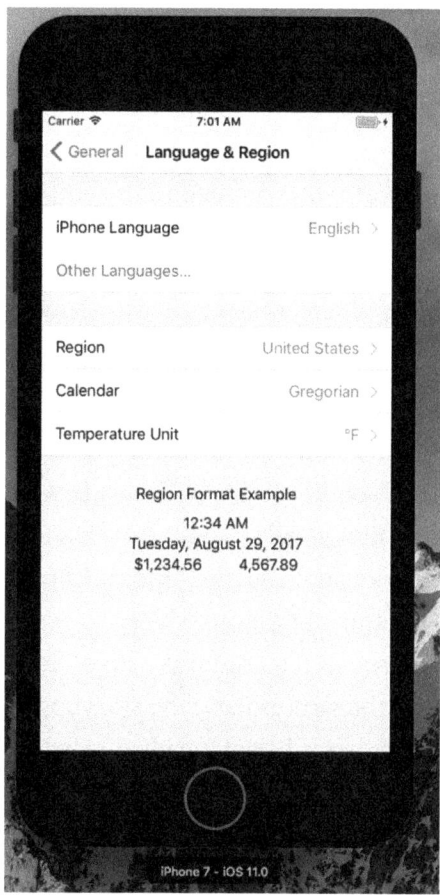

Figure 7-13. *Changing the language or region setting*

Tap iPhone Language to reveal the list of languages into which iOS has been localized, and then find and select the entry for French (which appears in French, as *Français*). You can also change the Region to France for complete authenticity, although that's not necessary for this example since we're not using numbers, dates, or times in our code. Press Done and then confirm that you want the device language to be changed. This will cause the device to do a partial reboot, which will take a few seconds. Now run the app again and you'll see once again that the labels on the left side are showing the localized French text (see Figure 7-12). However, as before, the flag is missing and right-hand column of text is still wrong. We'll take care of those in the next section.

CHAPTER 7   TRANSLATING APPS USING LOCALIZATION

Generating and Localizing a Strings File

In Figure 7-12, the words on the right side of the view are still in SHOUT_ALL_CAPS style because we haven't translated them yet; what you are seeing are the keys that `NSLocalizedString()` is using to look for the localized texts. In order to localize those, we need to first extract the key and comment strings from the code. Fortunately, Xcode makes it easy to extract the text that needs to be localized from your project and put it all in a separate file for each language. Let's see how that works.

In the Project Navigator, select your project. In the editor, select either the project or one of its targets. Now choose Editor ➤ Export for Localization… from the menu. This opens a dialog where you choose which languages you want to localize and where the files for each language should be written. Select a suitable location for the file (for example, in a new folder called XLIFF in the project's root directory), ensure that the check boxes for Existing Translations and French are both selected, and press Save. Xcode creates a file called fr.xliff in a folder called `LocalizeMe` inside the folder that you chose. If you plan to use a third-party service to translate your application's text, it's likely that they can work with XLIFF files — all you should need to do is send them this file, have them update it with the translated strings, and re-import it into Xcode. For now, though, we are going to do the translation ourselves.

Open the fr.xliff file. You'll see that it contains a lot of XML. It breaks down into three different sections that contain the strings from the storyboard, the strings that Xcode found in your source code, and a number of localizable values from your application's Info.plist file. We'll talk about why you need to localize entries from Info.plist later in the chapter. For now, let's translate the text that comes from the application's code. Look through the file and you'll find that text embedded in some XML that looks like this:

```
<file original="LocalizeMe/Localizable.strings" source-language="en"
datatype="plaintext" target-language="fr">
    <header>
      <tool tool-id="com.apple.dt.xcode" tool-name="Xcode"
      tool-version="n.n.n" build-num="nnnnn"/>
    </header>
```

```xml
<body>
  <trans-unit id="FLAG_FILE">
    <source>FLAG_FILE</source>
    <note>Name of the flag</note>
  </trans-unit>
  <trans-unit id="LABEL_FIVE">
    <source>LABEL_FIVE</source>
    <note>The number 5</note>
  </trans-unit>
  <trans-unit id="LABEL_FOUR">
    <source>LABEL_FOUR</source>
    <note>The number 4</note>
  </trans-unit>
  <trans-unit id="LABEL_ONE">
    <source>LABEL_ONE</source>
    <note>The number 1</note>
  </trans-unit>
  <trans-unit id="LABEL_THREE">
    <source>LABEL_THREE</source>
    <note>The number 3</note>
  </trans-unit>
  <trans-unit id="LABEL_TWO">
    <source>LABEL_TWO</source>
    <note>The number 2</note>
  </trans-unit>
</body>
</file>
```

Notice that the `<file>` element has a `target-language` attribute that gives the language into which the text needs to be translated, and that there is a nested `<trans-unit>` element for each string that needs to be translated. Each of them contains a `<source>` element with the original text and a `<note>` element that contains the comment from the `NSLocalizedString()` call in the source code. Professional translators have software tools that present the information in this file and allow them

CHAPTER 7   TRANSLATING APPS USING LOCALIZATION

to enter the translations. We, on the other hand, are going to do it manually by adding <target> elements containing the French text, like this:

```
<file original="LocalizeMe/Localizable.strings" source-language="en" datatype="plaintext" target-language="fr">
    <header>
      <tool tool-id="com.apple.dt.xcode" tool-name="Xcode"
      tool-version="n.n.n" build-num="nnnnn"/>
    </header>
    <body>
      <trans-unit id="FLAG_FILE">
        <source>FLAG_FILE</source>
        <note>Name of the flag</note>
        <target>flag_france</target>
      </trans-unit>
      <trans-unit id="LABEL_FIVE">
        <source>LABEL_FIVE</source>
        <note>The number 5</note>
        <target>Cinq</target>
      </trans-unit>
      <trans-unit id="LABEL_FOUR">
        <source>LABEL_FOUR</source>
        <note>The number 4</note>
        <target>Quatre</target>
      </trans-unit>
      <trans-unit id="LABEL_ONE">
        <source>LABEL_ONE</source>
        <note>The number 1</note>
        <target>Un</target>
      </trans-unit>
      <trans-unit id="LABEL_THREE">
        <source>LABEL_THREE</source>
        <note>The number 3</note>
        <target>Trois</target>
      </trans-unit>
```

```
    <trans-unit id="LABEL_TWO">
      <source>LABEL_TWO</source>
      <note>The number 2</note>
      <target>Deux</target>
    </trans-unit>
  </body>
</file>
```

If you haven't already translated the storyboard strings, you can do that too. You'll find them in a separate block of `<trans-unit>` elements, which are easy to find because of the comments that include the links to the labels from which the text came. On the other hand, if you have done the translations already, you'll find that Xcode included them in the XLIFF file, like this:

```
<trans-unit id="GO5-hd-zou.text">
    <source>Third</source>
    <target>Troisième</target>
    <note>Class = "UILabel"; text = "Third"; ObjectID = "GO5-hd-zou";
    </note>
</trans-unit>
    <trans-unit id="NCJ-hT-XgS.text">
    <source>Second</source>
    <target>Deuxième</target>
    <note>Class = "UILabel"; text = "Second"; ObjectID = "NCJ-hT-XgS";
    </note>
</trans-unit>
```

Save your translations. The next step is to import the results back into Xcode. Make sure that the project is selected in the Project Navigator. Then, choose Editor ➤ Import Localizations in the menu bar, navigate to your file, and open it. Xcode will show you a list of keys that have been translated and their translations. Press Import to complete the import process. If you look at the Project Navigator, you'll see that two files have been added — InfoPlist.strings and Localizable.strings. Open Localizable.strings and you'll see that it contains the French translations of the strings that Xcode extracted from ViewController.swift:

```
/* Name of the flag */
"FLAG_FILE" = "flag_france";

/* The number 5 */
"LABEL_FIVE" = "Cinq";

/* The number 4 */
"LABEL_FOUR" = "Quatre";

/* The number 1 */
"LABEL_ONE" = "Un";

/* The number 3 */
"LABEL_THREE" = "Trois";

/* The number 2 */
"LABEL_TWO" = "Deux";
```

Now, build and run the app with French as the active language. You should see the labels on the right-hand side translated into French and at the bottom of the screen, you should now see the French flag, as shown in Figure 7-14.

CHAPTER 7 TRANSLATING APPS USING LOCALIZATION

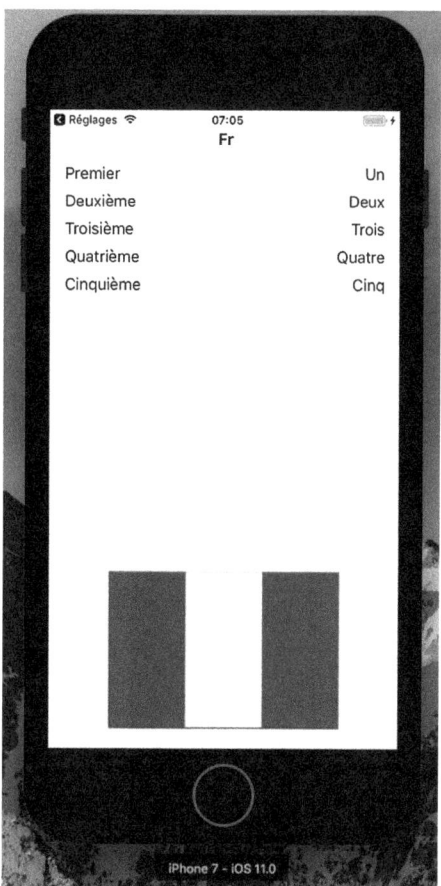

Figure 7-14. *Our properly localized app, for French, including the correct flag*

So are we done yet? Not quite. Rerun the app with English as the active language. You'll see the unlocalized version of the app shown in Figure 7-3. To make the app work in English, we have to localize it for English. To do that, select the Project in the Project Navigator and then select Editor ➤ Export for Localization… from the menu to export strings for localization again; but this time, choose Development Language Only and then press Save. This creates a file called en.xliff, where we'll add the localizations for English. Edit the file and make the following changes:

```
<file original="LocalizeMe/Localizable.strings" source-language="en"
datatype="plaintext">
  <header>
    <tool tool-id="com.apple.dt.xcode" tool-name="Xcode"
    tool-version="n.n.n" build-num="nnnnn"/>
  </header>
```

247

```xml
<body>
  <trans-unit id="FLAG_FILE">
    <source>FLAG_FILE</source>
    <note>Name of the flag</note>
    <target>flag_usa</target>
  </trans-unit>
  <trans-unit id="LABEL_FIVE">
    <source>LABEL_FIVE</source>
    <note>The number 5</note>
    <target>Five</target>
  </trans-unit>
  <trans-unit id="LABEL_FOUR">
    <source>LABEL_FOUR</source>
    <note>The number 4</note>
    <target>Four</target>
  </trans-unit>
  <trans-unit id="LABEL_ONE">
    <source>LABEL_ONE</source>
    <note>The number 1</note>
    <target>One</target>
  </trans-unit>
  <trans-unit id="LABEL_THREE">
    <source>LABEL_THREE</source>
    <note>The number 3</note>
    <target>Three</target>
  </trans-unit>
  <trans-unit id="LABEL_TWO">
    <source>LABEL_TWO</source>
    <note>The number 2</note>
    <target>Two</target>
  </trans-unit>
</body>
</file>
```

Import these changes back into Xcode using Editor ➤ Import Localizations.

Xcode creates a folder called en.lproj and adds to its files called InfoPlist.strings, Localizable.strings, and Main.strings that contain the English localization. What you have added is the reference to the image file for the flag and the text to replace the keys used in the `NSLocalizedString()` function calls in the code. Now if you run the app with English as your selected language, you'll see the correct English text and the U.S. flag.

The requirement to provide the flag image file name and the text strings for the base localization arises because we chose not to use localized text as the keys when calling `NSLocalizedString()`. Had we done something like this, the English text would appear in the user interface for any language for which there is no localization, even if we didn't provide a base localization:

```
labels[0].text = NSLocalizedString("One", comment: "The number 1")
labels[1].text = NSLocalizedString("Two", comment: "The number 2")
labels[2].text = NSLocalizedString("Three", comment: "The number 3")
labels[3].text = NSLocalizedString("Four", comment: "The number 4")
labels[4].text = NSLocalizedString("Five", comment: "The number 5")
let flagFile = NSLocalizedString("flag_usa", comment: "Name of the flag")
```

While this is perfectly legal, the downside is that if you need to change any of the English text strings, you are also changing the key used to look up the strings for all of the other languages, so you will need to manually update all of the localized .strings files so that they use the new key.

Localizing the App Display Name

We want to explore one final piece of localization that is commonly used: localizing the app name that's visible on the home screen and elsewhere. Apple does this for several of the built-in apps, and you might want to do so, as well. The app name used for display is stored in your app's Info.plist file, which you'll find in the Project Navigator. Select this file for editing, and you'll see that one of the items it contains, Bundle name, is currently set to ${PRODUCT_NAME}. In the syntax used by Info.plist files, anything starting with a dollar sign is subject to variable substitution. In this case, it means that when Xcode compiles the app, the value of this item will be replaced with the name of the product in this Xcode project, which is the name of the app itself. This is where we want to do some localization, replacing ${PRODUCT_NAME} with the localized name for each language. However, as it turns out, this doesn't quite work out as simply as you might expect.

CHAPTER 7　TRANSLATING APPS USING LOCALIZATION

The Info.plist file is sort of a special case, and it isn't meant to be localized. Instead, if you want to localize the content of Info.plist, you need to make localized versions of a file named InfoPlist.strings. Before you can do that, you need to create a Base version of that file. If you followed the steps in the previous section to localize the app, you'll already have English and French versions of this file that are empty. If you don't have these files, you can add one, as follows:

1. Select File ➤ New ➤ File…. In the iOS section, choose Resource and then Strings File (see Figure 7-15). Press Next, name the file InfoPlist.strings, assign it to the Supporting Files group in the LocalizeMe project, and create it.

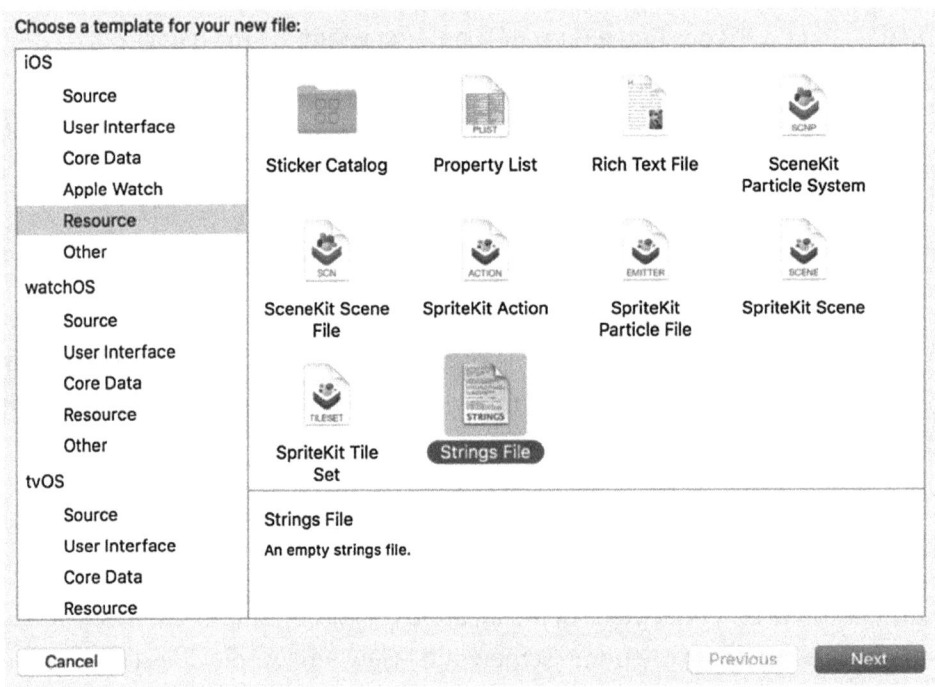

Figure 7-15. *The Strings File option under the iOS Resource file type selection*

2. Select the new file and, in the File Inspector, press Localize. In the dialog box that appears, have the file moved to the English localization. Back in the File Inspector, check the check box for French under Localizations. You should now see copies of this file for both French and English in the Project Navigator.

We need to add a line to each localized copy of this file to define the display name for the app. In the Info.plist file, we were shown the display name associated with a dictionary key called **Bundle name**; however, that's not the real key name. It's merely an Xcode nicety, trying to give us a friendlier and readable name. The real name is CFBundleName, which you can verify by selecting Info.plist, right-clicking anywhere in the view, and then selecting Show Raw Keys/Values. This shows you the true names of the keys in use. So, select the English localization of InfoPlist.strings and either add or modify the following line:

```
"CFBundleName" = "Localize Me";
```

This key may already exist if you followed the localization steps for English, because it's inserted as part of the process of importing an XLIFF file. In fact, another way to localize your app's name is to add the translation to the XLIFF file in the same way as we did for the other texts that we needed to translate — just look for the entry for CFBundleName and add a `<trans>` element with the translated name. Similarly, select the French localization of the InfoPlist.strings file and edit it to give the app a proper French name:

```
"CFBundleName" = "Localisez Moi";
```

Build and run the app, and then go back to the launch screen. And of course, switch the device or simulator you're using to French if it's currently running in English. You should see the localized name just underneath the app's icon, but sometimes it may not appear immediately. iOS seems to cache this information when a new app is added, but it doesn't necessarily change it when an existing app is replaced by a new version — at least not when Xcode is doing the replacing. So, if you're running in French and you don't see the new name — don't worry. Just delete the app from the launch screen, go back to Xcode, and then build and run the app again.

Warning   You won't see the localized app name if you are running the application with a custom scheme. The only way to see it is to switch the device or simulator language to French.

Now our application is fully localized for both French and English.

CHAPTER 7   TRANSLATING APPS USING LOCALIZATION

Adding Another Localization

To wrap up, we're going to add another localization to our application. This time, we'll localize it to Swiss French, which is a regional variation of French with language code **fr-CH.**

The basic principle is the same as before — in fact, now that you have done this once, it should go much faster this time. Start by selecting the project in the Project Navigator, and then select the project itself in the editor, followed by the Info tab. In the Localizations section, press + to add a new language. You won't see Swiss French in the menu, so scroll down and select Other. This opens a submenu with a very large number of languages to choose from — fortunately, they are in alphabetical order. If you scroll down, you will eventually find French (Switzerland), so select it. In the dialog that appears (which looks like Figure 7-6), change the Reference Language for all of the listed files to French, so that Xcode uses your existing French translations as the basis for the Swiss French localization, and then click Finish. Now if you look at the Project Navigator, you'll see that you have Swiss French versions of the storyboard, localizable strings, and InfoPlist.strings files. To demonstrate that this localization is distinct from the French one, open the Swiss French version of InfoPlist.strings and change the bundle name to this:

```
"CFBundleName" = "Swiss Localisez Moi";
```

Now build and run the application. Switch to the Settings application and go to Language & Region. You probably won't find Swiss French in the list of iPhone Languages. Instead, click Add Language... and scroll down (or search) until you find French (Switzerland); and then select it and press Done. This will bring up an action sheet in which you will be asked if you prefer Swiss French or your current language. Select Swiss French and let iOS reset itself. Go to the home screen and you should now see that our application is called **Swiss Localisez Moi** (in fact, you may not see the whole name, because it's too long, but you get the point). If you open the application, you'll see that the text is all in French. Unfortunately, the flag is also the French flag, not the Swiss one. By now, you should be able to figure out how to fix this by editing the Swiss localization files. So as an exercise, try downloading a Swiss flag image from the Internet and see if you can make it appear in the Swiss version of the application.

Summary

To maximize sales of your iOS application, you'll probably want to localize it as much as possible. Fortunately, the iOS localization architecture makes easy work of supporting multiple languages, and even multiple dialects of the same language, within your application. As you saw in this chapter, nearly any type of file that you add to your application can be localized.

Even if you don't plan on localizing your application, you should get in the habit of using `NSLocalizedString()` instead of just using static strings in your code. With the Xcode IDE's Code Sense feature, the difference in typing time is negligible. And, should you ever want to translate your application, your life will be much, much easier. Going back late in the project to find all text strings that should be localized is a boring and error-prone process, which you can avoid with a little effort in advance.

CHAPTER 8

Using Machine Learning

Artificial intelligence (AI) has been around since the 1960s. In those early days, computer scientists dreamed of intelligent computers that could think, but the reality proved far less breathtaking. The biggest obstacle to AI was that computer scientists had to mimic intelligence by anticipating all situations. In limited domains like chess, this worked, but when dealing with large amounts of data, this primitive solution failed because it's impossible to anticipate all possible situations that might encounter in most cases. That's why the latest developments in AI focus less on hand coding all possibilities and focuses more on machine learning.

Machine learning has proven valuable for creating "smarter" programs, especially when they must deal with previously unknown data. For example, credit card companies use machine learning to track your spending patterns. With so many customers, it's impossible for people to track each customer's spending patterns so that's why they rely on machine learning instead.

Machine learning can analyze your spending patterns and the moment it detects something unusual, such as a purchase in another country or a large, out of the ordinary purchase, the machine learning program flags that as suspicious. Since your spending patterns may change subtly over time, the machine learning program can adjust and recognize valid purchases while spotting suspicious ones. In this way, machine learning adapts to new situations and appears "smarter."

Machine learning is best used for dealing with data that can't be anticipated ahead of time although many programs can adapt machine learning to make the program easier to use. For example, when you type text to write an e-mail or a note, the virtual keyboard displays words and phrases it thinks you're likely to write. By tapping on a word or phrase, you can type faster without writing out the entire word or phrase.

Machine learning can make apps more responsive and versatile. In this chapter, you'll learn how to incorporate machine learning in iOS apps.

CHAPTER 8 USING MACHINE LEARNING

Understanding Machine Learning

The main idea behind machine learning is that computer scientists create generic algorithms that they train using large amounts of data. When the algorithm gets the problem right, it modifies its own code so it can identify similar types of problems in the future. When the algorithm gets the problem wrong, it also modifies its own code to reduce the chance of making the same mistake again. Such training and feedback creates a program that literally learns, hence the term machine learning. Best of all, the algorithm trains itself based on data it receives so there's no need for a human programmer to modify the algorithm by hand, which would be tedious and inefficient.

Machine learning lets programs deal with situations it has never encountered before. One common machine learning problem involves image recognition. You can train an algorithm to recognize a dog or a boat in a picture, but that algorithm must eventually learn to recognize dogs or boats in pictures it has never seen before.

Most people may be familiar with an early form of machine learning that appeared in spam filters for e-mail. It's impossible to identify all possible spam because spammers can simply modify their spam. As a result, spam filters use machine learning to identify possible spam. When you confirm that a message is spam, you're training the spam filter to recognize similar types of spam in the future. That's why over time, spam filters tend to get better simply because they keep getting trained by new data.

Machine learning involves three steps:

- Developing and writing algorithms.
- Training the algorithm with large amounts of data.
- Using the trained algorithm (called a machine learning model).

Creating algorithms can be difficult and training algorithms can be time-consuming. Fortunately, you don't have to do either task. Instead, you can take trained machine learning models and simply use them without writing your own algorithms or training it with large amounts of data.

The advantages of simply using a trained machine learning model are that you can add artificial intelligence to your iOS apps quickly and easily. The drawback is that you need to find trained machine learning models that do what you need. In addition, you cannot increase the trained machine learning model's intelligence. You're essentially taking a fixed machine learning model that won't improve over time.

Since most people aren't able to write machine learning algorithms and train it with large amounts of data, they must rely on machine learning models that others have created. There are two sources or machine learning models:

- Core ML models.
- Non-Core ML models.

When you add a machine learning model to an iOS project, it must be stored in a file format known as Core ML (which stands for Core Machine Learning). Since Core ML is a new file format, most machine learning models are stored in different file formats. Fortunately, Apple has converted some popular machine learning models into the Core ML format. That means you can use these machine learning models in your iOS apps right away.

The main purpose for adding machine learning to your iOS apps is so your app can anticipate the user's needs. When you type text in many iOS apps, you'll see a list of words or phrases the app thinks you want to type. Rather than type the entire word or phrase yourself, you can just tap on the suggested word or phrase displayed. Over time, the app will tend to suggest common words and phrases you use most often, so the app customizes itself to your behaviour, making typing text faster and easier for you.

Essentially machine learning lets your app become smarter. The smarter your app is able to respond to the user, the happier the user will be. Machine learning gives your app new capabilities without requiring you to exhaustively write instructions yourself.

What this chapter will focus on is finding Core ML machine learning models, adding them to iOS projects, and using them in your iOS app.

Finding a Core ML Model

The simplest way to find a Core ML model to use is to visit Apple's machine learning developer's site at https://developer.apple.com/machine-learning. Apple provides a growing library of tested Core ML models that you can add to an iOS project. While this list may be relatively small, it will grow over time.

Besides Apple's site, you may also be able to find Core ML models on third-party sites where people have created or converted other machine learning model formats into Core ML. For the truly adventurous, you can find Core ML conversion tools on Apple's developer's site. By using these Core ML conversion tools, you can search for other machine learning models stored in different file formats and convert them into the

Core ML format. This process of converting machine learning models into the Core ML format involves using the Python programming language and is beyond the scope of this chapter.

When evaluating different Core ML models to use, you need to look at what the machine learning model does and how large its file may be as shown in Figure 8-1.

The Core ML model described in Figure 8-1 tells you that it's an image recognition model that's 17.1 MB in size. The size of Core ML models can vary dramatically so you need to weigh the benefits of each model with its size. Adding 17.1 MB to the size of your iOS app may be reasonable, but adding 553.5 MB may not. There's often a trade-off between large file size and greater accuracy but sometimes smaller models can outperform larger ones so you may need to experiment with different models until you find the right one for your app that balances accuracy and file size.

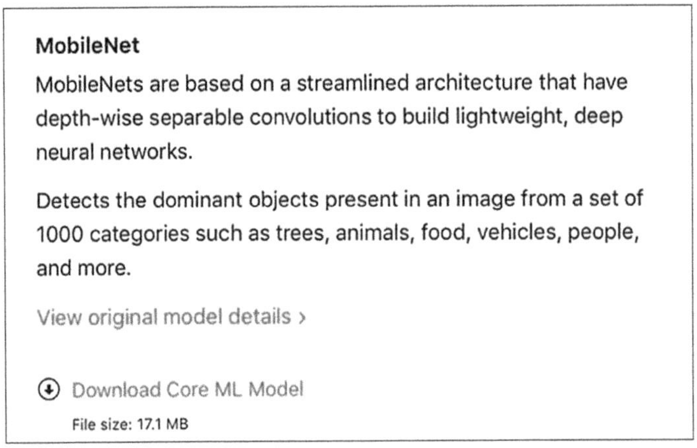

Figure 8-1. Core ML models briefly describe what the model does and how large its file is

Image Recognition

At the time of this writing, most of the Core ML models available on Apple's machine learning site focus on image recognition. This can work in two ways:

- Your app can load an image stored in the Photos app.
- Your app can view an item through the camera.

First, we'll start simple and add an image to an Xcode project. This will only allow us to recognize that single image hard-coded into the app, but it will let us focus on getting

CHAPTER 8   USING MACHINE LEARNING

the Core ML model working within an app. Once we know the Core ML model works, we can focus on the non-machine learning functions to retrieve an image from the Photos app or from the iPhone/iPad camera.

The first step is to download a Core ML model to your computer. Visit `https://developer.apple.com/machine-learning` and download the MobileNet and SqueezeNet models. Both models focus on image recognition and both are fairly small in size. By experimenting with two different Core ML models, you can see how accurate both of them might be and how using any Core ML model works in similar ways.

The second step is to visit any search engine and look for images of any object such as a car, dog, computer, or bird. The exact image doesn't matter but choose an image that has a blank background such as all white. By choosing an image that's isolated and not cluttered with other items, you'll improve the Core ML model's chance of recognizing it correctly.

Obviously in real apps, you can't always choose pictures that are easiest for the Core ML model to identify, but for our purposes, we just want to get the Core ML model working to identify items in a picture. Once you have downloaded the Core ML models (SqueezeNet and MobileNet) and a single image of any object, you're ready to create the Xcode project to use machine learning.

Creating the Image Recognition Application

First, use Xcode to create a new Single View Application project named ImageRecognition. This will be a simple app that loads the image you just downloaded of an object (such as a dog or a car) and then display a description from the machine learning model on the screen.

Now select the ViewController.swift file and add the following lines directly underneath the "import UIKit" line so the first three lines look like this:

```
import UIKit
import CoreML
import Vision
```

259

CHAPTER 8   USING MACHINE LEARNING

The "import CoreML" line simply lets your project recognize and use the Core ML model added to your project. The "import Vision" line lets your project use the Vision framework for recognizing items in an image. To add a Core ML model to a project, just drag and drop it from a Finder window to your Xcode project navigator. Start with the MobileNet Core ML model for now as shown in Figure 8-2.

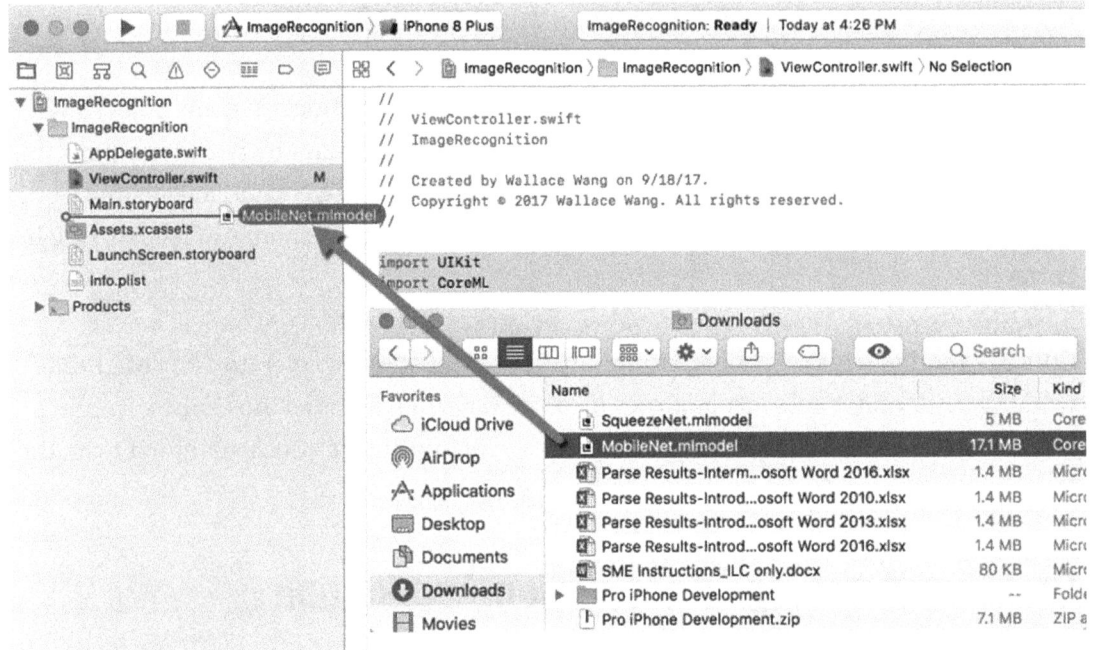

Figure 8-2. Drag and drop the Core ML model into Xcode

Now drag and drop an image into the Xcode Project navigator. Make sure this image file has a descriptive name such as "cat.jpg" or something similar. When dragging and dropping both the image and Core ML model, Xcode will display a window so make sure the "Copy items if needed" check box is selected.

Click on the image file you added to the Project navigator and Xcode will display that image. Look in the right pane under the Target Membership category and make sure the check box is selected. If you named your Xcode project ImageRecognition, then select the ImageRecognition check box under the Target Membership category.

Click on the MobileNet.mlmodel file in the Project navigator. The middle Xcode pane displays information about the machine learning model such as its authors and how it works. More importantly, the Model Evaluation Parameters describe the input the model expects and the data it outputs.

260

CHAPTER 8   USING MACHINE LEARNING

In the case of the MobileNet.mlmodel file, it expects an input of an image. Once it receives an image, it outputs a dictionary (a string and a double) that displays the probability that it accurately identified the image. It also outputs a string that identifies the image.

Even though you've physically added the Core ML model file to your Xcode project, you may need to take one additional step. On the far right, select the check box in the Target Membership category as shown in Figure 8-3. If you named your Xcode project ImageRecognition, then select the ImageRecognition check box under the Target Membership category.

***Figure 8-3.** Viewing the details of the MobileNet model*

For the user interface, click on the Main.storyboard file and then drag and drop a Label and an Image View. The label will display the machine learning model's description of the item in the image and the image view will display the actual image. In this case, the image view will simply display the image file you dragged and dropped in your project such as a file named "cat.jpg."

The exact position of the label and image view isn't important just as long as the label is wide and tall enough to display text such as shown in Figure 8-4.

CHAPTER 8   USING MACHINE LEARNING

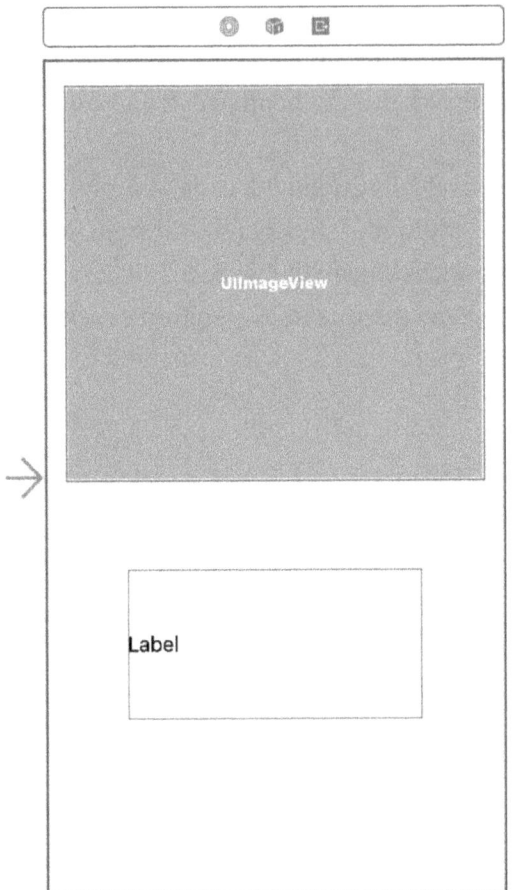

Figure 8-4. *Designing the user interface*

Click on the image view and then click View ➤ Utilities ➤ Show Attributes Inspector. Click on the Image text field and choose the file name of your image such as "cat.jpg". This will make the image view display the image you stored in your Xcode project.

Now click on the Content Mode text field and choose Aspect Fit. This will make the image appear correctly proportioned in the image view. At this point, you should see your chosen image appear in the image view.

Click on the label and make sure the Attributes Inspector is still visible. (If not, click View ➤ Utilities ➤ Show Attributes Inspector.) Click in the Lines text field and type 0. Defining 0 lines makes the label display as many lines as needed depending on the text you store in that label.

CHAPTER 8 USING MACHINE LEARNING

Once you've completed the user interface, open the Assistant Editor and Control-drag from the image view and label on the Main.storyboard file to the ViewController.swift file to create an IBOutlet for both the image view and the label. Give the IBOutlet names imageView and labelDescription so your code in the ViewController.swift file should look like this:

```swift
class ViewController: UIViewController {
    @IBOutlet var imageView: UIImageView!
    @IBOutlet var labelDescription: UILabel!
```

The machine learning model needs an image as input, so we need to identify the image file you added to your Xcode project. This involves two steps. First, you need to identify the file name, file extension of the image, and path of that image. Second, you need to store this information as a URL to give to the Core ML model.

To do both steps, you need two lines of code. The first line captures the file name, extension, and path like this:

```swift
let imagePath = Bundle.main.path(forResource: "cat", ofType: "jpg")
```

In the above code, the constant name is "imagePath" but you can choose any name you wish. The file name is "cat" but you need to replace this with the name of your image file. The file extension is "jpg" and you'll need to replace it with the file extension of your image file as well. The above code creates an optional variable.

The second line of code you need stores the image file's name, extension, and path in a URL such as:

```swift
let imageURL = NSURL.fileURL(withPath: imagePath!)
```

In the above code, the constant name is "imageURL" but you can choose any name you wish. The image path is identified as "imagePath," which must be identical to the constant you created using the Bundle.main.path command. Notice that you must explicitly unwrap the "imagePath" optional variable using the exclamation point.

Edit the viewDidLoad function in the ViewController file like this:

```swift
override func viewDidLoad() {
        super.viewDidLoad()
        
        let imagePath = Bundle.main.path(forResource: "cat", ofType: "jpg")
        let imageURL = NSURL.fileURL(withPath: imagePath!)
        
    }
```

263

CHAPTER 8 USING MACHINE LEARNING

Now that you've stored the image file, extension, and path in a constant ("imageURL"), it's time to work with the Core ML model. First, you need to create a constant to represent the Core ML model you added to your Xcode project, such as MobileNet.mlmodel. To do this, you need the following code:

```
let modelFile = MobileNet()
```

The "modelFile" constant can actually be any name you wish. MobileNet() identifies the MobileNet.mlmodel file added in your Xcode project. If you use a different Core ML model such as SqueezeNet.mlmodel, then you would replace "MobileNet" with "SqueezeNet".

Next, you need to tell your app to use your chosen Core ML model (identified by the "modelFile" constant) with the Vision framework. This means creating another constant with an arbitrary name (such as "model") as follows:

```
let model = try! VNCoreMLModel(for: modelFile.model)
```

At this point, the code in the viewDidLoad function inside the ViewController.swift file should look like Listing 8-1:

Listing 8-1. The viewDidLoad function code in the ViewController.swift File

```
override func viewDidLoad() {
    super.viewDidLoad()

    let imagePath = Bundle.main.path(forResource: "cat",
    ofType: "jpg")
    let imageURL = NSURL.fileURL(withPath: imagePath!)

    let modelFile = MobileNet()
    let model = try! VNCoreMLModel(for: modelFile.model)
}
```

The first two "let" statements store the image file and the second two "let" statements prepare the Core ML model to work with the Vision framework.

Now the next step is to let the Core ML model examine the image. We already defined the image name, extension, and path in the "imageURL" constant, so we can use this to define an image request like this:

```
let handler = VNImageRequestHandler(url: imageURL)
```

264

CHAPTER 8 USING MACHINE LEARNING

After requesting an image to examine, the next step is to request that your app actually use the Core ML model stored in the "model" constant. The Core ML model needs to examine the image and compare it to its trained data multiple times to maximize the chances of identifying it correctly. That means you need to request that the Core ML model run and provide it with a completion handler that defines what the Core ML model does when it identifies the image. To do this requires two more lines of code:

```
let request = VNCoreMLRequest(model: model, completionHandler: findResults)
try! handler.perform([request])
```

The entire code for the viewDidLoad function should look like Listing 8-2:

Listing 8-2. The completed viewDidLoad function code in the ViewController.swift File

```
    override func viewDidLoad() {
        super.viewDidLoad()

        let imagePath = Bundle.main.path(forResource: "cat", ofType: "jpg")
        let imageURL = NSURL.fileURL(withPath: imagePath!)

        let modelFile = MobileNet()
        let model = try! VNCoreMLModel(for: modelFile.model)

        let handler = VNImageRequestHandler(url: imageURL)
        let request = VNCoreMLRequest(model: model, completionHandler: findResults)

        try! handler.perform([request])
    }
```

The last step is to write the function for the completion handler, which is called "findResults." In the ViewController.swift file, create a function as follows:

```
        func findResults(request: VNRequest, error: Error?) {
        }
```

265

CHAPTER 8 USING MACHINE LEARNING

This findResults function runs when the Core ML model examines an image. The first step for this findResults function is to make sure it can examine the image. If not, it needs to prevent the rest of its code from running. To check if the Core ML model can successfully examine an image, we can use a guard statement like this:

```
guard let results = request.results as?
[VNClassificationObservation] else {
    fatalError("Unable to get results")
}
```

Assuming that the Core ML model can examine the image, we need to keep track of its guesses with two variables that can be any arbitrary name. For this example, we can call them "bestGuess" and "bestConfidence" as follows:

```
var bestGuess = ""
var bestConfidence: VNConfidence = 0
```

The "bestGuess" variable will hold the Core ML model's current prediction of what it thinks the item in an image might be. The "bestConfidence" variable will hold the confidence level. Note that the "bestConfidence" variable must be defined as a VNConfidence data type, which holds a decimal value.

Finally, we need a loop to exhaustively examine the image to determine the Core ML model's best guess of what that object might be. This loop assigns a confidence level and an identifier to the "bestConfidence" and "bestGuess" variables respectively. Each time it comes across a prediction with a higher confidence level, it stores it in the "bestGuess" variable. This loop looks like the following:

```
for classification in results {
    if (classification.confidence > bestConfidence) {
        bestConfidence = classification.confidence
        bestGuess = classification.identifier
    }
}
```

Finally after the loop has exhaustively searched through all possible predictions for what the item in the image might be, the loop stops and the "bestGuess" variable contains the guess and the "bestConfidence" variable contains that confidence level.

CHAPTER 8 USING MACHINE LEARNING

Now we need one last line of code to display this information in the label on the user interface like this:

```
labelDescription.text = "Image is: \(bestGuess) with confidence \(bestConfidence)) out of 1"
```

The entire findResults function should look like Listing 8-3:

Listing 8-3. The findResults function

```
    func findResults(request: VNRequest, error: Error?) {
       guard let results = request.results as? [VNClassificationObservation] else {
            fatalError("Unable to get results")
       }

       var bestGuess = ""
       var bestConfidence: VNConfidence = 0

       for classification in results {
           if (classification.confidence > bestConfidence) {
               bestConfidence = classification.confidence
               bestGuess = classification.identifier
           }
       }

       labelDescription.text = "Image is: \(bestGuess) with confidence \(bestConfidence) out of 1"
    }
```

267

CHAPTER 8   USING MACHINE LEARNING

If you run this app, you'll see your chosen image displayed and the Core ML model's guess underneath with its confidence level as shown in Figure 8-5.

Figure 8-5. *ImageRecognition running on the iPhone simulator*

If you modify your project by adding a different Core ML model, you'll notice that each Core ML model identifies the same object in slightly different ways with different confidence levels. You can also try modifying your project by adding different image files containing cars, trees, horses, or airplanes to see how accurately it identifies the displayed item. Machine learning models aren't perfect but you can see that we've created an app that can identify items with very little coding. Instead, we've let a trained machine learning model do all the hard work of identifying items in an image.

CHAPTER 8 USING MACHINE LEARNING

Note You'll find a completed version of this project in the ImageRecognition folder in the example source code.

Identifying Objects from the Camera

The first app we built in this chapter simply examined a single image file. If we wanted to examine a different image, we'd have to add that new image to the Xcode project, modify the code slightly to reflect the different image file name, and then run the app all over again.

A far more versatile solution is to simply use the built-in camera on an iPhone or iPad to aim and point at an object. Then have the Core ML model try to identify what that object might be. To do this, you'll need to physically connect an iPhone or iPad to your Macintosh while running Xcode since you cannot test the camera on the Simulator.

Create a new Xcode project using the iOS Single View App and give it a name of CameraRecognition. Now drag and drop a UILabel near the bottom of the view and a UIView so it fills out the top portion of the view as shown in Figure 8-6. The exact placement of the UIView and the UILabel doesn't need to be exact.

Figure 8-6. *Designing the user interface for the CameraRecognition app*

Open the Assistant Editor and Control-drag from the UIView and the UILabel into the ViewController.swift file to create two IBOutlets. Name the UIView videoFeed and the UILabel resultLabel so the two IBOutlets look like this:

```
class ViewController: UIViewController {
    @IBOutlet var videoFeed: UIView!
    @IBOutlet var resultLabel: UILabel!
```

Next create three variables that represent the camera output, the capture session, and the video preview layer. The camera output is what the iPhone/iPad camera receives. The capture session coordinates the flow of data from the camera. The video preview layer displays the video the iPhone/iPad camera captures. These three variables should appear underneath the two IBOutlets you just created as shown below.

```
class ViewController: UIViewController {

    @IBOutlet var videoFeed: UIView!
    @IBOutlet var resultLabel: UILabel!

    var cameraOutput : AVCapturePhotoOutput!
    var previewLayer : AVCaptureVideoPreviewLayer!
    var captureSession : AVCaptureSession!
```

Once we've created these IBOutlets and variables, we need to write a function that store and display data captured through the camera. The first step is to create an AVCaptureSession, which can capture different types of data such as audio or video. The second step is to capture photographic images through the camera using two lines of code like this:

```
        captureSession = AVCaptureSession()
        captureSession.sessionPreset = AVCaptureSession.Preset.photo
```

The next step is to store the captured video from the camera in the cameraOutput variable like this:

```
cameraOutput = AVCapturePhotoOutput()
```

CHAPTER 8 USING MACHINE LEARNING

Finally, we need to retrieve video and determine if it's successful or not. That involves creating a constant called "device" to capture video. Then we need to see an if statement to determine if the camera is successfully capturing video. This involves defining a "device" constant and then using an if statement like this:

```
let device = AVCaptureDevice.default(for: AVMediaType.video)
if let input = try? AVCaptureDeviceInput(device: device!) {

} else {
    print ("No video feed available")
}
```

If there is no video feed, then the else portion runs and prints "No video feed available." If there is video, then we need to check if the video can be successfully displayed in the UIView through its IBOutlet named videoFeed.

Once we know we can retrieve video, two more if statements check if it's possible to get input and output from the camera as follows:

```
if (captureSession.canAddInput(input)) {
    captureSession.addInput(input)

    if (captureSession.canAddOutput(cameraOutput)) {
        captureSession.addOutput(cameraOutput)
    }
}
```

Finally, we need to display the captured video onto the UIView on the user interface. To do this, we need to define the previewLayer to the captureSession (the video feed from the camera) and define how that video appears inside the UIView such as Aspect Fill like this:

```
previewLayer = AVCaptureVideoPreviewLayer(session: captureSession)
previewLayer.videoGravity = AVLayerVideoGravity.resizeAspectFill
```

The last step is to actually display the video inside the UIView, which is defined by the IBOutlet called videoFeed. First, we need to define the frame of the preview layer to match the size of the UIView on the user interface. Next, we need to add that

271

CHAPTER 8 USING MACHINE LEARNING

previewLayer to the UIView layer. Finally, we need to start capturing the video using the following code:

```
previewLayer.frame = videoFeed.bounds
videoFeed.layer.addSublayer(previewLayer)
captureSession.startRunning()
```

The entire function, named "useCamera," appears in Listing 8-4.

Listing 8-4. The useCamera Method Goes in the ViewController.swift File

```swift
func useCamera() {
    captureSession = AVCaptureSession()
    captureSession.sessionPreset = AVCaptureSession.Preset.photo
    cameraOutput = AVCapturePhotoOutput()

    let device = AVCaptureDevice.default(for: AVMediaType.video)
    if let input = try? AVCaptureDeviceInput(device: device!) {
        if (captureSession.canAddInput(input)) {
            captureSession.addInput(input)

            if (captureSession.canAddOutput(cameraOutput)) {
                captureSession.addOutput(cameraOutput)
            }

            previewLayer = AVCaptureVideoPreviewLayer(session: captureSession)
            previewLayer.videoGravity = AVLayerVideoGravity.resizeAspectFill
            previewLayer.frame = videoFeed.bounds
            videoFeed.layer.addSublayer(previewLayer)
            captureSession.startRunning()
        } else {
            print ("Could not get any input")
        }
    } else {
        print ("No video feed available")
    }
}
```

CHAPTER 8   USING MACHINE LEARNING

Now you just need to call this "useCamera" function inside the viewDidLoad method like this:

```
override func viewDidLoad() {
    super.viewDidLoad()
    useCamera()
}
```

Since this app needs access to an actual iOS device with a camera, you cannot test this app in the Simulator. Instead, you can only test this app by connecting an iOS device to your Macintosh through its USB cable. Then you need to click the Active Scheme icon at the top of the Xcode window to display a menu. At the top of this menu, choose your iOS device under the Device category as shown in Figure 8-7.

CHAPTER 8 USING MACHINE LEARNING

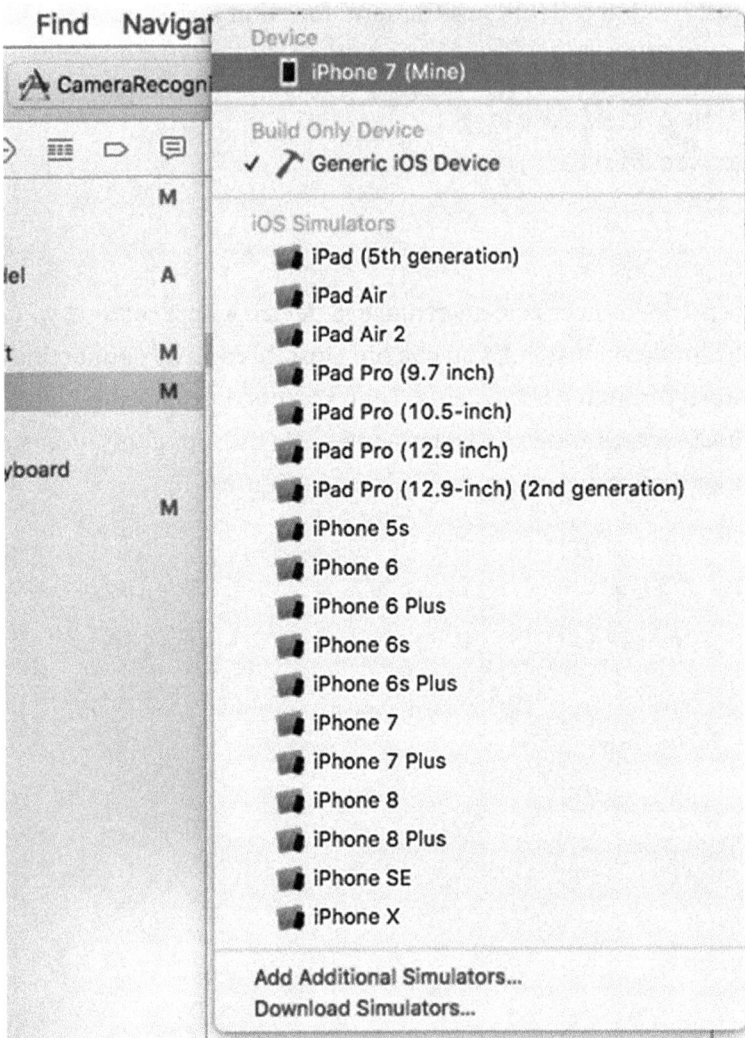

Figure 8-7. Choosing an iOS device from the Active Scheme icon

When you run this app through a connected iOS device, you should see the camera's video feed appear in the UIView of the user interface. Now the next step is to add the machine learning model to recognize items displayed in the camera.

Once you've defined an actual iOS device to run your Xcode CameraRecognition app, the last step is to give your app permission to access the camera. To do this, click on the Info.plist file in the Project navigator. Then click on any up/down arrow that appears to the right of any item in the Information Property List. Then click the + icon that appears.

CHAPTER 8   USING MACHINE LEARNING

This displays a pop-up menu so choose Privacy – Camera Usage Description as shown in Figure 8-8. Under the Value column, type a descriptive message that explains to the user why the app needs access to the camera. This message can be something simple like "App needs to access camera." The exact text does not matter as it will only appear the first time your app runs on an iOS device.

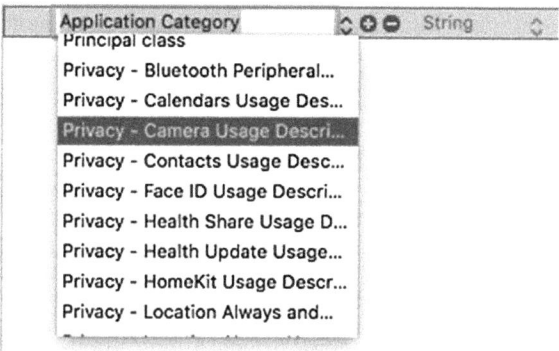

Figure 8-8. *Defining privacy settings to allow use of the camera*

Note   You'll need to test this project on an actual iPhone or iPad running iOS 11 to view the video feed.

Analyzing an Image

At this point the code in your project simply allows the app to retrieve video from a connected iOS device's camera and display it on the user interface. The next step is to actually capture and analyze an individual image from that video feed so the Core ML model can recognize the object viewed by the camera.

We'll need to create a function that retrieves an image from the video feed and another function to analyze that image using a Core ML model. First, we need to capture an image from the video feed with a function called recognizeImage(). Call that function at the end of the useCamera method. The last few lines of the userCamera method look like this:

```
    } else {
            print ("No video feed available")
        }
        recognizeImage()
    }
```

275

CHAPTER 8 USING MACHINE LEARNING

Now create the recognizeImage function underneath the userCamera() method like this:

```
@objc func recognizeImage() {

}
```

> **Note** The @obj keyword allows Swift and Objective-C code to work together. In this case, this allows Swift code to work with Objective-C code that's part of Apple's framework for creating apps.

The first step is to create an object that allows the capture of an image, which is an AVCapturePhotoSettings object. Then we need to capture the actual image and define its format. Finally, we need to capture an image so the code in the recognizeImage() function should look like this:

```
@objc func recognizeImage() {
    let settings = AVCapturePhotoSettings()

    settings.previewPhotoFormat = settings.embeddedThumbnailPhotoFormat

    cameraOutput.capturePhoto(with: settings, delegate: self)
}
```

After the recognizeImage() function retrieves an image from the video feed, we need another function to convert this image into a UIImage as follows:

```
    func photoOutput(_ output: AVCapturePhotoOutput,
didFinishProcessingPhoto photo: AVCapturePhoto, error: Error?) {
        if let error = error {
            print ("Error code: \(error.localizedDescription)")
        }

        if let imageData = photo.fileDataRepresentation(), let image =
        UIImage(data: imageData) {
            predictItem(image: image)
        }
    }
```

CHAPTER 8 USING MACHINE LEARNING

The photoOutput function stores the captured image as a UIImage and also calls a function called predictItem, which we'll need to write later. This predictItem function will need to use a Core ML model to analyze the image captured from the video feed.

Since the Core ML model needs to know where to find that image, we'll first need to write a function that returns a URL like this:

```swift
func getDocumentsDirectory() -> URL {
    let paths = FileManager.default.urls(for: .documentDirectory, in:
    .userDomainMask)
    let documentsDirectory = paths[0]
    return documentsDirectory
}
```

Now we can write the predictItem function like this:

```swift
func predictItem(image: UIImage) {
    if let data = UIImagePNGRepresentation(image) {
        let fileName = getDocumentsDirectory().
        appendingPathComponent("image.png")
        try? data.write(to: fileName)

        let modelFile = SqueezeNet()
        let model = try! VNCoreMLModel(for: modelFile.model)

        let request = VNCoreMLRequest(model: model, completionHandler:
        finalGuess)
        let handler = VNImageRequestHandler(url: fileName)
        try! handler.perform([request])
    }
}
```

This code uses the SqueezeNet Core ML model but you can substitute the name of a different Core ML model if you wish. By experimenting with different Core ML models, you can see how accurate (or poorly) different Core ML models are at recognizing and identifying items in a picture.

The predictItem function calls another function called finalGuess, which runs after the Core ML model analyzes the image. The finalGuess function runs each time the Core ML model guesses what an item is in an image. Each time the Core ML model makes a guess, it gives a confidence level between 0 and 1 where 1 is highly confident.

The finalGuess function simply analyzes each prediction by the Core ML model and checks its confidence level. If the Core ML model is more confident that it has found a better match, it uses that prediction instead. Eventually after the Core ML analyzes all possible items it can recognize, the one item with the highest confidence level will be left and that will be the answer displayed on the label on the user interface.

The finalGuess function uses the Timer function to capture new images every five seconds and looks like this:

```swift
func finalGuess(request: VNRequest, error: Error?) {
    guard let results = request.results as?
    [VNClassificationObservation] else {
        fatalError("Unable to get a prediction")
    }
    
    var bestGuess = ""
    var confidence: VNConfidence = 0
    for classification in results {
        if classification.confidence > confidence {
            confidence = classification.confidence
            bestGuess = classification.identifier
        }
    }
    resultLabel.text = bestGuess + "\n"
    Timer.scheduledTimer(timeInterval: 5.0, target: self, selector: #selector(self.recognizeImage), userInfo: nil, repeats: false)
}
```

Finally, make sure you import the CoreML, AVFoundation, and Vision frameworks so the complete code for ViewController.swift file is shown in Listing 8-5.

Listing 8-5. The complete ViewController.swift File

```swift
import UIKit
import AVFoundation
import CoreML
import Vision
```

```swift
class ViewController: UIViewController, AVCapturePhotoCaptureDelegate {

    @IBOutlet var videoFeed: UIView!
    @IBOutlet var resultLabel: UILabel!

    var cameraOutput : AVCapturePhotoOutput!
    var previewLayer : AVCaptureVideoPreviewLayer!
    var captureSession : AVCaptureSession!

    override func viewDidLoad() {
        super.viewDidLoad()
        useCamera()
    }

    override func didReceiveMemoryWarning() {
        super.didReceiveMemoryWarning()
        // Dispose of any resources that can be recreated.
    }

    func useCamera() {
        captureSession = AVCaptureSession()
        captureSession.sessionPreset = AVCaptureSession.Preset.photo
        cameraOutput = AVCapturePhotoOutput()

        let deviceCamera = AVCaptureDevice.default(for: AVMediaType.video)
        if let input = try? AVCaptureDeviceInput(device: deviceCamera!) {
            if (captureSession.canAddInput(input)) {
                captureSession.addInput(input)

                if (captureSession.canAddOutput(cameraOutput)) {
                    captureSession.addOutput(cameraOutput)
                }

                previewLayer = AVCaptureVideoPreviewLayer(session:
                captureSession)
                previewLayer.videoGravity = AVLayerVideoGravity.
                resizeAspectFill
                previewLayer.frame = videoFeed.bounds
                videoFeed.layer.addSublayer(previewLayer)
                captureSession.startRunning()
```

CHAPTER 8   USING MACHINE LEARNING

```swift
        } else {
            print ("Could not get any input")
        }
    } else {
        print ("No video feed available")
    }

    recognizeImage()
}

@objc func recognizeImage() {
    let settings = AVCapturePhotoSettings()

    let previewPixelType = settings._
    availablePreviewPhotoPixelFormatTypes.first!

    let previewFormat = [kCVPixelBufferPixelFormatTypeKey as String:
    previewPixelType, kCVPixelBufferWidthKey as String: 160,
    kCVPixelBufferHeightKey as String: 160]

    settings.previewPhotoFormat = previewFormat

    cameraOutput.capturePhoto(with: settings, delegate: self)

}

func photoOutput(_ output: AVCapturePhotoOutput,
didFinishProcessingPhoto photo: AVCapturePhoto, error: Error?) {
    if let error = error {
        print ("Error code: \(error.localizedDescription)")
    }

    if let imageData = photo.fileDataRepresentation(), let image =
    UIImage(data: imageData) {
        predictItem(image: image)
    }
}
```

```
func getDocumentsDirectory() -> URL {
    let paths = FileManager.default.urls(for: .documentDirectory, in:
    .userDomainMask)
    let documentsDirectory = paths[0]
    return documentsDirectory
}

func predictItem(image: UIImage) {
    if let data = UIImagePNGRepresentation(image) {
        let fileName = getDocumentsDirectory().
        appendingPathComponent("image.png")
        try? data.write(to: fileName)

        let modelFile = SqueezeNet()
        let model = try! VNCoreMLModel(for: modelFile.model)

        let request = VNCoreMLRequest(model: model, completionHandler:
        finalGuess)
        let handler = VNImageRequestHandler(url: fileName)
        try! handler.perform([request])
    }
}

func finalGuess(request: VNRequest, error: Error?) {
    guard let results = request.results as?
    [VNClassificationObservation] else {
        fatalError("Unable to get a prediction")
    }

    var bestGuess = ""
    var confidence: VNConfidence = 0
    for classification in results {
        if classification.confidence > confidence {
            confidence = classification.confidence
            bestGuess = classification.identifier
        }
    }
```

CHAPTER 8 USING MACHINE LEARNING

```
        resultLabel.text = bestGuess + "\n"
        Timer.scheduledTimer(timeInterval: 5.0, target: self, selector:
        #selector(self.recognizeImage), userInfo: nil, repeats: false)
    }

}
```

When you run this project on an iPhone or iPad connected to your Macintosh through a USB cable, you can point the camera at a nearby item to see what the Core ML model thinks that item might be as shown in Figure 8-9. (Don't be surprised if the accuracy of most Core ML models is surprisingly low.)

Figure 8-9. Identifying an item through the camera of an iPhone

Summary

As you can see, Core ML machine learning models can be impressive in giving your app the ability to recognize items in images, but they still have limitations in failing to recognize everything with perfect accuracy. Not all Core ML models are equal in accuracy or size, so you may need to experiment with different Core ML models until you find the one that works best with your app.

The main idea behind Core ML is that you can add the ability to deal with unknown data by simply using a trained machine learning model. Apple will continue adding new Core ML models that will likely offer different features beyond just image recognition. Over time, you'll be able to add these trained machine learning models to your apps and give your app artificial intelligence with little effort.

CHAPTER 9

Using Facial and Text Recognition

In the previous chapter, you learned about Core ML, which lets you use machine learning models in your apps. However, iOS also offers another form of artificial intelligence that doesn't require finding and adding a trained machine learning model to your app. Instead, you can simply use the Vision framework that can recognize objects in in pictures such as faces or text.

At the simplest level, facial recognition can identify the number of faces in a picture and also draw rectangles in an image to show exactly all the faces the app recognized. On a more advanced level, facial recognition can also identify eyes, noses, and mouths and other parts of a face as well.

Beyond recognizing faces in a picture, the Vision framework can also recognize and identify text in a picture by displaying a rectangle around text. Just remember that text recognition works best with text that's easy to see such as black text against a white background (or white text against a dark background). Text that appears too similar to the background may get overlooked.

Although facial recognition and text recognition may not be perfect, it can be accurate enough to give your app extra features that requires you to write little additional code on your own.

CHAPTER 9   USING FACIAL AND TEXT RECOGNITION

Recognizing Faces in Pictures

Create a new iOS Single View App and name it FacialRecognition. To use facial recognition, you must import the Vision framework. In this app we'll be analyzing pictures stored in the Photos app so you also need to import the Photos framework so the ViewController.swift file should contain three import lines like this:

```
import UIKit
import Vision
import Photos
```

Since this app will need to pick pictures stored in the Photos app, we'll need to import the Photos framework and make the ViewController.swift file adopt the UIImagePickerControllerDelegate along with the UINavigationControllerDelegate. Modify the class ViewController line like this:

```
class ViewController: UIViewController, UIImagePickerControllerDelegate, UINavigationControllerDelegate {
```

Click on the Main.storyboard file and let's design the user interface. This will consist of a UIButton, a UIImageView, and a UILabel. Change the button's title to something more descriptive such as "Get Image" and resize the UIImageView and the UILabel. The UIImageView will display your chosen picture while the UILabel will display a message on the screen as shown in Figure 9-1.

CHAPTER 9 USING FACIAL AND TEXT RECOGNITION

Figure 9-1. *A button, label, and Image View defines the user interface*

Regardless of how you designed your user interface items, choose Editor ➤ Resolve Auto Layout Issues ➤ Reset to Suggested Constraints under the All Views in the Container category. This will set constraints on all your user interface items.

Now open the Assistant Editor and Control-drag from the UILabel and the UIImageView to the ViewController.swift file to create two IBOutlets named pictureChosen and messageLabel like this:

```
@IBOutlet var pictureChosen: UIImageView!
@IBOutlet var messageLabel: UILabel!
```

Control-drag from the button to the ViewController.swift file and create an IBAction named getImage and modify its code like this:

```
@IBAction func getImage(_ sender: UIButton) {
    getPhoto()
}
```

287

The getImage IBAction method needs to call a function called getPhoto, which will let the user view and retrieve an image stored in the Photos app.

Now let's write some code in the ViewController.swift file, so feel free to close the Assistant Editor so you'll have more room to view the ViewController.swift file. First, write a function called getPhoto, which will retrieve an image from the Photos app:

```swift
func getPhoto() {
    let picker = UIImagePickerController()
    picker.delegate = self
    picker.sourceType = .savedPhotosAlbum
    present(picker, animated: true, completion: nil)
}
```

Note For the picker.sourceType, you can choose either .savedPhotosAlbum or .photoLibrary.

Once the user selects an image, the next step is to display that image in the UIView on the user interface and analyze that image to look for faces. To do this, we need to create another function called imagePickerController that runs after the user picks an image from the Photos album:

```swift
func imagePickerController(_ picker: UIImagePickerController,
didFinishPickingMediaWithInfo info: [String : Any]) {
    picker.dismiss(animated: true, completion: nil)
    guard let gotImage = info[UIImagePickerControllerOriginalImage] as?
    UIImage else {
        fatalError("No picture chosen")
    }
    
    pictureChosen.image = gotImage
    analyzeImage(image: gotImage)
}
```

This function first dismisses the image picker. Then it verifies that a picture has been chosen. Once it has verified that the user chose a picture, it displays that image in the UIView connected to the IBOutlet named pictureChosen. Finally it calls another function to analyze the image, called analyzeImage.

CHAPTER 9 USING FACIAL AND TEXT RECOGNITION

Create an analyzeImage function like this:

```
func analyzeImage(image: UIImage) {
    let handler = VNImageRequestHandler(cgImage: image.cgImage!,
    options: [ : ])

    messageLabel.text = "Analyzing picture..."

    let request = VNDetectFaceRectanglesRequest(completionHandler:
    handleFaceRecognition)
    try! handler.perform([request])
}
```

This function uses VNDetectFaceRectanglesRequest in the Vision framework to detect faces in a picture. After it analyzes a picture, it runs another function called handleFaceRecognition.

This handleFaceRecognition function simply displays the number of faces in the UILabel on the user interface. Keep in mind that the facial recognition feature may not always be accurate for images where faces may be too small or may appear to blend in with the background.

The complete ViewController.swift code should appear as shown in Listing 9-1.

Listing 9-1. The ViewController.swift code for the FacialRecognition project

```
import UIKit
import Vision
import Photos

class ViewController: UIViewController, UIImagePickerControllerDelegate,
UINavigationControllerDelegate {

    @IBOutlet var pictureChosen: UIImageView!
    @IBOutlet var messageLabel: UILabel!

    override func viewDidLoad() {
        super.viewDidLoad()
        // Do any additional setup after loading the view, typically from a nib.
    }
```

```swift
override func didReceiveMemoryWarning() {
    super.didReceiveMemoryWarning()
    // Dispose of any resources that can be recreated.
}

@IBAction func getImage(_ sender: UIButton) {
    getPhoto()
}

func getPhoto() {
    let picker = UIImagePickerController()
    picker.delegate = self
    picker.sourceType = .savedPhotosAlbum
    present(picker, animated: true, completion: nil)
}

func imagePickerController(_ picker: UIImagePickerController,
didFinishPickingMediaWithInfo info: [String : Any]) {
    picker.dismiss(animated: true, completion: nil)
    guard let gotImage = info[UIImagePickerControllerOriginalImage] as?
    UIImage else {
        fatalError("No picture chosen")
    }
    
    pictureChosen.image = gotImage
    analyzeImage(image: gotImage)
}

func analyzeImage(image: UIImage) {
    let handler = VNImageRequestHandler(cgImage: image.cgImage!,
    options: [ : ])
    
    messageLabel.text = "Analyzing picture..."
    
    let request = VNDetectFaceRectanglesRequest(completionHandler:
    handleFaceRecognition)
    try! handler.perform([request])
}
```

CHAPTER 9   USING FACIAL AND TEXT RECOGNITION

```
    func handleFaceRecognition(request: VNRequest, error: Error?) {
        guard let foundFaces = request.results as? [VNFaceObservation] else
{
            fatalError ("Can't find a face in the picture")
        }
        messageLabel.text = "Found \(foundFaces.count) faces in the
        picture"
    }
}
```

You can test this project on either the Simulator or on an actual iOS device connected to your Macintosh through a USB cable. If you want to test this project on the Simulator, you'll need to add pictures of people in the Photos app. To do this, run this project on the Simulator, and then click on the Home button of the simulated iPhone/iPad to display the Home screen.

Now click the Safari icon (and make sure your Macintosh has an Internet connection). This will load Safari and from there, visit any site that contains pictures of people. When you see an image that you want to store in the Photos app in the Simulator, move the mouse pointer over that image, hold down the mouse/trackpad button, and slide up until a menu appears at the bottom of the screen as shown in Figure 9-2.

CHAPTER 9   USING FACIAL AND TEXT RECOGNITION

Figure 9-2. *Saving an image in Safari running on the Simulator*

Tap the Save Image button. Now click the Home button on the Simulator and return to the FacialRecognition app. Click the Get Image button on your FacialRecognition app and select the image you just saved from within Safari.

If you connect an iPhone/iPad to your Macintosh through its USB cable, you can load any picture stored in the Photos app. Whether you run the project in the Simulator or on an actual iOS device, the app should display the number of faces it found in an image as shown in Figure 9-3.

CHAPTER 9   USING FACIAL AND TEXT RECOGNITION

Figure 9-3. *Running the FacialRecognition app in the Simulator*

Highlighting Faces in an Image

Just identifying the number of faces in an image is fine, but you can also highlight each face with a rectangle to show you exactly which parts of a picture the Vision framework recognized as a face. There are two parts to identify faces in a picture with a rectangle. First, you need to use the VNFaceLandmarkRegion2D class to identify the face in the image. In the Vision framework, landmarks are identifying parts of an image where the most obvious landmark to identify is a face.

Once you identify a landmark (face) in an image, the second step is to draw a rectangle around that landmark (face). The final step is to take this image, with rectangles around one or more faces, and display it on the UIView on the user interface.

CHAPTER 9   USING FACIAL AND TEXT RECOGNITION

To see how to identify faces in a picture by drawing a rectangle around them, either create a new iOS Single View App project or duplicate the FacialRecognition project. In either case, name this new project AdvancedFacialRecognition. This AdvancedFacialRecognition needs a button (titled Get Image), a UIView, and a label (see Figure 9-1).

You'll need to import the Vision and Photos frameworks along with adopting two delegates like this:

```
import Vision
import Photos

class ViewController: UIViewController, UIImagePickerControllerDelegate, UINavigationControllerDelegate {
```

Next, you'll need two IBOutlets and an IBAction method as follows:

```
@IBOutlet var messageLabel: UILabel!
@IBOutlet var pictureChosen: UIImageView!

@IBAction func getImage(_ sender: UIButton) {
    getPhoto()
}
```

The getPhoto function displays the image picker control to let the user choose an image and looks like this:

```
func getPhoto() {
    let picker = UIImagePickerController()
    picker.delegate = self
    picker.sourceType = .photoLibrary
    present(picker, animated: true, completion: nil)
}
```

You need another function to run once the user selects an image through the image picker. This function will display the chosen image in the UIView and then call a function called identifyFacesWithLandmarks like this:

```
func imagePickerController(_ picker: UIImagePickerController,
didFinishPickingMediaWithInfo info: [String : Any]) {
    picker.dismiss(animated: true, completion: nil)
```

CHAPTER 9 USING FACIAL AND TEXT RECOGNITION

```
    guard let gotImage = info[UIImagePickerControllerOriginalImage] as?
    UIImage else {
        fatalError("No picture chosen")
    }

    pictureChosen.image = gotImage
    identifyFacesWithLandmarks(image: gotImage)
}
```

This identifyFacesWithLandmarks function uses the VNDetectFaceLandmarksRequest function to look for faces in a picture like this:

```
func identifyFacesWithLandmarks(image: UIImage) {
    let handler = VNImageRequestHandler(cgImage: image.cgImage!,
    options: [ : ])

    messageLabel.text = "Analyzing picture..."

    let request = VNDetectFaceLandmarksRequest(completionHandler:
    handleFaceLandmarksRecognition)
    try! handler.perform([request])
}
```

Each time the identifyFacesWithLandmarks function identifies a face in a picture, it runs another function called handleFaceLandmarksRecognition. This function is the one that uses VNFaceLandmarkRegion2D to identify the faces in a picture. Using this information, another function called drawImage actually draws the rectangle around the faces:

```
func handleFaceLandmarksRecognition(request: VNRequest, error: Error?) {
    guard let foundFaces = request.results as? [VNFaceObservation] else {
        fatalError ("Problem loading picture to examine faces")
    }
    messageLabel.text = "Found \(foundFaces.count) faces in the picture"

    for faceRectangle in foundFaces {

        var landmarkRegions: [VNFaceLandmarkRegion2D] = []
```

CHAPTER 9   USING FACIAL AND TEXT RECOGNITION

```
            drawImage(source: pictureChosen.image!, boundary: faceRectangle.
            boundingBox, faceLandmarkRegions: landmarkRegions)

    }
}
```

The drawImage function does the actual work of drawing rectangles on the chosen image. By altering the fillColor property, you can choose to draw rectangles in various colors such as green or red. The complete drawImage function looks like this:

```
func drawImage(source: UIImage, boundary: CGRect, faceLandmarkRegions:
[VNFaceLandmarkRegion2D]) {
    UIGraphicsBeginImageContextWithOptions(source.size, false, 1)
    let context = UIGraphicsGetCurrentContext()!
    context.translateBy(x: 0, y: source.size.height)
    context.scaleBy(x: 1.0, y: -1.0)
    context.setLineJoin(.round)
    context.setLineCap(.round)
    context.setShouldAntialias(true)
    context.setAllowsAntialiasing(true)

    let rect = CGRect(x: 0, y:0, width: source.size.width, height:
    source.size.height)
    context.draw(source.cgImage!, in: rect)

    //draw rectangles around faces
    let fillColor = UIColor.green
    fillColor.setStroke()

    let rectangleWidth = source.size.width * boundary.size.width
    let rectangleHeight = source.size.height * boundary.size.height

    context.addRect(CGRect(x: boundary.origin.x * source.size.width,
    y:boundary.origin.y * source.size.height, width: rectangleWidth,
    height: rectangleHeight))
    context.drawPath(using: CGPathDrawingMode.stroke)

    let modifiedImage : UIImage =
    UIGraphicsGetImageFromCurrentImageContext()!
```

```
    UIGraphicsEndImageContext()
    pictureChosen.image = modifiedImage
}
```

The last step in this function displays the modified image (with rectangles around each person's face) in the pictureChosen UIView on the user interface. Running this project should now display rectangles around each person's face as shown in Figure 9-4.

Figure 9-4. *Displaying rectangles around faces in a picture*

CHAPTER 9　USING FACIAL AND TEXT RECOGNITION

The complete ViewController.swift code should appear as shown in Listing 9-2:

Listing 9-2. *The ViewController.swift code for the AdvancedFacialRecognition project*

```swift
import UIKit
import Vision
import Photos

class ViewController: UIViewController, UIImagePickerControllerDelegate,
UINavigationControllerDelegate {

    @IBOutlet var messageLabel: UILabel!
    @IBOutlet var pictureChosen: UIImageView!

    override func viewDidLoad() {
        super.viewDidLoad()
        // Do any additional setup after loading the view, typically from a nib.
    }

    override func didReceiveMemoryWarning() {
        super.didReceiveMemoryWarning()
        // Dispose of any resources that can be recreated.
    }

    @IBAction func getImage(_ sender: UIButton) {
        getPhoto()
    }

    func getPhoto() {
        let picker = UIImagePickerController()
        picker.delegate = self
        picker.sourceType = .photoLibrary
        present(picker, animated: true, completion: nil)
    }

    func imagePickerController(_ picker: UIImagePickerController,
    didFinishPickingMediaWithInfo info: [String : Any]) {
        picker.dismiss(animated: true, completion: nil)
```

CHAPTER 9 USING FACIAL AND TEXT RECOGNITION

```swift
    guard let gotImage = info[UIImagePickerControllerOriginalImage] as?
    UIImage else {
        fatalError("No picture chosen")
    }

    pictureChosen.image = gotImage
    identifyFacesWithLandmarks(image: gotImage)
}

func identifyFacesWithLandmarks(image: UIImage) {
    let handler = VNImageRequestHandler(cgImage: image.cgImage!,
    options: [ : ])

    messageLabel.text = "Analyzing picture..."

    let request = VNDetectFaceLandmarksRequest(completionHandler:
    handleFaceLandmarksRecognition)
    try! handler.perform([request])
}

func handleFaceLandmarksRecognition (request: VNRequest, error: Error?) {
    guard let foundFaces = request.results as? [VNFaceObservation] else {
        fatalError ("Problem loading picture to examine faces")
    }
    messageLabel.text = "Found \(foundFaces.count) faces in the picture"

    for faceRectangle in foundFaces {

        var landmarkRegions: [VNFaceLandmarkRegion2D] = []

        drawImage(source: pictureChosen.image!, boundary: faceRectangle.
        boundingBox, faceLandmarkRegions: landmarkRegions)

    }
}
```

CHAPTER 9   USING FACIAL AND TEXT RECOGNITION

```swift
func drawImage(source: UIImage, boundary: CGRect, faceLandmarkRegions:
[VNFaceLandmarkRegion2D]) {
    UIGraphicsBeginImageContextWithOptions(source.size, false, 1)
    let context = UIGraphicsGetCurrentContext()!
    context.translateBy(x: 0, y: source.size.height)
    context.scaleBy(x: 1.0, y: -1.0)
    context.setLineJoin(.round)
    context.setLineCap(.round)
    context.setShouldAntialias(true)
    context.setAllowsAntialiasing(true)
    
    let rect = CGRect(x: 0, y:0, width: source.size.width, height: source.size.height)
    context.draw(source.cgImage!, in: rect)
    
    //draw rectangles around faces
    let fillColor = UIColor.green
    fillColor.setStroke()
    
    let rectangleWidth = source.size.width * boundary.size.width
    let rectangleHeight = source.size.height * boundary.size.height
    
    context.addRect(CGRect(x: boundary.origin.x * source.size.width, y:boundary.origin.y * source.size.height, width: rectangleWidth, height: rectangleHeight))
    context.drawPath(using: CGPathDrawingMode.stroke)
    
    let modifiedImage : UIImage = UIGraphicsGetImageFromCurrentImageContext()!
    UIGraphicsEndImageContext()
    pictureChosen.image = modifiedImage
  }

}
```

Highlighting Parts of a Face in an Image

Besides identifying faces in an image with a rectangle, the Vision framework can also identify and highlight the following parts of a face:

- Contour of the face
- Nose and nose crest
- Inner and outer lips
- Eye, eyebrow, and pupil for both the left and right eyes
- Median line

Note To get a complete listing of all the parts of a face the Vision framework can identify, visit Apple's developer's web site at: https://developer.apple.com/documentation/vision/vnfacelandmarks2d.

To identify facial features, we need to modify the code in the AdvancedFacialRecognition project. Within the handleFacelandmarksRecognition function, we'll need to look for landmarks within a face in an image by using this code:

```
guard let landmarks = faceRectangle.landmarks else {
    continue
}
```

Next we'll need to look for specific landmarks such as a left eye or nose. Once we find a specific facial feature, we need to store this in the landmarkRegions array using code such as the following:

```
if let faceContour = landmarks.faceContour {
    landmarkRegions.append(faceContour)
}
if let leftEye = landmarks.leftEye {
    landmarkRegions.append(leftEye)
}
if let rightEye = landmarks.rightEye {
    landmarkRegions.append(rightEye)
}
```

```
        if let nose = landmarks.nose {
            landmarkRegions.append(nose)
        }
```

The complete handleFaceLandmarksRecognition function should look like this:

```
func handleFaceLandmarksRecognition(request: VNRequest, error: Error?) {
    guard let foundFaces = request.results as? [VNFaceObservation] else {
        fatalError ("Problem loading picture to examine faces")
    }
    messageLabel.text = "Found \(foundFaces.count) faces in the picture"
    
    for faceRectangle in foundFaces {
        
        guard let landmarks = faceRectangle.landmarks else {
            continue
        }
        
        var landmarkRegions: [VNFaceLandmarkRegion2D] = []
        
        if let faceContour = landmarks.faceContour {
            landmarkRegions.append(faceContour)
        }
        if let leftEye = landmarks.leftEye {
            landmarkRegions.append(leftEye)
        }
        if let rightEye = landmarks.rightEye {
            landmarkRegions.append(rightEye)
        }
        if let nose = landmarks.nose {
            landmarkRegions.append(nose)
        }
```

CHAPTER 9 USING FACIAL AND TEXT RECOGNITION

```
        drawImage(source: pictureChosen.image!, boundary: faceRectangle.
        boundingBox, faceLandmarkRegions: landmarkRegions)

    }
}
```

The drawImage function needs to be modified to highlight any chosen facial features. First, change the fillColor constant to a variable like this:

```
var fillColor = UIColor.green
```

Then define a color, such as red, to highlight facial features and draw those lines as follows:

```
        fillColor = UIColor.red
        fillColor.setStroke()
        context.setLineWidth(2.0)
        for faceLandmarkRegion in faceLandmarkRegions {
            var points: [CGPoint] = []
            for i in 0..<faceLandmarkRegion.pointCount {
                let point = faceLandmarkRegion.normalizedPoints[i]
                let p = CGPoint(x: CGFloat(point.x), y: CGFloat(point.y))
                points.append(p)
            }
            let facialPoints = points.map { CGPoint(x: boundary.origin.x *
            source.size.width + $0.x * rectangleWidth, y: boundary.origin.y
            * source.size.height + $0.y * rectangleHeight) }
            context.addLines(between: facialPoints)
            context.drawPath(using: CGPathDrawingMode.stroke)
        }
```

The complete drawImage function should look like this:

```
func drawImage(source: UIImage, boundary: CGRect, faceLandmarkRegions:
[VNFaceLandmarkRegion2D])  {
    UIGraphicsBeginImageContextWithOptions(source.size, false, 1)
    let context = UIGraphicsGetCurrentContext()!
    context.translateBy(x: 0, y: source.size.height)
    context.scaleBy(x: 1.0, y: -1.0)
```

CHAPTER 9 USING FACIAL AND TEXT RECOGNITION

```
context.setLineJoin(.round)
context.setLineCap(.round)
context.setShouldAntialias(true)
context.setAllowsAntialiasing(true)

let rect = CGRect(x: 0, y:0, width: source.size.width, height:
source.size.height)
context.draw(source.cgImage!, in: rect)

//draw rectangles around faces
var fillColor = UIColor.green
fillColor.setStroke()

let rectangleWidth = source.size.width * boundary.size.width
let rectangleHeight = source.size.height * boundary.size.height

context.addRect(CGRect(x: boundary.origin.x * source.size.width,
y:boundary.origin.y * source.size.height, width: rectangleWidth,
height: rectangleHeight))
context.drawPath(using: CGPathDrawingMode.stroke)

//draw facial features
fillColor = UIColor.red
fillColor.setStroke()
context.setLineWidth(2.0)
for faceLandmarkRegion in faceLandmarkRegions {
    var points: [CGPoint] = []
    for i in 0..<faceLandmarkRegion.pointCount {
        let point = faceLandmarkRegion.normalizedPoints[i]
        let p = CGPoint(x: CGFloat(point.x), y: CGFloat(point.y))
        points.append(p)
    }
    let facialPoints = points.map { CGPoint(x: boundary.origin.x *
    source.size.width + $0.x * rectangleWidth, y: boundary.origin.y
    * source.size.height + $0.y * rectangleHeight) }
    context.addLines(between: facialPoints)
    context.drawPath(using: CGPathDrawingMode.stroke)
}
```

CHAPTER 9   USING FACIAL AND TEXT RECOGNITION

```
    let modifiedImage : UIImage = UIGraphicsGetImageFromCurrent
    ImageContext()!
    UIGraphicsEndImageContext()
    pictureChosen.image = modifiedImage
}
```

Running this project will then highlight the face contour, nose, left, and right eye as shown in Figure 9-5.

Figure 9-5. *Highlighting facial features in a picture*

CHAPTER 9 USING FACIAL AND TEXT RECOGNITION

The complete code in the ViewController.swift file should look like Listing 9-3.

Listing 9-3. The ViewController.swift code for the AdvancedFacialRecognition project to recognize facial features

```
import UIKit
import Vision
import Photos

class ViewController: UIViewController, UIImagePickerControllerDelegate,
UINavigationControllerDelegate {

    @IBOutlet var messageLabel: UILabel!
    @IBOutlet var pictureChosen: UIImageView!

    override func viewDidLoad() {
        super.viewDidLoad()
        // Do any additional setup after loading the view, typically from a nib.
    }

    override func didReceiveMemoryWarning() {
        super.didReceiveMemoryWarning()
        // Dispose of any resources that can be recreated.
    }

    @IBAction func getImage(_ sender: UIButton) {
        getPhoto()
    }

    func getPhoto() {
        let picker = UIImagePickerController()
        picker.delegate = self
        picker.sourceType = .photoLibrary
        present(picker, animated: true, completion: nil)
    }

    func imagePickerController(_ picker: UIImagePickerController,
    didFinishPickingMediaWithInfo info: [String : Any]) {
        picker.dismiss(animated: true, completion: nil)
```

CHAPTER 9   USING FACIAL AND TEXT RECOGNITION

```
    guard let gotImage = info[UIImagePickerControllerOriginalImage] as?
    UIImage else {
        fatalError("No picture chosen")
    }

    pictureChosen.image = gotImage
    identifyFacesWithLandmarks(image: gotImage)
}

func identifyFacesWithLandmarks(image: UIImage) {
    let handler = VNImageRequestHandler(cgImage: image.cgImage!,
    options: [ : ])

    messageLabel.text = "Analyzing picture..."

    let request = VNDetectFaceLandmarksRequest(completionHandler:
    handleFaceLandmarksRecognition)
    try! handler.perform([request])
}

func handleFaceLandmarksRecognition(request: VNRequest, error: Error?) {
    guard let foundFaces = request.results as? [VNFaceObservation] else {
        fatalError ("Problem loading picture to examine faces")
    }
    messageLabel.text = "Found \(foundFaces.count) faces in the picture"

    for faceRectangle in foundFaces {

        guard let landmarks = faceRectangle.landmarks else {
            continue
        }

        var landmarkRegions: [VNFaceLandmarkRegion2D] = []

        if let faceContour = landmarks.faceContour {
            landmarkRegions.append(faceContour)
        }
```

```swift
            if let leftEye = landmarks.leftEye {
                landmarkRegions.append(leftEye)
            }
            if let rightEye = landmarks.rightEye {
                landmarkRegions.append(rightEye)
            }
            if let nose = landmarks.nose {
                landmarkRegions.append(nose)
            }
            
            drawImage(source: pictureChosen.image!, boundary: faceRectangle.
            boundingBox, faceLandmarkRegions: landmarkRegions)
            
        }
    }
    
    func drawImage(source: UIImage, boundary: CGRect, faceLandmarkRegions:
    [VNFaceLandmarkRegion2D]) {
        UIGraphicsBeginImageContextWithOptions(source.size, false, 1)
        let context = UIGraphicsGetCurrentContext()!
        context.translateBy(x: 0, y: source.size.height)
        context.scaleBy(x: 1.0, y: -1.0)
        context.setLineJoin(.round)
        context.setLineCap(.round)
        context.setShouldAntialias(true)
        context.setAllowsAntialiasing(true)
        
        let rect = CGRect(x: 0, y:0, width: source.size.width, height:
        source.size.height)
        context.draw(source.cgImage!, in: rect)
        
        //draw rectangles around faces
        var fillColor = UIColor.green
        fillColor.setStroke()
        
        let rectangleWidth = source.size.width * boundary.size.width
        let rectangleHeight = source.size.height * boundary.size.height
```

CHAPTER 9 USING FACIAL AND TEXT RECOGNITION

```
    context.addRect(CGRect(x: boundary.origin.x * source.size.width,
    y:boundary.origin.y * source.size.height, width: rectangleWidth,
    height: rectangleHeight))
    context.drawPath(using: CGPathDrawingMode.stroke)

    //draw facial features
    fillColor = UIColor.red
    fillColor.setStroke()
    context.setLineWidth(2.0)
    for faceLandmarkRegion in faceLandmarkRegions {
        var points: [CGPoint] = []
        for i in 0..<faceLandmarkRegion.pointCount {
            let point = faceLandmarkRegion.normalizedPoints[i]
            let p = CGPoint(x: CGFloat(point.x), y: CGFloat(point.y))
            points.append(p)
        }
        let facialPoints = points.map { CGPoint(x: boundary.origin.x *
        source.size.width + $0.x * rectangleWidth, y: boundary.origin.y
        * source.size.height + $0.y * rectangleHeight) }
        context.addLines(between: facialPoints)
        context.drawPath(using: CGPathDrawingMode.stroke)
    }

    let modifiedImage : UIImage =
    UIGraphicsGetImageFromCurrentImageContext()!
    UIGraphicsEndImageContext()
    pictureChosen.image = modifiedImage
   }
}
```

Recognizing Text in an Image

Besides recognizing text, the Vision framework can also recognize text in an image or through a camera. To see how the Vision framework can detect text, create a new iOS Single View App and name it TextRecognition. This app will use the camera so you can point at a sign and the app will identify text by drawing rectangles around it. To use

CHAPTER 9   USING FACIAL AND TEXT RECOGNITION

text recognition through the camera of an iOS device, you must import the Vision and AVFoundation frameworks. In addition, your ViewController.swift file will need to adopt a delegate for capturing video output, so in your TextRecognition project, click on the ViewController.swift file and make sure the first lines look like this:

```
import UIKit
import Vision
import AVFoundation

class ViewController: UIViewController,
AVCaptureVideoDataOutputSampleBufferDelegate {
```

Click on the Main.storyboard file in the Navigator pane and place a UIImageView on the user interface. The exact placement doesn't matter, but you'll want the UIImageView to be as large as possible because this is where you'll see the video output that identifies text.

After you have placed the UIImageView on the user interface, choose Editor ➤ Resolve Auto Layout Issues ➤ Reset to Suggested Constraints.

Open the Assistant Editor and Control-drag from the UIImageView to the ViewController.swift file and create an IBOutlet as follows:

```
@IBOutlet var textImage: UIImageView!
```

Now we need to create one variable to capture video from the camera and a second variable to analyze the image like this:

```
var session = AVCaptureSession()
var requests = [VNRequest]()
```

There are two steps to identifying text in an image through the camera. First, we need to get an image from the camera. Second, we need to identify text in that image. So modify the viewDidLoad function to call two functions called getVideo and detectText like this:

```
override func viewDidLoad() {
    super.viewDidLoad()
    // Do any additional setup after loading the view, typically from a nib.
    getVideo()
    detectText()
}
```

CHAPTER 9 USING FACIAL AND TEXT RECOGNITION

The getVideo function needs to define the camera to record video and then capture that video. Finally, it must display that video in the UIImageView using the textImage IBOutlet. Add a getVideo function like this:

```swift
func getVideo() {
    session.sessionPreset = AVCaptureSession.Preset.photo
    let camera = AVCaptureDevice.default(for: AVMediaType.video)

    let cameraInput = try! AVCaptureDeviceInput(device: camera!)
    let cameraOutput = AVCaptureVideoDataOutput()
    cameraOutput.videoSettings = [kCVPixelBufferPixelFormatTypeKey as String: Int(kCVPixelFormatType_32BGRA)]
    cameraOutput.setSampleBufferDelegate(self, queue: DispatchQueue.global(qos: DispatchQoS.QoSClass.default))
    session.addInput(cameraInput)
    session.addOutput(cameraOutput)

    let videoLayer = AVCaptureVideoPreviewLayer(session: session)
    videoLayer.frame = textImage.bounds
    textImage.layer.addSublayer(videoLayer)
    session.startRunning()
}
```

To capture an image from the camera, create a captureOutput function as follows:

```swift
func captureOutput(_ output: AVCaptureOutput, didOutput sampleBuffer: CMSampleBuffer, from connection: AVCaptureConnection) {
    guard let pixelBuffer = CMSampleBufferGetImageBuffer(sampleBuffer)
        else {
            return
    }

    var requestOptions:[VNImageOption : Any] = [:]

    if let cameraData = CMGetAttachment(sampleBuffer, kCMSampleBufferAttachmentKey_CameraIntrinsicMatrix, nil) {
        requestOptions = [.cameraIntrinsics:cameraData]
    }
```

CHAPTER 9   USING FACIAL AND TEXT RECOGNITION

```
        let imageRequestHandler = VNImageRequestHandler(cvPixelBuffer:
        pixelBuffer, orientation: CGImagePropertyOrientation(rawValue: 6)!,
        options: requestOptions)

        do {
            try imageRequestHandler.perform(self.requests)
        } catch {
            print(error)
        }
    }
```

All the code you've written so far simply gets the camera to work on an iOS device, but you won't be able to access the camera until the user gives your app permission to do so. The final step is to click on the Info.plist file in the Navigator pane and add the Privacy – Camera usage Description key. Under the Value column, type descriptive text such as "Need to use camera to view text" as shown in Figure 9-6.

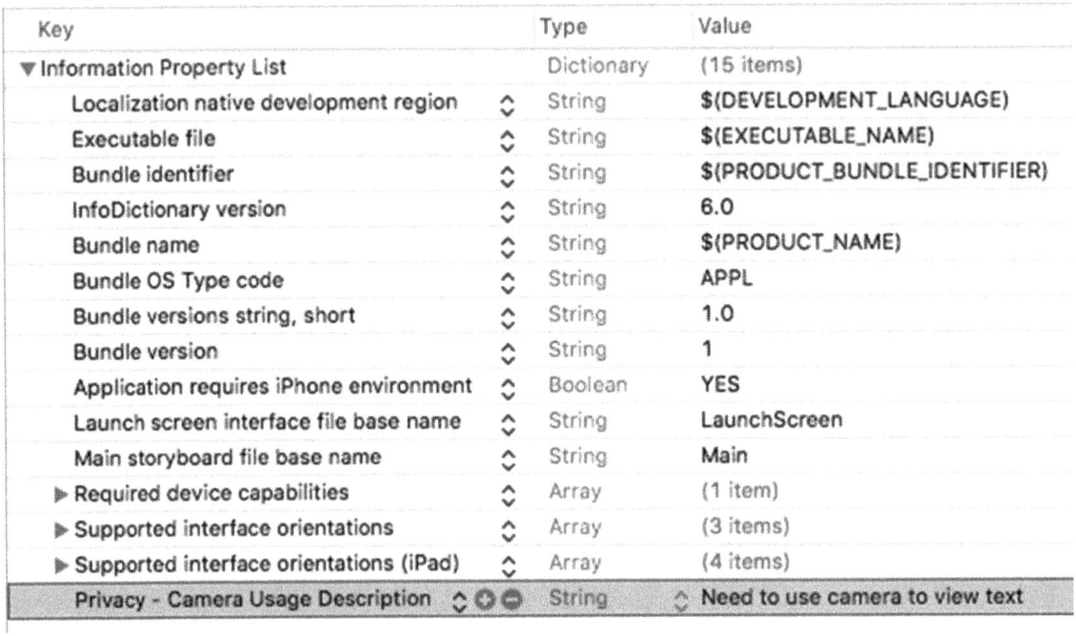

Key	Type	Value
▼ Information Property List	Dictionary	(15 items)
Localization native development region	String	$(DEVELOPMENT_LANGUAGE)
Executable file	String	$(EXECUTABLE_NAME)
Bundle identifier	String	$(PRODUCT_BUNDLE_IDENTIFIER)
InfoDictionary version	String	6.0
Bundle name	String	$(PRODUCT_NAME)
Bundle OS Type code	String	APPL
Bundle versions string, short	String	1.0
Bundle version	String	1
Application requires iPhone environment	Boolean	YES
Launch screen interface file base name	String	LaunchScreen
Main storyboard file base name	String	Main
▶ Required device capabilities	Array	(1 item)
▶ Supported interface orientations	Array	(3 items)
▶ Supported interface orientations (iPad)	Array	(4 items)
Privacy - Camera Usage Description	String	Need to use camera to view text

Figure 9-6. Editing the Info.plist file lets an app ask for permissiont to use the camera

CHAPTER 9 USING FACIAL AND TEXT RECOGNITION

The final step is to detect text in an image. First, write a detectText function like this to identify text using the VNDetectTextRectanglesRequest method:

```
func detectText() {
    let textRequest = VNDetectTextRectanglesRequest(completionHandler: handleText)
    textRequest.reportCharacterBoxes = true
    requests = [textRequest]
}
```

Once this function identifies text in an image, it calls a second function called handleText to define where to display a rectangle on the image. Another function called identifyWords does the actual work of drawing a rectangle where text appears. So create a handleText and identifyWords function like this:

```
func handleText(request: VNRequest, error: Error?) {
    guard let observations = request.results else {
        print ("No text found")
        return
    }

    let result = observations.map({$0 as? VNTextObservation})

    DispatchQueue.main.async() {
        self.textImage.layer.sublayers?.removeSubrange(1...)
        for region in result {
            guard let foundRegion = region else {
                continue
            }
            self.identifyWords(box: foundRegion)
        }
    }
}
func identifyWords(box: VNTextObservation) {
    guard let rectangle = box.characterBoxes else {
        return
    }
```

313

CHAPTER 9   USING FACIAL AND TEXT RECOGNITION

```
        var maxX: CGFloat = 9999.0
        var minX: CGFloat = 0.0
        var maxY: CGFloat = 9999.0
        var minY: CGFloat = 0.0

        for char in rectangle {
            if char.bottomLeft.x < maxX {
                maxX = char.bottomLeft.x
            }
            if char.bottomRight.x > minX {
                minX = char.bottomRight.x
            }
            if char.bottomRight.y < maxY {
                maxY = char.bottomRight.y
            }
            if char.topRight.y > minY {
                minY = char.topRight.y
            }
        }

        let xCord = maxX * textImage.frame.size.width
        let yCord = (1 - minY) * textImage.frame.size.height
        let width = (minX - maxX) * textImage.frame.size.width
        let height = (minY - maxY) * textImage.frame.size.height

        let outline = CALayer()
        outline.frame = CGRect(x: xCord, y: yCord, width: width, height: height)
        outline.borderWidth = 2.0
        outline.borderColor = UIColor.red.cgColor

        textImage.layer.addSublayer(outline)
}
```

Note   To test this app, you'll need to connect an iPhone or iPad with a camera to your Macintosh using a USB cable.

When you test this app on an actual iOS device, aim the camera at a sign. Whatever the camera sees appears inside the UIImageView on the user interface and displays rectangles around text. While the Vision framework may not always be accurate in identifying text in an image, it can recognize text in different languages as shown in Figure 9-7.

Figure 9-7. Identifying text on a sign through the iPhone camera

Summary

As you can see, the Vision framework contains enough artificial intelligence to identify and recognize faces in a picture. Not only can you identify the number of faces, but you can also identify the faces by drawing a rectangle around them in a picture.

Besides recognizing faces, the Vision framework can also identify specific facial features such as eyes, nose, and lips. If your app works with images containing people or text, you can use the Vision framework to identifying faces, facial features, and text (even in different languages) to give your app extra features without writing much code yourself.

CHAPTER 10

Using 3D Touch

When Apple introduced the iPhone, smartphones often displayed rows of buttons or sported keyboards that folded or flipped out. Having to display so many buttons meant that the smartphone couldn't display much of the screen. Fortunately, the iPhone changed the smartphone world when they introduced the touch screen interface. Instead of crowding the smartphone with physical buttons, the touch screen interface displayed a single screen that could offer virtual buttons.

Such virtual buttons meant the screen could adapt to the user's needs. If you were typing an e-mail message, the virtual keyboard could display characters to type. If you were browsing the Internet, the virtual keyboard could display commonly used keys such as the @ symbol or the .com extension. Virtual keyboards made the iPhone far more versatile than older smartphones that relied on physical buttons.

The touch screen interface of the iPhone initially focused on taps and gestures. Tapping an icon on the screen would select it while swiping on that same icon might make it move or slide away. While useful, such two-dimensional interaction can be limiting. That's why the latest iPhones offer a third way to interact with the touch screen called 3D Touch.

The idea behind 3D Touch is to add a third dimension to interaction with the touch screen: pressure. By pressing your finger on an icon for an extended period of time, 3D Touch can display shortcuts. By adding support for 3D Touch, your app can take advantage of the iPhone's latest touch gestures.

Note Only the iPhone 6s and later support 3D Touch. The iPad does not support 3D Touch.

CHAPTER 10   USING 3D TOUCH

Understanding 3D Touch

3D Touch first appeared on the iPhone 6s and has been a standard feature of every iPhone since then. The two most common ways to interact with 3D Touch is from the Home screen and from within your app itself. 3D Touch works by detecting the amount of pressure a user places on the touch screen.

When you use 3D Touch from the Home screen, a pop-up menu appears, listing several common actions you're most likely to want from that app. This pop-up menu can display shortcuts, called Quick Actions, that consist of up to two lines of text and an icon as shown in Figure 10-1.

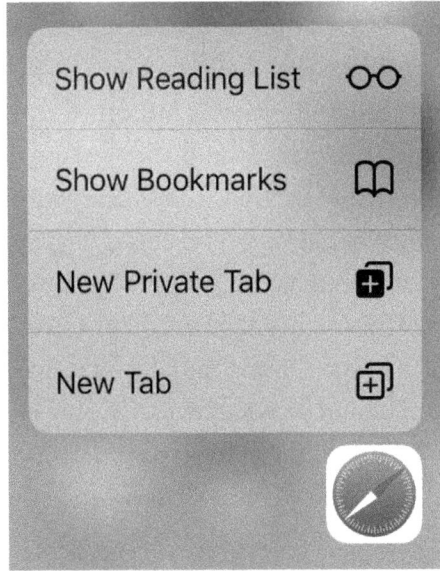

Figure 10-1. *3D Touch can display Quick Actions*

By tapping on a Quick Action, users can immediately access common features of an app. The second common way to use 3D Touch is within an app itself, which can involve three steps:

- Peek availability
- Peek
- Peek quick actions

CHAPTER 10 USING 3D TOUCH

When you first press on an item within an app, peek availability blurs the surrounding screen to show you that it supports 3D Touch as shown in Figure 10-2.

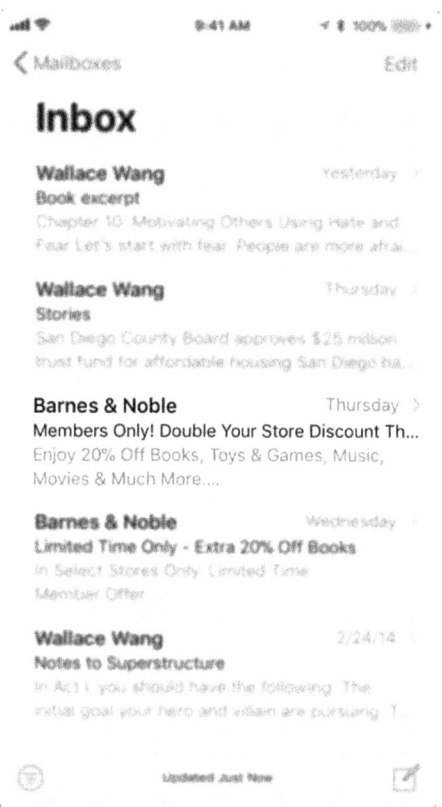

Figure 10-2. *Peek availability blurs the surrounding area to show that the app supports 3D Touch*

Once an app reveals that it supports 3D Touch through blurring the screen, the user can continue pressing to peek at more detailed information in a window that doesn't quite fill up the screen. This Peek action lets you view information without taking the time to open it as shown in Figure 10-3.

319

CHAPTER 10   USING 3D TOUCH

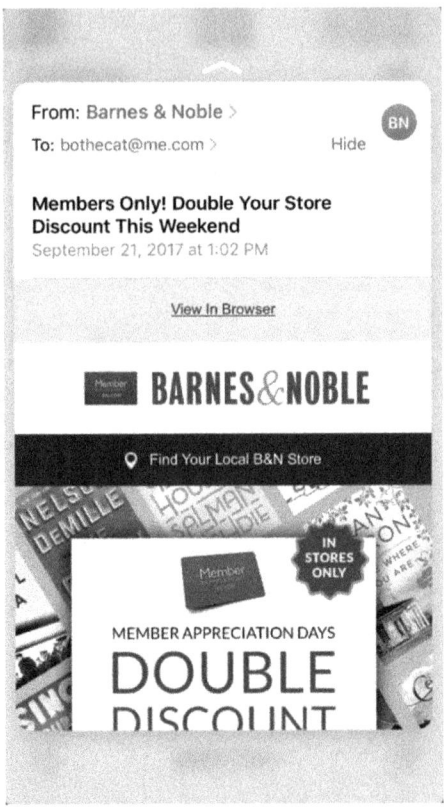

Figure 10-3. *Peek lets you view information without opening it fully in an app*

If you release your finger from the screen, this Peek information will disappear. However, if you swipe up, a menu of Peek Quick Actions appears at the bottom of the screen. This lets you perform common actions without opening the data within the app. At this point, the user can stop touching the screen to tap on one of the Peek Quick Actions as shown in Figure 10-4.

CHAPTER 10 USING 3D TOUCH

Figure 10-4. *A Peek Quick Action menu lets the user choose a common action for the displayed data*

To make this Peek Quick Action menu go away, the user can tap the top of the screen.

Detecting 3D Touch Availability

Since your app may be used on an iPad or iPhone model earlier than the iPhone 6s, your app must first check if a device supports 3D Touch or not. To see how 3D Touch works, create a new iOS Single View App project and name it 3D Touch.

CHAPTER 10 USING 3D TOUCH

Now click on the ViewController.swift file in the Project navigator and add the following function:

```
override func touchesMoved(_ touches: Set<UITouch>, with event:
UIEvent?) {
  if let touch = touches.first {
     if #available(iOS 9.0, *) {
        if traitCollection.forceTouchCapability == UIForceTouch
        Capability.available {
           print ("3D Touch available!")
        } else {
           print ("3D Touch not available")
        }
     } else {
        print ("Need iOS 9 or higher")
     }
  }
}
```

This code first detects a touch and then checks if the device is running iOS 9 or higher. That's because 3D Touch is only supported by iOS 9 and higher. The next if statement checks if 3D Touch capability is available. If 3D Touch is available and the device is running iOS 9 or higher, then the above code prints "3D Touch available!"

3D Touch first appeared on the iPhone 6s so any older iPhone model won't support 3D Touch. It's best to ensure a device can support 3D Touch to avoid possible crashes on older iPhone models.

Run this app in the Simulator and make sure the Simulator mimics an iPhone 6s or newer model. This will display the message "3D Touch available!" in the Debug area window. Then change the target device to an older iPhone model such as iPhone 5s. When running on a simulated iPhone 5s, the message "3D Touch not available" will appear.

Note Users can also turn off 3D Touch on their iOS device in Settings ➤ General ➤ Accessibility ➤ 3D Touch.

Detecting Pressure

Once you know that a device offers 3D Touch, you may want to detect the pressure from the user pressing down on the screen. To simulate 3D Touch, you need to run your app on one of the following:

- In the Simulator running on a laptop Macintosh with a touch pad or a desktop Macintosh with a Magic Trackpad.

- On an iPhone 6s or later connected to a Macintosh through its USB cable.

The two properties for detecting the pressure of 3D Touch include "force" and "maximumPossibleForce." The force property measures the current amount of pressure while the maximumPossibleForce property defines the maximum pressure iOS can recognize.

To measure the pressure from a 3D Touch, drag and drop a UILabel on the Main.storyboard file. Then open the Assistant Editor and Control-drag from the UILabel to the ViewController.swift file to create an IBOutlet and name this IBOutlet forceLabel. This will create an IBOutlet as follows:

```
@IBOutlet var forceLabel: UILabel!
```

Now modify the touchesMoved function as follows:

```
override func touchesMoved(_ touches: Set<UITouch>, with event: UIEvent?) {
    if let touch = touches.first {
        if #available(iOS 9.0, *) {
            if traitCollection.forceTouchCapability == UIForceTouchCapability.available {
                //print ("3D Touch available!")
                let force = touch.force/touch.maximumPossibleForce
                forceLabel.text = "\(force * 100)% force"
            } else {
                print ("3D Touch not available")
            }
```

```
        } else {
            print ("Need iOS 9 or higher")
        }
    }
}
```

This modified code retrieves the pressure on the screen from the touch.force property. Then it divides this value by the maximumPossibleForce property. Finally, it displays this value as a percentage in the label on the app's user interface.

When you run this app, you can press on your Macintosh trackpad or on the iPhone screen itself to see how hard you pressed on the screen as shown in Figure 10-5.

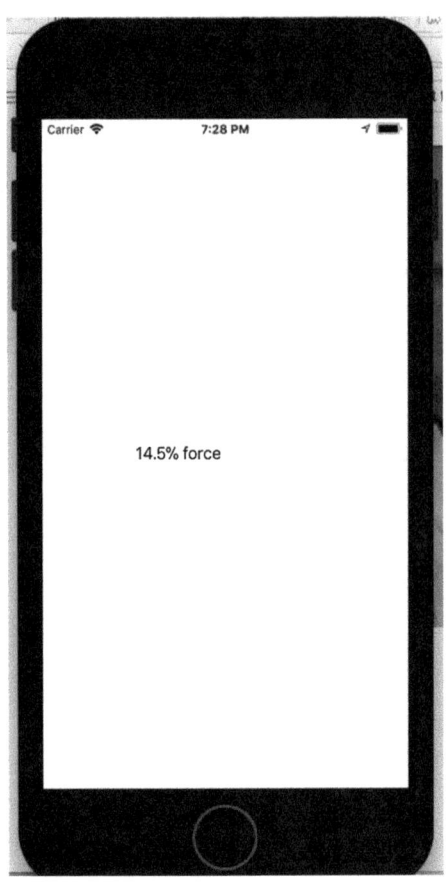

Figure 10-5. *Running the 3D Touch app to detect pressure*

Creating Home Screen Quick Actions

Quick Actions give the user the option of opening an app using different options. For example, when you use Quick Actions on the Safari icon on the Home Screen, you'll have the option of opening a new tab, a privacy tab, a reading list, or a list of bookmarks (see Figure 9-1). Quick Actions provide shortcuts to commonly used features in an app.

There are two parts to creating Quick Actions. First, you need to create a menu of up to four Quick Actions by defining multiple strings in a dictionary stored in the info.plist file. Each Quick Action can display a title, a subtitle, and an icon. Second, you need to write Swift code in a method to handle every Quick Action.

Click on the Info.plist file in the Navigator pane. This displays the Information Property List of your app. Click the mouse pointer over the up/down arrow icons that appear to the right of any key item in the property list. A + and a – icon appear to the right of the up/down arrow.

Click the + key to create a new property list item and name this UIApplicationShortcutItems. Make sure its Type is an Array.

Repeat the above steps to create two items numbered Item 0 and Item 1. This will create two Home Screen Quick Actions. Create three additional rows under each Item and name these three items as follows:

- UIApplicationShortcutItemTitle – Defines the Quick Action shortcut title

- UIApplicationShortcutItemSubtitle – Defines the Quick Action shortcut subtitle that appears in a smaller font size under the title text (optional).

- UIApplicationShortcutItemType – Defines a required string to create a Quick Action shortcut menu.

For our 3D Touch app, we'll just create two Quick Action shortcuts, so create nine new rows in the Information Property List that looks like the table below and Figure 10-6:

CHAPTER 10　USING 3D TOUCH

Key	Type	Value
▼ Information Property List	Dictionary	(15 items)
Localization native development region	String	$(DEVELOPMENT_LANGUAGE)
Executable file	String	$(EXECUTABLE_NAME)
Bundle identifier	String	$(PRODUCT_BUNDLE_IDENTIFIER)
InfoDictionary version	String	6.0
Bundle name	String	$(PRODUCT_NAME)
Bundle OS Type code	String	APPL
Bundle versions string, short	String	1.0
Bundle version	String	1
Application requires iPhone environment	Boolean	YES
▼ UIApplicationShortcutItems	Array	(2 items)
▼ Item 0	Dictionary	(3 items)
UIApplicationShortcutItemTitle	String	View
UIApplicationShortcutItemSubtitle	String	View favorite items
UIApplicationShortcutItemType	String	$(PRODUCT_BUNDLE_IDENTIFIER).First
▼ Item 1	Dictionary	(3 items)
UIApplicationShortcutItemTitle	String	Share
UIApplicationShortcutItemSubtitle	String	Share items with friends
UIApplicationShortcutItemType	String	$(PRODUCT_BUNDLE_IDENTIFIER).Second
Launch screen interface file base name	String	LaunchScreen
Main storyboard file base name	String	Main
▶ Required device capabilities	Array	(1 item)
▶ Supported interface orientations	Array	(3 items)
▶ Supported interface orientations (iPad)	Array	(4 items)

Figure 10-6. Defining Quick Action shortcuts in the Information Property List

Key	Type	Value
UIApplicationShortcutItems	Array	(2 items)
Item 0	Dictionary	(3 items)
UIApplicationShortcutItemTitle	String	View
UIApplicationShortcutItemSubtitle	String	View favorite items
UIApplicationShortcutItemType	String	$(PRODUCT_BUNDLE_IDENTIFIER).First
Item 1	Dictionary	(3 items)
UIApplicationShortcutItemTitle	String	Share
UIApplicationShortcutItemSubtitle	String	Share items with friends
UIApplicationShortcutItemType	String	$(PRODUCT_BUNDLE_IDENTIFIER).Second

Run this app in the Simulator (if your Macintosh has a touch pad or Magic Trackpad) or on an iPhone 6s or higher. When the app runs, click the Home button to return to the Home Screen and look for the 3D Touch icon. Press and hold over this 3D Touch icon and you'll see your defined Quick Action shortcut menu as shown in Figure 10-7.

Figure 10-7. *Displaying the Quick Action shortcut menu*

If you notice the Quick Action menu, the title appears in large font and the subtitle appears in a smaller font. However, you may notice a black dot. This is where you can define an icon to appear. Apple provides icons to represent common tasks such as sharing, adding, or choosing a favorite item. To view a complete list of available icons, visit `https://developer.apple.com/documentation/uikit/uiapplicationshortcuticontype`.

To define an icon, you need to create an additional row for each Quick Action shortcut that defines UIApplicationShortcutItemIconType. Then define this as an icon using UIApplicationShortcutIconTypeFavorite and UIApplicationShortcutIconTypeShare as shown in Figure 10-8.

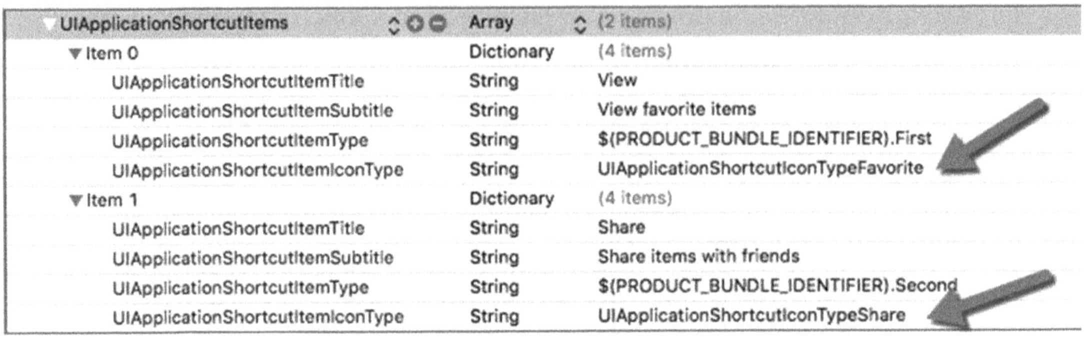

UIApplicationShortcutItems	Array	(2 items)
▼ Item 0	Dictionary	(4 items)
UIApplicationShortcutItemTitle	String	View
UIApplicationShortcutItemSubtitle	String	View favorite items
UIApplicationShortcutItemType	String	$(PRODUCT_BUNDLE_IDENTIFIER).First
UIApplicationShortcutItemIconType	String	UIApplicationShortcutIconTypeFavorite
▼ Item 1	Dictionary	(4 items)
UIApplicationShortcutItemTitle	String	Share
UIApplicationShortcutItemSubtitle	String	Share items with friends
UIApplicationShortcutItemType	String	$(PRODUCT_BUNDLE_IDENTIFIER).Second
UIApplicationShortcutItemIconType	String	UIApplicationShortcutIconTypeShare

Figure 10-8. Adding icons to the Quick Action menu items

Note Make sure you spell everything (including upper- and lowercase letters) exactly right. Be especially careful when defining an icon type. Under the Key column heading, you must use UIApplicationShortcutItemIconType (UI Application Shortcut Item Icon Type) but under the Value column heading, you need to use UIApplicationShortcutIconType (UI Application Shortcut Icon Type) followed by the icon name you want to use such as Share or Favorite.

Run this project on the Simulator or on an iPhone 6s or later. When the app runs, click the Home button to return to the Home screen and then press the 3D Touch icon. Notice that the Quick Actions menu items now display icons as shown in Figure 10-9.

CHAPTER 10 USING 3D TOUCH

Figure 10-9. *Displaying icons in the Quick Action menu items*

Responding to Quick Action Items

Once you've created a list of Quick Action menu items, the last step is to write Swift code to respond to the Quick Action the user chose. To do that, you need to write Swift code in the AppDelegate.swift file of your project. The AppDelegate.swift file needs to contain an enumeration that identifies each Quick Action item with a descriptive name.

There are two parts to creating an enumeration. First, you must create an enumeration that has an equal number of Quick Actions you want to display. So if you want to respond to four Quick Actions, you must have four items defined in the enumeration.

329

In our project, we just have two Quick Action menu items, so our enumeration only needs to define two items like this:

```
enum MenuItems: String {
    case First
    case Second
}
```

The exact name of your enumeration is arbitrary (such as MenuItems). Also the name you give for each item in the enumeration is also arbitrary (First and Second). Next, we need to initialize the enumeration items using the following code as part of the enumeration:

```
enum MenuItems: String {
    case First
    case Second

    init?(fullType: String) {
        guard let last = fullType.components(separatedBy: ".").last
        else { return nil }

        self.init(rawValue: last)
    }

    // MARK: Properties

    var type: String {
        return Bundle.main.bundleIdentifier! + ".\(self.rawValue)"
    }
}
```

To respond to Quick Action items, you need to create a variable of the type UIApplicationShortcutItem in the AppDelegate.swift file like this:

```
var launchedShortcutItem: UIApplicationShortcutItem?
```

In the AppDelegate.swift file, you need to write two application functions. The first application function runs when the user selects a Quick Action item. This function stores the selected Quick Action selection in the launchedShortcutItem variable like this:

```
func application(_ application: UIApplication, didFinishLaunching
WithOptions launchOptions: [UIApplicationLaunchOptionsKey: Any]?) ->
Bool {
    if let shortcutItem = launchOptions?[UIApplicationLaunchOptions
    Key.shortcutItem] as? UIApplicationShortcutItem {
    
        launchedShortcutItem = shortcutItem
    }
    
    return true
}
```

The second application function does nothing more than call a function to handle the completion of the user choosing a Quick Action item:

```
func application(_ application: UIApplication, performActionFor
shortcutItem: UIApplicationShortcutItem, completionHandler: @escaping
(Bool) -> Void) {

    completionHandler(handleShortCutItem(shortcutItem))
}
```

The above function calls a function called handleShortCutItem (this name is arbitrary and can be anything you want to call it). This handleShortCutItem function does the actual work of deciding how to respond to which Quick Action item the user chose.

Now let's write the handleShortCutItem function to respond to the Quick Action the user chose. There are two ways to identify the user's chosen Quick Action. One way is to identify the choice defined by the enumeration. The second way is to identify the localizedTitle property, which identifies the UIApplicationShortcutItemTitle for the Quick Action shortcut you defined in the Info.plist file.

However you want to identify the Quick Action the user chose, you'll likely need a switch statement to identify the chosen Quick Action and then respond to it. In our

331

CHAPTER 10   USING 3D TOUCH

project, we'll just identify the Quick Action chosen. Add the handleShortCutItem function to the AppDelegate.swift file as follows:

```swift
func handleShortCutItem(_ shortcutItem: UIApplicationShortcutItem) -> Bool {
    var handled = false

    guard MenuItems(fullType: shortcutItem.type) != nil else {
        return false
    }

    guard let shortCutType = shortcutItem.type as String? else {
        return false
    }

    switch (shortCutType) {
    case MenuItems.First.type:
        print ("View favorites")
        handled = true
    case MenuItems.Second.type:
        print ("Share")
        handled = true
    default:
        break
    }

    let alertController = UIAlertController(title: "Shortcut Chosen", message: "\"\(shortcutItem.localizedTitle)\"", preferredStyle: .alert)
    let okAction = UIAlertAction(title: "OK", style: .default, handler: nil)
    alertController.addAction(okAction)
    window!.rootViewController?.present(alertController, animated: true, completion: nil)

    return handled
}
```

First, we need to declare a Boolean variable called handled and set it to false. Then we have two guard statements to ensure that a Quick Action was actually chosen. The switch statement identifies the chosen Quick Action by its enumeration value. Then an alert dialog appears to display the chosen Quick Action by its UIApplicationShortcutItemTitle value as shown in Figure 10-10.

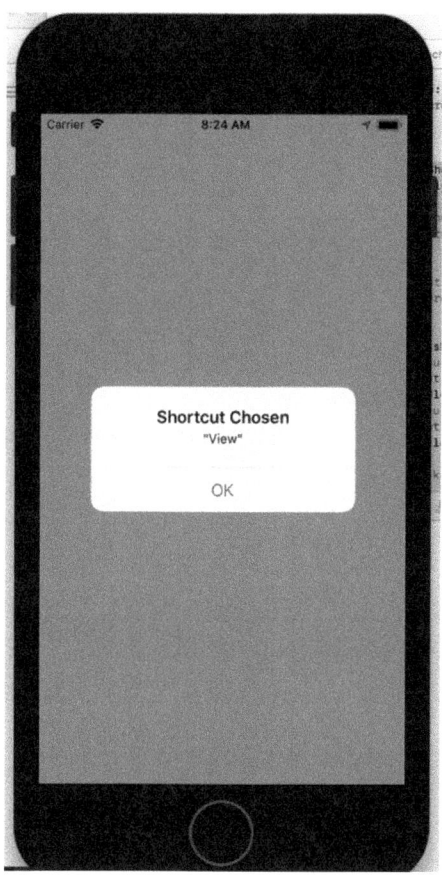

Figure 10-10. *An alert dialog shows the Quick Action shortcut the user chose*

Adding Dynamic Home Screen Quick Actions

The two Quick Actions we defined so far are known as static actions because they appear all the time. A second type of Quick Action is known as Dynamic Quick Actions, which you can create in Swift code to appear after your app is already running. This allows the Quick Action menu to display different options depending on what the user might be doing at the moment.

Note Remember, you can only have a maximum of four Quick Actions such as one static Quick Action and three Dynamic Quick Actions or four static Quick Actions and zero Dynamic Quick Actions.

To add Dynamic Quick Actions, you must modify the enumeration for each Dynamic Quick Action you want to add. In our project, we had two items in our enumeration so we need to add two more for the two Dynamic Quick Actions we want to add such as:

```
enum MenuItems: String {
    case First
    case Second
    case Third
    case Fourth

    init?(fullType: String) {
        guard let last = fullType.components(separatedBy: ".").last
        else { return nil }

        self.init(rawValue: last)
    }

    // MARK: Properties

    var type: String {
        return Bundle.main.bundleIdentifier! + ".\(self.rawValue)"
    }
}
```

Note The Quick Action defined by the top enumeration value will appear at the bottom of the Quick Action menu. So the Quick Action defined by Fourth will appear at the top, the one defined by Third will appear second, the one defined by Second will appear third, and the one defined by First will appear at the bottom as shown in Figure 10-11.

CHAPTER 10 USING 3D TOUCH

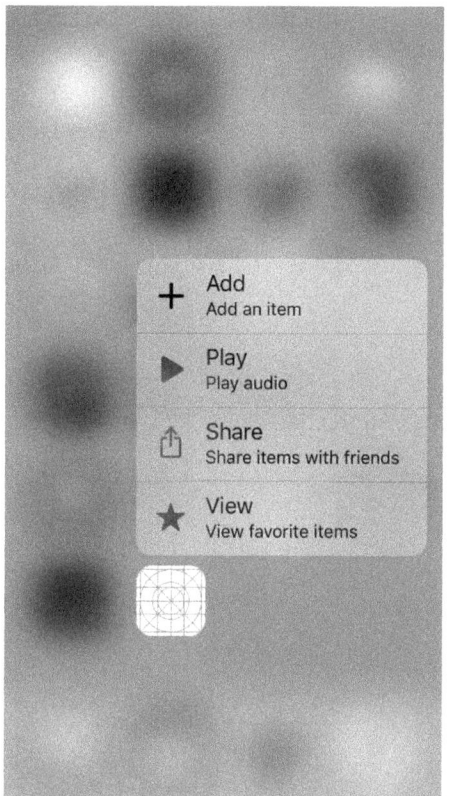

Figure 10-11. *Displaying the Quick Action menu*

Now we need to modify the existing application didFinishLaunchingWithOptions functions in two ways. First, we need to define each Dynamic Quick Action. By identifying its place in the enumeration list (such as Third and Fourth), giving it a localizedTitle and localizedSubtitle, and a corresponding icon (UIApplicationShortcutIcon) such as:

```
let shortcut3 = UIMutableApplicationShortcutItem(type: MenuItems.
Third.type, localizedTitle: "Play", localizedSubtitle: "Play
audio", icon: UIApplicationShortcutIcon(type: .play)
)

let shortcut4 = UIMutableApplicationShortcutItem(type: MenuItems.
Fourth.type, localizedTitle: "Add", localizedSubtitle: "Add an
item", icon: UIApplicationShortcutIcon(type: .add)
)
```

335

Finally, we need to add these two Quick Action shortcuts to a shortcutItems array like this:

```
application.shortcutItems = [shortcut3, shortcut4]
```

The complete AppDelegate.swift file should look as shown in Listing 10-1.

Listing 10-1. The AppDelegate.swift file for the complete 3D Touch project

```
import UIKit

@UIApplicationMain
class AppDelegate: UIResponder, UIApplicationDelegate {

    var window: UIWindow?

    var launchedShortcutItem: UIApplicationShortcutItem?

    enum MenuItems: String {
        case First
        case Second
        case Third
        case Fourth

        init?(fullType: String) {
            guard let last = fullType.components(separatedBy: ".").last
            else { return nil }

            self.init(rawValue: last)
        }

        // MARK: Properties

        var type: String {
            return Bundle.main.bundleIdentifier! + ".\(self.rawValue)"
        }
    }
```

```swift
func handleShortCutItem(_ shortcutItem: UIApplicationShortcutItem) ->
Bool {
    var handled = false

    guard MenuItems(fullType: shortcutItem.type) != nil else {
        return false
    }

    guard let shortCutType = shortcutItem.type as String? else {
        return false
    }

    switch (shortCutType) {
    case MenuItems.First.type:
        print ("View favorites")
        handled = true
    case MenuItems.Second.type:
        print ("Share")
        handled = true
    default:
        break
    }

    let alertController = UIAlertController(title: "Shortcut Chosen",
    message: "\"\(shortcutItem.localizedTitle)\"", preferredStyle: .alert)
    let okAction = UIAlertAction(title: "OK", style: .default,
    handler: nil)
    alertController.addAction(okAction)
    window!.rootViewController?.present(alertController, animated: true,
    completion: nil)

    return handled
}

func application(_ application: UIApplication, performActionFor
shortcutItem: UIApplicationShortcutItem, completionHandler: @escaping
(Bool) -> Void) {

    completionHandler(handleShortCutItem(shortcutItem))
}
```

CHAPTER 10   USING 3D TOUCH

```
func application(_ application: UIApplication, didFinishLaunching
WithOptions launchOptions: [UIApplicationLaunchOptionsKey: Any]?) ->
Bool {
    // Override point for customization after application launch.

    // If a shortcut was launched, display its information and take the
    appropriate action
    if let shortcutItem = launchOptions?[UIApplicationLaunchOptionsKey.
    shortcutItem] as? UIApplicationShortcutItem {

        launchedShortcutItem = shortcutItem
    }

    // Install our two extra dynamic Quick Actions.
    if let shortcutItems = application.shortcutItems, shortcutItems.
    isEmpty {
        // Construct the items.

        let shortcut3 = UIMutableApplicationShortcutItem(type: MenuItems.
        Third.type, localizedTitle: "Play", localizedSubtitle: "Play
        audio", icon: UIApplicationShortcutIcon(type: .play)
        )

        let shortcut4 = UIMutableApplicationShortcutItem(type: MenuItems.
        Fourth.type, localizedTitle: "Add", localizedSubtitle: "Add an
        item", icon: UIApplicationShortcutIcon(type: .add)
        )

        // Update the application providing the initial 'dynamic'
        shortcut items.
        application.shortcutItems = [shortcut3, shortcut4]
    }

    return true
}
}
```

By modifying the shortcutItems array, your app can dynamically change the Quick Actions displayed in the Quick Action menu such as adding or removing items as long as the total number of Quick Action items never exceeds four.

Adding Peeking, Popping, and Previewing

The final use of 3D Touch is to add peeking to our project. Peeking lets the user press on an item to focus just on that item (see Figure 10-2). Holding a finger over that item pops up a new view of itself in a smaller form (see Figure 10-3). Previewing lets you view a menu of items to perform a task of some kind (see Figure 10-4).

Peeking and popping involves two different views. The first view displays an item and when the user presses on an item, a second view pops up. Because you're working with two different views, you need to write code in the view controller files connected to each view (such as ViewController.swift).

To see how peeking, popping, and previewing work, create a new Single View App iOS project and name it 3D PeekPop. Click on the Main.storyboard file and place a UIButton in the middle of the view. Give this button a descriptive title such as "Touch Me to Peek," and change the background color to make it easier to see.

Change the background color of the UIButton to make it easier to see. Finally, choose Editor ➤ Resolve Auto Layout Issues ➤ Reset to Suggested Constraints. This creates a simple user interface as shown in Figure 10-12.

CHAPTER 10 USING 3D TOUCH

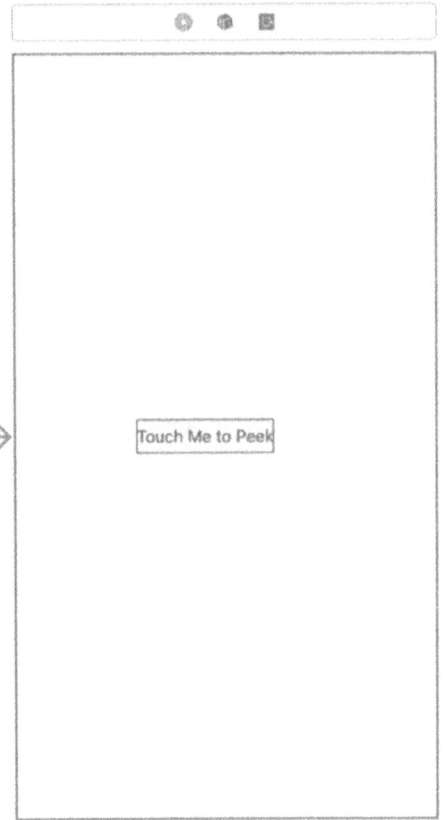

Figure 10-12. The initial user interface of the 3D PeekPop project

Open the Assistant Editor and Control-drag to create an IBOutlet and give it a descriptive name such as peekButton. To implement peeking, popping, and previewing, we need the view controller to adopt the UIViewControllerPreviewingDelegate protocol like this:

```
class ViewController: UIViewController, UIViewControllerPreviewingDelegate {

    @IBOutlet var peekButton: UIButton!
```

Inside the viewDidLoad function, we need to make sure 3D Touch is available. If so, then call the registerForPreviewing function as follows:

```
    override func viewDidLoad() {
        super.viewDidLoad()

        if traitCollection.forceTouchCapability == .available {
            registerForPreviewing(with: self, sourceView: view)
        }
    }
```

CHAPTER 10   USING 3D TOUCH

The UIViewControllerPreviewingDelegate requires two previewingContext functions to work. The first function runs when the user first presses down on an item. This function must identify a second view to appear and verify that the user pressed within on an item such as our UIButton. Then this function needs to define a smaller size for displaying the second view. The complete code looks like this:

```swift
func previewingContext(_ previewingContext: UIViewControllerPreviewing,
    viewControllerForLocation location: CGPoint) -> UIViewController? {
    guard let showMyView = storyboard?.instantiateViewController(with
        Identifier: "PeekVC"), peekButton.frame.contains(location) else {
            return nil
    }
    showMyView.preferredContentSize = CGSize(width: 0.0, height: 300.0)
    return showMyView
}
```

Note that the second view (which we haven't created yet) needs a Storyboard ID of "PeekVC." The second function runs when the user continues pressing down and simply looks like this:

```swift
func previewingContext(_ previewingContext: UIViewControllerPreviewing,
    commit viewControllerToCommit: UIViewController) {
    show(viewControllerToCommit, sender: self)
}
```

The complete code for the ViewController.swift file looks like Listing 10-2:

Listing 10-2. The ViewController.swift file for the complete 3D PeekPop project

```swift
import UIKit

class ViewController: UIViewController, UIViewControllerPreviewingDelegate {

    @IBOutlet var peekButton: UIButton!

    override func viewDidLoad() {
        super.viewDidLoad()

        if traitCollection.forceTouchCapability == .available {
            registerForPreviewing(with: self, sourceView: view)
        }
```

```
    // Do any additional setup after loading the view, typically
    from a nib.
}

override func didReceiveMemoryWarning() {
    super.didReceiveMemoryWarning()
    // Dispose of any resources that can be recreated.
}

// Runs when user first presses down
func previewingContext(_ previewingContext: UIViewControllerPreviewing,
viewControllerForLocation location: CGPoint) -> UIViewController? {
    guard let showMyView = storyboard?.instantiateViewController(with
        Identifier: "PeekVC"), peekButton.frame.contains(location) else {
            return nil
            }
    showMyView.preferredContentSize = CGSize(width: 0.0, height: 300.0)
    return showMyView
}

// Runs if the user continues pressing down
func previewingContext(_ previewingContext: UIViewControllerPreviewing,
commit viewControllerToCommit: UIViewController) {
    show(viewControllerToCommit, sender: self)
}

}
```

Now the next part is to create a new view in the storyboard and a file to hold Swift code. Click on the Main.storyboard file in the Navigator pane and drag and drop a View Controller next to the existing view. Drag a UILabel near the top of this new view and resize it. Give it a title of "Touch Me to Peek," and change its background color to make it easy to see. Make sure you place this UILabel near the top of the view and do not place constraints on this UILabel. This second view will pop up in a condensed form and should look like Figure 10-13.

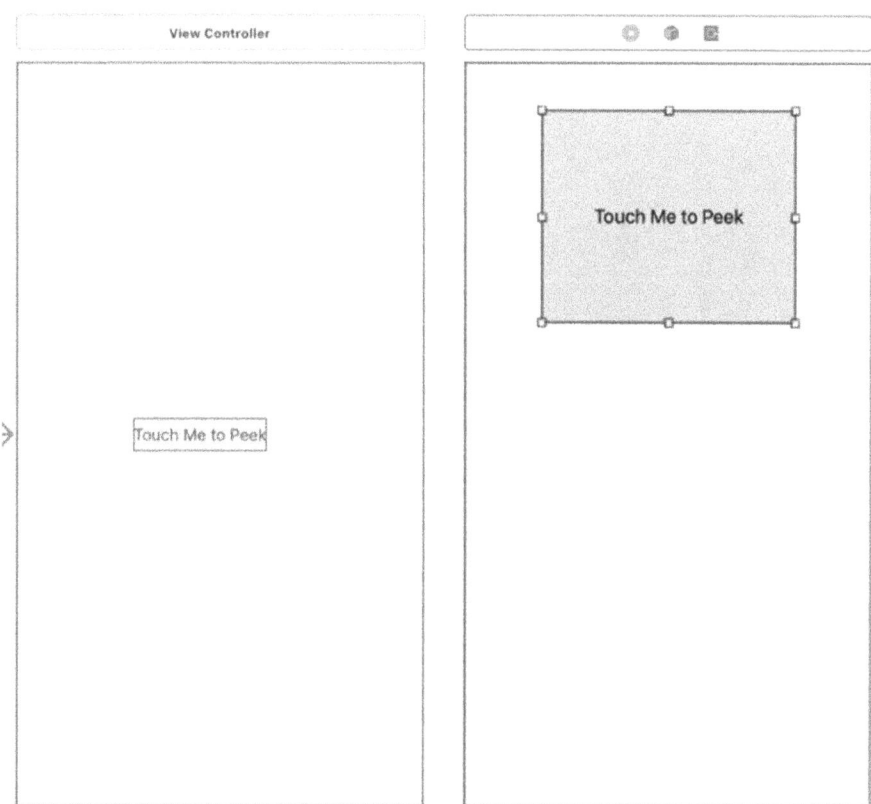

Figure 10-13. *The second view of the 3D PeekPop project*

Click the yellow circle at the top of the second view and choose View ➤ Utilities ➤ Show Identity Inspector. In the Storyboard ID, type "PeekVC" as shown in Figure 10-14.

CHAPTER 10 USING 3D TOUCH

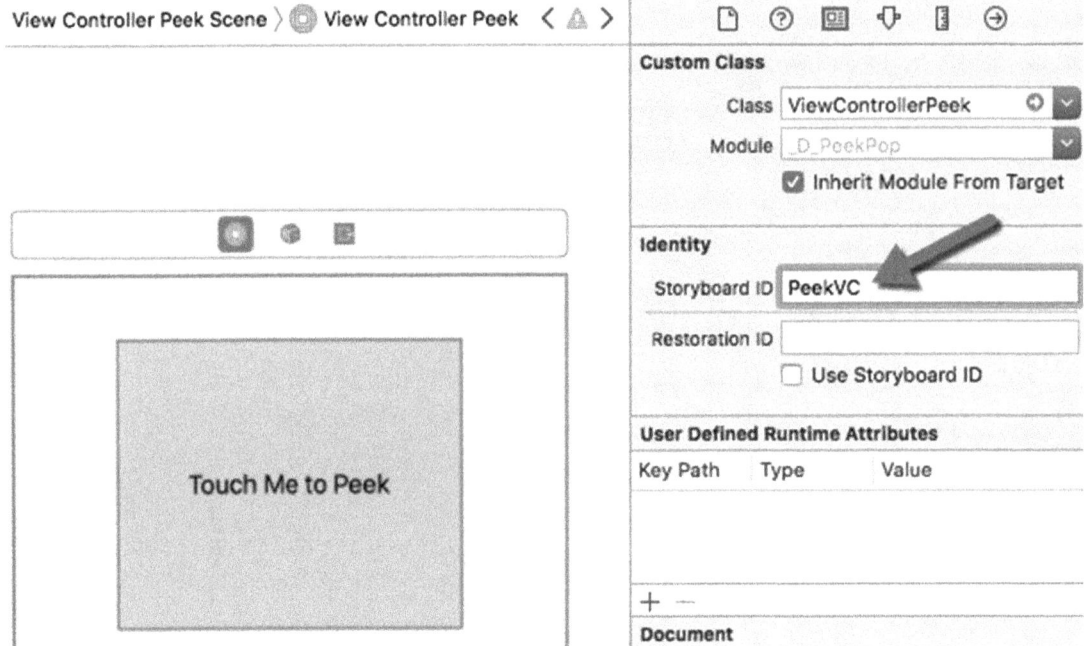

Figure 10-14. Identifying the second view as PeekVC

Now we need to create a file to hold Swift code for this second view. Choose file ➤ New ➤ File, choose Cocoa Touch Class under the iOS category, name it ViewControllerPeek, and make sure it's a subclass of UIViewController and uses the Swift language.

With the Identity Inspector pane still visible, click in the Class list box and choose ViewControllerPeek. This connects the view with the ViewControllerPeek.swift file.

The ViewControllerPeek.swift file needs to contain code to define preview menu items that appear if the user holds and swipes up on the popped item. When you display menu items, you have a choice of different styles to choose: default, selected, or destructive where all preview menu items get stored in an array.

The default style simply displays a menu title. The selected style displays a check mark next to the menu title. The destructive style displays a menu title in red to warn the user of a possibly destructive action such as deleting an item as shown in Figure 10-15.

CHAPTER 10 ■ USING 3D TOUCH

Figure 10-15. *Displaying three different types of preview menu items*

The entire ViewControllerPeek.swift file looks like this:

```
import UIKit

class ViewControllerPeek: UIViewController {

    override func viewDidLoad() {
        super.viewDidLoad()

        // Do any additional setup after loading the view.
    }

    override func didReceiveMemoryWarning() {
        super.didReceiveMemoryWarning()
        // Dispose of any resources that can be recreated.
    }

    override var previewActionItems : [UIPreviewActionItem] {

        let defaultAction = UIPreviewAction(title: "Default style",
        style: .default) { (action, viewController) -> Void in
            print("Default")
        }

        let selectAction = UIPreviewAction(title: "Selected style",
        style: .selected) { (action, viewController) -> Void in
            print("Selected")
        }

        let destructiveAction = UIPreviewAction(title: "Destructive style",
        style: .destructive) { (action, viewController) -> Void in
            print("Destructive")
        }
```

345

```
        return [defaultAction, selectAction, destructiveAction]
    }
}
```

Run this project on the Simulator or connected to an iPhone and you should see the first view appear, displaying a button. If you hold and press on this button, the second view appears. If you swipe up from this second view, a list of preview menu items appears.

Summary

3D Touch is a new way to interact with the iPhone (but not with current versions of the iPad). Since iPhone users will likely get used to 3D Touch, it's important that your apps can run both with and without 3D Touch depending on the type of iPhone users might own. As you can see, adding support for 3D Touch is fairly straightforward. Now it's up to your imagination to add 3D Touch features in your apps.

CHAPTER 11

Using Speech

The Speech framework lets apps recognize audio commands as a supplement to taps and gestures. In addition, the Speech framework can also transcribe speech into text. By adding speech recognition features, your app can offer more ways for the user to interact in a natural manner that's easy for everyone to do.

Before an app can use speech recognition, the user must give permission for the app to access the microphone and use speech recognition. You may also want to make your users aware that speech recognition may send audio data to Apple's servers over the Internet to improve accuracy. That's why it's important to get the user's permission to use the microphone and use speech recognition due to privacy concerns.

By adding speech recognition to your app, your user interface is no longer limited to the touch screen. Speech recognition may never replace the touch screen, but it can give users another way to interact with your app by just speaking to it out loud.

Note You can only test speech recognition on an actual iOS device. You cannot test speech recognition with the Simulator program.

Converting Speech to Text

The Speech framework that Apple provides can convert spoken words into printed text, even in different languages based on your current location. To see how this speech-to-text recognition feature works, create a new Single View App iOS project and name it Speech2Text.

Chapter 11   Using Speech

The first step for any app that uses the microphone or the Speech framework is to ask the user's permission to access the microphone and use speech recognition. To do this, click on the Info.plist file in the Navigator pane and add two privacy settings by clicking on the + icon to create a new row and then choose the Privacy – Microphone Usage Description and Privacy – Speech Recognition Usage Description as shown in Figure 11-1.

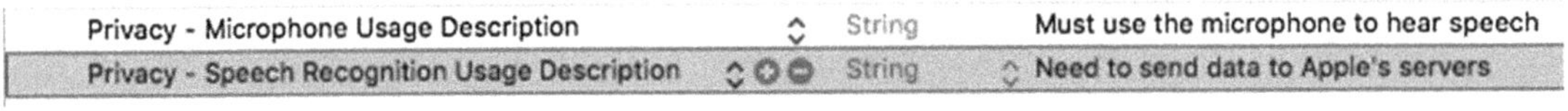

| Privacy - Microphone Usage Description | | String | Must use the microphone to hear speech |
| Privacy - Speech Recognition Usage Description | | String | Need to send data to Apple's servers |

Figure 11-1. *Adding two privacy settings in the Info.plist file*

After choosing both privacy settings, add descriptive text under the Value column to briefly describe to the user why the app needs access to the microphone and speech recognition.

Now it's time to create the user interface. Drag and drop a UILabel and two UIButtons on to the user interface. Change the text on the top UIButton to something more descriptive like "Start Recognizing Speech" and the text on the bottom UIButton to "Stop Recording." Resize the UILabel so it's tall and wide enough to display text as shown in Figure 11-2. Also modify the number of lines in the UILabel to 0 in the Attributes Inspector. This will let the UILabel display as multiple lines of text. Then choose Editor ➤ Resolve Auto Layout Issues ➤ Reset to Suggested Constraints at the bottom of the menu to define constraints for all items.

CHAPTER 11   USING SPEECH

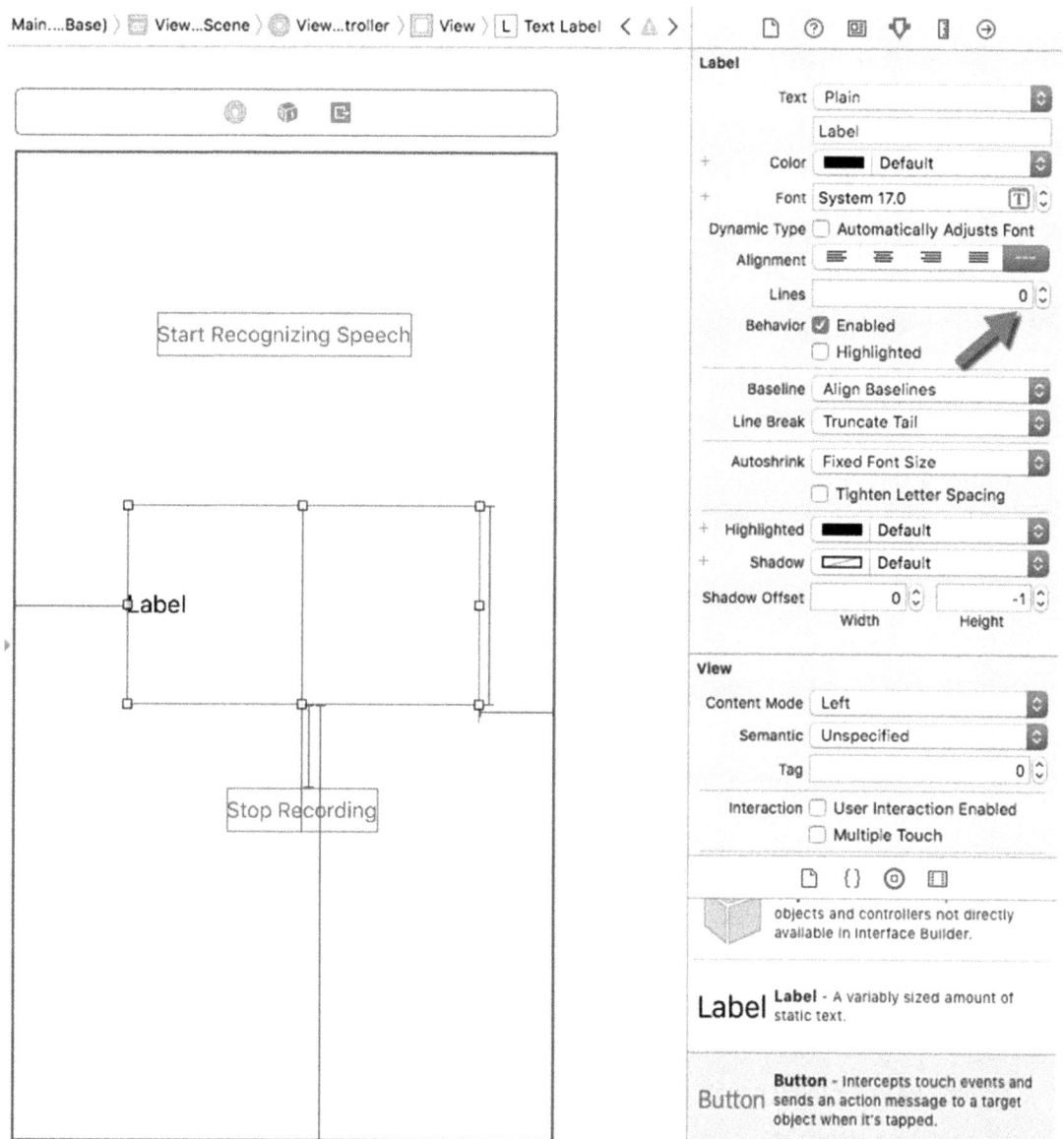

Figure 11-2. *Designing the Speech2Text user interface with a label and two buttons*

CHAPTER 11 USING SPEECH

Open the Assistant Editor and Control-drag from the UIButton and UILabel to create three IBOutlets named recordButton, stopButton, and textLabel like this:

```
@IBOutlet var recordButton: UIButton!
@IBOutlet var textLabel: UILabel!
@IBOutlet var stopButton: UIButton!
```

Control-drag from the top UIButton to the ViewController.swift file to create an IBAction and name it buttonTapped like this:

```
@IBAction func buttonTapped(_ sender: UIButton) {
}
```

Control-drag from the bottom UIButton to the ViewController.swift file to create an IBAction and name it stopTapped like this:

```
@IBAction func stopTapped(_ sender: UIButton) {
}
```

You can choose Editor ➤ Resolve Auto Layout Issues ➤ Reset to Suggested Constraints to constrain the label and the two buttons on the user interface.

Click on the ViewController.swift file in the Navigator pane. We need to import the Speech framework and adopt the SFSpeechRecognizerDelegate protocol, so modify the ViewController.swift file like this:

```
import UIKit
import Speech

class ViewController: UIViewController, SFSpeechRecognizerDelegate {
```

In the ViewController.swift file, create an instance of the AVAudioEngine class like this:

```
let audioEngine = AVAudioEngine()
```

Next, we need to create the speech recognizer and define a location to detect a specific type of language such as English like this:

```
let speechRecognizer = SFSpeechRecognizer(locale: Locale(identifier: "en-US"))
```

Now we need a request to detect spoken audio:

```
let request = SFSpeechAudioBufferRecognitionRequest()
```

Finally we need an optional variable to store the recognition task. It needs to be an optional variable since the task may or may not succeed. The three constants and one variable should look like this:

```
let audioEngine = AVAudioEngine()
let speechRecognizer = SFSpeechRecognizer(locale: Locale(identifier: "en-US"))
let request = SFSpeechAudioBufferRecognitionRequest()
var recognitionTask : SFSpeechRecognitionTask?
```

Modify the IBAction method you created for the two UIButton as follows:

```
@IBAction func buttonTapped(_ sender: UIButton) {
    recordButton.isEnabled = false
    stopButton.isEnabled = true
    recognizeSpeech()
}
@IBAction func stopTapped(_ sender: UIButton) {
    recordButton.isEnabled = true
    stopButton.isEnabled = false
    stopRecording()
}
```

We'll need to write a stopRecording function like this:

```
func stopRecording() {
    audioEngine.stop()
    request?.endAudio()
    recognitionTask?.cancel()
    audioEngine.inputNode.removeTap(onBus: 0)
}
```

The next function we need to create is the recognizeSpeech function. The audio engine processes data in nodes, so we need to get that data and create a request to recognize speech. The first few lines of code in the recognizeSpeech function look like this:

```
    let node = audioEngine.inputNode

    request = SFSpeechAudioBufferRecognitionRequest()
    guard let recognitionRequest = request else {
```

```
        fatalError ("Can not create a recognition request")
    }
    recognitionRequest.shouldReportPartialResults = true

    let recordingFormat = node.outputFormat(forBus: 0)
    node.installTap(onBus: 0, bufferSize: 1024, format:
    recordingFormat) { (buffer, _) in
        self.request?.append(buffer)
    }
```

Next we need to catch potential errors in case the audio engine can't start or if the speech recognizer cannot be accessed:

```
    audioEngine.prepare()
    do {
        try audioEngine.start()
    } catch {
        return print (error)
    }
    guard let recognizeMe = SFSpeechRecognizer() else {
        return
    }
    if !recognizeMe.isAvailable {
        return
    }
```

Finally, we need to recognize the spoken speech and transcribe it to text, which will appear in the textLabel IBOutlet:

```
    recognitionTask = speechRecognizer?.recognitionTask(with: request!,
    resultHandler: {result, error in
        if let result = result {
            let transcribedString = result.bestTranscription.formattedString
            self.textLabel.text = transcribedString
        } else if let error = error {
            print(error)
        }
    })
```

The entire ViewController.swift file should look like Listing 11-1.

Listing 11-1. The ViewController.swift file for the Speech2Text project

```swift
import UIKit
import Speech

class ViewController: UIViewController, SFSpeechRecognizerDelegate {

    @IBOutlet var recordButton: UIButton!
    @IBOutlet var textLabel: UILabel!
    @IBOutlet var stopButton: UIButton!

    let audioEngine = AVAudioEngine()
    let speechRecognizer = SFSpeechRecognizer(locale: Locale(identifier: "en-US"))
    var request : SFSpeechAudioBufferRecognitionRequest? = nil
    var recognitionTask : SFSpeechRecognitionTask?

    override func viewDidLoad() {
        super.viewDidLoad()
        // Do any additional setup after loading the view, typically from a nib.
        stopButton.isEnabled = false
    }

    override func didReceiveMemoryWarning() {
        super.didReceiveMemoryWarning()
        // Dispose of any resources that can be recreated.
    }

    @IBAction func buttonTapped(_ sender: UIButton) {
        recordButton.isEnabled = false
        stopButton.isEnabled = true
        recognizeSpeech()
    }

    @IBAction func stopTapped(_ sender: UIButton) {
        recordButton.isEnabled = true
        stopButton.isEnabled = false
        stopRecording()
    }
```

CHAPTER 11   USING SPEECH

```swift
func stopRecording() {
    audioEngine.stop()
    request?.endAudio()
    recognitionTask?.cancel()
    audioEngine.inputNode.removeTap(onBus: 0)
}

func recognizeSpeech() {
    let node = audioEngine.inputNode
    
    request = SFSpeechAudioBufferRecognitionRequest()
    guard let recognitionRequest = request else {
        fatalError ("Can not create a recognition request")
    }
    
    recognitionRequest.shouldReportPartialResults = true
    
    let recordingFormat = node.outputFormat(forBus: 0)
    node.installTap(onBus: 0, bufferSize: 1024, format: recordingFormat) { (buffer, _) in
        self.request?.append(buffer)
    }
    
    audioEngine.prepare()
    do {
        try audioEngine.start()
    } catch {
        return print (error)
    }
    
    guard let recognizeMe = SFSpeechRecognizer() else {
        return
    }
    
    if !recognizeMe.isAvailable {
        return
    }
```

CHAPTER 11 USING SPEECH

```
    recognitionTask = speechRecognizer?.recognitionTask(with: request!,
    resultHandler: {result, error in
        if let result = result {
            let transcribedString = result.bestTranscription.formattedString
            self.textLabel.text = transcribedString
        } else if let error = error {
            print(error)
        }
    })
   }
}
```

If you run this project on an iPhone or iPad connected to your Macintosh through a USB cable, you can tap the Start Recognizing Speech button at the top of the screen, speak a brief sentence, and see the transcribed text appear in the UILabel. Then you can tap the Stop Recording button when you're done. The transcribed text may make mistakes, but in general, you'll find it's fairly accurate in transcribing common words into text as shown in Figure 11-3.

Figure 11-3. Running the Speech2Text project on an iPhone

CHAPTER 11 USING SPEECH

Recognizing Spoken Commands

Besides transcribing spoken speech into text, the Speech framework can also recognize specific spoken words that you identify ahead of time. This gives your app the ability to respond to spoken commands as a way to interact with the user.

Just be aware that in most languages, words may sound alike but be spelled differently. For example in English, "red" and "read" sound the same and "too," "to," and "two" also sound alike. When identifying spoken commands, be aware of words that sound alike but may have completely different meanings.

To recognize spoken commands, we simply need to use a switch statement to detect a specific word or phrase. Create a new function called checkSpokenCommand like this:

```
func checkSpokenCommand (commandString: String) {
    switch commandString {
    case "Purple":
        textLabel.backgroundColor = UIColor.purple
    case "Green":
        textLabel.backgroundColor = UIColor.green
    case "Yellow":
        textLabel.backgroundColor = UIColor.yellow
    default:
        textLabel.backgroundColor = UIColor.white
    }
}
```

If the user says "purple," "green," or "yellow," the app will change the UILabel background to a different color. If the user says anything else, the UILabel background will turn to white.

Now we need to call this checkSpokenCommand function inside the recognizeSpeech function like this:

```
func recognizeSpeech() {
    let node = audioEngine.inputNode

    request = SFSpeechAudioBufferRecognitionRequest()
    guard let recognitionRequest = request else {
        fatalError ("Can not create a recognition request")
    }
```

```
recognitionRequest.shouldReportPartialResults = true

let recordingFormat = node.outputFormat(forBus: 0)
node.installTap(onBus: 0, bufferSize: 1024, format:
recordingFormat) { (buffer, _) in
    self.request?.append(buffer)
}

audioEngine.prepare()
do {
    try audioEngine.start()
} catch {
    return print (error)
}

guard let recognizeMe = SFSpeechRecognizer() else {
    return
}

if !recognizeMe.isAvailable {
    return
}

recognitionTask = speechRecognizer?.recognitionTask(with: request!,
resultHandler: {result, error in
    if let result = result {
        let transcribedString = result.bestTranscription.formattedString
        self.textLabel.text = transcribedString

        // Check for spoken command
        self.checkSpokenCommand(commandString: transcribedString)

    } else if let error = error {
        print(error)
    }
})
}
```

CHAPTER 11　USING SPEECH

Run this project on an iOS device connected to your Macintosh and say one of the three words ("purple" "green" or "yellow"), which will change the background color of the UILabel. When the app recognizes one of these three command words, it changes the label background color as shown in Figure 11-4.

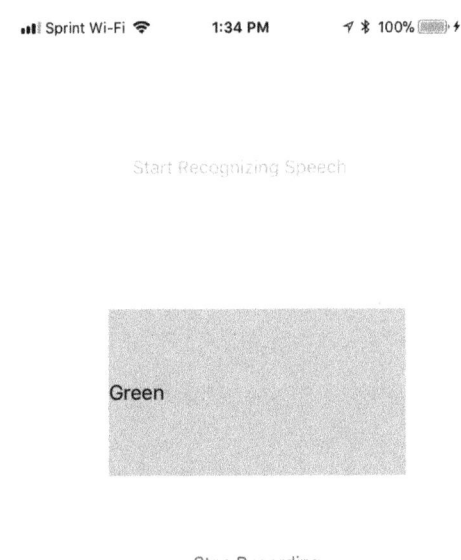

Figure 11-4. Running the Speech2Text project on an iPhone to change the background color of the label

Turning Text to Speech

Just as Swift can recognize spoken commands and convert spoken words into text, so can Swift do it the other way around by reading text out loud. To read text out loud, you need to use the AVFoundation framework, which gives your app access to a speech synthesizer.

This speech synthesizer is based on your current location and default language such as American English, Australian English, or United Kingdom English. Then the speech synthesizer can read text stored in a string that can be read at a fast or slow rate.

CHAPTER 11 USING SPEECH

To see how to use the speech synthesizer, create a new Single View App iOS project and name it Text2Speech. Then click on the Main.storyboard file and drag and drop three items on the user interface:

- UITextView
- UISlider
- UIButton

Place the three items near the top of the user interface and double-click in the UITextView to type some text. Change the title on the UIButton to "Read Text Out Loud." Then choose Editor ➤ Resolve Auto Layout Issues ➤ Reset to Suggested Constraints at the bottom of the menu to define constraints for all items. Your user interface should look similar to Figure 11-5.

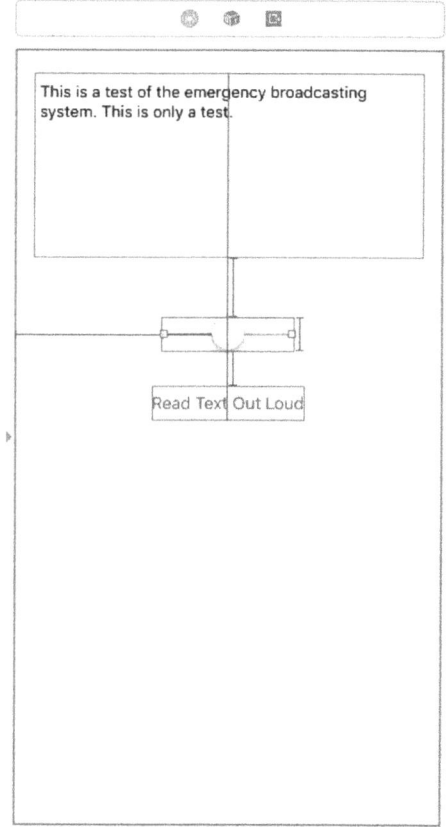

Figure 11-5. *The user interface for the Text2Speech project*

Open the Assistant Editor and Control-drag to the ViewController.swift file to create two IBOutlets for the UITextView and the UISlider. Give the UITextView IBOutlet a descriptive name like textView and the UISlider IBOutlet a name like rateSlider like this:

```
@IBOutlet var textView: UITextView!
@IBOutlet var rateSlider: UISlider!
```

Control-drag from the UIButton to the ViewController.swift file to create an IBAction method called readText:

```
@IBAction func readText(_ sender: UIButton) {
}
```

To access the speech synthesizer, we need to import the AVFoundation framework like this:

```
import AVFoundation
```

To use the speech synthesizer, we need to use the AVSpeechSynthesizer class like this:

```
let audio = AVSpeechSynthesizer()
```

Then we need to use the AVSpeechUtterance class, which will define the text to read out loud:

```
var convertText = AVSpeechUtterance(string: "")
```

Now edit the readText function like this:

```
@IBAction func readText(_ sender: UIButton) {
    convertText = AVSpeechUtterance(string: textView.text)
    convertText.rate = rateSlider.value
    audio.speak(convertText)
}
```

This function first retrieves any text stored in the textView IBOutlet. Then it retrieves the value defined by the UISlider, which varies from 0 to 1.0 to define the rate that the speech synthesizer will speak. A low number makes the speech synthesizer speak slowly while a higher number makes the speech synthesizer speak faster.

Finally the speech synthesizer uses the rate and text to read the text out loud. The entire ViewController.swift file should look like Listing 11-2.

Listing 11-2. The ViewController.swift file for the Text2Speech project

```swift
import UIKit
import AVFoundation

class ViewController: UIViewController {

    @IBOutlet var textView: UITextView!
    @IBOutlet var rateSlider: UISlider!

    let audio = AVSpeechSynthesizer()
    var convertText = AVSpeechUtterance(string: "")

    override func viewDidLoad() {
        super.viewDidLoad()
        // Do any additional setup after loading the view, typically from a nib.
    }

    override func didReceiveMemoryWarning() {
        super.didReceiveMemoryWarning()
        // Dispose of any resources that can be recreated.
    }

    @IBAction func readText(_ sender: UIButton) {
        convertText = AVSpeechUtterance(string: textView.text)
        convertText.rate = rateSlider.value
        audio.speak(convertText)
    }
}
```

Run this project in the Simulator or on an actual iOS device. You'll be able to type and edit text in the UITextView and drag the UISlider left or right to adjust the speaking rate. Then click on the Read Text Out Loud button to hear the speech synthesizer read the text displayed in the UITextView.

CHAPTER 11 USING SPEECH

Summary

Adding speech recognition requires the Speech framework while adding a speech synthesizer to read text out loud requires the AVFoundation framework. Speech recognition gives users another way to interact with your app while the speech synthesizer gives your app to read short strings or even long amounts of text out loud. This can be handy for people with visibility problems or to provide information to users if they can't look at the iPhone screen, such as when they're driving.

By adding speech recognition and speech synthesis, your app can use audio as another part of its user interface to allow users to give and receive data from your iPhone app.

# CHAPTER 12

Understanding SiriKit

In the last chapter, you learned how to do simple speech recognition. However since there are multiple ways to say the same thing, recognizing voice commands can be difficult when commands get more complex than simple one word options. To help your app recognize more complicated voice commands, you can add the features of Siri to your app through the SiriKit framework.

Siri essentially takes care of the difficult task of recognizing words and turning them into commands. Then your app has the task of responding to voice commands identified through Siri. Once your app identifies a user's intent through recognized voice commands, your app may need to ask additional questions to clarify the user's intent. Finally, your app can respond intelligently using Siri as its user interface. By using SiriKit, your app can gain the power of Siri with little additional work on your part.

The main limitation is that SiriKit restricts your app to one of several domains that define the user's intent such as sending a message, making a call, browsing through photos, sending money, or making an appointment with a ride-sharing service.

Note To view a list of all possible Intent domains SiriKit can recognize, visit https://developer.apple.com/documentation/sirikit.

Intent domains make it easier for Siri to understand what the user says. For example, if you said, "Send 25 dollars to Fred" within a money payment app, Siri could correctly identify the recipient (Fred) and the amount of money to send (25 dollars). At this point, your app would need to do the actual work of sending money to Fred along with verifying that Fred was a valid person and that your account had enough money to send in the first place.

SiriKit works by recognizing speech, extracting possible actions within a limited domain, asking the user for additional information if necessary, then converting that spoken speech into text for your app to process.

CHAPTER 12 UNDERSTANDING SIRIKIT

How SiriKit Works

SiriKit works with an app through two types of files called extensions. An Intents App extension contains Swift code to respond to the user's voice commands after they're interpreted by Siri. An Intents UI App extension allows your app to customize the appearance of data displayed within Siri. At the very least, every app that connects to SiriKit needs an Intents App extension. An Intents UI App extension simply makes your app look more professional but isn't absolutely necessary.

To see how to add an Intents App extension to an Xcode iOS project, create a new Single View App iOS project and name it SiriTest. Now choose File ➤ New ➤ Target. Click on the iOS category and click on the Intents Extensions icon as shown in Figure 12-1. Then click Next.

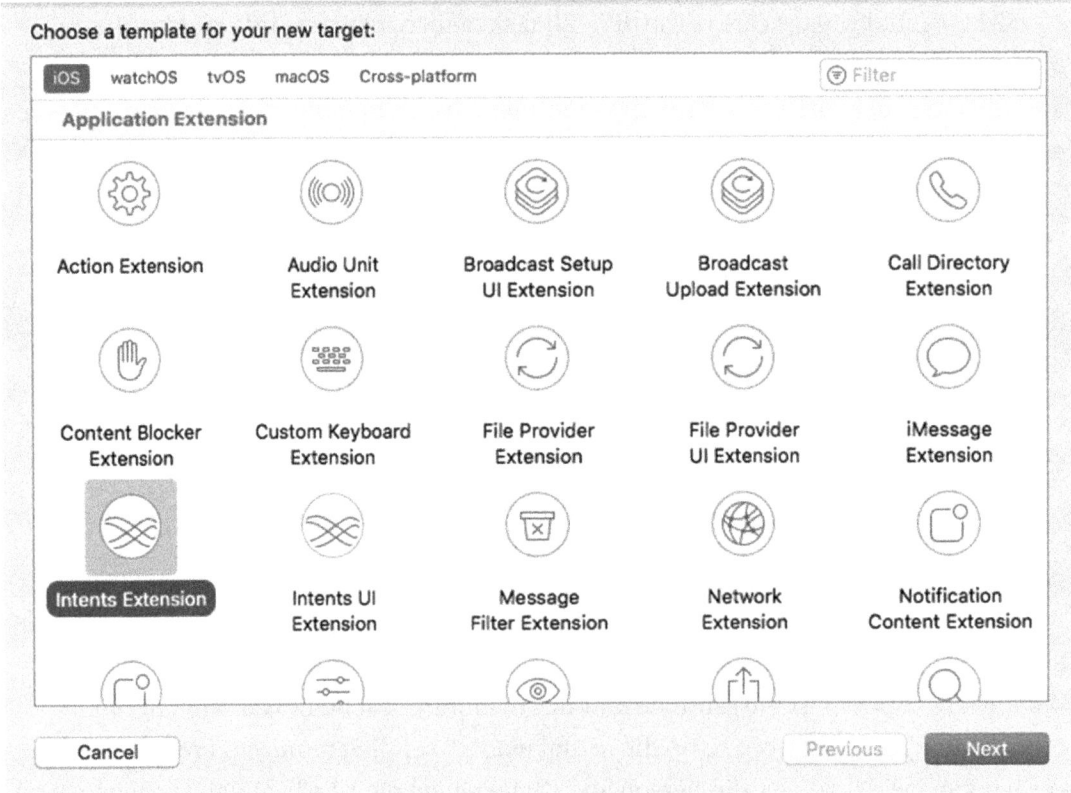

Figure 12-1. Adding an Intents Extension file to a project

When Xcode asks for a product name for your extension, type MessageExtension. Make sure you select the "Include UI Extension" check box and click the Finish button.

CHAPTER 12　UNDERSTANDING SIRIKIT

A dialog may appear, asking to activate the scheme. Click the Activate button. This creates two new folders called MessageExtension and MessageExtensionUI as shown in Figure 12-2.

Figure 12-2. Xcode adds two new folders for your Intents Extension

The MessageExtension folder contains an IntentHandler.swift file. This is where you write code to handle commands captured by Siri.

The MessageExtensionUI folder contains a MainInterface.storyboard file along with an accompanying IntentViewController.swift file. The Main.storyboard file appears within Siri to let users know they're interacting with your app through Siri. If you do not customize this Main.storyboard file, your app will display a generic dialog within Siri.

Creating an IntentExtension target file creates template code for working with messaging. Connect an iPhone or iPad to your Macintosh through its USB cable and run your project. A dialog appears, asking you to choose an app to run as shown in Figure 12-3.

CHAPTER 12 UNDERSTANDING SIRIKIT

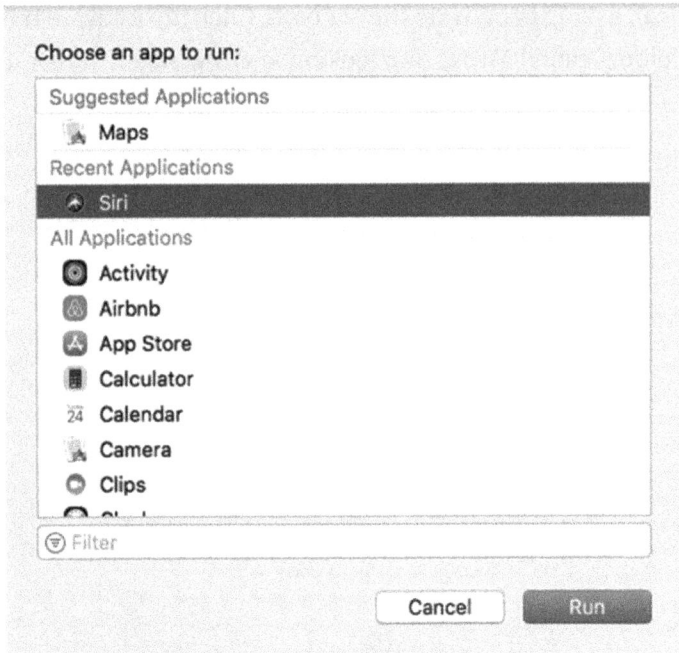

Figure 12-3. *Choosing Siri to run your app*

Click on Siri and click the Run button. Siri appears and waits for you to speak. At this point, you need to give Siri a command, so say, "Send a message using SiriTest." Remember, if you chose a different name for your project instead of SiriTest, say that name instead.

Note When choosing the name of your app when working with Siri, try to choose a distinctive name that's easy to pronounce and won't be easily confused with other words. For example, an app named "RedRight" could be interpreted incorrectly by Siri as "Read Write." If Siri can't identify your app name, it will be difficult for users to use your app within Siri.

When Siri appears and you give the command "Send a message with SiriTest," Siri will request more information. First, Siri will ask who do you want to send your message to. Notice that a generic SiriTest dialog appears in Siri as shown in Figure 12-4.

CHAPTER 12 UNDERSTANDING SIRIKIT

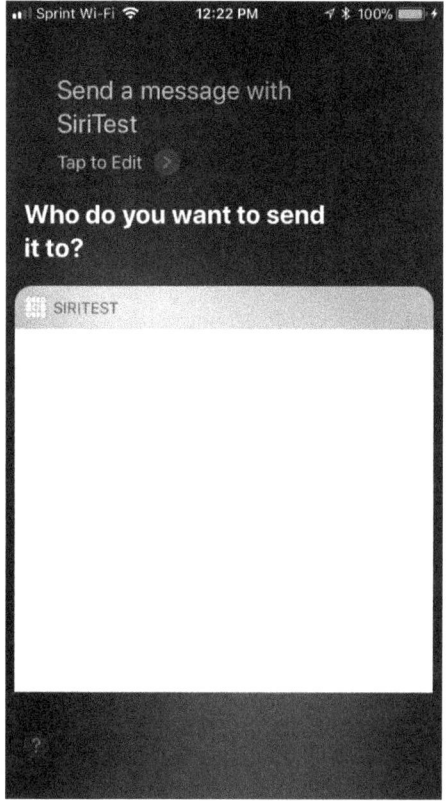

Figure 12-4. Your SiriTest app appears within Siri

This generic SiriTest dialog is what's defined by the Main.storyboard file under the MessageExtensionUI folder. State a name stored in your Contacts app. Siri will then ask for the message to send. Recite any message you like. Notice that Siri may not always understand the words you speak accurately.

Siri will then ask for confirmation to send it. Although Siri will say it sent the message, nothing will actually be sent. Within Xcode on your Macintosh, click the Stop button to stop running your app on your iPhone or iPad.

Just with this short demo, you can see how SiriKit works by integrating your app in Siri and allowing Siri to work as your app's user interface.

Now let's go back to Xcode and understand the details of your SiriTest project and how it works.

367

CHAPTER 12 UNDERSTANDING SIRIKIT

Defining How Siri Interacts with the User

In both the MessageExtension and MessageExtensionUI folder of your SiriTest project, you'll see an Info.plist file. Each of these files defines what Siri recognizes and responds to.

In each Info.plist file, click under the NSExtension heading, then the NSExtensionAttributes, and finally under IntentsSupported. The Info-plist file under the MessageExtension folder supports three intents as shown in Figure 12-5:

- INSendMessageIntent
- INSearchForMessagesIntent
- INSetMessageAttributeIntent

Figure 12-5. The Info.plist contents under the MessageExtension folder

This means that Siri will let you send, search for, and modify the attributes of a message such as whether it's been marked as read or not.

If you were creating an app in a different domain such as making payments or creating notes, you would need to change the IntentsSupported items to something else such as INSendPaymentIntent or INCreateNoteIntent. The exact intent you'd add depends on the intent domain your app will handle and which intents your app will support. By looking up a particular SiriKit domain, such as creating notes, you can see all possible intents available as shown in Figure 12-6.

CHAPTER 12 UNDERSTANDING SIRIKIT

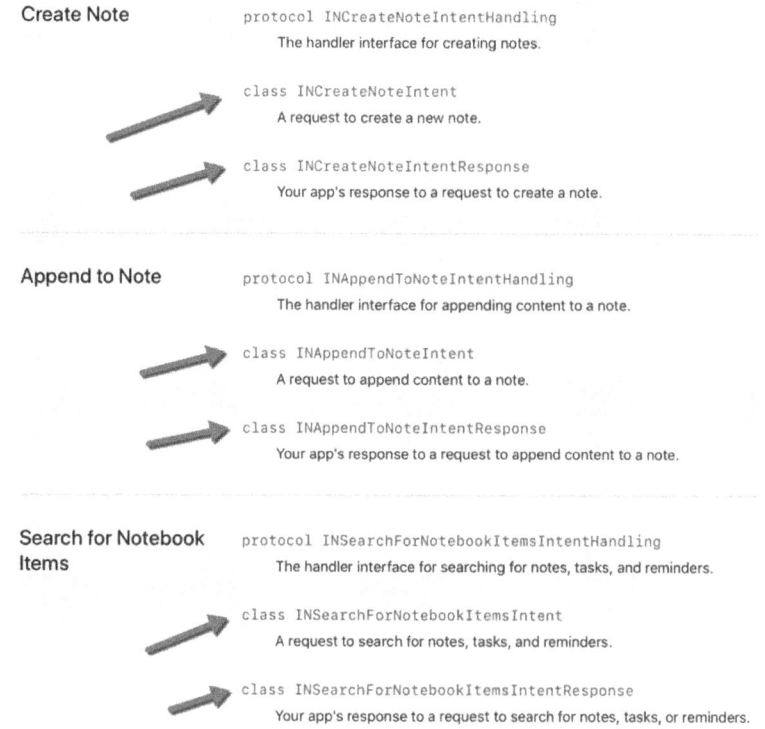

Figure 12-6. *Apple's documentation lists all possible intents for a particular domain such as note creation*

Click on the Info.plist file in the MessageExtensionUI folder. If you expand NSExtension, NSExtensionAttributes, and IntentsSupported, you can see that the user interface of Siri supports the INSendMessageIntent as shown in Figure 12-7.

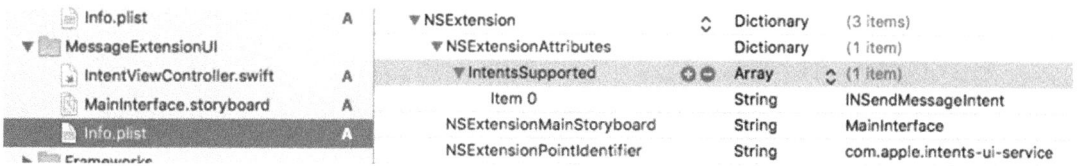

Figure 12-7. *The Info.plist file in the MessageExtensionUI folder*

In any app that works with SiriKit, make sure you modify the Info.plist files to define the intents your app will support for a particular domain such as ride booking, messaging, or photos.

369

CHAPTER 12 UNDERSTANDING SIRIKIT

One final Info.plist file you may need to modify is the one stored in your main project's folder. For example, if your app will work with SiriKit to allow searching of photos stored in the Photos album, you'll need to modify the Info.plist file to allow photo library usage as shown in Figure 12-8.

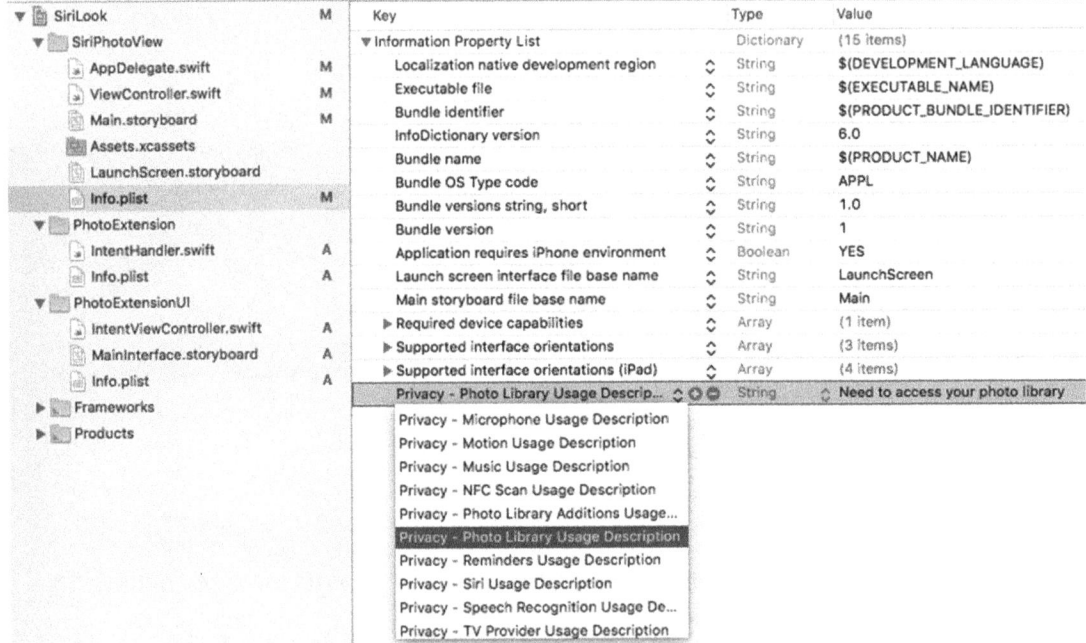

Figure 12-8. Adding privacy settings in the Info.plist of the main project

Some common privacy settings you may need to modify include the following:

- Calendar usage
- Contacts access
- Music library access
- Photo library access
- Reminders usage

Understanding the IntentHandler.swift File

Once you have modified the Info.plist files for any privacy settings and to define the intents your app will handle through Siri, the next step is to modify the IntentHandler.swift file located in the Extension folder (not the ExtensionUI folder).

The IntentHandler.swift file imports the Intents framework, but you may need to import additional frameworks. For example, if your app needs access to the Photos Library, you'll need to import the Photos framework. If your app makes VoIP calls, you'll need to import the CallKit framework. Make sure you import the proper framework your app needs.

After importing any additional frameworks, the next step is to make sure your IntentHandler class adopts handling protocols for your chosen domain. In our SiriTest project, our IntentHandler class adopts protocols for sending, searching, and modifying messages as follows:

```
class IntentHandler: INExtension, INSendMessageIntentHandling,
INSearchForMessagesIntentHandling, INSetMessageAttributeIntentHandling {
```

If your app is not working in the messaging domain, delete the code in the IntentHandler.swift file and adopt the IntentHandler class to different protocols such as the INStartAudioCallIntentHandling protocol to work with VoIP calling or the INStartWorkoutIntentHandling protocol. (SiriKit protocols typically end with the word "Handling.") The following code adopts protocols for the workout domain:

```
class IntentHandler: INStartWorkoutIntentHandling,
INPauseWorkoutIntentHandling, INResumeWorkoutIntentHandling,
INCancelWorkoutIntentHandling, INEndWorkoutIntentHandling {
```

Regardless of the specific SiriKit protocols your IntentHandler class adopts, you'll need to create functions to conform to those protocols. In our SiriTest project, the IntentHandler.swift file contains code for working with messaging. When working with SiriKit with messaging or any other domain such as workouts or payments, users can give commands in several ways. Ideally, users will give complete commands that identify at least three items:

- The name of your app
- The recipient of your action
- The content of your action

CHAPTER 12   UNDERSTANDING SIRIKIT

If your app used Siri to work in the payment domain, users could give a command like "Pay Fred ten dollars using SiriTest." In this example, Fred is the recipient of the action, ten dollars is the content of your action, and SiriTest is the name of the app the user wants to use.

However, most times users will not give complete commands. Instead, they may give a partial command like "Use SiriTest to pay Fred." When Siri hears the name of the app, it knows which app to use. Then it uses the person's name (Fred) as the recipient, assuming Fred is stored in your Contacts app and you have given the app permission to access the Contacts app database.

However, Siri won't know the amount, so at this point, it will need to ask an additional question for the amount. When the user states the amount, then Siri can complete the action. When Siri doesn't have complete information, it needs to ask for the missing information, which is called disambiguation.

Note   Although the IntentHandler.swift file uses a switch statement to verify names, it doesn't contain any code to actually access or verify if a name is stored in the Contacts app database or not.

In our SiriTest project, Siri need to resolve two possible pieces of missing information:

- Who the recipient is
- What the message may be

In the IntentHandler.swift file of our SiriTest project, there are two functions to handle these issues. The first function is called resolveRecipients. Notice there's a switch statement that deals with three cases. First is if the user gives a name that matches multiple people. For example, if you want to send a message to Fred but you have a Fred Johnson, Fred Murray, and Fred Billingsly in your contacts database, Siri will need to ask the user which person in particular:

```
case 2 ... Int.max:
    // We need Siri's help to ask user to pick one from the
    matches.
    resolutionResults += [INPersonResolutionResult.
    disambiguation(with: matchingContacts)]
```

If the user gives one name and that name matches exactly one person in the contact app, then the app can perform the complete action:

```
case 1:
    // We have exactly one matching contact
    resolutionResults += [INPersonResolutionResult.
    success(with: recipient)]
```

Of course, the user may give a name that isn't in the contacts database. In that case, the code will need to let Siri know that the task cannot be completed. This means Siri will need to inform the user of this and ask for a new name:

```
case 0:
    // We have no contacts matching the description provided
    resolutionResults += [INPersonResolutionResult.
    unsupported()]
```

The IntentHandler.swift file contains another function called resolveContent. This function checks if the user specifies a message to send. For example, the user could say, "Send a message with SiriTest to Fred." This identifies the app to use (our SiriTest project) and the recipient (Fred). But since the user didn't specify a message, Siri will need to resolve this by asking for a message. That's the purpose of the resolveContent function:

```
func resolveContent(for intent: INSendMessageIntent, with completion:
@escaping (INStringResolutionResult) -> Void) {
    if let text = intent.content, !text.isEmpty {
        completion(INStringResolutionResult.success(with: text))
    } else {
        completion(INStringResolutionResult.needsValue())
    }
}
```

Once Siri has a valid recipient and message to send, it uses a confirm function to ask the user to verify everything is ready.

> **Note** The template code in the IntentHandler.swift file does not actually send out messages even though Siri will claim that it has sent the message. To actually send a message, you'll need to write additional code.

```
func confirm(intent: INSendMessageIntent, completion: @escaping
(INSendMessageIntentResponse) -> Void) {
    // Verify user is authenticated and your app is ready to send a
    message.

    let userActivity = NSUserActivity(activityType: NSStringFromClass
    (INSendMessageIntent.self))
    let response = INSendMessageIntentResponse(code: .ready,
    userActivity: userActivity)
    completion(response)
}
```

Finally, the handle function actually takes action after Siri has gotten the recipient's name and message from the user. The handle function in the IntentHandler.swift file looks like this:

```
func handle(intent: INSendMessageIntent, completion: @escaping
(INSendMessageIntentResponse) -> Void) {
    // Implement your application logic to send a message here.

    let userActivity = NSUserActivity(activityType: NSStringFromClass
    (INSendMessageIntent.self))
    let response = INSendMessageIntentResponse(code: .success,
    userActivity: userActivity)
    completion(response)
}
```

Note that all of these functions include the keywords INSendMessageIntent or INSendMessageIntentResponse. If you look at the bottom of the IntentHandler.swift file, there are two handle functions but one is designed to deal with searching for messages (INSearchForMessageIntent), and the second is designed to deal with changing attributes of a message (INSetMessageAttributeIntent).

Understanding the ExtensionUI Folder

The IntentHandler.swift file in the Extension folder contains code to link your app to Siri. To customize the appearance of your app within Siri, you have the option of customizing a storyboard file that appears within Siri. The purpose of this storyboard file is to display information to the user within Siri. By default, your app will display a generic user interface inside Siri, but if you can, display a custom user interface by modifying the two files inside the ExtensionUI folder.

The IntentViewController.swift file contains Swift code for customizing your app's user interface within Siri. The MainInterface.storyboard file defines the actual user interface as shown in Figure 12-9.

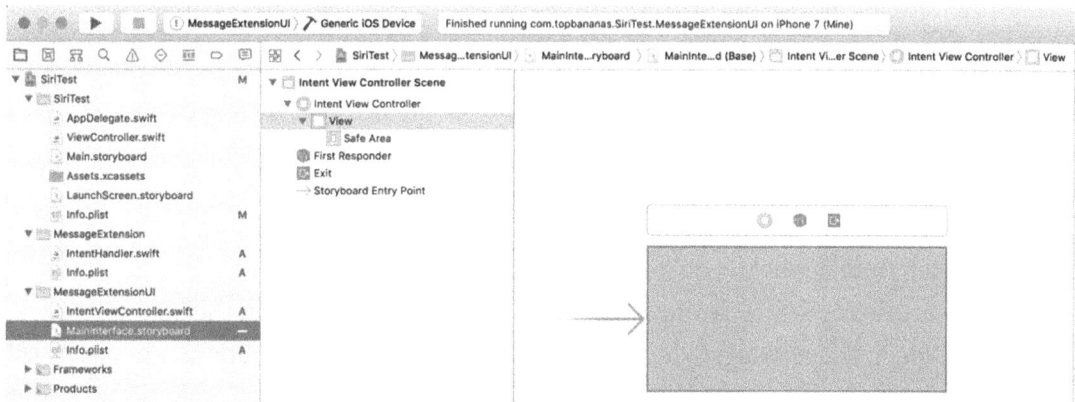

Figure 12-9. The MainInterface.storyboard file defines your app's user interface in Siri

If you want to define a custom user interface that appears inside Siri, you'll need to write Swift code in the IntentViewController.swift file and add user interface items on to the MainInterface.storyboard file such as a UILabel or UITextView. Then you'll need to create IBOutlets between the .storyboard file and the IntentViewController.swift file.

After customizing the .storyboard file and adding IBOutlets to the IntentViewController.swift file, the next step is to make the IntentViewController class adopt the INUIHostedViewsSiriProviding protocol as follows:

```
class IntentViewController: UIViewController, INUIHostedViewControlling,
INUIHostedViewSiriProviding {
```

CHAPTER 12 UNDERSTANDING SIRIKIT

Next, you'll need to set one of three variables to true:

- displaysMap – Used to replace a default Map interface if your app relies on Maps app such as ride booking

- displaysMessage – Used to display a custom interface if your app works with messages

- displaysPaymentTransaction – Used to display a custom interface if your app works with payments

Since our SiriTest project works with messages, we need to use the displaysMessage variable and set it to true like this:

```
var displaysMessage: Bool {
    return true
}
```

The final step is to modify the configure function to display your .storyboard file within Siri. Remember, each time Siri asks a question to the user, it will display your .storyboard file so you need to define what type of information to display in the user interface each time Siri asks a question.

To see how to display a custom user interface within Siri, click on the MainInterface. storyboard file in the MessageExtensionUI folder and drag a UILabel on to the view. Center it and expand its width so it looks like Figure 12-10.

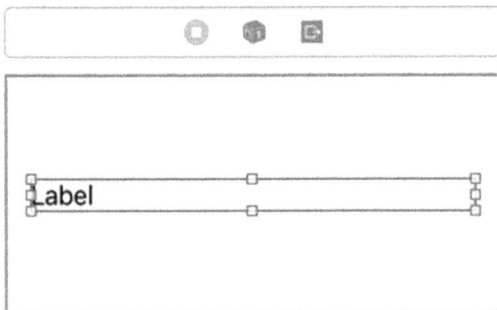

Figure 12-10. *Placing a UILabel on the MainInterface.storyboard file*

Open the Assistant Editor and Control-drag form the UILabel to the IntentViewController.swift file to create an IBOutlet for the UILabel and name it messageLabel:

```
@IBOutlet var messageLabel: UILabel!
```

376

Now modify the configure function as follows:

```
func configureView(for parameters: Set<INParameter>, of interaction:
INInteraction, interactiveBehavior: INUIInteractiveBehavior, context:
INUIHostedViewContext, completion: @escaping (Bool, Set<INParameter>,
CGSize) -> Void) {
    // Do configuration here, including preparing views and calculating
    a desired size for presentation.
    
    if let messageIntent = interaction.intent as? INSendMessageIntent {
        
        guard messageIntent.content != nil else {
            return completion(true, parameters, CGSize.zero)
        }
        
        messageLabel.text = "Your message = \(messageIntent.content ?? "")"
    }
    completion(true, parameters, self.desiredSize)
}
```

Essentially this function checks if the user has added content to a message. If not, then display the MainInterface.storyboard file as size zero, which effectively hides it from view and allows Siri to display its default interface as shown in Figure 12-11.

CHAPTER 12   UNDERSTANDING SIRIKIT

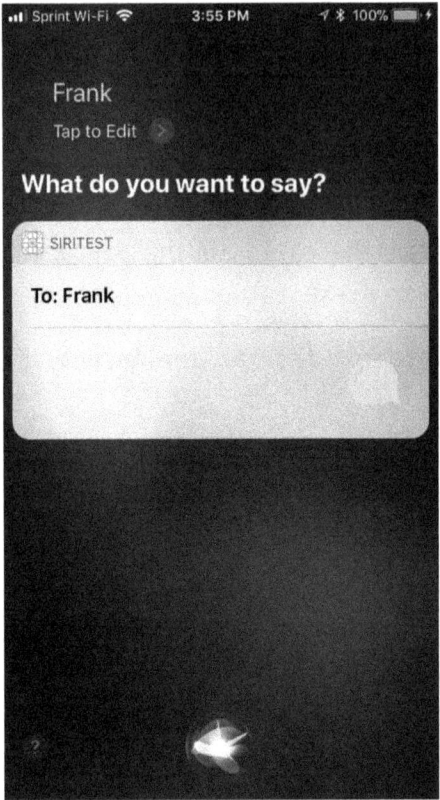

Figure 12-11. *Displaying the default user interface within Siri*

Once the user tells Siri the message content, then the MainInterface.storyboard file appears as shown in Figure 12-12.

CHAPTER 12 UNDERSTANDING SIRIKIT

Figure 12-12. *The MainInterface.storyboard appears within Siri*

The entire contents of the IntentViewController.swift file should look like this:

```
import IntentsUI

class IntentViewController: UIViewController, INUIHostedViewControlling,
INUIHostedViewSiriProviding {

    @IBOutlet var messageLabel: UILabel!

    override func viewDidLoad() {
        super.viewDidLoad()
        // Do any additional setup after loading the view.
    }
```

```swift
    override func didReceiveMemoryWarning() {
        super.didReceiveMemoryWarning()
        // Dispose of any resources that can be recreated.
    }

    // MARK: - INUIHostedViewControlling

    // Prepare your view controller for the interaction to handle.
    func configureView(for parameters: Set<INParameter>, of interaction:
    INInteraction, interactiveBehavior: INUIInteractiveBehavior, context:
    INUIHostedViewContext, completion: @escaping (Bool, Set<INParameter>,
    CGSize) -> Void) {
        // Do configuration here, including preparing views and calculating
        a desired size for presentation.

        if let messageIntent = interaction.intent as? INSendMessageIntent {
            guard messageIntent.content != nil else {
                return completion(true, parameters, CGSize.zero)
            }

            messageLabel.text = "Your message = \(messageIntent.content ?? "")"
        }
        completion(true, parameters, self.desiredSize)
    }

    var desiredSize: CGSize {
        return self.extensionContext!.hostedViewMaximumAllowedSize
    }

    var displaysMessage: Bool {
        return true
    }

}
```

Run this SiriTest project on an iOS device connected to your Macintosh through a USB cable. When you run the SiriTest project, a window will appear, asking you which app to use (see Figure 12-3). Click on Siri and click the Run button. Siri will appear.

CHAPTER 12 UNDERSTANDING SIRIKIT

Say, "Send a message using SiriTest." Siri will respond by asking who you want to send the message to.

Say a name such as Frank. Siri will display the name within the default user interface (see Figure 12-11). Then Siri will ask what you want to say, so state a message such as "Happy birthday." Siri will now display your MainInterface.storyboard file (see Figure 12-12).

Creating a Payment App with Siri

In our SiriTest project, we simply used code created by Xcode to send a message. In this project, we're going to create a simple payment app that works with Siri so you can see the differences between this project and the previous SiriTest project along with seeing what you need to modify when working with an app outside of the messaging domain.

Create a new Single View App iOS project and name it CatPay. Choose File ➤ New ➤ Target and click on the Intents Extension icon and click the Next button. Give this extension a name like PayExtension and make sure the "Include UI Extension" check box is selected. Click the Finish button. This creates a PayExtension folder (containing the IntentHandler.swift file) and the PayExtensionUI folder (containing the IntentViewController.swift file and the MainInterface.storyboard file).

For our simple payment app, we're only going to allow sending a payment, so we need to modify the Info.plist file in both the PayExtension and PayExtensionUI folders. You'll need to expand NSExtension, NSExtensionAttributes, and IntentsSupported.

By default, the items in the Info.plist file will contain message-sending intents such as INSendMessageIntent, but our app will be sending payments instead. Delete all items except for one and replace that remaining item with INSendPaymentIntent as shown in Figure 12-13.

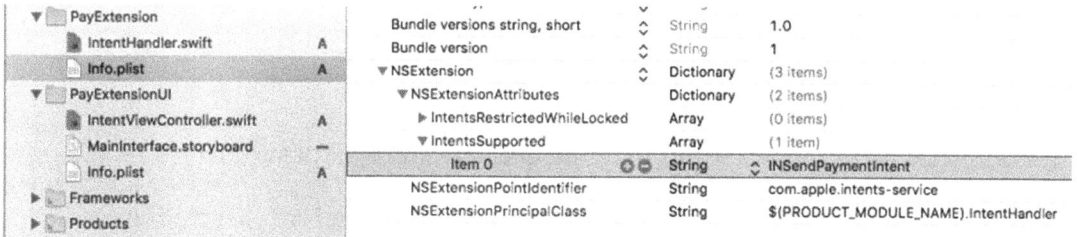

Figure 12-13. *Modifying the Info.plist file to support INSendPaymentIntent*

Make sure you modify the Info.plist file in both the PayExtension and PayExtensionUI folders. This tells your app and Siri to support sending payments.

381

CHAPTER 12 UNDERSTANDING SIRIKIT

The next step is to modify the IntentHandler.swift file. First, make the class declaration at the top of the file focus on INSendPaymentIntentHandling instead of messages like this:

```
class IntentHandler: INExtension, INSendPaymentIntentHandling {
```

Now edit the handle function to deal with the INSendPaymentIntent like this:

```
func handle(intent: INSendPaymentIntent, completion: @escaping
(INSendPaymentIntentResponse) -> Void) {
    let userActivity = NSUserActivity(activityType: NSStringFromClass
(INSendMessageIntent.self))
    completion(INSendPaymentIntentResponse(code: .success,
    userActivity: userActivity))
}
```

Just as you need to modify the handle function to work with INSendPaymentIntent (instead of INSendMessageIntent), so you need to also modify the confirm function to deal with the INSendPaymentIntent like this:

```
func confirm(intent: INSendPaymentIntent, completion: @escaping
(INSendPaymentIntentResponse) -> Void) {
    let userActivity = NSUserActivity(activityType: NSStringFromClass
(INSendPaymentIntent.self))
    let response = INSendPaymentIntentResponse(code: .ready,
    userActivity: userActivity)
    completion(response)
}
```

The entire IntentHandler.swift file should look like this:

```
import Intents

class IntentHandler: INExtension, INSendPaymentIntentHandling {

    func handle(intent: INSendPaymentIntent, completion: @escaping
    (INSendPaymentIntentResponse) -> Void) {
        let userActivity = NSUserActivity(activityType: NSStringFromClass
        (INSendMessageIntent.self))
```

CHAPTER 12 UNDERSTANDING SIRIKIT

```
        completion(INSendPaymentIntentResponse(code: .success,
        userActivity: userActivity))
    }

    func confirm(intent: INSendPaymentIntent, completion: @escaping
    (INSendPaymentIntentResponse) -> Void) {
        let userActivity = NSUserActivity(activityType: NSStringFromClass
        (INSendPaymentIntent.self))
        let response = INSendPaymentIntentResponse(code: .ready,
        userActivity: userActivity)
        completion(response)
    }

    override func handler(for intent: INIntent) -> Any {
        // This is the default implementation.  If you want different
        objects to handle different intents,
        // you can override this and return the handler you want for that
        particular intent.

        return self
    }
}
```

Now it's time to create a custom user interface for appearing within Siri. Place a UILabel in the middle of the view on the MainInterface.storyboard (see Figure 12-10). Open the Assistant Editor and Control-drag from the UILabel to the IntentViewController.swift file to create an IBOutlet named contentLabel:

`@IBOutlet weak var contentLabel: UILabel!`

To make the MainInterface.storyboard appear within Siri, we need to modify the IntentViewController.swift file in two ways. First, we need to make it adopt the INUIHostedViewSiriProviding protocol like this:

`class IntentViewController: UIViewController, INUIHostedViewControlling, INUIHostedViewSiriProviding {`

CHAPTER 12 UNDERSTANDING SIRIKIT

Second, we need to define the displaysPaymentTransction variable to true like this:

```
var displaysPaymentTransaction: Bool {
    return true
}
```

Finally we need to modify the configure function so it displays the MainInterface.storyboard within Siri like this:

```
func configure(with interaction: INInteraction, context:
INUIHostedViewContext, completion: @escaping ((CGSize) -> Void)) {
    
    if let paymentIntent = interaction.intent as? INSendPaymentIntent {
        
        guard let amount = paymentIntent.currencyAmount?.amount else {
            return completion(CGSize.zero)
        }
        
        let paymentDescription = "Sending \(amount) \(paymentIntent.
        currencyAmount?.currencyCode ?? "dollars") worth of cats"
        contentLabel.text = paymentDescription
    }
    completion(self.desiredSize)
}
```

The guard statement checks if the user specified an amount for payment. If not, then the user interface size is set to zero, which makes the default user interface appear instead.

If the user has specified an amount, then it displays a string in the UILabel defined by the IBOutlet called contentLabel. Notice that currencyCode represents the currency used in your region, but you need to specify a default value (in this case "dollars") in case your app can't define the region's currency code.

The complete IntentViewController.swift file should look like this:

```
import IntentsUI

class IntentViewController: UIViewController, INUIHostedViewControlling,
INUIHostedViewSiriProviding {
    
    @IBOutlet weak var contentLabel: UILabel!
```

```
func configure(with interaction: INInteraction, context:
INUIHostedViewContext, completion: @escaping ((CGSize) -> Void)) {

    if let paymentIntent = interaction.intent as? INSendPaymentIntent {

        guard let amount = paymentIntent.currencyAmount?.amount else {
            return completion(CGSize.zero)
        }

        let paymentDescription = "Sending \(amount) \(paymentIntent.
        currencyAmount?.currencyCode ?? "dollars") worth of cats"
        contentLabel.text = paymentDescription
    }
    completion(self.desiredSize)
}

var desiredSize: CGSize {
    return self.extensionContext!.hostedViewMaximumAllowedSize
}

var displaysPaymentTransaction: Bool {
    return true
}

}
```

When you run the CatPay project on an iOS device connected to your Macintosh through a USB cable, Siri will appear. Say "Send twenty-five dollars using CatPay." Siri will display the MainInterface.storyboard user interface as shown in Figure 12-14.

Chapter 12   Understanding SiriKit

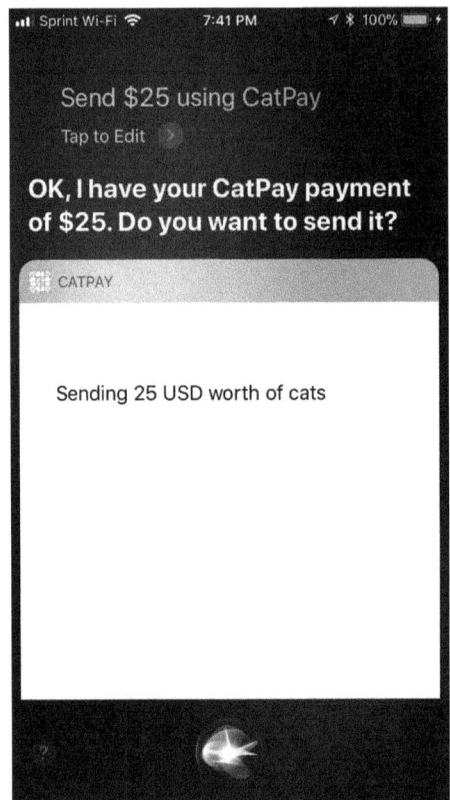

Figure 12-14. *The MainInterface.storyboard appears within Siri*

When Siri asks if you want to send the payment, say "Send" and Siri will say it sent payment (although it really doesn't because you haven't written any code to define who to send the money to or how to withdraw funds from an account).

Although you customized the MainInterface.storyboard with a UILabel, you could easily add pictures or text that represent your app's logo. That way users can recognize your app within Siri.

Summary

SiriKit gives your apps the ability to connect to Siri so users can interact with your app using voice commands. Just remember that SiriKit can only handle a limited range of domains such as messaging, ride booking, VoIP calling, or payments.

When you create a target file for your project, Xcode creates template code for working with the messaging domain to send messages. You'll need to delete most of this code in the IntentHandler.swift file to customize it for a different domain such as photos or workouts.

Make sure you edit the Info.plist files in the Extension and ExtensionUI folders to define the specific domain intents your app will handle such as INSendPaymentIntent or INSendMessageIntent.

To customize your user interface within Siri, you'll need to modify the MainInterface.storyboard file and the IntentViewController.swift file.

By adding SiriKit to your app, you can make your app easier to use through the natural language processing capabilities of Siri.

CHAPTER 13

Understanding ARKit

One of the most popular mobile games in recent years was Pokemon Go, which displayed Pokemon characters overlaid over actual places when viewed through the iPhone camera. By aiming your iPhone camera at a park bench or a bush, you could see a Pokemon cartoon character as if it were really there.

This technology of displaying virtual objects over actual physical objects is known as augmented reality (AR). The idea behind augmented reality is to let you combine real-world objects with virtual objects that appear on your iPhone screen.

One use for augmented reality is to point your iPhone at a street so you can see street names and names of businesses in the surrounding area. Another use is to show you walking directions complete with arrows to show you how to navigate around large public places such as airport terminals or museums.

In the past, creating augmented reality apps required writing mathematic equations to track real-world objects and position virtual objects in the real world. Fortunately, Apple has made augmented reality much easier to create through a new software framework called ARKit. By using ARKit along with other frameworks such as SceneKit, you can create augmented reality apps quickly and easily.

> **Note** You can only test and run ARKit apps on an iPhone 6s or higher, or an iPad Pro.

How ARKit Works

At the simplest level, ARKit works by identifying surrounding areas called feature points. Once ARKit understands the physical objects viewed by an iOS device camera, it can then overlay a virtual object on top of the real image displayed by the camera.

CHAPTER 13   UNDERSTANDING ARKIT

To see an example of ARKit in action, create a new iOS project. However, make sure you click the Augmented Reality App project as shown in Figure 13-1. Then click Next.

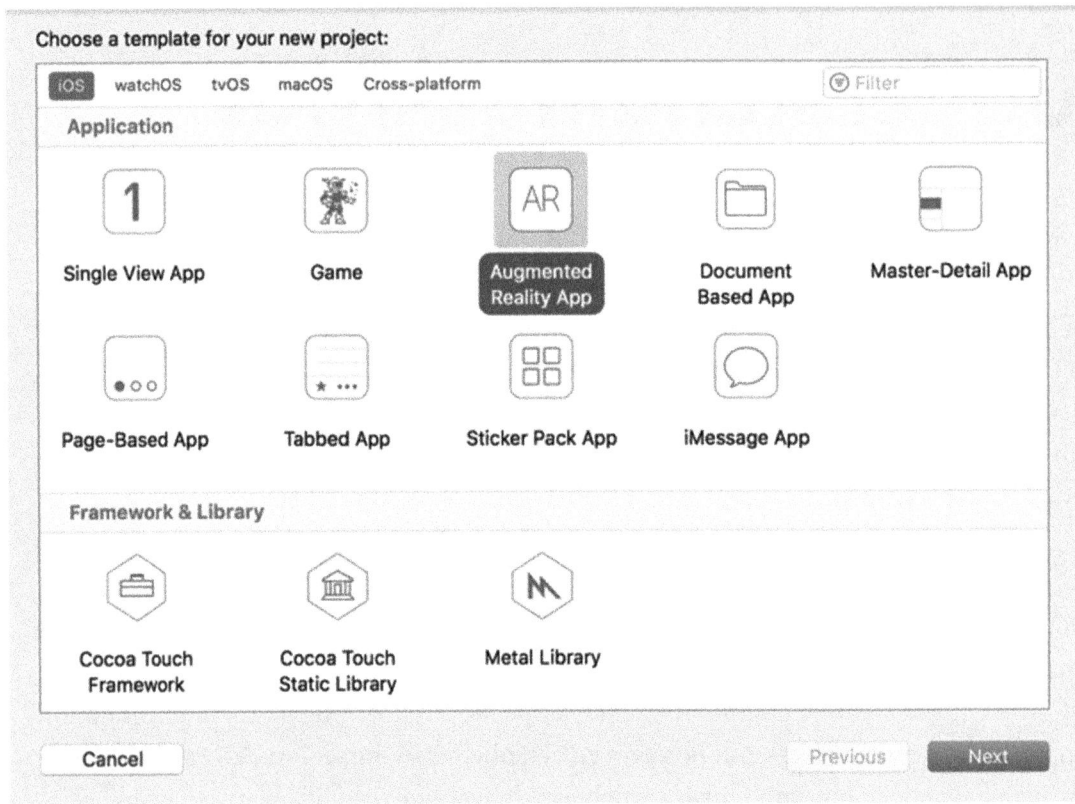

Figure 13-1. The Augmented Reality App template

When Xcode asks for a product name for your project, type ARTest. Make sure the Content Technology pop-up menu displays SceneKit. (The other two options in the Content Technology pop-up menu are Metal and SpriteKit. SpriteKit is designed for 2-D images while Metal is designed for advanced users who prefer to create their own code to create graphics. In most cases, you'll want to use SceneKit to display 3-D images.)

When you click the Finish button, Xcode creates a standard iOS project that consists of an AppDelegate.swift file, a ViewController.swift file, and a Main.storyboard user interface.

Click on the ViewController.swift file and you'll see code already written for you to create an augmented reality app. Notice that the ViewController.swift file contains three import statements:

```
import UIKit
import SceneKit
import ARKit
```

UIKit creates an iOS app. SceneKit lets you display three-dimensional objects. ARKit lets you add augmented reality to your app.

Next, notice that the ViewController class adopts the ARSCNViewDelegate:

```
class ViewController: UIViewController, ARSCNViewDelegate {
```

This protocol lets you display SceneKit images as augmented reality objects overlaid over real-world objects. Next, notice that the ViewController.swift file already contains a single IBOutlet named sceneView:

```
@IBOutlet var sceneView: ARSCNView!
```

If you click on the Main.storyboard file, you can see an ARKit SceneKit View already on the user interface as shown in Figure 13-2. This ARSCNView displays 3D SceneKit images on a camera background.

CHAPTER 13 UNDERSTANDING ARKIT

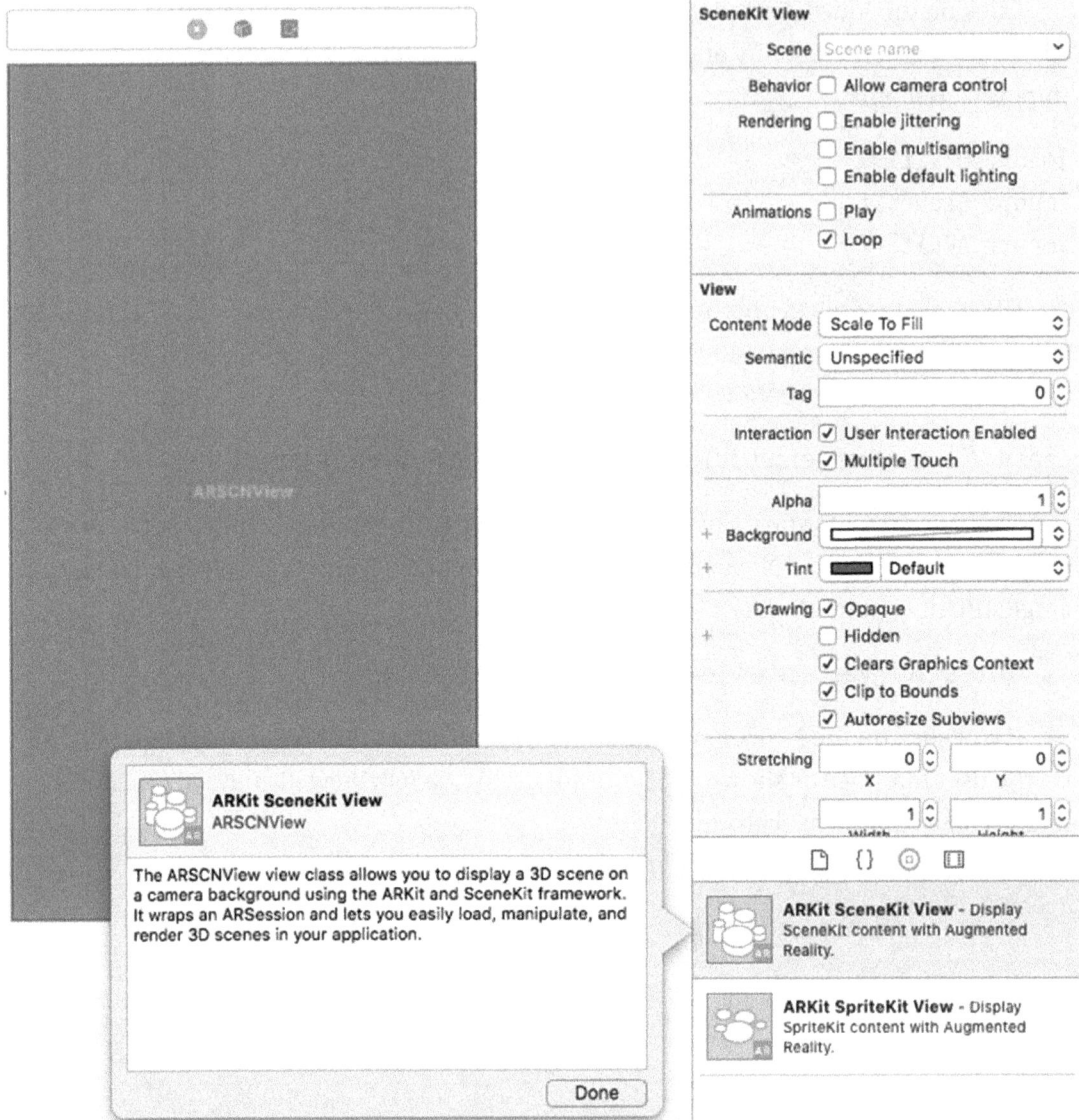

Figure 13-2. *An ARKit SceneKit View already appears on the user interface*

In the ViewController.swift file, look in the viewWillAppear function and you'll see two lines of code that help create augmented reality in the app. The first line creates a constant called configuration, which represents an ARWorldTrackingConfiguration object. This object tracks an iOS device's orientation and position as well as detecting real-world surfaces.

```
let configuration = ARWorldTrackingConfiguration()
```

CHAPTER 13 UNDERSTANDING ARKIT

The second line actually displays the augmented reality image overlaid on the view displayed by the camera:

    sceneView.session.run(configuration)

Now look in the viewDidLoad function of the ViewController.swift file. First, there's a line that defines the ViewController.swift file as its delegate. Second, there's a line that displays frames per second (fps) and timing data at the bottom of the screen:

    sceneView.showsStatistics = true

If you look in the Navigator pane, you'll see an art.scnassets folder. If you expand this folder, you'll see that it contains two files: ship.scn and texture.png. The ship.scn file contains a three-dimensional object that you can modify to change its appearance. The texture.png file contains graphics that appear on the ship.scn shape as shown in Figure 13-3.

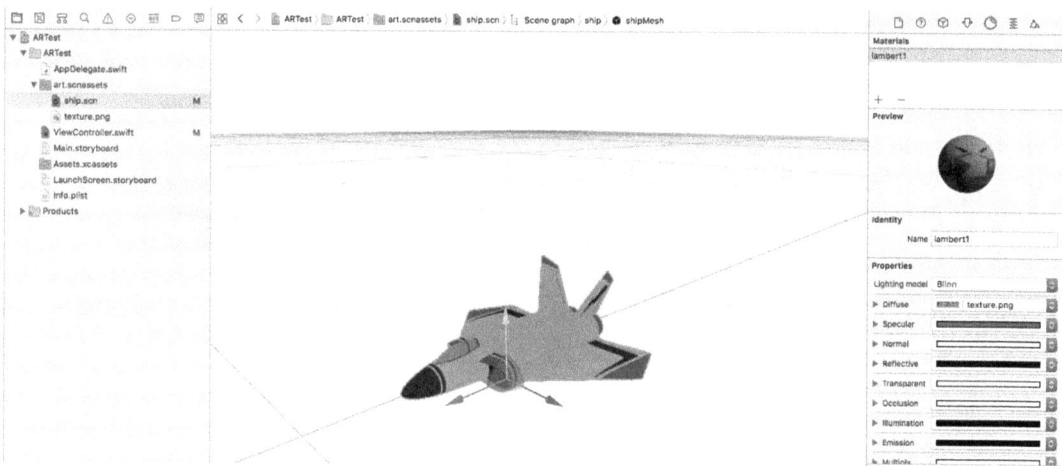

Figure 13-3. Viewing the ship.scn file in Xcode

Note A .scn file stands for a SceneKit file format. Most 3D digital imaging programs can save files in a .dae (Digital Asset Exchange) file format. If you add a .dae file to Xcode, you can convert it to a .scn file format by adding the .dae file to the Navigator pane and then choosing File ➤ Export and save the file as a .scn file. If you want to create .dae files, you can use the free, open source Blender program (www.blender.org). You can also find free, public domain .dae files on the Internet as well.

393

CHAPTER 13 UNDERSTANDING ARKIT

Virtual objects consist of a shape (in this case, the ship.scn file) and a texture (texture.png) that gets applied on the shape. If you click on the texture.png file, you'll see the color and graphics that appear on the ship.scn file.

Click on the ship.scn file and click on the plane image in the Xcode window. Click on the Show the Materials Inspector icon (or choose View ➤ Utilities ➤ Show the Materials Inspector). This display the Materials Inspector pane, which lets you modify the appearance of the shape.

Click on the Diffuse pop-up menu in the Properties category and you can see that the texture.png is chosen as shown in Figure 13-4. Click on Black or White to remove the texture so you can see how removing the texture.png file from the shape changes the ship.scn file's appearance.

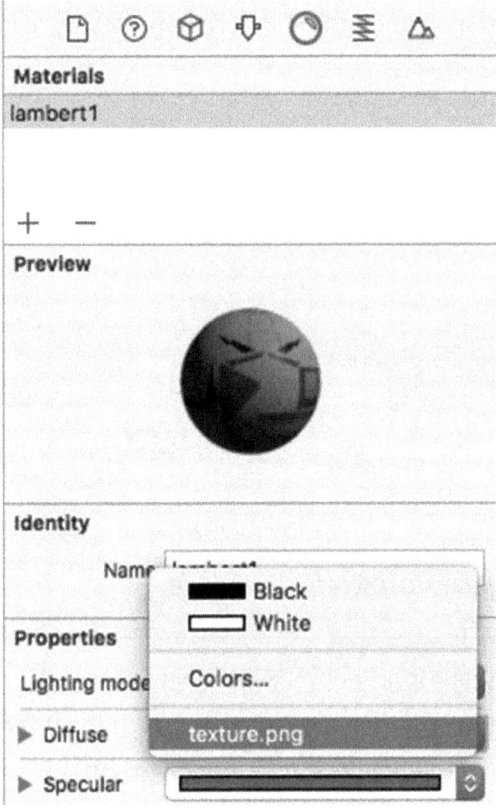

Figure 13-4. The Diffuse pop-up menu defines the outer appearance of the ship.scn file

394

CHAPTER 13   UNDERSTANDING ARKIT

Make sure the Diffuse pop-up menu displays the texture.png again. Connect an iOS device to your Macintosh through a USB cable and point your iOS device camera anywhere. The virtual image of the ship.scn file should now appear over the real-world objects viewed by the camera as shown in Figure 13-5.

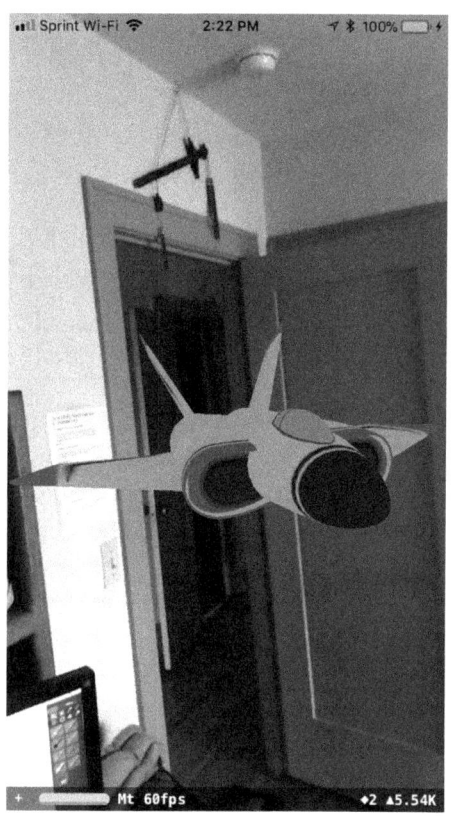

Figure 13-5. *Running the ARTest project in an iPhone*

As you move your iOS device around, you should see different angles of the ship.scn image as if it were a real object in front of you. Also note that the bottom of the screen displays statistics about the augmented reality image such as its frames per second (fps).

Back in Xcode, choose Product ➤ Stop or click the Stop icon to stop the ARTest project from running. At this point, you've seen a simple demonstration of how augmented reality works. By adding different texture files or replacing the ship.scn file with a different image, you can display custom images as seen through the iOS device camera.

CHAPTER 13 UNDERSTANDING ARKIT

Go back and edit the ViewController.swift file. First, comment out the two lines that define the ship.scn file and then loads that scene:

```
//let scene = SCNScene(named: "art.scnassets/ship.scn")!
//sceneView.scene = scene
```

Now add the following line to display feature points and the world origin overlaid over the camera image:

```
sceneView.debugOptions = [ARSCNDebugOptions.showWorldOrigin,
    ARSCNDebugOptions.showFeaturePoints]
```

Feature points appear as yellow dots that highlight surface areas that ARKit recognizes. The world origin appears as an x-, y-, z-axis where the x-axis goes right, the y-axis goes up, and the z-axis points out of the screen toward the user.

Note ARKit works best in clear lighting conditions with multiple objects visible so it can detect surface areas of tables, floors, and walls. Poor lighting conditions will hinder ARKit's ability to identify surface areas along with pointing the camera at a blank wall or floor.

Your entire viewDidLoad function should look like this:

```
override func viewDidLoad() {
    super.viewDidLoad()

    // Set the view's delegate
    sceneView.delegate = self

    // Show statistics such as fps and timing information
    sceneView.showsStatistics = true

    // Create a new scene
    //let scene = SCNScene(named: "art.scnassets/ship.scn")!

    // Set the scene to the view
    //sceneView.scene = scene

    sceneView.debugOptions = [ARSCNDebugOptions.showWorldOrigin,
        ARSCNDebugOptions.showFeaturePoints]
}
```

CHAPTER 13 UNDERSTANDING ARKIT

When you run this modified version of the ARTest project, you'll see the origin displayed along with yellow dots on nearby areas that represent feature points as shown in Figure 13-6.

Figure 13-6. *The debugOptions line displays the origin and feature points*

Drawing Augmented Reality Objects

By replacing the ship.scn file with your own images, you can display anything you want as an augmented reality object. However, you can also display simple geometric shapes as well. Some of the available shapes you can draw include:

- SCNBox – draws a box
- SCNCapsule – draws a cylinder whose ends are capped with hemispheres
- SCNCone – draws a cone

CHAPTER 13 UNDERSTANDING ARKIT

- SCNCylinder – draws a cylinder
- SCNFloor – draws an infinite plane that can optionally reflect a scene
- SCNPlane – draws a rectangular plane of a specific width and height
- SCNPyramid – draws a pyramid
- SCNSphere – draws a sphere
- SCNTorus – draws a torus, ring-shaped object
- SCNTube – draws a cylinder with a hole along its central axis

When displaying geometric shapes, you need to define three features:

- The object's physical dimensions such as its height and width
- The object's appearance such as its color
- The object's position relative to the world origin

Once you define an object's size, appearance, and position, you need to place it on the view displayed by the camera. To do this, you need to define a node. To see how this works, we'll need to add the following code to the existing viewDidLoad function in the ViewController.swift file:

Underneath the sceneView.debugOptions line, add the following:

```
let node = SCNNode()
node.geometry = SCNPyramid(width: 0.1, height: 0.2, length: 0.1)
node.geometry?.firstMaterial?.diffuse.contents = UIColor.cyan
node.position = SCNVector3(0, -0.2, 0)
sceneView.scene.rootNode.addChildNode(node)
```

This first line creates a node, which defines where a geometric shape will appear. The second line defines a SCNPyramid with a width, height, and length.

The third line defines the color of the shape, which is cyan.

The fourth line defines the pyramid's position relative to the world origin. In this case, the base of the pyramid appears below the origin at -0.2.

The fifth line adds the node to the scene so a cyan pyramid appears directly under the world origin as shown in Figure 13-7.

CHAPTER 13   UNDERSTANDING ARKIT

Figure 13-7. *Displaying a pyramid as an augmented reality object*

Experiment by changing the values for the node.position along with the pyramid's width, height, and length. Also change the color of the pyramid from cyan to red or yellow. Rather than display a pyramid, choose a different shape such as a SCNBox, SCNTub, or SCNCone.

Resetting the World Origin

We created the ARTest project using the Augmented Reality App template, but we can easily give augmented reality capabilities to any project just by adding the ARKit and SceneKit frameworks. Create a new project and create a new Single View App. Give it a name of ARReset.

CHAPTER 13   UNDERSTANDING ARKIT

When you first run any AR app, it will define the world origin at the current location of your iPhone or iPad. If you take a few steps back, you'll see the origin displayed on the screen (see Figure 13-6). Unfortunately, the world origin will remain fixed until you run the app again.

To fix this problem, the next project you'll create will show a Reset button that will let you move your iPhone/iPad to a new location and redefine the origin at your new location. In this way, you can redefine the world origin position without having to restart the app.

Click the ViewController.swift file and add the SceneKit and ARKit frameworks like this:

```
import SceneKit
import ARKit
```

Modify the ViewController class to adopt the ARSCNViewDelegate like this:

```
class ViewController: UIViewController, ARSCNViewDelegate {
```

Click on the Info.plist file and add a Privacy – Camera Usage Description key. If you fail to do this, your app won't have access to the camera and won't be able to run.

Click on the Main.storyboard file and add an ARKit SceneKit View to the user interface as shown in Figure 13-8.

CHAPTER 13   UNDERSTANDING ARKIT

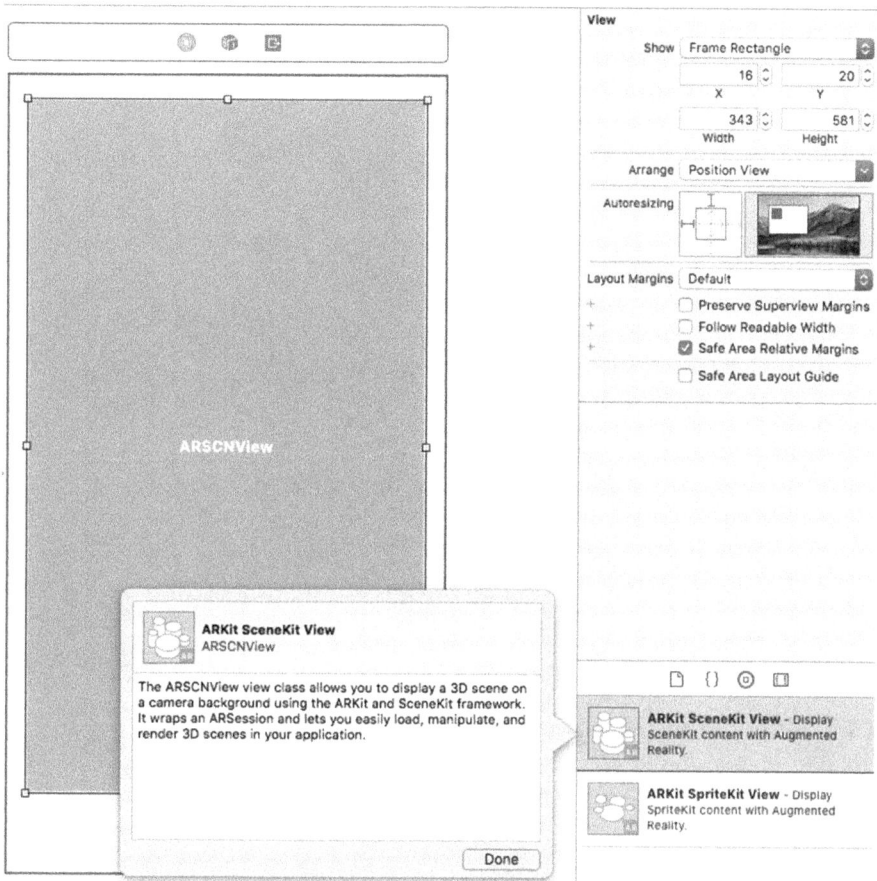

Figure 13-8. *The ARKit SceneKit View displays augmented reality objects*

Drag a UIButton to the bottom of the screen underneath the ARKit SceneKit View so it stretches the width of the view. Give this button a title of "Reset" as shown in Figure 13-9. Then choose Editor ➤ Resolve Auto Layout Issues ➤ Reset to Suggested Constraints.

401

CHAPTER 13   UNDERSTANDING ARKIT

Figure 13-9. *Placing a UIButton on the user interface*

Open the Assistant Editor and Control-drag from the ARSCNView to create an IBOutlet named sceneView:

```
@IBOutlet var sceneView: ARSCNView!
```

Now Control-drag from the UIButton to create an IBAction method named resetAR and add code like this:

```
@IBAction func resetAR(_ sender: UIButton) {
    sceneView.session.pause()
    sceneView.session.run(configuration, options: [.resetTracking,
    .removeExistingAnchors])
}
```

The entire ViewController.swift file should look like this:

```
import UIKit
import SceneKit
import ARKit
```

```swift
class ViewController: UIViewController, ARSCNViewDelegate {
    
    @IBOutlet var sceneView: ARSCNView!
    
    // Create a session configuration
    let configuration = ARWorldTrackingConfiguration()
    
    override func viewDidLoad() {
        super.viewDidLoad()
        
        sceneView.delegate = self
        
        // Show statistics such as fps and timing information
        sceneView.showsStatistics = true
        
        // Show origin and feature points
        sceneView.debugOptions = [ARSCNDebugOptions.showWorldOrigin,
        ARSCNDebugOptions.showFeaturePoints]
    }
    
    override func viewWillAppear(_ animated: Bool) {
        super.viewWillAppear(animated)
        
        // Run the view's session
        sceneView.session.run(configuration)
    }
    
    override func viewWillDisappear(_ animated: Bool) {
        super.viewWillDisappear(animated)
        
        // Pause the view's session
        sceneView.session.pause()
    }
    
    override func didReceiveMemoryWarning() {
        super.didReceiveMemoryWarning()
        // Dispose of any resources that can be recreated.
    }
```

```
    @IBAction func resetAR(_ sender: UIButton) {
        sceneView.session.pause()
        sceneView.session.run(configuration, options: [.resetTracking,
        .removeExistingAnchors])
    }
}
```

When you run this app, take a few steps back and you'll see the world origin displayed in front of you. Move to a new location and tap the Reset button, then step backwards. You should now see the world origin defined in your new location.

Drawing Custom Shapes

ARKit offers common geometric shapes you can create such as cylinders, cones, pyramids, boxes, and spheres. If none of those geometric shapes meet your needs, you can draw your own by defining a starting point and then adding lines to create a shape. Drawing lines to define a shape creates what's called a Bezier path.

The four main steps to creating a Bezier path include:

- Defining a Bezier path.
- Defining a starting point for drawing.
- Drawing one or more lines.
- Define a SCNShape based on the Bezier path lines you've defined.

To create a Bezier path, you need to define a BezierPath object like this:

```
let path = UIBezierPath()
```

Once you've created a Bezier path, you need to define its starting point like this:

```
path.move(to: CGPoint(x: 0, y: 0))
```

Now we need to draw one or more lines using the addLine method that defines the ending point of that line like this:

```
path.addLine(to: CGPoint(x: 0.2, y: 0.2))
```

CHAPTER 13 UNDERSTANDING ARKIT

Finally, we need to turn that Bezier path into a shape:

```
let shape = SCNShape(path: path, extrusionDepth: 0.1)
```

Once we have a shape, we can display it as an augmented reality object by defining it as a node with a color and position. Then we can finally add that node to the augmented reality view:

```
let node = SCNNode()
node.geometry = shape
node.geometry?.firstMaterial?.diffuse.contents = UIColor.yellow
node.position = SCNVector3(0,0, -0.4)
sceneView.scene.rootNode.addChildNode(node)
```

Modify the ViewController.swift file in your ARReset project so its entire contents look like this:

```
import UIKit
import SceneKit
import ARKit

class ViewController: UIViewController, ARSCNViewDelegate {

    @IBOutlet var sceneView: ARSCNView!

    // Create a session configuration
    let configuration = ARWorldTrackingConfiguration()

    override func viewDidLoad() {
        super.viewDidLoad()

        sceneView.delegate = self

        // Show statistics such as fps and timing information
        sceneView.showsStatistics = true

        // Show origin and feature points
        sceneView.debugOptions = [ARSCNDebugOptions.showWorldOrigin,
        ARSCNDebugOptions.showFeaturePoints]

        let path = UIBezierPath()
        path.move(to: CGPoint(x: 0, y: 0))
```

405

```swift
            path.addLine(to: CGPoint(x: 0.2, y: 0.2))
            path.addLine(to: CGPoint(x: 0.4, y: -0.2))
            let shape = SCNShape(path: path, extrusionDepth: 0.1)
            let node = SCNNode()
            node.geometry = shape
            node.geometry?.firstMaterial?.diffuse.contents = UIColor.yellow
            node.position = SCNVector3(0,0, -0.4)
            sceneView.scene.rootNode.addChildNode(node)
        }

        override func viewWillAppear(_ animated: Bool) {
            super.viewWillAppear(animated)

            // Run the view's session
            sceneView.session.run(configuration)
        }

        override func viewWillDisappear(_ animated: Bool) {
            super.viewWillDisappear(animated)

            // Pause the view's session
            sceneView.session.pause()
        }

        override func didReceiveMemoryWarning() {
            super.didReceiveMemoryWarning()
            // Dispose of any resources that can be recreated.
        }

        @IBAction func resetAR(_ sender: UIButton) {
            sceneView.session.pause()
            sceneView.session.run(configuration, options: [.resetTracking,
            .removeExistingAnchors])
        }

    }
```

If you run this modified ARReset project on an iOS device connected to your Macintosh, you should see a yellow triangular shape past the world origin as shown in Figure 13-10.

CHAPTER 13   UNDERSTANDING ARKIT

Figure 13-10. *Drawing a custom shape using a Bezier path*

Modifying the Appearance of Shapes

Up until now, we've just created a shape and applied a color to it, but there are other ways to modify the appearance of a shape. Some ways to modify the appearance of a shape include changing the lighting, transparency, or texture. Lighting makes a shape look differently depending on the type of lighting and location of the light source. Transparency defines whether a shape appears solid or see-through. Texture applies a graphic image on the sides of a shape such as making a shape appear to be made out of bricks or sand. By modifying the appearance of a shape, you can make that shape more visually interesting.

To experiment with modifying the appearance of shapes, create a new Augmented Reality App project and name it ARAppearance. Make sure the Content Technology uses SceneKit. The first way we're going to modify the appearance of an object is to use a graphic image that appears over that shape.

CHAPTER 13 UNDERSTANDING ARKIT

Search the Internet for "public domain texture images" and you'll find plenty of images that you can freely download and use. Texture images typically display a regular pattern such as bricks, water, fields, or materials such as wood or stone as shown in Figure 13-11.

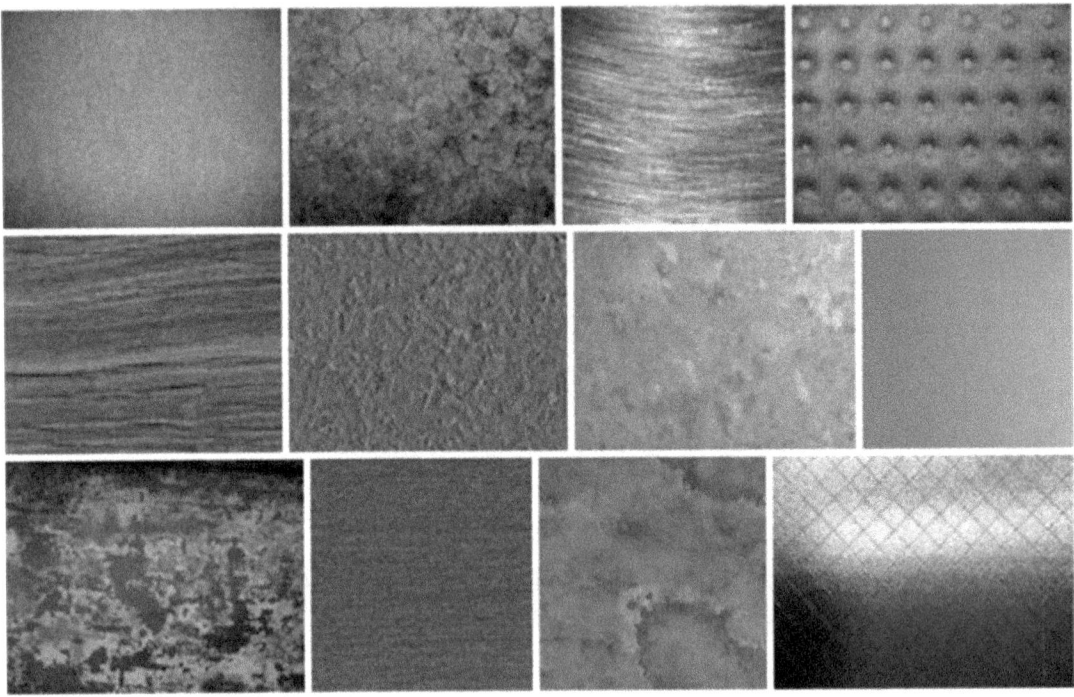

Figure 13-11. Searching for public domain texture images

Download a texture image and make sure it's stored in either the .png or .jpg file format. Then drag and drop it into the Navigator pane as shown in Figure 13-12.

CHAPTER 13 UNDERSTANDING ARKIT

Figure 13-12. *Placing a texture image file in the Navigator pane*

Modify the ViewController.swift file so it appears as follows:

```
import UIKit
import SceneKit
import ARKit

class ViewController: UIViewController, ARSCNViewDelegate {

    @IBOutlet var sceneView: ARSCNView!

    override func viewDidLoad() {
        super.viewDidLoad()

        // Set the view's delegate
        sceneView.delegate = self

        // Show statistics such as fps and timing information
        sceneView.showsStatistics = true
```

409

CHAPTER 13 UNDERSTANDING ARKIT

```swift
        sceneView.debugOptions = [ARSCNDebugOptions.showWorldOrigin,
        ARSCNDebugOptions.showFeaturePoints]

        let box = SCNBox(width: 0.1, height: 0.1, length: 0.2,
        chamferRadius: 0.01)
        let node = SCNNode()
        let material = SCNMaterial()
        material.diffuse.contents = UIImage(named: "stone.jpg")
        box.materials = [material]

        node.geometry = box
        node.position = SCNVector3(0, 0, -0.3)

        sceneView.scene.rootNode.addChildNode(node)

    }

    override func viewWillAppear(_ animated: Bool) {
        super.viewWillAppear(animated)

        // Create a session configuration
        let configuration = ARWorldTrackingConfiguration()

        // Run the view's session
        sceneView.session.run(configuration)
    }

    override func viewWillDisappear(_ animated: Bool) {
        super.viewWillDisappear(animated)

        // Pause the view's session
        sceneView.session.pause()
    }

    override func didReceiveMemoryWarning() {
        super.didReceiveMemoryWarning()
        // Release any cached data, images, etc that aren't in use.
    }
```

CHAPTER 13 UNDERSTANDING ARKIT

```swift
    // MARK: - ARSCNViewDelegate

/*
    // Override to create and configure nodes for anchors added to the
    view's session.
    func renderer(_ renderer: SCNSceneRenderer, nodeFor anchor: ARAnchor)
    -> SCNNode? {
        let node = SCNNode()

        return node
    }
*/

    func session(_ session: ARSession, didFailWithError error: Error) {
        // Present an error message to the user

    }

    func sessionWasInterrupted(_ session: ARSession) {
        // Inform the user that the session has been interrupted, for
        example, by presenting an overlay

    }

    func sessionInterruptionEnded(_ session: ARSession) {
        // Reset tracking and/or remove existing anchors if consistent
        tracking is required

    }
}
```

This code defines a SCNBox geometric shape and also defines a SCNMaterial array. That's because a shape can have multiple materials. Then the code defines a graphic file called "stone.jpg" as its first material, which creates a stone image around the shape as shown in Figure 13-13.

CHAPTER 13   UNDERSTANDING ARKIT

Figure 13-13. *A stone image appears as material around a box shape*

Another way to modify the appearance of a shape is to change its transparency using a value between 0 (invisible) to 1 (solid). Add a line of code to define a transparency value so your entire viewDidLoad function looks like this:

```
override func viewDidLoad() {
    super.viewDidLoad()

    // Set the view's delegate
    sceneView.delegate = self

    // Show statistics such as fps and timing information
    sceneView.showsStatistics = true

    sceneView.debugOptions = [ARSCNDebugOptions.showWorldOrigin,
    ARSCNDebugOptions.showFeaturePoints]
```

```
    let box = SCNBox(width: 0.1, height: 0.1, length: 0.2,
    chamferRadius: 0.01)
    let node = SCNNode()
    let material = SCNMaterial()
    material.diffuse.contents = UIImage(named: "stone.jpg")
    material.transparency = 0.7
    box.materials = [material]

    node.geometry = box
    node.position = SCNVector3(0, 0, -0.3)

    sceneView.scene.rootNode.addChildNode(node)
}
```

The above code defines two features in the material array. First, it displays the "stone.jpg" image around the box. Second, it defines a transparency of 0.7 so the box appears semi-transparent as shown in Figure 13-14.

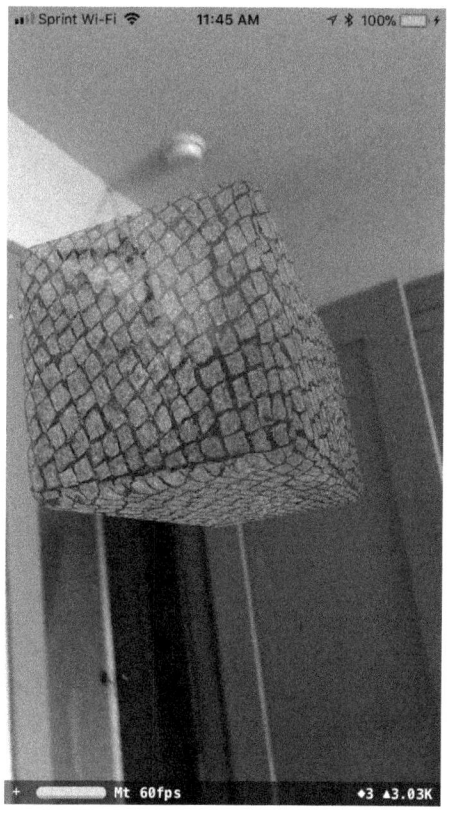

Figure 13-14. *Changing the transparency value makes a shape look less solid*

CHAPTER 13 UNDERSTANDING ARKIT

Besides applying textures and defining a transparency level, another way to change the appearance of a shape is through lighting. Lighting lets you create a light source that illuminates nearby shapes. Depending on the lighting you choose and the position of that light, you can create different types of visual effects on a shape.

To create a light source, you need to do the following:

- Define an SCNLight object
- Define the SCNLight type
- Assign the SCNLight object to an SCNNode
- Define the position of the SCNNode
- Add the SCNNode to the scene

To define an SCNLight object, you just need to create a constant like this:

```
let spotLight = SCNLight()
```

Now define one of the following lighting types:

- ambient
- directional
- IES
- probe
- spot

Each type of lighting type highlights a shape in different ways, so let's start by experimenting with the directional lighting type:

```
spotLight.type = .directional
```

Now that you've defined a lighting type, you need to create a SCNNode like this:

```
let spotNode = SCNNode()
spotNode.light = spotLight
```

The first line creates an SCNNode object and the second line defines its light source as the spotlight (SCNLight) object that we created earlier.

CHAPTER 13 UNDERSTANDING ARKIT

Finally, we can position the SCNNode object based on the world origin. That means you need to define an X, Y, and Z value such as:

```
spotNode.position = SCNVector3(0, 0.2, 0)
```

The above code places the light source 0.2 meters above the origin so the light shines down on the box we're going to create.

The final step is to add this light source node to the augmented reality scene:

```
sceneView.scene.rootNode.addChildNode(spotNode)
```

The entire viewDidLoad function should look like this:

```
override func viewDidLoad() {
    super.viewDidLoad()

    // Set the view's delegate
    sceneView.delegate = self

    // Show statistics such as fps and timing information
    sceneView.showsStatistics = true

    sceneView.debugOptions = [ARSCNDebugOptions.showWorldOrigin,
    ARSCNDebugOptions.showFeaturePoints]

    let box = SCNBox(width: 0.1, height: 0.1, length: 0.1,
    chamferRadius: 0.01)
    let node = SCNNode()
    let material = SCNMaterial()
    // material.diffuse.contents = UIImage(named: "stone.jpg")
    // material.transparency = 0.7

    let spotLight = SCNLight()
    spotLight.type = .directional
    let spotNode = SCNNode()
    spotNode.light = spotLight
    spotNode.position = SCNVector3(0, 0.2, 0)

    material.diffuse.contents = UIColor.orange
    box.materials = [material]
```

415

```
        node.geometry = box
        node.position = SCNVector3(0, 0, -0.3)

        sceneView.scene.rootNode.addChildNode(node)
        sceneView.scene.rootNode.addChildNode(spotNode)
    }
```

If you run this project, it will create an orange box placed 0.3 meters behind the origin. Then the light source will appear 0.2 meters above the origin shining down on the orange box. Because the light type is directional, it only highlights the face of the box as shown in Figure 13-15.

Figure 13-15. *Directional lighting focuses on the front of the orange box*

CHAPTER 13 UNDERSTANDING ARKIT

To see how a different light type changes the appearance of a shape, change the light type from directional to omni like this:

```
//spotLight.type = .directional   // illuminates only the front of
                                  the box
spotLight.type = .omni   // illuminates the front and top of the box
```

Now if you run this project, the omni lighting type highlights the front and the top of the box as shown in Figure 13-16.

Figure 13-16. *An omni light type illuminates the front and top of the orange box*

Apple's documentation defines how the different light types should behave so experiment with changing the light type and the position of the light source. By changing the position of a light source, you can illuminate different areas of a shape. By simply changing the light type, you can illuminate an object in different ways as shown in Figure 13-17.

417

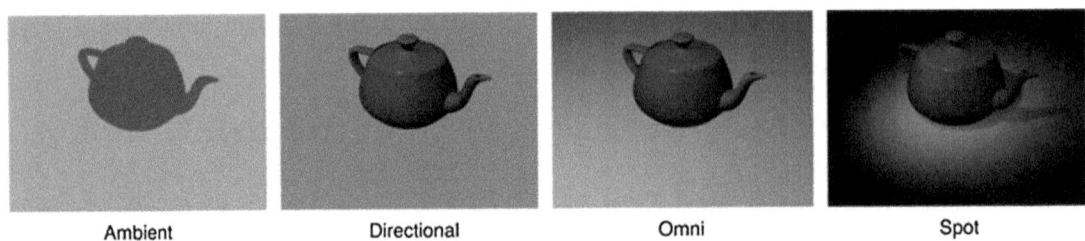

Figure 13-17. *How different lighting types work in highlighting a shape*

Summary

In this chapter, you've learned the basics of creating augmented reality objects using ARKit. You've learned how to place an augmented reality object on a scene and how to alter the appearance of an object by changing its color, transparency, and texture. In addition, you also learned how to draw your own objects and illuminate an object using a light source.

Augmented reality gives your apps the ability to overlay virtual objects over an actual scene. In the next chapter, you'll learn how to interact with augmented reality objects so that you can control and manipulate them.

CHAPTER 14

Interacting with Augmented Reality

Displaying virtual objects on a real-world scene can be interesting, but you'll likely want to do more than just overlay static images on a scene. Besides displaying virtual objects on a scene, ARKit can also make virtual objects move on the screen and gives users the ability to interact with virtual objects through touch gestures such as taps or swipes.

For example, a user might want to tap on a virtual object to make it move or respond in some way such as changing its appearance or moving on the screen. By making augmented reality interactive, your app can be more visually interesting and responsive to the user.

> **Note** You can only test and run ARKit apps on an iPhone 6s or higher, or an iPad Pro.

Let's create a new Augmented Reality App project and name it ARGesture. This project will contain an AppDelegate.swift file, a ViewController.swift file, and a Main.storyboard file along with an art.scnassets folder that contains a ship.scn object and a texture.png file.

Our goal is to create a geometric shape and display it on the screen. Then the user can swipe on that shape and make it rotate. To do this, we'll need to learn several skills.

First, most people are familiar with manipulating geometric shapes using degrees, but Apple's SceneKit framework uses radians instead. We could write our own formula to convert degrees to radians but Apple provides a mathematical framework called GLKit, which contains a function that can perform this calculation. As a general rule, it's always best to rely on Apple's frameworks as much as possible rather than write your own functions because Apple's frameworks are tested so you won't have to spend time debugging and testing your own functions.

At the top of the ViewController.swift file, add the following line to import the GLKit framework:

```
import GLKit
```

Your ViewController.swift file should import the GLKit, UIKit, SceneKit, and ARKit frameworks for a total of four import statements.

Next, we need to create a node that will represent the geometric shape we want to add to the screen. This means creating an SCNNode object. Since we'll need to access this object in more than one function, create this as a property under the IBOutlet, so the top of the ViewController.swift file should look like this:

```
import UIKit
import SceneKit
import ARKit
import GLKit

class ViewController: UIViewController, ARSCNViewDelegate {

    @IBOutlet var sceneView: ARSCNView!

    let node = SCNNode()
```

In the viewDidLoad function, we can add the debug options that will display the world origin on the screen. You may not want to display the world origin in a final app, but it can be helpful to show you where your virtual objects appear on the screen while developing your app. Add the following lines in the viewDidLoad function:

```
sceneView.debugOptions = [ARSCNDebugOptions.showWorldOrigin,
    ARSCNDebugOptions.showFeaturePoints]
```

Storing and Accessing Graphic Assets

Now we need to create a geometric shape. In this case, we want to create a pyramid so we'll need to define its width, height, and length. In addition, we also want to apply a texture over our pyramid.

The Augmented Reality App project comes with two graphic files: ship.scn and texture.png. We won't be displaying the ship.scn file so you can delete the code that displays this ship.scn on the screen. However, we do want to use the texture.png file.

CHAPTER 14 INTERACTING WITH AUGMENTED REALITY

In the previous chapter, you saw how to apply a texture graphic image by simply defining its name like this:

```
let material = SCNMaterial()
material.diffuse.contents = UIImage(named: "stone.jpg")
```

Defining the graphic file name is fine, but if you misspell the name or move the file, then Xcode won't know where to find that file. A safer approach is to store the graphic image in the Assets.xcassets folder and give it a descriptive name. Then you can reference this graphic image any time by using its descriptive name instead.

Click on the Assets.xcassets folder in the Navigator pane to open a pane. Near the bottom-left corner of this pane, click on the + icon to display a pop-up menu as shown in Figure 14-1.

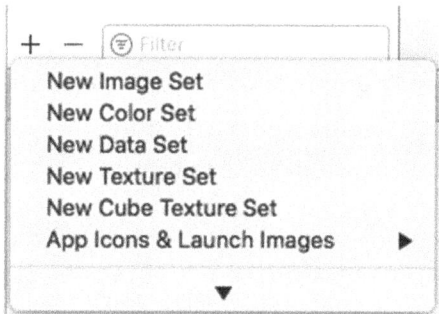

Figure 14-1. Creating a new Image Set

Click New Image Set. Xcode display an Image name along with different magnification size images you can store as shown in Figure 14-2.

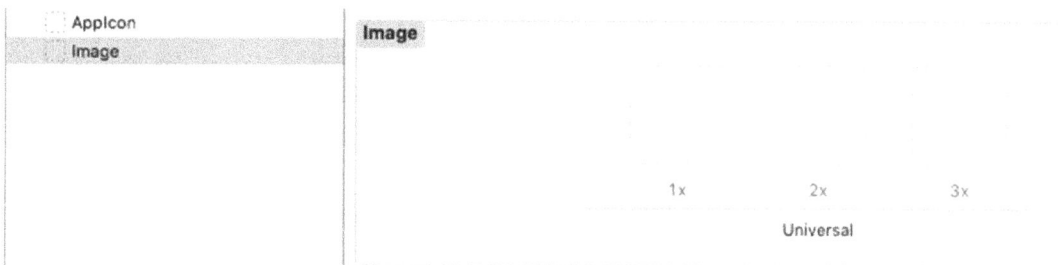

Figure 14-2. Viewing an Image Set

421

CHAPTER 14 INTERACTING WITH AUGMENTED REALITY

Click on Image under the AppIcon set and press Return. Xcode highlights the Image name so you can type a more descriptive name. For our purposes, type "Texture" and press Return.

Now drag and drop the texture.png from the Navigator pane onto the 1x dotted line box as shown in Figure 14-3.

Figure 14-3. Displaying a graphic image in an image set

At this point, we've stored a graphic image and we can now refer to this image by using its descriptive image set name, which is Texture.

Click in the ViewController.swift file and in the viewDidLoad function, add the following:

```
node.geometry = SCNPyramid(width: 0.15, height: 0.2, length: 0.1)
```

This defines a pyramid. Now to apply the texture, type the following:

```
node.geometry?.firstMaterial?.diffuse.contents = T
```

Because you've defined your graphic image under the descriptive image set name of Texture, Xcode can recognize it in a pop-up menu as shown in Figure 14-4.

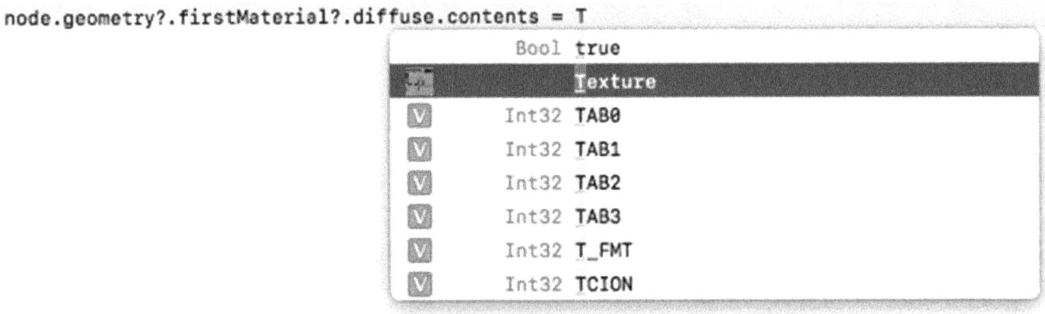

Figure 14-4. Xcode can recognize an image set name

422

CHAPTER 14 INTERACTING WITH AUGMENTED REALITY

Click on Texture. Notice that instead of displaying the name Texture, Xcode shows a thumbnail image of the graphic file represented by the Texture image set name. Not only does this method of referencing a graphic file avoid typos, but it also shows you visually what the graphic file looks like. The two lines of code to define the pyramid and add a texture to it should look like this:

```
node.geometry = SCNPyramid(width: 0.15, height: 0.2, length: 0.1)
node.geometry?.firstMaterial?.diffuse.contents =
```

Working with Touch Gestures

Once we've created a pyramid and applied a texture to it so it appears on the screen, the next step is to recognize when the user touches the pyramid. To do this, we need to create a gesture recognizer. There are several types of gestures you can recognize such as a swipe, tap, long press, pinch, or rotation motion. In our project, we're going to detect a right swipe gesture. When the user right swipes on the pyramid, we want the pyramid to rotate.

To detect a touch gesture, we need to create a constant that recognizes a specific type of gesture and defines a function to respond to that touch gesture. In the viewDidLoad, add the following two lines:

```
let swipeGesture = UISwipeGestureRecognizer(target: self, action: #selector(handleSwipe))
sceneView.addGestureRecognizer(swipeGesture)
```

The first line creates a gesture recognizer constant that calls a handleSwipe function to deal with the swipe gesture.

The second line adds the gesture recognizer so the scene view can recognize the swipe gesture.

The entire viewDidLoad function should look like this:

```
override func viewDidLoad() {
    super.viewDidLoad()
    
    // Set the view's delegate
    sceneView.delegate = self
    
    // Show statistics such as fps and timing information
    sceneView.showsStatistics = true
```

423

CHAPTER 14 INTERACTING WITH AUGMENTED REALITY

```
        sceneView.debugOptions = [ARSCNDebugOptions.showWorldOrigin,
        ARSCNDebugOptions.showFeaturePoints]

        node.geometry = SCNPyramid(width: 0.15, height: 0.2, length: 0.1)
        node.geometry?.firstMaterial?.diffuse.contents
        = imageLiteral(resourceName: "Texture")

        let swipeGesture = UISwipeGestureRecognizer(target: self, action:
        #selector(handleSwipe))
        sceneView.addGestureRecognizer(swipeGesture)

        node.position = SCNVector3(0, -0.2, 0)
        sceneView.scene.rootNode.addChildNode(node)

    }
```

The viewDidLoad function displays statistics such as the frame rate at the bottom of the screen. Then it displays debug options like the world origin and feature points.

Next, the viewDidLoad function creates a pyramid shape and covers its surface with the texture.png graphic image. Then it defines a swipe gesture recognizer on the scene view. Finally, it places the pyramid below the world origin and adds it to the scene view.

When we created a gesture recognizer, we also defined a function to handle the swipe when it's recognized. Now we need to create the handleSwipe function like this:

```
    @objc func handleSwipe(sender: UISwipeGestureRecognizer) {
        let swipeArea = sender.view as! SCNView
        let touchCoordinates = sender.location(in: swipeArea)
        let touchedShape = swipeArea.hitTest(touchCoordinates, options: nil)

        if (sender.direction == .right) && (touchedShape.isEmpty != true) {
            print ("Right swipe")

            let degrees: Float = 45
            let radians = GLKMathDegreesToRadians(degrees)

            let action = SCNAction.rotateBy(x: 0, y: CGFloat(radians), z: 0,
            duration: 5)
            node.runAction(action)

        }
```

CHAPTER 14 INTERACTING WITH AUGMENTED REALITY

This function retrieves the coordinates where the user swiped. Then it checks if the swipe gesture is to the right and within the pyramid boundaries. If so, then it prints "Right swipe" and defines degrees as a Float type with a value of 45.

Using the GLKMathDegreesToRadians function in the GLKit framework, it converts 45 degrees to radians and stores this value in the radians constant.

Then it defines an SCNAction to rotate by a fixed number of radians. In this case, rotation only occurs around the y-axis so the pyramid appears to spin around. The time duration to spin completely around is defined as five seconds.

This rotation action is then applied to the node (pyramid) using the runAction method. When you run this app, the pyramid appears under the world origin, covered with the texture.png graphic image as shown in Figure 14-5. Right swipe on the pyramid and it will rotate for five seconds before stopping.

Figure 14-5. Running the ARGesture project in an iPhone

425

CHAPTER 14 INTERACTING WITH AUGMENTED REALITY

Right now, the pyramid rotates for five seconds and then stops. If you want the pyramid to rotate and never stop, replace the last two lines in the viewDidLoad function like this:

```
let forever = SCNAction.repeatForever(action)
node.runAction(forever)
```

The complete ViewController.swift file should look like this:

```
import UIKit
import SceneKit
import ARKit
import GLKit

class ViewController: UIViewController, ARSCNViewDelegate {

    @IBOutlet var sceneView: ARSCNView!

    let node = SCNNode()

    override func viewDidLoad() {
        super.viewDidLoad()

        // Set the view's delegate
        sceneView.delegate = self

        // Show statistics such as fps and timing information
        sceneView.showsStatistics = true

        sceneView.debugOptions = [ARSCNDebugOptions.showWorldOrigin,
        ARSCNDebugOptions.showFeaturePoints]

        node.geometry = SCNPyramid(width: 0.15, height: 0.2, length: 0.1)
        node.geometry?.firstMaterial?.diffuse.contents
            = imageLiteral(resourceName: "Texture")

        let swipeGesture = UISwipeGestureRecognizer(target: self, action:
        #selector(handleSwipe))
        sceneView.addGestureRecognizer(swipeGesture)

        node.position = SCNVector3(0, -0.2, 0)
        sceneView.scene.rootNode.addChildNode(node)

    }
```

CHAPTER 14 INTERACTING WITH AUGMENTED REALITY

```swift
override func viewWillAppear(_ animated: Bool) {
    super.viewWillAppear(animated)
    
    // Create a session configuration
    let configuration = ARWorldTrackingConfiguration()
    
    // Run the view's session
    sceneView.session.run(configuration)
}

@objc func handleSwipe(sender: UISwipeGestureRecognizer) {
    let swipeArea = sender.view as! SCNView
    let touchCoordinates = sender.location(in: swipeArea)
    let touchedShape = swipeArea.hitTest(touchCoordinates, options: nil)
    
    if (sender.direction == .right) && (touchedShape.isEmpty != true) {
        print ("Right swipe")
        
        let degrees: Float = 45
        let radians = GLKMathDegreesToRadians(degrees)
        
        let action = SCNAction.rotateBy(x: 0, y: CGFloat(radians), z: 0, duration: 5)
        //let forever = SCNAction.repeatForever(action)
        node.runAction(action)    //node.runAction(forever)
    }
    
}

override func viewWillDisappear(_ animated: Bool) {
    super.viewWillDisappear(animated)
    
    // Pause the view's session
    sceneView.session.pause()
}

override func didReceiveMemoryWarning() {
    super.didReceiveMemoryWarning()
    // Release any cached data, images, etc that aren't in use.
}
```

CHAPTER 14 INTERACTING WITH AUGMENTED REALITY

```
    // MARK: - ARSCNViewDelegate

/*
    // Override to create and configure nodes for anchors added to the
    view's session.
    func renderer(_ renderer: SCNSceneRenderer, nodeFor anchor: ARAnchor)
    -> SCNNode? {
        let node = SCNNode()

        return node
    }
*/

    func session(_ session: ARSession, didFailWithError error: Error) {
        // Present an error message to the user

    }

    func sessionWasInterrupted(_ session: ARSession) {
        // Inform the user that the session has been interrupted, for
        example, by presenting an overlay

    }

    func sessionInterruptionEnded(_ session: ARSession) {
        // Reset tracking and/or remove existing anchors if consistent
        tracking is required

    }
}
```

Detecting a Horizontal Plane

Up until now, our augmented reality apps can appear at specific locations on the screen and can even respond to gestures such as a swipe. To make augmented reality more versatile, we're going to learn about plane detection.

Plane detection allows an iOS device to recognize a horizontal plane such as a table top or a floor. Once your app recognizes a horizontal surface, then it can place a virtual object on that surface such as a chair or a coffee mug. In this app, you'll learn how to detect horizontal planes and how to use tap gestures to place a virtual object on a horizontal plane.

CHAPTER 14 INTERACTING WITH AUGMENTED REALITY

Create a new Augmented Reality App project and name it ARPlane. This will automatically create an art.scnassets folder with the ship.scn and texture.png art files. We'll be using the ship.scn file to place on a flat surface.

To detect horizontal planes, add the following line in the viewWillAppear function:

```
configuration.planeDetection = .horizontal
```

The entire viewWillAppear function should look like this:

```
override func viewWillAppear(_ animated: Bool) {
    super.viewWillAppear(animated)
    
    // Create a session configuration
    let configuration = ARWorldTrackingConfiguration()
    
    //
    configuration.planeDetection = .horizontal
    
    // Run the view's session
    sceneView.session.run(configuration)
}
```

Add the following line inside the viewDidLoad function to display the world origin and feature points:

```
sceneView.debugOptions = [ARSCNDebugOptions.showFeaturePoints,
ARSCNDebugOptions.showWorldOrigin]
```

When our app detects a horizontal plane, we want to tap on that area to add a virtual object. In this case, the virtual object will be the ship.scn image. To add a tap gesture, we need to create a tap gesture and then add it to the scene. Add the following two lines to the viewDidLoad function:

```
let tapGesture = UITapGestureRecognizer(target: self, action:
#selector(handleTap))
sceneView.addGestureRecognizer(tapGesture)
```

The first line defines a tap gesture that will be handled by a function called handleTap. The second line adds that tap gesture to the scene view.

CHAPTER 14 INTERACTING WITH AUGMENTED REALITY

Now we need to create the handleTap function to respond to the tap gesture. Add the following handleTap function inside the ViewController.swift file:

```
@objc func handleTap(sender: UITapGestureRecognizer) {
    let sceneView = sender.view as! ARSCNView
    let location = sender.location(in: sceneView)
    let hitTest = sceneView.hitTest(location, types:
    .estimatedHorizontalPlane)
    if !hitTest.isEmpty {
        addObject(hitTestResult: hitTest.first!)
    }
}
```

The first line defines the handleTap function as an Objective-C function as defined by the @obj keyword. Then it retrieves the tap gesture.

The second line creates a sceneView constant that receives the data as an ARSCNView.

The third line identifies the location on the screen.

The fourth line checks if the tapped location appears within a horizontal plane.

The fifth line checks if the user tapped within a horizontal plane. If so, then it runs an addObject function that sends it the data where the user tapped (hitTest.first!). Now we need to create this addObject function like this:

```
func addObject (hitTestResult: ARHitTestResult) {
    let scene = SCNScene(named: "art.scnassets/ship.scn")!
    let node = (scene.rootNode.childNode(withName: "ship", recursively: false))!

    let transform = hitTestResult.worldTransform.columns.3
    node.position = SCNVector3(transform.x, transform.y, transform.z)
    sceneView.scene.rootNode.addChildNode(node)
}
```

This function defines the ship.scn as the object to add to a scene. The data received by this function contains the coordinates of where the user tapped, which is stored in a 4x4 matrix (worldTransform). The third column in this matrix contains the x, y, and z coordinates where the user tapped.

The final two lines of code above define the position of the node (the ship.scn image) and add it to the scene. The entire ViewController.swift file should look like this:

```swift
import UIKit
import SceneKit
import ARKit

class ViewController: UIViewController, ARSCNViewDelegate {

    @IBOutlet var sceneView: ARSCNView!

    override func viewDidLoad() {
        super.viewDidLoad()

        // Set the view's delegate
        sceneView.delegate = self

        // Show statistics such as fps and timing information
        sceneView.showsStatistics = true

        //
        sceneView.debugOptions = [ARSCNDebugOptions.showFeaturePoints,
        ARSCNDebugOptions.showWorldOrigin]

        //
        let tapGesture = UITapGestureRecognizer(target: self, action:
        #selector(handleTap))
        sceneView.addGestureRecognizer(tapGesture)

    }

    @objc func handleTap(sender: UITapGestureRecognizer) {
        let sceneView = sender.view as! ARSCNView
        let location = sender.location(in: sceneView)
        let hitTest = sceneView.hitTest(location, types:
        .estimatedHorizontalPlane)
        if !hitTest.isEmpty {
            addObject(hitTestResult: hitTest.first!)
        }
    }
```

CHAPTER 14 INTERACTING WITH AUGMENTED REALITY

```swift
func addObject (hitTestResult: ARHitTestResult) {
    let scene = SCNScene(named: "art.scnassets/ship.scn")!
    let node = (scene.rootNode.childNode(withName: "ship", recursively:
    false))!

    let transform = hitTestResult.worldTransform.columns.3
    node.position = SCNVector3(transform.x, transform.y, transform.z)
    sceneView.scene.rootNode.addChildNode(node)
}

override func viewWillAppear(_ animated: Bool) {
    super.viewWillAppear(animated)

    // Create a session configuration
    let configuration = ARWorldTrackingConfiguration()

    //
    configuration.planeDetection = .horizontal

    // Run the view's session
    sceneView.session.run(configuration)
}

override func viewWillDisappear(_ animated: Bool) {
    super.viewWillDisappear(animated)

    // Pause the view's session
    sceneView.session.pause()
}

override func didReceiveMemoryWarning() {
    super.didReceiveMemoryWarning()
    // Release any cached data, images, etc that aren't in use.
}

// MARK: - ARSCNViewDelegate
```

```
/*
    // Override to create and configure nodes for anchors added to the
    view's session.
    func renderer(_ renderer: SCNSceneRenderer, nodeFor anchor: ARAnchor)
    -> SCNNode? {
        let node = SCNNode()
        
        return node
    }
*/
    func session(_ session: ARSession, didFailWithError error: Error) {
        // Present an error message to the user
        
    }
    
    func sessionWasInterrupted(_ session: ARSession) {
        // Inform the user that the session has been interrupted, for
        example, by presenting an overlay
        
    }
    
    func sessionInterruptionEnded(_ session: ARSession) {
        // Reset tracking and/or remove existing anchors if consistent
        tracking is required
        
    }
}
```

Modifying an Image

Right now if you run the ARPlane project, it will add the ship.scn image as a virtual object. However, this image will appear too large. When you add virtual images to appear in an augmented reality app, you may need to modify that image by rotating it or scaling its size, which is what we need to do.

CHAPTER 14 INTERACTING WITH AUGMENTED REALITY

In the Navigator pane, open the art.scnassets folder and click on the ship.scn file. Xcode displays the image so you can see its appearance. Click on the Node Inspector icon or choose View ➤ Utilities ➤ Show Node Inspector. Now you can see the position, Euler angles, and scale of the ship.scn as shown in Figure 14-6.

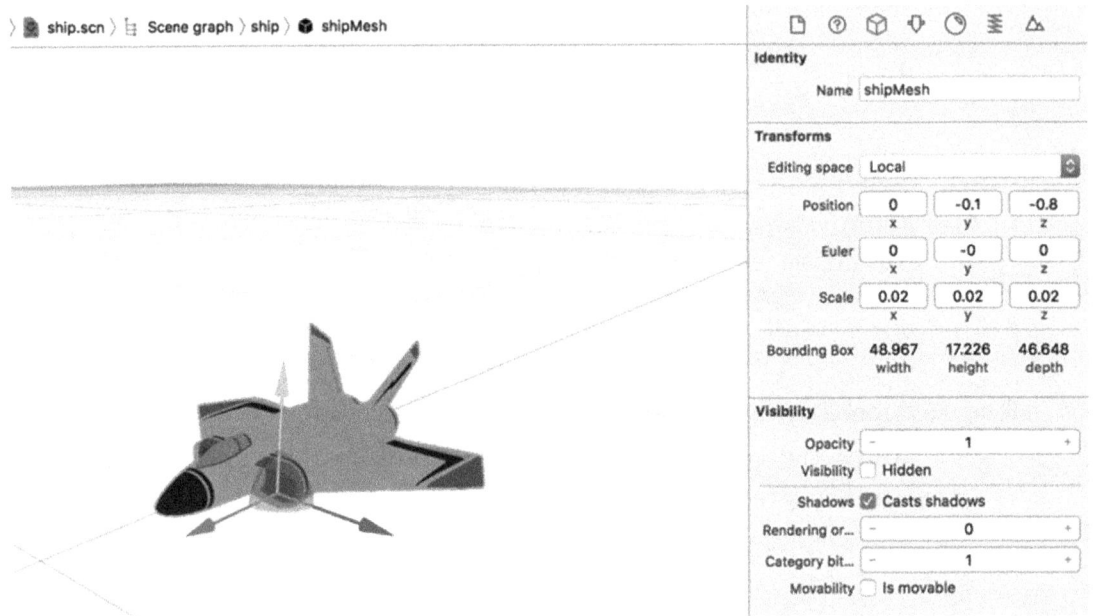

Figure 14-6. *Editing an image with the Node Inspector*

The Position coordinates define the image's position based on the world origin.

The Euler coordinates define the rotation of the image around the x-, y-, and z-axis (also known as the pitch, yaw, and roll respectively).

The Scale coordinates define the size of the image. Right now the scale is 0.02, which is too large. Change all three scale options (x, y, and z) to 0.005. This will shrink the image down to a reasonable size.

Note When adding virtual image files to an Xcode project, you may need to modify that virtual image's position, rotation, and scale in the Node Inspector to suit your needs. Most virtual image files will not be perfectly sized and oriented for your augmented reality apps.

CHAPTER 14　INTERACTING WITH AUGMENTED REALITY

Run this ARPlane project now and aim your iOS device at a horizontal surface. You can tell when the ARPlane app detects a horizontal surface when lots of yellow feature point dots appear on a surface.

As soon as you see lots of feature point dots on a horizontal surface, tap that area and the ship.scn file appears in that spot as shown in Figure 14-7.

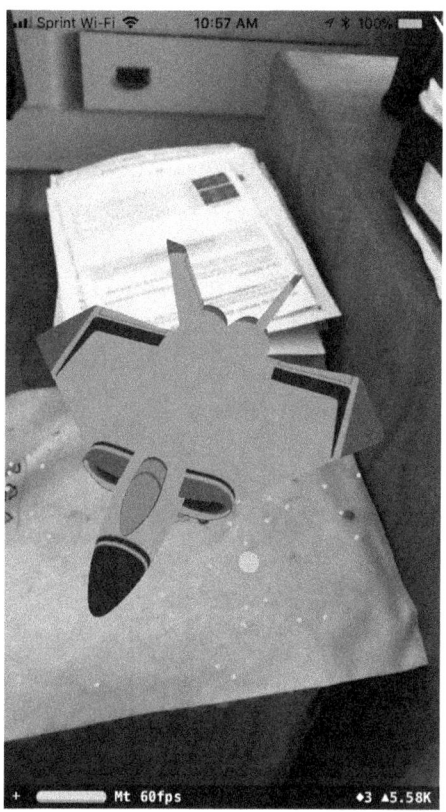

Figure 14-7.　*Displaying the ship.scn file on a horizontal surface*

Creating Virtual Objects

In the last project, we used the ship.scn file that automatically comes with any project created using the Augmented Reality App project. In this next project, we're going to learn how to create simple virtual objects using common geometric shapes.

We've already seen how to create virtual objects out of common geometric shapes like cylinders, boxes, and pyramids using Swift code. Now we're going to see how to create common shapes and modify them to create simple virtual objects visually. You can create virtual objects and then modify them using Swift code later if you wish.

CHAPTER 14   INTERACTING WITH AUGMENTED REALITY

Create a new Augmented Reality App project and name it ARCreateShapes. The code will be exactly the same as the last project (ARPlane). The only difference is that we'll create a .scn virtual image from scratch and learn more about designing virtual objects using common geometric shapes.

Click on the art.scnassets folder and delete the ship.scn and texture.png files by clicking on each file and pressing the Delete key (or choosing Edit ➤ Delete). Now click on the ARCreateShapes folder and choose File ➤ New ➤ File. A template window appears. Click the iOS category and scroll down until you see the Resource category as shown in Figure 14-8.

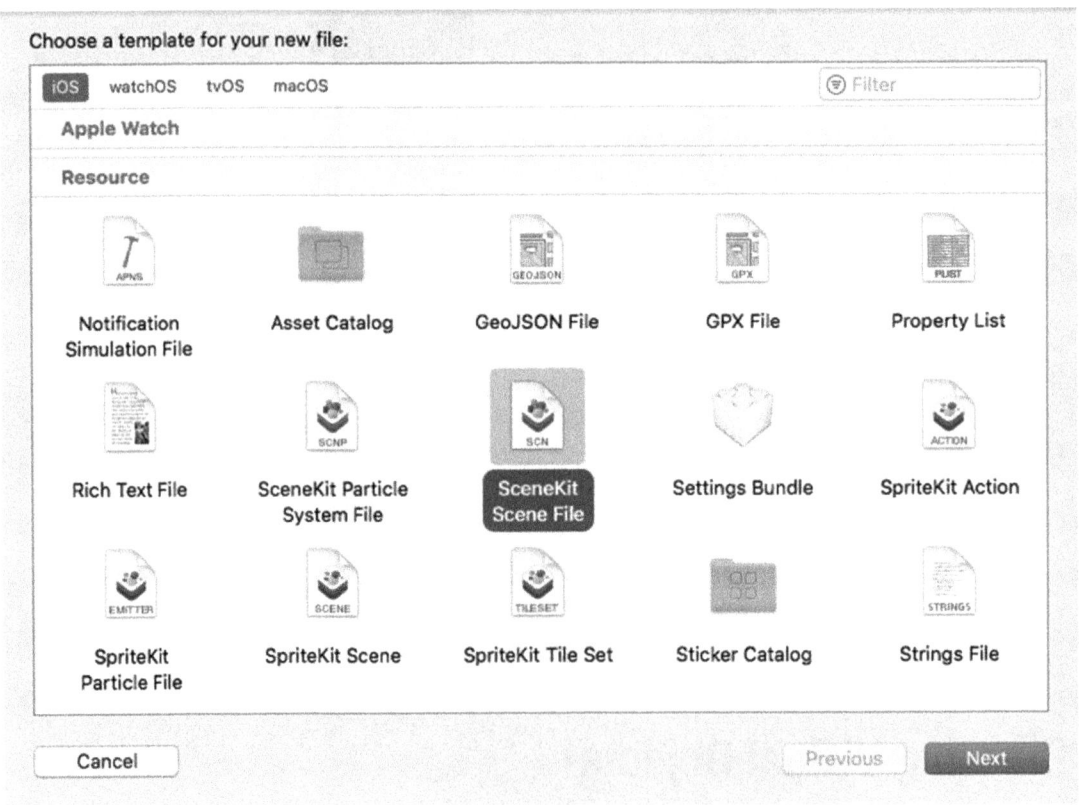

Figure 14-8. *Choosing a SceneKit Scene File in the template window*

Click the SceneKit Scene File icon and choose Next and when a Save As dialog appears, give your file a descriptive name such as MyShape and then click Create. This creates an empty .scn file for us to modify. Drag and drop your newly created .scn file into the art.scnassets folder.

CHAPTER 14 INTERACTING WITH AUGMENTED REALITY

Make sure the Object Library window is open (choose View ➤ Utilities ➤ Show Object Library) and you should see a variety of different objects and modifications you can add to your .scn file as shown in Figure 14-9.

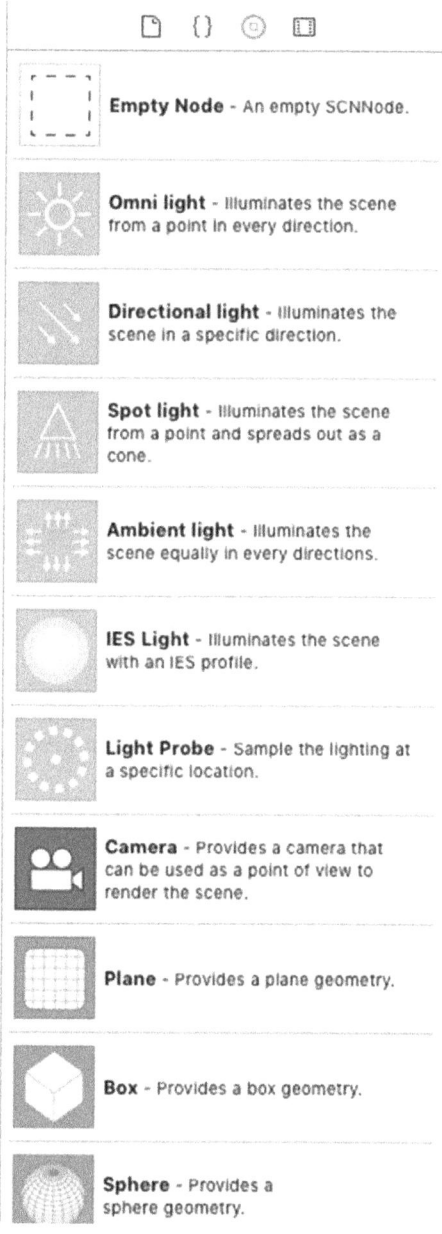

Figure 14-9. *The Object Library displays different items to add to a .scn file*

To create a virtual object, we need to start with an empty node, so click the Empty Node icon in the Object Library and drag and drop it on the scene. This displays an x-, y-, and z-axis on the scene as shown in Figure 14-10.

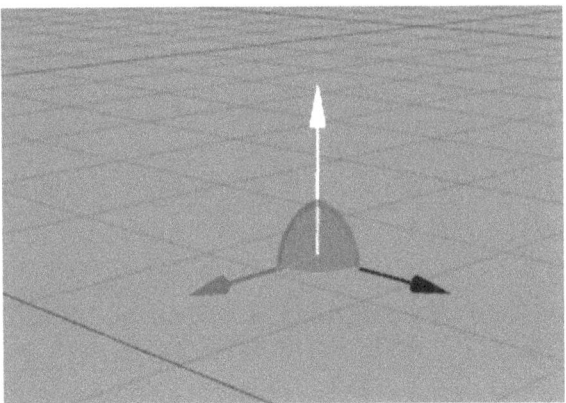

Figure 14-10. *Placing an Empty Node on a scene displays an x-, y-, and z-axis*

Click on the Node Inspector icon (or choose View ➤ Utilities ➤ Show Node Inspector). From the Node Inspector, you can define the following:

- The name of the node (used for identification purposes)
- The position of the node
- The Euler coordinates of the node (its rotation around the x-, y-, and z-axis)
- The scale of the node
- The opacity (how visible the node is)

We'll be creating virtual objects out of multiple shapes so let's create a house that will consist of a box and a pyramid on top with a plane to represent the door. With the Node Inspector visible, click in the Name text field under the Identity category and type House. If you click the Show/Hide the Scene Graph View icon, you can see that the node you named appears with House appearing in the Scene Graph View and the Name text field in the Node Inspector pane as shown in Figure 14-11.

CHAPTER 14 INTERACTING WITH AUGMENTED REALITY

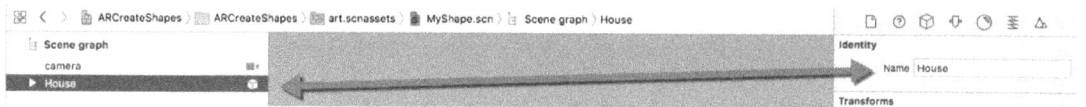

Figure 14-11. Defining a name for a node

In the Object Library pane, you'll need to add the following:

- Box
- Pyramid
- Plane

Click on the Show/Hide the Scene Graph View icon to make sure the Scene Graph View pane is visible as shown in Figure 14-12.

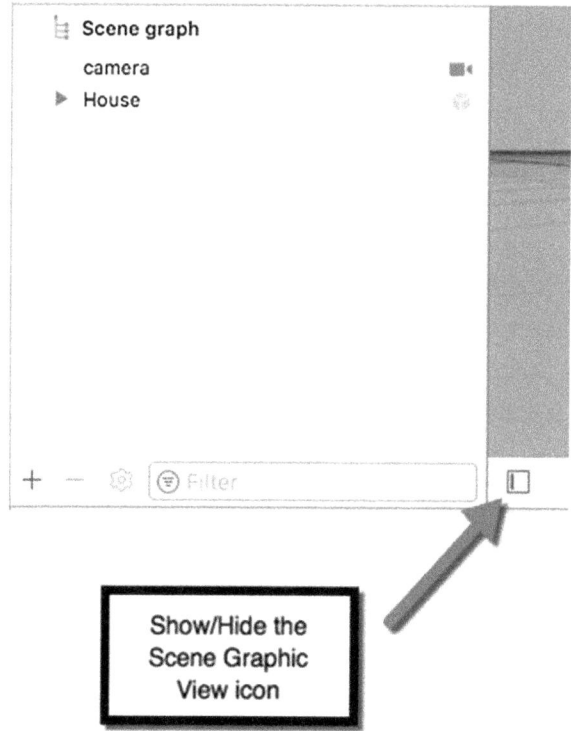

Figure 14-12. The Show/Hide the Scene Graph View icon

439

Drag and drop the Box in the Scene Graph View pane directly and indented under the House title as shown in Figure 14-13.

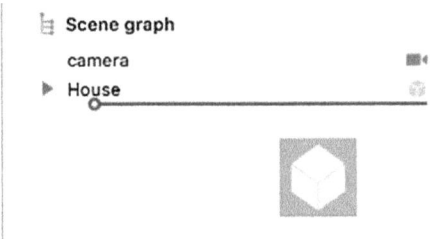

Figure 14-13. Make sure a blue line appears indented under the House category when dragging and dropping items

After you add a box, you may need to scroll around to find a white box displayed on the screen. Since white can be hard to see, let's change the box's color. Click on the box name in the Scene Graph View pane and click the Material Inspector icon (or choose View ➤ Utilities ➤ Show Material Inspector).

Click on the Diffuse pop-up menu to display a Colors window, and click on a color such as Turquoise.

Now we need to position the box in a specific location so click the Node Inspector icon (or choose View ➤ Utilities ➤ Show Node Inspector). Change the x, y, and z text boxes in the Position category to 0. You should now have a box appearing in your chosen color at positions 0, 0, 0.

Add a pyramid by dragging and dropping it in the Scene Graph View pane so it appears indented under the House title. This creates a white pyramid. Let's move this pyramid so it has a color and appears on top of the box.

Click on pyramid in the Scene Graphic View pane and click the Materials Inspector icon (or choose View ➤ Utilities ➤ Show Material Inspector). Click on the Diffuse pop-up menu and choose a different color such as Salmon. Now we need to move the pyramid on top of the box.

Click the Node Inspector icon (or choose View ➤ Utilities ➤ Show Node Inspector). Change the x and z text boxes in the Position category to 0 but make the y value 0.5. This should place the pyramid on top of the box.

CHAPTER 14　INTERACTING WITH AUGMENTED REALITY

Finally, we need to add a plane to create a door to the side of the box. Drag and drop a plane indented under the House title. Click the Node Inspector icon (or choose View ➤ Utilities ➤ Show Node Inspector). Change the x text boxes in the Position category to 0. Change the y text box value to -0.25. Change the z text box value to 0.52. This value of 0.52 places the plane slightly in front of the box so it's visible.

Click the Attributes Inspector icon (or choose View ➤ Utilities ➤ Show Attributes Inspector). In the Size text boxes, change the width to 0.25 and the height to 0.5.

Finally, click on House in the Scene Graph View pane and then click the Node Inspector icon (or choose View ➤ Utilities ➤ Show Node Inspector). Change the x, y, and z values in the Scale category to 0.2. This shrinks the entire house image so it's much smaller. The final result should show a house with a pyramid on top of a box and a plane in one side as shown in Figure 14-14.

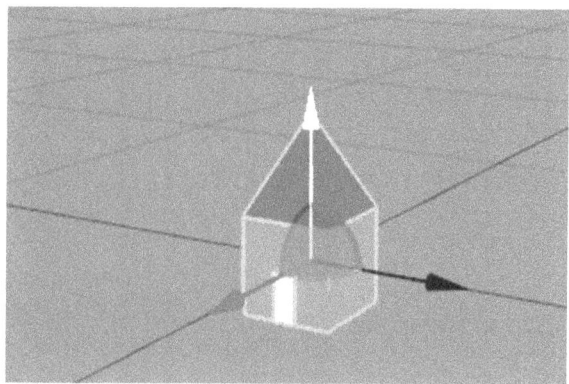

Figure 14-14. *Creating a house out of a pyramid, box, and a plane*

Copy all the functions from the previous ARPlane project's ViewController.swift file. Since we now want to display the House image (instead of the ship.scn image), modify the first two lines of the addObject function as follows:

```
let scene = SCNScene(named: "art.scnassets/MyShape.scn")!
let node = (scene.rootNode.childNode(withName: "House",
recursively: false))!
```

CHAPTER 14   INTERACTING WITH AUGMENTED REALITY

Notice that the first line defines the actual MyShape.scn file. Then the second line defines the node, which we named "House." Your entire ViewController.swift file should look like this:

```
import UIKit
import SceneKit
import ARKit

class ViewController: UIViewController, ARSCNViewDelegate {

    @IBOutlet var sceneView: ARSCNView!

    override func viewDidLoad() {
        super.viewDidLoad()

        // Set the view's delegate
        sceneView.delegate = self

        // Show statistics such as fps and timing information
        sceneView.showsStatistics = true

        //
        sceneView.debugOptions = [ARSCNDebugOptions.showFeaturePoints,
        ARSCNDebugOptions.showWorldOrigin]

        //
        let tapGesture = UITapGestureRecognizer(target: self, action:
        #selector(handleTap))
        sceneView.addGestureRecognizer(tapGesture)

    }

    @objc func handleTap(sender: UITapGestureRecognizer) {
        let sceneView = sender.view as! ARSCNView
        let location = sender.location(in: sceneView)
        let hitTest = sceneView.hitTest(location, types:
        .estimatedHorizontalPlane)
        if !hitTest.isEmpty {
            addObject(hitTestResult: hitTest.first!)
```

CHAPTER 14 INTERACTING WITH AUGMENTED REALITY

```swift
        }
    }

    func addObject (hitTestResult: ARHitTestResult) {
        let scene = SCNScene(named: "art.scnassets/MyShape.scn")!
        let node = (scene.rootNode.childNode(withName: "House",
        recursively: false))!

        let transform = hitTestResult.worldTransform.columns.3
        node.position = SCNVector3(transform.x, transform.y, transform.z)
        sceneView.scene.rootNode.addChildNode(node)
    }

    override func viewWillAppear(_ animated: Bool) {
        super.viewWillAppear(animated)

        // Create a session configuration
        let configuration = ARWorldTrackingConfiguration()

        // Run the view's session
        sceneView.session.run(configuration)
    }

    override func viewWillDisappear(_ animated: Bool) {
        super.viewWillDisappear(animated)

        // Pause the view's session
        sceneView.session.pause()
    }

    override func didReceiveMemoryWarning() {
        super.didReceiveMemoryWarning()
        // Release any cached data, images, etc that aren't in use.
    }
    // MARK: - ARSCNViewDelegate
```

443

CHAPTER 14 INTERACTING WITH AUGMENTED REALITY

```
/*
    // Override to create and configure nodes for anchors added to the
    view's session.
    func renderer(_ renderer: SCNSceneRenderer, nodeFor anchor: ARAnchor)
    -> SCNNode? {
        let node = SCNNode()
 
        return node
    }
*/
    func session(_ session: ARSession, didFailWithError error: Error) {
        // Present an error message to the user
        
    }
    
    func sessionWasInterrupted(_ session: ARSession) {
        // Inform the user that the session has been interrupted, for
        example, by presenting an overlay
        
    }
    
    func sessionInterruptionEnded(_ session: ARSession) {
        // Reset tracking and/or remove existing anchors if consistent
        tracking is required
        
    }
}
```

If you run this ARCreateShapes project, point your iOS device's camera at a horizontal surface and tap the screen. This will display the house image you created as shown in Figure 14-15.

CHAPTER 14 INTERACTING WITH AUGMENTED REALITY

Figure 14-15. *Displaying a house image in augmented reality*

There are two ways to design virtual objects. One way is to define everything using Swift code. The second way is to design virtual objects visually, which can make it easier to create objects out of multiple geometric shapes such as a pyramid on a box to create a house.

If you need to create realistic images, you'll likely need a 3D image editor, but for simple shapes, creating virtual objects can be simple and easy.

445

Summary

In this chapter, you learned more about working with augmented reality objects. First, you learned how to store images by name and access them without typing the entire file name and extension. Next, you learned how to use a gesture to swipe on a virtual object and make it move.

You also learned how to detect horizontal planes in the real world and how to edit and modify virtual images by changing its position, size, rotation, and scale. More importantly, you also learned how to create geometric shapes visually and combine them to create new objects. By knowing how to modify, store, and create virtual objects, you can now create anything you wish to display in augmented reality.

Index

A

Accelerometer
    acceleration and gravity, 167
    CMMotionManager, 180–181
    graphic representation, 168
    shakes, 188
applicationDidBecomeActive(), 21
applicationWillEnterForeground(), 21
applicationWillResignActive(), 21
applicationWillTerminate(), 21
ARKit
    ARSCNView, 391
    augmented reality (AR), 390, 397–399
    Bezier path, 404–407
    configuration, 392
    debugOptions line, 397
    Diffuse pop-up menu, 394–395
    execution in iPhone, 395
    feature points, 389
    Navigator pane, 393
    SceneKit, 392
    shape appearance
        directional lighting, 416
        lighting, 407, 414, 418
        material array, 413
        omni lighting type, 417
        SCNBox geometric shape, 411
        SCNLight object, 414
        SCNMaterial array, 411
        SCNNode object, 415
        texture and transparency, 407–409, 412–413
        ViewController.swift file, 409
        viewDidLoad function, 415
    ship.scn file, 393–396
    SpriteKit, 390
    ViewController.swift file, 391
    viewDidLoad function, 396–397
    Virtual objects, 394
    world origin, 400, 402–404
Augmented Reality (AR)
    geometric shape, 420
    gesture recognizer, 423
    GLKit, 419
    graphic files, 420
    horizontal plane, 428, 430, 432–433
    image modification, 434–435
    Image Set, 422–423
    touch gesture
        gesture recognizer, 424
        GLKMathDegreesToRadians function, 425
        in iPhone, 425
        runAction method, 425
        swipe gesture, 423–424
        ViewController.swift file, 426–428
    viewDidLoad function, 420
    Virtual Objects, creation (*see* Virtual objects)

INDEX

B

Background state
  applicationDidEnterBackground(), 40–43
  resource management, 33–34, 36
  saving and restoration mechanism, 37, 39
Ball
  accelerometer, 188
  BallView, 191–194
  Images and Sounds, 189
  movement, 195–197
  viewDidLoad(), 190–191
Bezier path, 404–407
BulletNode, 68–69

C

Camera
  creation, 205–208
  implementation, 210–215
  privacy, 208–209
CameraRecognition
  Active Scheme, 274
  privacy, 275
  UILabel, 269
  UIView, 270–271
  ViewController, 272
CLLocation, 143–144, 146
CLLocationManagerDelegate, 143
CMMotionManager
  accelerometer, 180–181
  attitude, 179–180
  gyroscope, 179–180
  modes, 169
  motion access, 176, 178–179
  MotionMonitor (*see* MotionMonitor)

Collision-handling method
  EnemyNode, 81
  GameScene, 77
  PhysicsCategories, 78
  playerLives, 82
  SKNode, 79–80

D

Development base language, 218
3D Touch
  detection, 321–322
  peek, 320
  peek availability, 319
  peeking, popping and previewing, 339–346
  peek quick action, 321
  pressure detection, 323–324
  Quick Actions, 318

E

EnemyNode
  creation, 63, 65
  GameScene, 65–66
ExtensionUI
  default interface, 377–378
  IntentViewController.swift, 379–380
  MainInterface.storyboard, 375
  UILabel, 376

F

FacialRecognition
  AdvancedFacialRecognition, 301–309
  analyzeImage, 288
  identifyFacesWithLandmarks, 293–295, 297–300

imagePickerController, 288
Save Image, 291-293
UIImageView, 286-287
ViewController, 289, 291

G, H

GameScene
    didMoveToView(), 51
    modifications, 52-53
    SKLabelNode, 54
    SKView, 56
    viewDidLoad, 55-56
Gesture recognizer, 104
GLKit, 419
Grand Central Dispatch (GCD)
    background processing, 17-18
    challenges, 2
    life cycle, 19
    queue, 9
    SlowWorker Application
        (*see* SlowWorker)
    state-change notifications
        Background (*see* Background state)
        delegate methods, 20-21
        execution states, 26
        exploring states, 23-25
        Inactive (*see* Inactive state)
        State Lab, 22-23
Graphic files, 420-422

I, J, K

Image picker controller
    implementation, 203-205
    uses, 200-203
Image recognition
    Attributes Inspector, 262

camera
    CameraRecognition
        (*see* CameraRecognition)
    Core ML models, 258-259
    findResults function, 267-268
    image
        recognizeImage()
            (*see* recognizeImage())
    MobileNet model, 260-261
    user interface, 261-262
    viewDidLoad, 263-266
Inactive state
    implicit animation, 29
    State Lab, 30
    ViewController.swift, 31
    viewDidLoad, 27-28, 32
IntentHandler.swift file
    INSendMessageIntent, 374
    INSendMessageIntentResponse, 374
    Photos framework, 371
    resolveContent, 373
    resolveRecipients, 372
    SiriKit, 371-372

L

Localization
    project/folder, 218
LocalizeMe
    Attributes Inspector, 224
    capitalizedStringWithLocale(), 227
    display name, 249, 251
    language and region settings, 223, 226
        custom scheme, 238-240
        device/simulator, 240-241
    localization, 252
    NSLocale, 222
    NSLocalizedString(), 227, 229

LocalizeMe (*cont.*)
    Project, localizing, 230–234
    storyboard
        Assistant Editor, 236–237
        translator, 235
    strings file (*see* Strings files)
    viewDidLoad, 225
Location manager
    cell ID location, 139
    CLLocationManager, 140
    Core Location, 139
    delegate
        CLLocation, 143–144, 146
        error notifications, 147
        updates, 143
    desired accuracy, 140
    distance filter, 141
    Map Kit, 139
    requestLocation(), 142
    start polling, 142
    users permission, 142

M, N, O

Machine learning (ML)
    advantages, 256
    core model, 257–258
    image recognition (*see* Image recognition)
MotionMonitor
    CMAccelaration, 174
    CMDeviceMotion, 174
    positions, sizes and lables, 171
    ViewController, 170, 172–173
Multitouch screen
    allTouches(), 109
    gesture recognizer, 104
    tap, 104
    touch, 104
    UISwitch, 108

P

Particle system
    EnemyExplosion, 85–86
    EnemyNode, 87
    massive explosion, 84
    missile explosion, 85
    PlayerNode, 88–89
    spark, 84
Payment app
    INSendPaymentIntent, 381–382
    IntentViewController.swift, 383–385
    MainInterface.storyboard, 384–386
Physics engine
    BulletNode, 68–69
    definition, 67–68
    EnemyNode, 73–74
    GameScene, 70, 72
    unit vector, 70
PinchMe, 132–134
PlayerNode
    Geometry, 61–62
    scene, 58–59
    SKLabelNode, 58
    SKNode, 57
    touch location, 60–61
    wobble cycles, 62–63

Q

Quick Actions
    Dynamic Quick Actions, 333–338
    Home Screen, 325–329
    responding, 329, 331–333

R

recognizeImage()
    finalGuess, 278
    predictItem, 277
    UIImage, 277
    userCamera, 275
    ViewController, 279-282
Responder chain
    events, 105-106
    gesture, 107

S

Shakes
    accelerometer, 188
    baked-in shaking, 182
    ball application (*see* Ball)
    break application, 183, 185-187
    MotionMonitor, 182
SiriKit
    execution, 365-366
    ExtensionUI folder (*see* ExtensionUI)
    IntentHandler.swift file
        (*see* IntentHandler.swift)
    Intents Extensions, 364
    limitation, 363
    MessageExtensionUI, 365, 368-369
    payment app (*see* Payment app)
    privacy, 370
    SiriTest, 366-367
SKNode Inspector, 50
SlowWorker
    creation, 3-4
    doWork()
        dispatch_group_async(), 15
        dispatch_group_notify(), 15
        execution, 15-16
        modifications, 11-13
        Spinner Functions, 14-15
    GCD, 9
    main thread, 8
    mutex, 7
    thread-safe, 8
    units of work, 8-9
    ViewController.swift, 4-7
Speech2Text
    privacy, 348
    recognize spoken commands, 356-358
    Start Recognizing Speech, 348-349
    Stop Recording, 348-349
    ViewController, 350-353, 355
SpriteKit, 390
    scene graph, 45
    TextShooter (*see* TextShooter)
SpriteKit Level Designer, 49
StartScene, 92-95
State Lab, 22-23
Strings files
    generating and localizing, 242, 244-245, 247, 249
    literals and constants, 220
    localized, 221-222
Syroscope sensor, 169

T

Text2Speech
    UIButton, 359-360
    UISlider, 360-361
    UITextView, 359-361
TextRecognition
    handleText and identifyWords, 313-314
    sign identifyication, 315
    UIImageView, 310-311

INDEX

TextShooter
    collision-handling method
        (*see* Collision-handling method)
    EnemyNode (*see* EnemyNode)
    GameOverScene, 90-92
    GameScene class (*see* GameScene)
    GameViewController, 47
    goToNextLevel(), 75
    Particle system (*see* Particle system)
    physics categories (*see* Physics engine)
    PlayerNode (*see* PlayerNode)
    radial gravity fields, 97-100
    scaleMode property, 50
    SKNode Inspector, 50
    SKScene, 48
    SKView, 48
    sound effects, 95-96
    SpriteKit Level Designer, 49
    StartScene, 92-95
    updateEnemies(), 74-75
TouchExplorer
    continuous gesture recognizer, 131
    multiple taps, 125-128, 130-131
    pinching and rotation, 135-136
    PinchMe, 132-134
    swipes
        creation, 116
        detecting, 116-120
        gesture recognition, 120-121
        multiple, 122-125
    ViewController, 111-115
Touch gesture
    gesture recognizer, 424
    GLKMathDegreesToRadians
        function, 425
    in iPhone, 425
    runAction method, 425
    swipe gesture, 423-424
    ViewController.swift file,
        426-428

U

UIImagePickerController, *see* Image
    picker controller

V

viewDidLoad function, 420
Virtual objects
    ARKit, 394
    Attributes Inspector, 441
    geometric shapes, 436
    house creation, 441-445
    Node Inspector, 438, 440
    object library, 437
    Scene Graph View pane, 439-440
    SceneKit Scene File, 436

W, X, Y, Z

WhereAmI
    CLLocationManager, 149
    location manager, 155-159
    Locations Services, 164-165
    Map Kit, 159-163
    UI layout, 151
    user permission, 153
    ViewController, 148
    viewDidLoad(), 152, 154

Get the eBook for only $5!

Why limit yourself?

With most of our titles available in both PDF and ePUB format, you can access your content wherever and however you wish—on your PC, phone, tablet, or reader.

Since you've purchased this print book, we are happy to offer you the eBook for just $5.

To learn more, go to http://www.apress.com/companion or contact support@apress.com.

Apress®

All Apress eBooks are subject to copyright. All rights are reserved by the Publisher, whether the whole or part of the material is concerned, specifically the rights of translation, reprinting, reuse of illustrations, recitation, broadcasting, reproduction on microfilms or in any other physical way, and transmission or information storage and retrieval, electronic adaptation, computer software, or by similar or dissimilar methodology now known or hereafter developed. Exempted from this legal reservation are brief excerpts in connection with reviews or scholarly analysis or material supplied specifically for the purpose of being entered and executed on a computer system, for exclusive use by the purchaser of the work. Duplication of this publication or parts thereof is permitted only under the provisions of the Copyright Law of the Publisher's location, in its current version, and permission for use must always be obtained from Springer. Permissions for use may be obtained through RightsLink at the Copyright Clearance Center. Violations are liable to prosecution under the respective Copyright Law.

CPI Antony Rowe
Chippenham, UK
2019-05-16 15:56